STUDIES IN EARLY MODERN CULTURAL,
POLITICAL AND SOCIAL HISTORY

Volume 10

COMMUNE, COUNTRY AND COMMONWEALTH
THE PEOPLE OF CIRENCESTER, 1117–1643

Studies in Early Modern Cultural, Political and Social History

ISSN: 1476–9107

Series editors

I
Women of Quality
Accepting and Contesting Ideals of Femininity in England, 1690–1760
Ingrid H. Tague

II
Restoration Scotland, 1660–1690
Royalist Politics, Religion and Ideas
Clare Jackson

III
Britain, Hanover and the Protestant Interest, 1688–1756
Andrew C. Thompson

IV
Hanover and the British Empire, 1700–1837
Nick Harding

V
The Personal Rule of Charles II, 1681–85
Grant Tapsell

VI
Royalism, Print and Censorship in Revolutionary England
Jason McElligott

VII
The English Catholic Community, 1688–1745
Politics, Culture and Ideology
Gabriel Glickman

VIII
England and the 1641 Irish Rebellion
Joseph Cope

IX
Culture and Politics at the Court of Charles II, 1660–1685
Matthew Jenkinson

COMMUNE, COUNTRY AND COMMONWEALTH

THE PEOPLE OF CIRENCESTER, 1117–1643

David Rollison

THE BOYDELL PRESS

First published 2011
The Boydell Press, Woodbridge

ISBN 978–1–84383–671–1

The Boydell Press is an imprint of Boydell & Brewer Ltd
PO Box 9, Woodbridge, Suffolk IP12 3DF, UK
and of Boydell & Brewer Inc.
668 Mt Hope Avenue, Rochester, NY 14620, USA
website: www.boydellandbrewer.com

A catalogue record for this book is available from the British Library

Papers used by Boydell & Brewer Ltd are natural, recyclable products made from wood grown in sustainable forests

Printed in Great Britain by
CPI Antony Rowe, Chippenham and Eastbourne

Contents

List of maps and tables vi
Preface: 'A phoenix in flames' vii
Abbreviations xi

Introduction: Commune at the crossroads 1

1. A domination of abbots 17
2. The crisis of the early fourteenth century 26
3. Classes of the commune before the Black Death 33
4. The struggle continues, 1335–99 44
5. A turning-point: the generation of 1400 50
6. Highpoint of vernacular religion: building a church, 1400–1548 64
7. Classes of the commune in 1522 89
8. Surviving Reformation: the rule of Robert Strange, 1539–70 95
9. 'The tyranny of infected members called papists': the Strange regime under challenge, c.1551–80 103
10. Phoenix arising: crises and growth, 1550–1650 119
11. Only the poor will be saved: the preacher and the artisans 133
12. Gentlemen and commons of the Seven Hundreds 149
13. Immigrants 171
14. The revival of the parish 189
15. 'More than freeholders ought to have voices': parliamentarianism in one '*countrey*', 1571–1643 208
16. 'Moments of decision', August 1642 to February 1643 225

Afterword: Rural sunrise 246

Bibliography 269
Index 279

Illustrations

Maps

1	The 'Countrey': detail from Christopher Saxton's map of Gloucestershire, showing towns and villages of the Seven Hundreds	4
2	Johannes Kip, 'Cirencester the Seat of Allen Bathurst Esq.'	246

Tables

3.1	Taxpayers in 1327	34
3.2	Surname types in 1327	40
7.1	Wealth distribution in 1522	89
7.2	Wealth distribution of two towns compared: Cirencester and Tewkesbury, 1522	90
7.3	Wealth distribution in 1559–60	94
10.1	Population estimates, 1404–1801	123
10.2	Weddings, baptisms and burials, 1561–1709	125
10.3	Categories of persons buried, May 1577 to January 1579	129
12.1	The social and military formation of the Seven Hundreds, 1608	152
12.2	Occupations at Cirencester in 1608	155
15.1	Freeholders of six rural hundreds in 1712 and 1801	213
A1	1671 Hearth Tax	256
A2	Occupations in 1768	259
A3	Expenditure on poor relief in four rural hundreds, 1776 and 1803	264

Preface

'A phoenix in flames'

> The arms of the town are said to be a Phoenix in Flames … alluding to the old town having been burnt by sparrows, and this rising out of its ashes, as the young Phoenix is fabled to proceed from the ashes of the old one.
>
> Samuel Rudder, *The History of the Town of Cirencester* (Cirencester, 1800), 222

Once upon a time, long ago, one Gormund, an invading Dane, frustrated by the stubborn resistance of the Saxons of Cirencester, promised an earldom to any who could put an end to it. A 'heathen knight' stepped forward. He ordered his followers to net hundreds of sparrows and collect nut-shells from the neighbouring forest. He filled the nut-shells with burning tinder and tied them to the feet of the sparrows. 'The sparrows took their flight, and flew to their holes over the burgh, where they ere were inhabiting … Anon, as the fire was hot, as the sparrows inner crept, the wind came with the night, and the fire kindled, and the burgh … [be]gan her to burn.' The Saxons 'leapt out of the walls and [Gormund's] men slew them all'. Another authority traced the story even further back, attributing the stratagem to the Anglo-Saxon king Ceawlin, 'who lived in the sixth century'.[1]

The American scholar who, in 1925, traced and reported these legends, observed that 'it would be rash for the modern investigator to treat legends as idle fictions. If they are not based on historical truth, they may be at best based on mythological truth, that is, on ancient customs or beliefs which crystallized into historical legends and entered the works of medieval chroniclers.' Eighteenth-century Cirencastrian author and printer Samuel Rudder does not say where he got his version, but it seems more likely to have been contemporary oral tradition than the Welsh translation of Geoffrey of Monmouth's twelfth-century *History*, to which Alexander Haggerty Krappe traced the legend of Gormund the Dane's ingenious 'knight'. Rudder was, anyway, less interested in when and where the fabled event took place than in what happened next. He fancied the idea of Cirencester as a phoenix

1 Alexander Haggerty Krappe, 'The Sparrows of Cirencester', *Modern Philology* 23:1 (August 1925), 8–9, 12.

'rising out of its ashes' alluded to an abiding truth embodied in the *history* of the town he loved.[2]

The phoenix is a more than apt symbol of the struggles of an English commune, from the twelfth century to the outbreak of the English Revolution, to continue to be a lively and strategic inland entrepot, through five centuries of changing regional, national and international circumstances, and to achieve independent, self-governing status. The book is itself something of a phoenix: it is a long time since my first encounter with the town records. In late 1979 I was at the Gloucestershire County Records Offices, working my way through the parish registers of a selection of Gloucestershire's clothworking towns. Counting burials at Cirencester, I stumbled into evidence of a mortality crisis that carried away a third of its population in about eighteen months. It was a powerful experience, reading and transcribing the endless lists of burials: impossible not to wonder how the inhabitants felt, living through it. How did they respond? That evening I crossed Gloucester to the City Library to see what they had on the town in the years of crisis. In the Library's 'Gloucestershire Collection' (now at the Gloucestershire Archives), I discovered an unusually eloquent source, a book of fiery sermons preaching salvation to the 'manuary craftworkers' of the town in 1586. Yet to contextualize such a telling episode, and to do justice to what, it soon appeared, was an extremely eventful *longue durée*, would require months (decades) of focused study. I marked it as a very interesting but as yet unexplored story and returned to the larger study I was trying to complete at the time.

The history of Cirencester has haunted me ever since. The events of the 1570s and 1580s have gradually merged into the larger story I encountered first in an exceptionally rich town historiography: Rudder, the proud and outspoken eighteenth-century citizen; the great English country writer, Richard Jefferies, author of *Hodge and his Masters*; his contemporary E.A. Fuller, incumbent and author of what remain great essays on medieval constitutional struggles; the prolific, cosmopolitan gentleman-scholar from Painswick, Welbore St Clair Baddeley; and the invaluable K.J. Beecham – to name only the leading town scholars of the eighteenth to early twentieth centuries. The town was one of H.P.R. Finburg's superb *Gloucestershire Studies*. In what is still a definitive piece of English economic and social history, an article published half a century ago, A.J. and R.H. Tawney identified Cirencester as a capital of a region where industrial capitalism and the 'protestant ethic' were born. The innovative English Marxist scholar, R.H. Hilton, noted it as something of a hot-spot in the thirteenth to fifteenth

2 Rudder, *History of Cirencester*, 248, also reports that 'a phenix in flames' was carved 'over one of the pillars' of the nave; possibly it was carved when the nave was rebuilt in the early sixteenth century. This raises the fascinating possibility that the townspeople responsible for the rebuilding saw the phoenix as an apt symbol for their activities: for the story and context of the rebuilding, see below, Chapter 6.

centuries. If we take in Sir Robert Atkyns, who knew the town very well indeed (he lived next door), some excellent members of local and national branches of the historian's craft have been noting and applying themselves to the history of the town for three centuries. Some of it was plain parochial affection, and none the worse for it, but, the main thing, they all noted that Cirencester punched well above its weight in the constitutional history of England, from the twelfth to seventeenth centuries. It is a legendary town and still, on a dark night, looks like one.

This is a social and political history. Cirencester attracts English Whigs, Tories and Socialists. R.H. Tawney, a great historian and a Christian socialist, was local, North Cotswolds; Tawneys were living near Stow on the Wold in the 1630s. At that time Sapperton House, Atkyns' residence, was occupied by Sir Henry Poole, whose family figures largely in the social and political history of the town and the Seven Hundreds of Cirencester in the century before the civil wars of the 1640s. Americans interested in the constitutional cultures of early American colonies could do a lot worse than study sixteenth-century Gloucestershire, a region that cradled and developed a great many communal experiments.

The Gloucestershire County Records Office is now the 'Gloucestershire Archives' and the 'Gloucestershire Collection' has now joined the rest of the local archive there. I am deeply grateful for the help and friendship given me over the years by the staffs of the Gloucestershire Archives and the Gloucester City Library. I must again acknowledge lasting debts of gratitude to Brian Frith, John Wyatt, Tom Bowers, Nick Herbert and John Fendley.

I have referred in passing to bits and pieces of the story in several publications. A master craftsman, Keith Wrightson, cast a critical and helpful eye over my first (1990) effort to 'reconstitute' the history of Cirencester from 1570 to 1643 and persuaded me the story was already too big to compress into a chapter of *The Local Origins of Modern Society: Gloucestershire 1500–1800* (1992). Pat Hudson invited me to give a talk on regions in early modern England at a conference at Liverpool University in 1995, and I responded with a study based on what I knew at that time of Cirencester's region. Comparative work on the history of early modern Liverpool during a Visiting Research Fellowship in the Department of Economic and Social History, University of Liverpool, led me, circuitously yet inexorably, back to the Cirencester archives. An early draft of several chapters, then called 'The Class-Struggles at Cirencester, 1117–1643', was referred to in a footnote to an article based partly on Cirencester sources published in *Social History* in 1999. My good friend Andy Wood read those draft chapters, which I still felt failed to do justice to their subject, discussed them with me and invited me to finish and publish the book in this series. Charles Zika invited me to talk about Jones the Preacher at a conference marking the end of the second millennium of Christianity, at Melbourne in 2000, followed by a chapter in Ellen Warne and Charles Zika (eds), *God, the Devil and a Millennium of Christian Culture* (Melbourne 2005). Dave Postles is an historian with a unique grasp of medieval and early modern social history and its sources, and shares my view that there is a significant gap in the new social and political historiography where towns like Cirencester are concerned; he kindly read the penultimate draft and offered many valuable suggestions. There are *vignettes* of the town's most dramatic appearances in traditional narratives of the nation, in 1400 and 1643, in *A Commonwealth of the People: Popular Politics and England's Long Social Revolution, 1066–1649* (2010). My hope is that what follows, entirely my own responsibility of course, does justice to the epic struggles of the commune of Cirencester in centuries that, for good and evil, saw the formation of the English nation.

Abbreviations

BL	British Library
Cal Close Rolls	Calendar of Close Rolls, various volumes
Cal Pat Rolls	Calendar of Patent Rolls, various volumes
Econ Hist Rev	*Economic History Review*
EEBO	Early English Books Online
Eng Hist Rev	*English History Review*
GA	Gloucestershire Archives
GCL	Gloucester City Library
GDR	Gloucestershire Diocesan Records
GHS	*Gloucestershire Historical Studies*
Hockaday	'Hockaday Abstracts': abstracts of (mainly) ecclesiastical records relating to Gloucestershire, compiled by F.S. Hockaday
TNA	The National Archives
Trans BGAS	Transactions of the Bristol and Gloucestershire Archaeological Society
VCH	*Victoria County History of Gloucestershire*

for our grandchildren

Introduction
Commune at the crossroads

It is a purpos'd thing, and grows by plot,
To curb the will of the nobility.
Shakespeare, *Coriolanus*, III, i

The place called *Corinium* by the Romans, and many variants of 'Cirencester' – 'armed camp by the River Churn' – after they left, replaced a nearby Celtic tribal capital, Bagendon, in the second and third centuries of the Christian era.[1] The change of location was determined by the crossing of three Roman roads, Akeman and Ermin Streets, and the Fosseway.[2] Like many old English towns, Cirencester owes its existence to Roman landscape engineering and a *pax romana* that imposed and protected movements of people, ideas and commodities throughout *Magna Britannia*. Later empires capable of restoring the roads and protecting the traffic depended on places like it to fill all the needs of the inter-regional traffic that converged on the space it occupied.

In the sense that it always belonged to an 'imperial' system, Cirencester was, and is, an imperial 'city'. Henceforth it owed its existence, not to the location of a lordship, a castle or a monastic foundation, but to the ability of its inhabitants, generation after generation, to maintain numerous functions within changing, larger, social systems. Its prosperity and happiness depended on the ability of its inhabitants to connect the town's wealthy rural hinterlands with the larger, national and international networks to which its strategic crossroads led. This inescapable fact was at the heart of the struggles of the commonalty of Cirencester against a succession of lords imposed on the town by succeeding states. The inhabitants described themselves differently at different times ('the fellowship of the town', 'the poor townspeople', 'resiants' and 'inhabitants'), usually implying the existence of

1 For the provenance of the name, see K.J. Beecham, *History of Cirencester and the Roman City of Corinium* (1887, repr. Stroud 1978), 3–4; from the fourteenth to the seventeenth centuries the name was frequently shortened to 'Ciciter' or 'Cisseter'.

2 Richard Reece and Christopher Catling, *Cirencester: Development and Buildings*, *British Archaeological Reports* 12 (Oxford 1975), 3–4 and Fig. 1.

a collective entity that was distinct from lordship and institutional governance. This fellowship embodied realistic, practical knowledge of why the town existed, what it was and what had to be done to keep its communal heart beating. Successive states and local lords resisted its formal incorporation for at least six centuries. The outcome is the subject of this book, an epic, stubborn, trans-generational struggle between two visions of religious, political and constitutional sovereignty.

We are dealing with simple ideas, always more easily transmitted than complex, nuanced paradoxes and contradictions, and not necessarily false. Imperial vision, let us say, is big-picture and top-down, hierarchical. Sovereignty was vested in a monarch, who then parcelled it out to a great chain of lesser mortals, from abbots and magnate lords down to village freemen. Urban merchants and village esquires, gentlemen and yeomen (or their earlier equivalents) saw to the everyday management of the subject, working people, delegating specific policing and licensing functions to men lower in the hierarchy. Constables and beadles, tithingmen and wardsmen, aletasters, bread-weighers, leather-stampers, overseers of various collective enterprises like repairing roads and bridges, were drawn from lower down: husbandmen, innkeepers, drapers, tailors and (very occasionally) labourers served as jurors in local manor courts and vestrymen in the parishes. The perspective of Empire was that authority descended. Kings and lords were sovereign. Empires look down on their parts, their subjects look up.

The other extreme is that authority ascends from the people. The movement explored in this book was not for popular sovereignty in the modern sense. Its basis was communal, not individualist. Communitarian popular sovereignty arose from the precept that everything depended on the morale and well-being of the communities of those who worked. The word 'commonweal', conjoining the Norman-French 'commune' and the Anglo-Saxon *weal*, was coined to denote this constitutional vision from below, in the generation of William Langland, Geoffrey Chaucer, John Wyclif and John Ball. This book is an interpretation of sources of the history of a town and its 'country', the Seven Hundreds of Cirencester, from the establishment of the 'domination of abbots', in the twelfth century, to the defeat of the parliamentarian commune in February 1643, with an Afterword offering some hypotheses concerning later developments. It privileges struggles for communal harmony and independence on the part of those who tilled the fields, built the houses, manufactured and exchanged the goods, saw to the care of thousands of churches and, collectively, organized the localities where the work went on. The operational contexts of the vast majority of the commonalty, or subject population, were local, but never exclusively so. The function of the inhabitants of the commune was to keep themselves and the inhabitants of its 'country' (the Seven Hundreds) in touch with matters that concerned them in the wider world.

What made Cirencester a regional capital – the capital of a distinctive *countrey* – was its location as a crossroads between other regions and countries of England.[3] Cirencester connected London and the East, Bristol, Exeter and the South West, Coventry and the Midlands, the Forest of Dean, Gloucester, Shrewsbury and Wales. During the period covered in this book – the twelfth to eighteenth centuries – it funnelled commodities from its hinterlands up the Thames Valley to London. It is structurally and mythically important that the Isis (Thames) rises in the ancient Hundred of Cirencester. From the fourteenth to seventeenth centuries the town transmitted bales of wool and bundles of cloth from their producers in the town and Seven Hundreds for distribution to other parts of England and, via Bristol, Southampton and, in time overwhelmingly, London, for export overseas. Wool and cloth made ten generations of inhabitants of the town and Seven Hundreds of Cirencester wealthy: only ever a small minority, it must be added, yet it always made a difference that, in a society riddled with class and status hierarchies, the rule of the comparatively rich was judged by their service to commune, *countrey* and commonweal.

Early modern Cirencester's 'country' was 'heartland England'. Its sources testify to the more or less continuous presence of all the 'sorts of people' described by the great Tudor constitutional writer, Sir Thomas Smith, in *A Discourse of the Commonweal of this Realm of England* (1549) and *De Republica Anglorum* (written 1560s, first published 1583) – and in roughly the same proportions. As such the town and its district were atypical, very different from another type of heartland England, John Smyth of Nibley's yeoman-dominated Hundred of Berkeley, or, different again, the fishermen and mariners of Over Severn and the proudly independent free miners of the Forest of Dean. To the north and northwest, Shakespeare's Stratford upon Avon, impoverished Winchcombe and Cheltenham, and bustling, enterprising Tewkesbury, were different again. Across the South Wolds lay Bristol, to the west across the Wolds and down the Edge at Birdlip snaked the road to the southernmost bridging point on the Severn, the county town and seat of the diocese of Gloucester. No two towns or villages anywhere in this region were alike, but some generalizations are possible.

Towns were where the persistent division of the common people of England into three or four broad classes, rich, upper- and lower-middling and poor, stood out most clearly. This simple class structure is qualified by sources throughout, yet describes well enough how members of the commonalty saw and classified themselves, as against how they were classified by their betters ('common'). Class and, at times, class-*struggle* divided the commonalty in every century spanned in these pages. I argue that in the long run another theme was as strong and sometimes stronger: a countervailing, trans-generational effort to make all the inhabitants work together as one 'fellowship'. When these efforts weakened, class and factional struggle came to the fore.

[3] For 'country', see Rollison, *The Local Origins of Modern Society*, 15–17, and below, 79, 208.

Map 1. Detail from Christopher Saxton's map of Gloucestershire, showing towns and villages of the Seven Hundreds (Courtesy of Gloucestershire Archives)

Map 1 shows a section of Christopher Saxton's map of Gloucestershire that corresponds to the '*countrey*' centred on Cirencester from the thirteenth to seventeenth centuries. 'Cirencester/Ciceter' is located in the southeastern corner, upriver from Cricklade. Roughly, my study is of the region encircled by the towns of Lechlade, Burford, Winchcombe, Tewkesbury, Gloucester, Dursley and Tetbury. This is slightly larger than the medieval and early modern 'Seven Hundreds of Cirencester'. Saxton shows that the countryside around the town was thickly settled with villages. The Seven Hundreds contained a hundred or so parishes, several chapelries, the gradually coalescing township of 'Stroyde' (Stroud), wealthy Painswick and compact, wool-trading Northleach. It was thickly settled because it was a varied, fertile, efficiently farmed and industrious country. Great flocks of sheep grazed the hills, industrious villagers husbanded and settled the valleys. In the fourteenth and fifteenth centuries large-scale cloth manufacturing developed in the Hundreds of Longtree and Bisley to the west of the town beyond 'Okeley wood' and the traditional power house at Sapperton. The western limits of the Seven Hundreds of Cirencester are where the hills end between Birdlip and 'Stroyde'. Part of the aim of this book is to explain why Cirencester was 'universally esteemed the (strategic) key' to control of this region for so many centuries, up to the constitutional wars of the seventeenth century.

The wealth attracted by the commune was always very unevenly distributed. I suggest in Chapters 3, 7 and 12 that from Edward III's first national tax in 1327 to the hearth taxes of the 1670s, between forty and sixty percent of households were judged too poor to pay taxes. At the other end of the social spectrum, 'big men' (exceptionally wealthy individuals) figured largely in the leadership of the commune, and gentlemen were thick on the ground in the villages. National tax assessments of the fourteenth to seventeenth centuries delineate these classes: in the town, a small elite of never more than a dozen very wealthy wholesalers and merchants; a small 'upper middle' class of lesser merchants, clothiers and the better-off master craftsmen; a larger 'lower middle' class consisting mainly of (often younger) artisans, retailers and miscellaneous shopkeepers, bakers and butchers. These were the taxpaying inhabitants. Then comes an extremely various 'fourth sort', Shakespeare's 'many headed monster', a class described by polite society in the eighteenth century as 'the multitude around us'. Above them all was the lord of the manor. From 1117 to 1539, this was a wealthy, resident Augustinian abbot.

The communities of the Seven Hundreds changed in response to shifting regional orientations, but the reason for its existence never changed. Beyond the critical fertility and enterprise of their 'cantons', towns like Cirencester depend on the vitality and integrity of the larger systems – provinces, kingdoms, federations of kingdoms, the nation, Christendom – to which, irrevocably, their fates were connected. As a consequence, it was an abiding rule never to neglect and lose connection with the local, national and international networks that, continuously and profitably, joined the commune to the larger business, political and religious communities of succeeding ages. There was never a time in the centuries spanned by this study when these connections were not being assiduously and enterprisingly maintained.

If national and regional traffic ebbed or flooded away, as it did from time to time, the commune contracted in size. This may have happened in the fifth and sixth centuries, after the fall of Rome.[4] Social memory, continuously prompted by visible ruins and monuments, meant the Roman capital was never entirely forgotten. I suggest the commune of Cirencester possessed a collective, 'corporate' identity that was transmitted, continuously, from one generation to the next. Its customs, first recorded in the early thirteenth century, fuelled resistance to the more oppressive aspects of the states and empires to which it was, irrevocably, annexed.

Another structural theme is that at no time from the early fourteenth to mid-seventeenth centuries was Cirencester able to reproduce the functions it served without routine and occasionally large-scale immigration. Bacteria-carrying traffic of various kinds probably washed along ill-repaired

4 See Chris Whickham, *Framing the Early Middle Ages: Europe and the Mediterranean, 400–800* (Oxford 2005), 339–551.

Roman roads in the fifth and sixth centuries, enough of it, perhaps, to keep a few hostelries open and a few households (blacksmith, wheelwright, saddler, shoemaker, possibly a priest and a musician or two) clustered around the place where the three great roads crossed. Carriers from local villages continued to gather there at certain times to pick up specialist items (and gossip) from wholesalers from other parts. Welsh cattlemen, wool drivers and buyers, innkeepers, smiths, victuallers, musicians and actors, painters, masons and sculptors and all sorts of other vocations and occupations depended, across the centuries, on the volume and regularity of regional and national traffic. The continuing existence of this lively crossroads meant that a little *civitas*, with all its ambitions and memories of struggle, was always ready to spring back into existence as the capital of its own wealthy little province and as a meeting place of hills and lowlands, Wales and the West Country, the Midlands and the South, London and the East. The commune was connected to its country, or (the French equivalent) *pays*, by chains of association and kinship.[5] It connected its country to the whole commonwealth of England – and the worlds beyond.

This book is a study of an open, trans-generational community, grounded in pragmatic knowledge of what was necessary for the commune to reproduce itself and prosper.[6] The line between the townspeople and the lord and his retainers was always elastic, but whenever they attempted to name their community (as 'the fellowship of the town', 'the poor townspeople of Cirencester', 'the poor inhabitants' and so on) they posited that the inhabitants, for all their gross inequalities, had one thing in common: they were 'poor' (in 'estate': wealth, power and institutionalized authority) in relation

5 In defining the town as a 'commune', a particular kind of 'collectivity', I am guided by W.G. Runciman, *Social Science and Political Theory* (Cambridge 1969), 7–8, who writes that 'What we are talking about when we say a collectivity exists is a "probability of action" appropriate in a specified way to the meaning attached to the collectivity… When a sociologist formulates a proposition about such a collectivity he must be able to specify the concrete social action which the proposition denotes. By this means he can not only see how a given proposition might in principle, at least, be falsified, but we can also avoid treating a collectivity as if it were a tangible object – the "fallacy of reification" which incenses the individualists.'

6 F.W. Maitland, 'The Corporation Sole', *Law Quarterly Review* 16 (1900): the great English constitutional historian called it 'corporateness'. 'The essence of corporateness,' wrote Maitland, was 'the permanent existence of [an] organized group, the "body" of "members", which remains the same body though its particles change.' I argue that, historically if not legally, the commonalty or community of Cirencester was such a body. Its existence was never completely independent of its 'particles', be they generations or individuals and families living at a specific time. Particularly enterprising individuals and associations could and did make a difference. Yet the town's structural dependence on larger fields of force (regional, national, international) ensured a certain continuity of practical problems and questions that remained in play throughout the five centuries and fifteen or more generations whose records and remains are the evidential base of this book.

to successive lords of Cirencester manor. And they continuously reinvented memories of a time when 'the poor townspeople' *had* governed themselves. One reading of Cirencester's history from the twelfth to nineteenth centuries is that the lords successfully resisted this unrelenting, trans-generational movement to make the town an independent, self-governing borough.

What emerges from the composition of the inhabitants is an underlying, recurring pattern. Where the distribution of wealth is concerned, not much changed from the earliest source (1327) to the Hearth Tax of 1671. Wealth was grossly and systematically unequal throughout. Social relations of production evident in the more systematic sources of the century before the civil wars can, I suggest, be projected back into the fifteenth, fourteenth and thirteenth centuries. The biological regime also remained much the same from the advent of plague, in 1349, to the late eighteenth century. Endemic bacteria mutated constantly, but the threat of death by endemic or epidemic disease remained a feared and taken-for-granted structure of life throughout. Famine may have left English shores in the sixteenth century, as demographers have suggested, but dearth and hunger emphatically did not, especially in old towns like Cirencester and new manufacturing districts like the neighbouring Stroudwater Valleys. Total wealth increased in the long run, but gross class differences were systemic and continuous. The language used to describe, legitimize, neutralize or criticize the inequality changed, the underlying class structure, I suggest, did not.[7]

Much of what follows is about what sources tell us did change: 'event-history' and collective consciousness. 'Events', January 1400 (Chapter 5), the papal 'fatwah' of 1570 (Chapter 9) and February 1643 (Chapter 16), I show, mobilized and dramatized underlying communitarian impulses and actual constitutions of the five hundred or so households that formed the town and its relations and communications with surrounding districts and beyond. Two structural changes stand out. First, after c.1300, a mode of production Marx called 'manufacturing' imposed its stamp on two previously rural hundreds, Bisley and Longtree. Cirencester was the central place of the new industrial districts until Stroud replaced it in the later seventeenth century. Clothmaking probably doubled the amount of wealth routinely brought back into the Seven Hundreds by the production and export of its prized commodities (traditionally wool, after c.1400 wool and cloth).

Second, sixteenth-century tax and militia surveys trace the emergence of gun-culture: guns replaced bows as the weapon of choice in the borough, market towns and villages of the Seven Hundreds sometime between 1522 and 1608. Guns figure prominently – and were probably decisive – in the

7 'Structures of society' is used throughout to mean abiding modes or systems of production, social relations of production, settlement patterns, means of communications, connectivity with other regions, religion, common language and ideas.

defeat of February 1643, told in Chapter 16. These changes were structural in the sense that they eventually transformed military and economic life.

The presentation is chronological. I construct a narrative of a highly formative period in Cirencester's (and thus, by definition, England's) history, from the twelfth to seventeenth centuries. Chapter 1 describes the arrival of an 'empire', a dominion that shaped urban politics for half a millennium: Henry I's endowment of an Augustinian abbey. It chronicles the expansion and intensification of the abbey's lordship from 1117 to roughly 1300. Chapter 2 describes violent struggles between lord and commune during the general crisis of the reign of Edward II. Chapter 3 delineates the classes of the commune on the basis of a tax assessment of 1327, in order to gain a clearer impression of the membership of what contemporaries called 'the fellowship of the town' and 'the poor men of Cirencester'. Chapter 4 takes the story of the abbots' empire and commonalty's resistance up to 1399. The dominion of the abbey from the twelfth to late fourteenth centuries is evidenced by the resistance of its corollary, a community that local jurors of the first decade of the thirteenth century termed 'the fellowship of the town'. Eruptions of this 'fellowship' generated the documentation on which the narrative of empire rests.

From the thirteenth to seventeenth centuries the lords of the manor did their best to incorporate the whole of communal life into the jurisdiction of the manor. The community or 'fellowship of the town' resisted incorporation. Mundane, circumstantial motives played a part in the struggles, but one precept was continuous: the belief that the community of the town existed as a separate, practical entity independent of alien institutions like lords of manors.

Chapter 5 examines an 'event', the townspeople's bloody intervention in English dynastic politics, in January 1400. Contemporaries noticed the symbolic as well as merely practical implications of that exceedingly timely intervention of the people at a traditional juncture in the history of the English state. Under the shadow of the church, within sight and earshot of the abbey, the bowmen of Cirencester utterly defeated, arrested and beheaded two senior noblemen of the kingdom. It was recognized at the time as an event with unanticipated constitutional implications. Chapter 6 shows that, in response to their eventual (predictable) betrayal by Henry of Lancaster and his son, the 'generation of 1400' created a vibrant and sensuous religious life that, testamentary and chantry sources reveal, retained its beauty and vigour for a century and a half, right up to the 'two dissolutions' of 1539 and 1547–8. They conceived and built one of the great English 'perpendicular' churches. The burghers and businessmen of Cirencester and the Seven Hundreds were never more enterprising than in this 'long fifteenth century'.

The parish church of St John the Baptist still witnesses the confidence, skill, capital and communal vision of the generations who built it. From the completion of the tower in 1415 to the construction of the nave a century later, the business community of Cirencester led its region in the way a capital town ought to lead. The dissolutions, of the abbey in 1539 and the chantries in 1548, removed the common enemy and confiscated capital that underpinned the communal religion of the fifteenth century. These seismic shocks explain why communal reconstruction took time – about a generation. A survivalist cabal led by the last abbot's bailiff, Robert Strange, policed the town for absentee lords from 1539 until the 1570s (Chapters 8 and 9). These chapters describe the disintegration of the religious commune founded in the late fourteenth and early fifteenth centuries. Gross inequality was intrinsic to the early modern commune: the challenge, always, was to create and maintain communal initiatives designed to minimize the ill effects of everyday class and factional struggle. For a time it was not clear who or what would emerge to fill the vacuum left by the disintegration of the medieval parish. The rules governing parishes and churches changed bewilderingly in the 1540s and 1550s. Chapters 5 forward are, in part, studies of the long English Reformation. The actual formation of the religious sects that, henceforth, were intrinsic to the history of the town is not strictly my brief here. Sects like 'Anabaptists', 'Congregationalists', 'Independents', 'Presbyterians' and 'Quakers' began to harden in the later 1640s and 1650s, as suggested in the Afterword. My account ends in February 1643, a signpost at the crossroads between one epoch and the next, as explained in the Afterword. Modern, 'rural' Cirencester was the form the new phoenix took, rising gradually out of the flames of frustrated resistance, rebellion and revolution.

In the epoch of communal resistance, constantly aggressive state religious policies eventually animated local communities by convincing them that the prescribed order in church and state could not be trusted to serve their needs. Cirencester's response in the later sixteenth century was as it had been in the past. Beginning with a timely petition of 'poor townspeople' against their 'papist' bailiff in 1570, the phoenix of communal governance was born again in the later decades of the sixteenth century. The 1560s and 1570s saw the emergence of opposition on two fronts. As Robert Strange grew old and the legitimacy of his regime weakened, sectaries defied his religious governance and a well-organized and well-funded movement of retailers and craftworkers tried to have the town reconstituted as a borough with what would later be called a 'leveller' franchise. In 1571 the town was made a parliamentary borough with the right to return two members to the House of Commons.

In decades when the parliamentary franchise became an issue, out of the ashes of the second failure of a movement to establish a Guild Merchant, rose a broadly unifying movement comparable with the parish revival of the fifteenth century. Bequests began flowing into the parish treasury again in the 1580s and 1590s and were sustained in the decades before the civil wars of the 1640s. An oligarchy of gentlemen, merchants and leading craftsmen initiated schemes to provide 'manuary workers' with loans to set themselves up as independent householders, funds for apprenticing poor children, money for raw materials to 'set the poor on work', and alms for the 'deserving poor', the sick, widows, orphans and the like.

This revived parish was fully operational by 1610, when its 'constitution' was discussed, formulated, committed to the minutes of the Vestry and presented to 'the better sort' for ratification. I argue the reforms of the late sixteenth and early seventeenth centuries were not opportunist or piecemeal; they derived from a systematic and lucid vision of an English commonwealth that dovetailed business, religion and secular governance. One aim was to create prosperity by harnessing capital and labour; another was to relieve tensions between rich and poor by judicious and systematic investment of carefully managed funds in apprenticeships, small businesses, make-work schemes and, above all, preaching.

Chapters 10 to 16 also describe a town and a region rising out of the ashes of the constitutional culture that had dominated them for five centuries. The focus changes slightly, partly to accommodate more systematic sources. The commune remains central but its 'canton' or 'country' is delineated in a little more detail. These chapters take in a region comprising the borough and about a hundred parishes within 'the Seven Hundreds of Cirencester'. They suggest the richer documentation of the later period sheds light on the condition of the region in earlier, less well-documented centuries.

Two more 'dates' or 'events' bracket the period from 1571 to February 1643. As noted above, Cirencester became a parliamentary borough in 1571. The serial demographic and economic contexts are addressed in Chapter 10. After c.1550 (the epidemics of the 1550s may mark an early sign that the supply of necessities was declining relative to total population) the ecology of England was unbalanced by a burst of sustained population growth. Chapter 10 chronicles the paradoxical pattern of 'crises and growth' in the town and Seven Hundreds from c.1560 to 1660. Chapter 11 focuses on a social movement that may well have been decisive in the generation of 1400, but only leaves ambiguous documentary traces in the earlier period: the struggles, in the 1570s and 1580s, of the middle and lower middle ranks of inhabitants, mainly 'independent' artisans and small retailers, against the social and constitutional hegemony of 'the rich'. This chapter includes analysis of an extraordinarily vehement series of sermons preached against 'the rich' and proclaiming that only 'poor manuary craftsmen' would be saved. As throughout the book, it is necessary to determine who exactly the terms 'rich' and 'poor' were intended to mean, in the light of contemporary theories of commonwealth.

Chapter 12 complements earlier chapters on social structure to delineate the variable 'constitutions' of the town and the hundred or so villages and markets of the Seven Hundreds. It tests and qualifies the near-contemporary constitutional anatomies of Sir Thomas Smith and Thomas Wilson in the light of incomparably rich muster lists of 1608, arguing that the latter offer a useful guide to the 'inhabitants' of the region as contemporaries used that word. As social historian Henry French explains, 'inhabitant' meant more, in the late sixteenth and seventeenth centuries, than the mere fact of residency. It referred to the members of broader constituencies that expected to be, and, in the interests of communal harmony, often were consulted and engaged by 'the better sort' (a term used at Cirencester in the early seventeenth century to denote the wealthier householders from whom churchwardens were selected) in processes of local governance. I suggest the basic unit of 'inhabitancy' in this sense was the 'independent' household, understood as a unit the decisive (but not only) qualification of which was *not* property ownership, but the ability to live on its own resources, usually (for most) the produce of a smallholding and/or wages. This chapter contextualizes the emergence, from 1571 to 1640, of commune and 'country' as self-conscious and socially deep constituencies of parliament, the franchises of which are enumerated and explored in Chapter 15. Chapter 13, based on aggregation and cross-referencing of parish registers and the muster lists, describes the social movement from which this loaded sense of 'inhabitancy' took its meaning: the tides of migrant labour on which Cirencester had always depended to maintain its size and functions.

Chapter 14 explores the response of a new, vehemently protestant elite – 'the gentlemen of town and country', as one of its leaders put it – to the disintegration of the post-1539 'survivalist' regime and the movement of the middling and lesser artisans in the 1570s and 1580s. It describes, first, the initiatives of two assiduously well-connected reformers, each of whom left a decisive mark on the corporate constitution and social memory. Philip Marner (?–1587) is remembered by his unusual brass in the nave of the church. When John Coxwell (1516–1617) died 'Abbot Street' was renamed 'Coxwell Street', in memory of his contributions to civic life. I quantify the bequests that formed the economic base of the parish revival they inspired, detail its constitution in the 1610s and suggest that the whole movement was based on 'communal capitalism', involving intense valorization of relations between relatively wealthy employers and 'the poor'. The result was a new, very businesslike Jerusalem, a prosperous 'commonwealth' driven by an alliance of godly, enterprising businessmen, 'the gentlemen of town and country' and the rank and file 'manuary (manual) workers'. The revival of the parish was never without vociferous, 'separatist', opponents, but, I argue, it was able to achieve a remarkable communal unity that only fell apart as a result of the civil war.

Chapter 15 enumerates and chronicles the final ingredient of the 'new communalism'. It shows that, in the period 1571–1640, connections between local and national reform movements intensified: first, by a quite dramatic increase in the number of 'voices' entitled to be heard in local shire and, especially, borough elections; second by the purchase of the Rectory of Cirencester, in 1627, by the London-based, puritan Feoffees for Impropriations; thirdly, by the active involvement in local affairs of influential committees of the House of Commons. The result, intensified by Charles I's secular and religious policies in the 1630s, was that by 1640, commune and country were intimately connected into parliamentarian religious and mercantile networks (usually the same men and organizations) that spearheaded national opposition to the prerogatives of the crown.

Chapter 16 narrates the local impact of the tremendous national social drama that resulted, locally and nationally, in the disintegration of the class alliances on which the new communalism was based. It opens with the attempt of George Brydges, sixth lord Chandos of Sudeley, to present the king's commission of array at Cirencester in August 1642, and ends with the siege of February 1643 and its demoralizing aftermath.

An Afterword presents images of the new, rural, magnate-dominated Cirencester that emerged in the eighteenth and nineteenth centuries, offers some source-based hypotheses relating to its development, and suggests some directions for further research on a part of the story that has yet to be told.

The operation of communal ethics: tyranny and the common good

As succeeding historians of medieval Cirencester have noted, the town's most dramatic occasions had to do with the community's enduring struggle with the its lords. These struggles, I argue, derived from collective precepts concerned with the evaluation of leadership and lordship that were ingrained in the constitutional culture of late medieval England. In the past few decades some of the most important insights into the constitutions of early modern England have been achieved in a growing body of local studies of cultures of governance operating below the level of the state. Marjorie Macintosh suggests local communities often anticipated reforms of governance and ideas that were only later, often much later, taken up by the state.[8] In developing ideas of Keith Wrightson and earlier generations of social historians, Steve Hindle shows that these localized 'cultures of government' drew on 'a common fund of ideas approaching the status of moral orthodoxy'.[9] The communal movements documented in this book were driven by a baseline 'moral orthodoxy' that, in times of crisis (which were many), took precedence over everything else.

The collective mentality of Cirencester from the thirteenth to seventeenth centuries was shaped by a simple yet highly responsive form of communalism.

Its first precept was that the whole takes precedence over the parts. Every community, neighbourhood, family, household and individual belonged to a greater 'commonwealth'. Any part or 'member' that pursued its own interests at the expense of the greater whole was a tyrant. Commonweal/th theory was not unique to England, of course. It had classical origins in the writings, among others, of Plato, Aristotle and Cicero. As I argue in *A Commonwealth of the People* (2010), its pervasive and frequently decisive influence in England dated back at least to the baronial wars of the thir-

8 Marjorie Keniston Macintosh, *Controlling Misbehaviour in England, 1370–1600* (Cambridge 1998).

9 Steve Hindle, *The State and Social Change in Early Modern England, 1550–1640* (Basingstoke 2000), 220, qf. Ian Breward, 'The Direction of Conscience', in Breward (ed.), *The Work of William Perkins* (Abingdon 1970), 75.

teenth century, when rebellious barons justified their resistance to Henry III by claiming to represent *all* the people, including the 'middling sort' and the commonalty. It became entrenched as a result of its use as justification for the spectacular depositions of Edward II (1327) and Richard II (1399).

The theory was developed and given considerable impetus by two widely read treatises of Sir Thomas Smith (1549, 1583), and, increasingly, by a new generation of theologians, preachers and lecturers, who infused medieval vocationalism with renewed theological legitimacy.[10] 'A vocation or calling', wrote influential Calvinist preacher and theologian, William Perkins, 'is a certain kind of life, ordained and imposed on man by God, *for the common good*.' The idea that every soul is projected into the world, by God, with an ultimately unique vocation, was thoroughly traditional and widely, perhaps universally believed from the thirteenth century up to the Puritan Revolution. If every person pursues his or her inborn vocation, the common good will follow. 'The final cause or end of every calling' was breathtakingly simple, universal and easily remembered: it had to be 'for the common good'. Perkins said this meant 'for the benefit and state of mankind', but most of those who heard his sermons and read his books would have understood it to mean their own localities in relation to the whole commonwealth of England.[11] Preachers spread lucid versions and applications of commonwealth theory to hearers rather than readers. But no-one understood the way commonwealth ideology worked in sixteenth-century England better than Sir Thomas Smith, son of a common burgher of Saffron Walden, a town like Cirencester, a 'capital' of its own *countrey*.

Smith followed Aristotle, who wrote that all constitutions were variable mixtures of three 'types': rule by one, rule by few and 'the thirde where the multitude doth rule', as Smith put it. A 'parte oor member of the common-weal is said to rule whiche doth controwle, correct, all other members of the common-wealth.'[12] A just commonweal is one in which 'that part which doth beare the rule, doe command that which is profitable to [the commonwealth]'.[13]

As in Aristotle's paradigm, Smith's ideal forms, Monarchy, Aristocracy and Polity, had just and tyrannical forms or tendencies. 'The just man' in each type (monarch, noble or citizen of the multitude), always aims to put right 'that which is amisse, and help the common wealthe, and doe good unto it'. Just constitutions are when the ruling part, whatever its type, 'doe

10 Sir Thomas Smith, *A Discourse of the Commonweal of this Realm of England, attributed to Sir Thomas Smith*, ed. Mary Dewar (Charlottesville 1969); Smith, *De Republica Anglorum*, ed. Mary Dewar (Cambridge 1982); Mary Dewar, *Sir Thomas Smith: A Tudor Intellectual in Office* (London 1984).

11 William Perkins, *A Treatise on the Vocation or Calling of men*, in M.J. Kitch, *Capitalism and the Reformation* (London 1969), 153.

12 *De Republica*, Ch. 2.

13 *Ibid*, Ch. 3.

command that which is profitable to [the commonwealth]'. 'King' was the name given to a 'good and just' monarch; at the other extreme 'they call [an evil and unjust king]… a tyrant'. Aristocracy was 'a governing of the best men… or *Remp. Optimatum*', its tyrannical form government by 'a few gentlemen, or a few of the richer and stronger sort' who disdained consultation with the others ('counsel') and were concerned only to do themselves good at the expense of the commonwealth. 'Where the multitude doth govern' the good form 'they call a commonwealth by the general name of the rule of the people'. The bad form was 'the rule or the usurping of the popular or rascall and viler sort.'[14] Informed as English public opinion was by these easily remembered tools of constitutional thought (constantly alluded to in popular sermons and lectures, and central to all variants of 'puritanism'), people of all ranks and classes were bound to ask what type of rule prevailed in their worlds, especially in frequent crises that affected everyone, albeit in different ways.

The implications of this ubiquitous ideology were very different from those of modern constitutional theory and ideology. Modern political ideology tends to assume that democracy (Aristotle and Smith's third form) is to be preferred over all others – thus reversing the medieval and early modern convention that monarchy was the best form. Aristotelian theory places content above form: any of the three forms, or any mixture of the forms, is good, if and only if the ruling part consults and rules in the interests of the whole commonwealth. In commonwealth ideology, no type is inherently superior. What mattered was not form but content. Was a king, noble, gentleman or common inhabitant perceptibly motivated by love of the commonwealth? If s/he was, all was well.

Popular love of monarchy, for example, implied judgement by very high standards. A king who, it seemed, did not return the people's love and did not listen to their counsel, was like a false lover. Because of the frequency of popular rebellions, late medieval and early modern English people were acutely aware that Hell hath no fury like a people scorned. What determined constitutional success was not the system of government but the perceived public-spiritedness of the governor(s). Clearly it was never going to be easy to live by such high ideals, but that rarely stopped subjects from observing and, even in private, comparing observations. The legitimacy of government was determined by the observable quality of those in authority, as measured by the commonwealth quality test. Was authority exercised for personal or class interests, or was it for the commonwealth?

Sources report that every major and most minor rebellions of the people, notably in 1381, 1450, 1536 and 1549, rose in the name of the 'common weal'. Having raised the subject of tyranny, Smith addressed the burning question: 'whether… obedience [to an evill governed common wealth] be

14 *Ibid*, Ch. 4, 50–1.

just'; or, to put it the other way around, was resistance and rebellion justified? How should people living under tyranny respond? Was resistance or rebellion against tyrants permissible? Smith was tactfully evasive. People of his generation knew from experience that popular rebels justified themselves in terms of commonwealth ideology. Smith's first *Discourse* on the constitution was written in the wake of the popular rebellions of 1549. Right or wrong, the belief that oppressed subjects had a right, even a duty, to resist and rebel against tyrants 'hath bein cause of many commotions in common wealthes', he wrote. 'The judgement of the common people is according to the event and success,' he added, suggesting that popular memory discriminated between rebellions that were successful in restoring good order and others that were not. In other words, he was too aware of historical precedents to rule out resistance. 'Certain it is,' he concluded, 'that it is always a doubtful and hazardous matter to meddle with the changing of the lawes and government, or to disobey the orders of the rule of government.' Rebellions, depositions and changes of regime happened, as all Smith's contemporaries knew. They would probably happen again, for any 'commonwealth must turn and alter as before from one to a few, so now from a few to many and the most part' (1:14, 200).

Smith's *De Republica Anglorum* was reprinted many times in many forms in the decades between its first publication in 1583 and the civil wars. This was a time when an escalating number of highly educated preachers and lecturers, always adapting their message to the status and education of their congregations, drew together the theories of the day and gave them sharp, practical applications. They were the adult educators of their day. Tyranny theory, they assumed, did not apply only to kings. What made the tyranny theory of fourteenth to seventeenth-century England different from classical models was that it was thought to apply to *all* persons who exercised power and authority. The result was that English communities had to be *convinced* that those who exercised authority did so in the interests of the whole community, and not for anything less. It was also why, for centuries, the wealthy merchants and tradesmen of Cirencester, in their continuing resistance to the lords and their officials, represented themselves as 'the poor townspeople'. In using this phrase they identified themselves with the whole commonalty, the vast majority of whom *were* 'poor' in any meaning of the word.

1

A domination of abbots

The Augustinian abbey of St Mary, Cirencester, was 'perhaps the order's most important individual house' in England.[1] It was 'exceptionally well-founded' by Henry I in 1117, and in 1131 the first abbot, Serlo, was consecrated.[2] Four centuries later, in 1535, 'its revenues were much greater than those of all other Austin houses save Waltham and Leicester', an observation that applies to its earlier history, since it acquired little property beyond the town and Seven Hundreds of Cirencester after its foundation.[3] It became a casualty of the Henrician Reformation 'on the morning of 19 December 1539'.[4] The abbey's lordship over the town lasted 422 years. It took about two centuries to achieve its high-point of supremacy, in the early fourteenth century. How that hegemony was achieved, and efforts to subvert it began, are the subjects of this chapter.

The constitutional status of Cirencester was disputed through four centuries of monastic domination, and has been a subject of controversy among historians. When the abbey was founded the town's key institutions, the market and the parish church, had existed for centuries. The long economic boom of the twelfth and thirteenth centuries had yet to make a mark on its vocations and composition; at this time the residents appear to have been farmers and gardeners with other skills that could be of service to passing traffic: victuallers, inn- and tavern-keepers, smiths and carpenters also seem certain to have been present, all of them perhaps, at this time, part-time agriculturalists. There is little sign of a town in *Domesday Book* and what would, two centuries later, be villages, appear more like estates of the king or some lesser lord, manned by a

1 C.D. Ross, The Cartulary of Cirencester Abbey, Vol. 1 (London 1964), Editor's Introduction, xxi.

2 It is not clear if this is the same 'Serlo of Gloucester, a monk of St Michel, who rebuilt on a grand scale the abbey (Gloucester) which he had found almost extinct, mentioned by David Knowles, *The Monastic Order in England … 940–1216* (Cambridge 1963), 113; see also Knowles, *The Religious Orders in England*, Vol. 2 (Cambridge 1955), 259. Cirencester, with Oseney, Leicester and Plympton abbeys, were the largest houses, with 40–50 canons.

3 Ross, *Cartulary*, xxi.

4 Richard Reece, 'The Abbey of St Mary, Cirencester', *Trans BGAS* 81 (1962), 199. The date is when ownership left the church and was taken into the hands of the crown.

few villeins and slaves. Duntisbourne, for example, was 'a manor of five hides' with '3 ploughs and 8 villeins with five ploughs' in demesne. Completing the inventory were '16 slaves'.[5] Fifty-seven tenants are recorded in the documentation prepared some time before 1155.[6] Described as 'the king's men', they were not slaves,[7] but 'there was no man so free but he (was) bound to plough and to carry with a wagon if he have one, or with a cart'. Before the abbey came, they were 'by their birth villeins of our lord, the king'. This standard formula resonates controversially through the documentation of the next four centuries, when a relentless succession of abbots tried to convert (and legally succeeded in converting) the townspeople into villeins of the abbey as well as of the king. The political history of the town would turn upon resistance to this unwelcome constitutional middle-man until Henry VIII dissolved the abbey in December 1539.

Godfrey Cuppe, John the Smith, Robert Hurt, Richard Knit and William Croce had names familiar enough to pass modern notice. Segrim, who 'carried much hay' for the king in the last harvest, Heregrim, Redegold, Alketil of Tidret, Thuribert and Eilmar, Hereward, Wulfric, Wolveric, Osbert of Walebarew, Angod and even Robert the sluggard are exotics to a modern ear, cosmopolitan reminders that the *burgh* or *villata*[8] of Cirencester, like all of England, already had a multicultural history.[9] At first sight the lists of names that provide our main evidence of the composition of Cirencester's commonalty during the centuries of monastic dominion are unpromising. Yet, as David Postles points out, the history of names has 'been widely adduced as a primary indicator' of important 'medieval cultural transitions'.[10] As we shall see throughout these early chapters, the analysis of lists and names yield valuable clues to the changing structure and composition of the commonalty of Cirencester from the early twelfth to the late fourteenth centuries.

5 *Domesday Book: A Complete Translation* (Penguin, London 2003), 455, 460.

6 'Customs and services', doc. 20 in Ross, *Cartulary*.

7 According to Domesday Book, as cited in Orlando Patterson, *Freedom*, Vol. 1: *Freedom on the Making of Western Culture* (New York 1991), 349–50, 'Nine percent of the counted population of England consisted of slaves in the late eleventh century, and in several of the western counties, such as Cornwall and Gloucestershire, the slave population exceeded 20 percent, larger than the percentage found in several of the slave states of the antebellum South.'

8 Both terms occur in contemporary documents, signifying the terrain on which the town's struggles were to occur for the next five centuries – as follows.

9 'Customs and services of the tenants of Cirencester', in Ross, *Cartulary*, doc. 20, 16; translation in E.A. Fuller, 'Tenures of Land by the Customary Tenants in Cirencester', *Trans BGAS* 2 (1877–8), 286–7; repr. Welbore St Clair Baddeley, *A History of Cirencester* (Cirencester 1924), 106–7. The quote regarding their status is from an inquisition dated 1209–10, *ibid*, 138–40. Baddeley illuminates the 'Dark Ages' carefully discriminating fact from myth, 1–87.

10 David Postles, *Naming the People of England, c.1100–1350* (Cambridge 2006), 11. See also the papers in Postles (ed.), *Naming, Society and Regional Identity* (Oxford 2002).

The list included Acelin the Priest, who was also bound to plough and carry for the king. He was a member of the community, listed willy-nilly among the other tenants. Beyond his name (Acelin), vocation (priest) and status (kingsman, i.e. 'freeman') we can only speculate. In later, better-documented times, priests were absolutely central to the quality of community life and the condition of the parish. Cirencester was essentially a one-parish town: the whole community was centred on the church of St John the Baptist, and the marketplace over which it presided. These were its central places. A conscientious parish priest routinely met his parishioners in the church and market.[11] In later, better-documented, centuries the community had high expectations of its priests. Priests (and canons) who consistently failed to live up to certain ideals and failed to convince the people that they put the spiritual and material well-being of the community before their own or other partial interests, were always challenged. King's-men like Acelin answered to two lords (the monarch and God), and sometimes the two did not agree. A priest could lead, or encourage a community to resist other lords, including the king, in the name of God. The question of whose side the priests were on reverberates through the centuries surveyed in this book.

Among Acelin's neighbours, 'Wulfric's widow' was obliged 'to mow one acre of corn and do haymaking work'; Geoffrey's widow had to 'pay one penny', perhaps in lieu of labour services. Women could be heads of households, perhaps even 'elders', though this role in the community's eyes was, the evidence shows, usually occupied by men. There is no mention in the document of what were their rights and liberties, simply what they owed their lord the king. All were expected to do 'boon works', regular labour and services, for the king. The question that vexed Cirencester for the next four centuries was what happened when the king granted his estate to a middle-man?

These were some of the members of the commonalty when, in 1117, the king founded an abbey at Cirencester, and endowed it with local manors and liberties. The document informs us as to their relationship to their lord, the king (*villeins*), some of what it implied in terms of customary obligations, but very little else. Some of their children and grandchildren may have been

[11] There may have been three churches at Cirencester in the twelfth and thirteenth centuries – St Lawrence, St Ciceley and St John the Baptist; K.J. Beecham, *History of Cirencester and the Roman City of Corinium* (1887, repr. Stroud 1978), 5, is uncertain when St John the Baptist became the sole parish church, but it was by 1242, after which St Lawrence and St Cecily were, at best, 'chapels of ease' to the parish of St John; St Cecily was 'clene down' when Leland visited in the early sixteenth century. Throughout this book 'the parish' refers to the parish of St John the Baptist, for a map of which see Richard Reece and Christopher Catling, *Cirencester: Development and Buildings, British Archaeological Reports* 12 (Oxford 1975), 10, Fig. 3: 'Cirencester: the medieval parish'. It is of great significance that the jurisdictions and territories of manor (or borough) and parish were not the same, as the map in Reece and Catling shows very clearly; relations between the two institutions varied from time to time, but the parish was the people's (or 'commonalty's') institution, the manor was the lord's: see below, Chapter 5.

among those who, in 1155, complained to Henry II that his canons were abusing the 'liberties' granted 38 years earlier. The circumstances leading to the petition are unknown, but whatever they were the king issued a proclamation instructing his 'fee-fermor' the abbot 'not unjustly to vex the king's men of Cirencester for their free tenements which they hold of the king'. Nor was he 'unjustly to exact from them any other customs or services than those which they were sworn to perform for their tenements when the king gave the town to the Abbey in alms, or than the men and their forebears were wont to perform in the days of his grandfather'.[12] The abbey was not to 'vex the king's men'. The silent implication of this formula was that he could 'vex' his own tenants. For the next four centuries, the contention of the townspeople was that even if all but a few local households were his tenants, they were *all* king's-men and wished to be subject to no other. In the twenty-two years since the consecration of the first abbot in 1133, the abbey had, in trying to pay for the building works and consolidate their estate, offended the holders of 'free tenements' as well as their own tenants. The new abbey was flexing its muscles, and the case was a first test of whether it could get the support of the king. Henry told the canons to act with prudence and charity.

The foundation charter of Henry I used the term 'burgesses', and Richard I's strengthening of the abbot's liberties in the 1190s, perhaps carelessly, calls Cirencester *burgus*, a borough. This was as the townspeople wished themselves to be, and as the great thirteenth-century jurist, Henry de Bracton, saw them.[13] Henry II's scribe, possibly a canon of the abbey, called it *villata*, a mere town. The king's proclamation warning the abbot 'not... to vex the king's men' only referred to 'customs or services (other) than those which they were sworn to perform for their tenements when the king gave the town to the abbey in alms, or than the men and their forebears were wont to perform in the days of his grandfather'.[14] Once again, there is nothing specific about the liberties of the townspeople, only evidence that (1) they believed they had them, or ought to have them, and (2) they felt the abbey was engrossing them. Royal tax-

12 'Writ of Henry II prohibiting the abbot and canons of Cirencester from troubling wrongfully his men of Cirencester touching their free tenements in the vill of Cirencester', Ross, *Cartulary*, doc. 75, 58; Fuller, 'Cirencester: the Manor and the Town', *Trans BGAS* 10 (1884–5), 317; 'Writ of the king, given at the Abbey in 1176 or 1188', in Baddeley, *A History*, 119–20.

13 'It is attested that Cirencester is a borough... A royal charter had recognised that Cirencester had risen to (*sic*) the status of a borough. When this change in status took place, whether the land had previously been ancient demesne or not, the villein inhabitants automatically ceased to be villeins and became freemen capable of enjoying the freemen's remedies in the royal courts of law': D.M. Stenton (ed.), *Rolls of Justice in Eyre (Gloucestershire, Warwickshire and Staffordshire 1221, 1222)*, Selden Society (London 1940), xvii–iii.

14 'Writ of Henry II... ', Ross, *Cartulary*, doc. 75, 58; Fuller, 'Cirencester: The Manor and the Town', 317; 'Writ of the king, given at the abbey' in 1176 or 1188, in Baddeley, *A History*, 119–20.

collectors were habitually confused as to Cirencester's status: in parliamentary tax-returns between 1294 and 1336 the town is described six times as *burgus* and five times as *vill.*[15] This was not just carelessness or confusion; rather, it represented the opinion of whichever side of the struggle was instrumental in generating documentation. It would be a very long argument that implied at least a grain of truth in the townspeople's claim. Legally they were villeins of the land held by the abbot of the king, but, in Bracton's view, at some point in the eleventh century 'a royal charter had recognised… that Cirencester is a borough' whereupon 'the villein inhabitants… became freemen capable of enjoying the freemen's remedies in the royal courts of law'.[16] This practical ambiguity imposed an ongoing structure to subsequent struggles, in which the townspeople appealed to the king to support them in their resistance to what they saw as the encroachments of their local lord. Only Henry IV came close to taking their side, but that never stopped them trying.

The charter disappeared in the thirteenth century. The townspeople claimed all copies had been obtained by the abbot and burned. New charters were signed by succeeding kings who were ignorant of, or did not care that, their predecessors had sealed parchments promising other things to the townspeople. In 1198, Henry's heir (Richard I) needed funds for a crusade to the Holy Land. Among the many transactions conducted by his financial advisers was a charter 'making over to the Abbot the town and manor of Cirencester in fee-farm in perpetuity, with all its manorial rights, customs, and its weekly market, together with the jurisdiction of the Seven Hundreds' – the town's 'canton'.[17] The right to exclude the sheriff of Gloucester from the liberties was purchased in 1203, and seven years later Henry III sold the abbot a licence to build a jail.[18] 'The trade of the town, which increased very rapidly in the twelfth and thirteenth centuries, was entirely under the Abbot's control.'[19] 'At all times (the abbots) worked entirely for (their) abbey's interests without divulging beyond (their) convent walls what these were, nor what privileges (they) had privately purchased in London.'[20] The twelfth century saw the emergence of a powerful new presence at the heart of Cirencester's region: a lord whose line was not affected by the vagaries of heredity and kinship, and who, unlike most secular lords of the day, was 'always with them, armed not

15 'The alleged borough status of Cirencester', in Ross, *Cartulary*, xxxviii.

16 R.H. Hilton, *A Medieval Society: the West Midlands at the End of the Thirteenth Century* (London 1966), 156–7, observes that there were 'effectively two communities at Cirencester: one of merchants and artisans and the other of agricultural tenants. Both communities were fighting for a higher social and legal status than the abbey was prepared to give them.'

17 Baddeley, *A History*, 131.

18 *VCH Gloucestershire*, Vol. 2, ed. William Page (London 1907), 80.

19 *Ibid.*

20 Baddeley, *A History*, 176.

merely with secular powers, but with fearsome powers spiritual which might even threaten the life hereafter'.[21]

Under Richard I, John and Henry III, the abbots added to their already deep chest of charters the rights to return of the king's writs, custody of prisoners, and the right to levy tallage whenever the king did so – thus doubling labour services and/or financial exactions. Once the townspeople had only two lords, the king and God. Now it had three.

As was to be the case repeatedly in the future, local tensions flared in times of general crisis. The region experienced 'extensive break-down of public order' during the 'Barons Wars' of the early thirteenth century. In 1215 the prior of Cirencester received a letter from a tenant at Wotton complaining that 'while this disturbance of the realm lasts many perils threaten travellers and make their journeys difficult; it is scarcely ever possible to go from one place to another without being robbed'.[22]

Struggles within the ruling classes presented an opportunity for the community to challenge the now well-entrenched 'new regime'. Resistance flared in 1209, six years before the signing of Magna Carta, when 'certain young men of Cyrencester, by their birth villeins of our lord the king, also certain others from without, but sojournant there … made plaint to the Sheriff … against Richard, Abbot of Cyrencester … the king's fee-fermor', concerning the abbot's encroachment on their liberties. 'Nineteen lawfull elders of the men of Cyrencester' were called before the Abbot's Court to testify as to the customs of the town as they remembered them from what older generations had taught them, and what they had learned, as children, from *their* 'elders'. The elders assured the king's commissioners they were happy to maintain the canons, as laid down in the original charter of Henry I, and confirmed by the charter of the present king's father. Every *nativi* was bound to serve three *bederipes* (seasonal harvest works) a year, on the abbot's land. In this conception, the king gave the abbots some land and the charity of the households that lived on it. This meant helping out in the fields at certain labour-intensive times of the year, and for the rest of the time getting with the businesses of making and maintaining a town.

In return for the harvest works, and the payment 'once and for all at Michaelmas to the king, or his fee-fermor, twopence-halfpenny as chepingavel' (market tolls),[23] the elders testified that custom licensed any member of the community 'to buy and sell freely without toll of any sort of merchandise to be found in the town-market all the year round, saving horses'. The market was Cirencester's heart. These men and their networks were the life-

21 *Ibid*, 133.

22 Colin Morris, 'A Note on the Troubles under King John', *Trans* BGAS 87 (1968), 206, 208.

23 The document from Abbey Register A, f. 88a, transcribed and translated in Fuller, 'Tenures of Land by the Customary Tenants in Cirencester', 308–9; this trans. from Baddeley, A *History*, 138–41.

blood of the market: the merchants, the craftworkers, the agricultural workers of the town's hinterlands, the petty-traders and shopkeepers, the journeymen, apprentices, servants, musicians, innkeepers and tapsters, beerbrewers, and not least the weavers and shoemakers who made the town entirely different from all its surrounding villages and market towns, altogether more 'connected' and dynamic. The elders of 1209 called this community 'the fellowship of the town'. They conceded the abbot's right to a local monopoly over trade in the age's most formidable allies in peace and war, horses.

The reference to 'sojourners' shows that immigrants, temporary or permanent, were embodied in the customs of the manor, at least as they understood them. The elders of 1209 expanded on this crucial point. 'As to strangers, resident or sojournant in Cyrencester', they testified that 'if a stranger coming hither slept in Cyrencester on midsomer night, and afterwards stayed there till the king or his fee-fermor had his corn reaped …'

> … then, whosoever he might be, whether freeman or bondman, male or female, he (*sic*) must needs do three bederipes to the king, or to his fee-fermor, for the fellowship that is of the town (*pro communitate videlicet ville*), which the said man had used and had enjoyed up till that day.

To obtain a settlement, immigrants had to 'use and enjoy … the fellowship of the town' from mid-July to mid-September, and perform the customary *bederipes*. Fellowship was open to 'bondmen', and remarkably free of the expected gender prejudice in that membership was also open to women. An expanding 'commonalty' of merchants and artisans existed in constant tension with a powerful, well-connected lord who never died.

In this conception, the right to trade freely belonged to anyone accepted by the community, although it is not said how such consensus was arrived at and acted on. Once membership was granted it became hereditary. Immigrants' children could engage in trade as soon as they were no longer 'beneath the rod and authority of their fathers or maintained by their parents': once they 'attained their own power, and lived of their own labour, and were become reapers … every one of them shall have license to buy and sell freely without toll of any sort …', in return for the customary three harvest works.[24] 'The rod and authority of their fathers' rings with patriarchy, rule by the old men, the "elders".' This would be another abiding theme.

24 *Ibid*, 139. Although Baddeley is in no doubt that the claims – I would suggest that it amounts to a political programme on the part of the trading community in the town – were legally outrageous, he does note (144) an earlier scholar's observation 'that in every instance, even in the lowest class, it was now the land that owed the service, and not the person, the condition of the whole land of the manor was that of villeinage; so that without special exemption every dweller thereon had to perform certain services': Fuller, 'Tenures of Land by the Customary Tenants in Cirencester', 301.

Other less formalized 'customs' dealt with the problem of getting rid of sojourners who, for one reason or another, were rejected by the 'fellowship', the community as they envisaged it: doubtless, when manorial officials and jurors couldn't or didn't take care of an unpopular sojourner, summer sprites, lords of misrule, boycott, rough music and other institutions of community expression were called into play. The central, pivotal, issue was sovereignty; the community believed in self-regulation under the king. If the form in which it has come down to us is anything to go by, the elders put their case with remarkable clarity. They made it perfectly clear that the abbey had to respect customary arrangements with regard to a communalist sovereignty that, in their minds, had served them and their ancestors, time out of mind.

Whatever the extent of its resistance at this time, the 'fellowship of the town' was not able to turn the tide. The abbey's foothold in the parish church was established when, in 1222, it purchased the rectory to add to its already extensive list of 28 benefices as far afield as London, Northants, Bucks, Wilts and Worcs.[25] The ownership and government of the Grammar School was in dispute, in 1242, between the abbots of Cirencester and Gloucester. The latter appears to have founded the school and endowed it with property in the Cotswolds and the Forest of Dean, thus giving the Benedictine abbot of Gloucester an irritating little toe-hold in the Augustinian abbot of Cirencester's domain.[26] In 1225 there was yet another enquiry into the customary services of the tenants of the manor, showing that the constitutional issue smouldered on. Once again, the king's court found in favour of the abbot.[27]

By the mid-thirteenth century, Cirencester Abbey was the rich and powerful lord of a flourishing little region. There was a setback when the abbey fell into the clutches of a certain William de Haswell, the prior to a weak or negligent abbot, Henry de Munden. Haswell was eventually found by the bishop of Worcester to be 'a man of evil life' who used his position to enrich his friends and family, but not until he had almost bankrupted the abbey. Following a thorough investigation of the abbey's affairs, in 1276, the bishop concluded that even 'the most discreet Abbot would find difficulty in redeeming its fortunes'.[28] It was a bad time to be negligent, for the whole of Western Europe had, by the late thirteenth century, reached the high tide of the great economic and demographic boom of the eleventh to thirteenth centuries. The abbey did restore its estate, but its strategies led inexorably to renewed and occasionally violent resistance on the part of the commonalty.

25 Baddeley, *A History*, 148, 158–60; the significance of the abbot's acquisition of the Rectory was that 'the township... was the inhabited portion of the royal manor... and had no relation to the area of the parish', which included Chesterton, Wigwold and Baunton: E.A. Fuller, 'Cirencester Guild Merchant', *Trans BGAS* 18 (1893–4), 53.

26 Baddeley, *A History*, 151.

27 *Ibid*, 152.

28 A.K.B. Evans, 'Cirencester Abbey: from Heyday to Dissolution', *Trans BGAS* 111 (1993), 126.

For four centuries, against repeated experience, the townspeople clung tenaciously to an ideal monarchy, which could and one day possibly would dissolve the constitutional middle-man and trust the citizens of the place to govern themselves. It was second nature for movements of the commonalty to aim at reducing the ranks of feudal society to a confederation of independent communities under an 'absolute imperial monarchy'; in a word, to get rid of intermediary lords. The testimony of the elders of 1209 takes us a little closer to ideals of commonweal sustained by what Chaucer was to call *commune opinoun*. In this town it represented itself as a kind of 'civil society', a community that, in its own eyes, possessed the right to constitute itself, to manufacture and to trade, independently of the lord. It possesses its own 'liberties' that were separate from and independent of those of the lords, and subject only to the king.

2

The crisis of the early fourteenth century

The reign of Edward II marks one of the great turning-points of English history. Demographic historians have shown that at some point in the reign of his father Edward I (1274–1307), the population of England reached a peak of nearly six million. Since the time of his mysterious disappearance and suspected murder, in 1327, Edward II has been regarded as a weak king. His contemporaries eventually judged him to be a tyrant (and therefore, according to contemporary constitutional theory, fit to be deposed). Yet Edward II was at least as unlucky, historically speaking, as he was weak and tyrannical. His reign coincided with the rapid termination of a long period of growth and the advent of a long demographic depression.[1]

The population of England fell rapidly, from a peak of about six million in c.1300, to a final low of two and a half to three million in c.1500. Coming as he did at the end of a long secular boom, Edward II inherited a remarkably integrated kingdom. Traffic was heavy and news spread rapidly. This country had emerged from two centuries of growth. Hundreds of market towns, all over the country, revived or sprang into new existence, linking the increasingly populous and enterprising villages of their hinterlands. Traffic steadily built up along the trunk-roads, interconnecting the provinces of England into a system increasingly centred on London and Westminster. The two centuries following Henry I's endowment of St Mary's Abbey saw Cirencester grow steadily to meet the needs of the inter-regional traffic along Akeman and Ermine Streets, the Fosseway and the White Way. Because of its location, the town was a hot-spot (a 'transformer', as Fernand Braudel characterized such places) in an expanding and intensifying greater economy and constitution. The issues of the day concentrated there and were sufficiently focused, well-defined, and commonly understood to be given regular expression.

In the early fourteenth century the peace that guaranteed the traffic broke down. Gloucestershire Assize rolls for the first decade leave an impression of the violent tenor of life. In 1302 Richard the clothmiller of Sapperton killed

[1] For a recent account of the crisis of 1315–22, see Bruce M.S. Campbell, 'Nature as Historical Protagonist: Environment and Society in Preindustrial England', *Econ Hist Rev* 63:2 (May 2010), part III.

Ralph the son of Thomas in a fight at Cirencester. This tells us incidentally that local cloth was already being finished in at least one village within walking distance of the town. Another man named John Atayse broke into the abbey and stole ten pounds from a coffer belonging to a man named Philip le Ken. This points to another function of the abbey, looking after people's money. No-one of that name is listed under *Villa Cyrencestre* in the Gloucestershire Subsidy Roll of 1327, but Willo. Kene paid the second-highest tax in the town, a penny behind John of Cirencester, who paid twenty-one shillings and a penny.[2] Several men siezed the church of Minety (part of the abbots' manor of Cirencester), kept possession of it for three weeks, and broke the arms and legs of two men who came to reason with them. Atayse was probably an unemployed soldier returned from the wars in Flanders with a small gang of retainers. The abbot made discretion the better part of valour by employing him for his own purposes. Atayse was accused in 1302 of visiting Cirencester Fair with Robert of Sandford, a cleric, where the two men beat Roger Queordelyoum 'nearly to death'.[3] He sounds like a hired thug, a 'hit-man' who got out of hand. At root, the episodes were symptoms of general crisis reverberating through the ranks of society – a crisis that marked both the end of the beginning and the beginning of the end of Norman-Angevin feudalism.

In circumstances like these, lords had to be able to protect their 'liberties', with force if necessary. The abbey was virtually on a war footing with the town throughout the second and third decades of the fourteenth century. On 3 September 1311, a commission was sent to inquire into an allegation that Abbot Brokenbury personally led a gang of armed men to claim 'tithes corn and other goods' relating to a holding called 'the Frith' in the forest of Windsor.[4] In 1316 a commission of oyer and terminer heard a complaint by Henry Tyas, keeper of the manor of Tetbury, that

> Adam [Brokenbury], Abbot of Cirencester, John of Lollebroke, a lay brother of the house, William of Pulham, John Clement, Roger of Pennbrigge, Reginald of Lollebrook, Richard of the Sale of Up Amney, Richard David, William parson of the church of Cotes, Thomas Helyon and Adam le Mareschal, with others, entered the free warren of the said heir at Tettburie and took rabbits, killed four colts of the price of 20 marks, carried away his goods and assaulted his servants.

The commissioners decided that Abbot Brokenbury had overstepped his authority and fined him 100s.[5]

Abbot Brokenbury made it clear that anyone who tried to erode *his* estate would have a fight on their hands. As for relations with the town, Brokenbury lived up to his name. The strategy of two generations of canons, following

2 GA: Gloucestershire Subsidy Roll, 1 Edw. III, 1327.
3 Fuller, 'Cirencester: the Manor and the Town', 313–15.
4 Cal Close Rolls, 4 Edw. II, 331.
5 *Ibid*, 499: 16 May 1316.

the depravations of the wicked prior, William of Haswell, was to tighten 'liberties' such as the exclusive right to mill grain, and to consolidate its lordship by purchasing every house, shop, stall, field, farmstead, wood or other resource at or near Cirencester that came on to the market. Since the bishop of Worcester's devastating judgement on the abbey's prospects in 1276, it had accumulated no fewer than 56 of these properties in the town and many more in the suburban hamlet of Minety. Engrossing tenancies into the 'dead hand' (*mortmain*) of an estate that would probably never have to sell them on was forbidden by royal statute. Accordingly, the abbey set about winning the king's forgiveness and support for its acquisitions.

Sustained engrossing of smallholdings and 'burgages' was at the root of increasingly turbulent relations between the abbey and the commonalty. In 1300, 'the poor men of Cirencester' complained to the king that the abbot had hired a gang of armed retainers to bully them into accepting novel impositions and encroachments. The abbot's thugs entered their homes, extorted 'great sums of money', consumed their goods and impounded their beasts. The abbot justified his actions to the king's justices at Gloucester by the townspeople's refusal to have their corn ground at his mills and using grinding-mills in their own homes. The justices confirmed the abbot's claim and ordered the townspeople to pay him a fine of 100 marks for having been forced to go to the trouble of having them beaten up.[6]

In 1312 Nicholas of Stratton, a village on the outskirts of town, charged Abbot Brokenbury in the king's exchequer, for an illegal tallage. This was probably 'Nicholas the Proctor', named in the 1313 mortmain list as the late holder of property recently acquired by the abbey. Proctors were elected, appointed or nominated by villages, townships and other communities that, like Cirencester, were constantly involved in negotiations and transactions with lords and other outside interests. It looks as though Nicholas of Stratton was a leader of the communal resistance that had been building up in the later thirteenth and early fourteenth centuries. Brokenbury abolished the proctorate, making Nicholas the last official leader of the townspeople, the last proctor. How proctors were elected or appointed varied from place to place; everywhere it was a key institution of the commonalty for negotiating with lords. Nicholas the proctor died in the name of the townspeople against the abbey's relentless encroachment on their unquenchable desire to run their affairs without external interference.

In challenging economic times, Brokenbury was also an encloser of common land: in the centre of town, he built a new street on the north side of what may, until then, have been a large Roman-style forum at the crossroads under the church, where the highways met. On the outskirts he enclosed 'the Querns', a place with mystical as well as practical uses for local people. Brokenbury defended his estate on every front: the piecemeal acquisition (or

6 *VCH Glos*, Vol. 2, 81.

reacquisition), in straitened economic circumstances, of urban tenancies was strategic. If the abbey owned all the buildings there was no-one left even to claim to be a burgess. Thus the abbey recovered its estate. A shrinking pool of freeholders and wealthier sort probably led the opposition to Brokenbury's plan to impose an urban landscape more convenient to the centrality of his abbey. Nicholas the Proctor took up the people's cause, but 'was cudgelled by the abbot's men, and presently died of his injuries'. An inquiry was held before Edward II's officials; in 1313, 1314 and 1315, unknown to the townspeople, the abbot 'quietly procured ... royal pardons' for his cudgelling encroachments, in return for a payment of £200.[7]

On 26 July 1313, an entry in the Patent Rolls records the sale by the king of a royal pardon to the abbot of Cirencester 'for acquiring in mortmain... divers small parcels of land, tenements, mills, shops and messuages, with the appurtenances in Cirencester' from 53 named individuals, five women and 48 men. 'Surnames in the thirteenth century', wrote R.H. Hilton, 'were seldom hereditary.' They offer clues to specific attributes of some of the individuals named, and to an important contemporary movement:

> A man's permanent name was what we would call his christian name, but since medieval parents were conservative in the names they gave their children ... it was necessary to identify a person more precisely. If he was not a native of the place in which he dwelt he would be called after the place from which he came. He might be called by his occupation. And sometimes he was given a nickname, frequently a physical characteristic.[8]

In this phase of the recording and labelling by the state of its subjects, a person's name often referred much more directly to what or who (s)he was, in the eyes of the community, than would be the case today. A place or occupational surname was a reminder to everyone that even if you didn't come from that place or do that specific trade, your father or grandfather probably did. In time surname-giving, initially a weapon of tax-collectors and legal scribes, turned out to have obvious advantages in everyday life. It became entrenched and institutionalized in English localities during the fourteenth century, as we shall see.

7 Cal Pat Rolls, 7 Edw. II (26 July 1313): royal pardon to abbot upon fine made by the abbot for acquiring in mortmain in the time of the late king, divers small parcels of land, tenements, mills, shops and messuages, with the appurtenances in C Viz: from [53 names] ... By fine of £200. *Ibid*, 127, 24 June 1314: pardon for acquiring in mortmain without licence lands in Minety from [18 names, two women] ... By fine of 100s. *Ibid*, 364, 24 Oct. 1315: another pardon for their trespass in acquiring in fee divers lands and tenements in Mynty from Richard son of Hugh of Mynty, and also divers lands, messuages and shops in C from [57 names, including 13 women and 'Nicholas the Proctor'] ... and entering thereon without licence of the said king after the publication of the statute of mortmain. By fine of 100s.

8 Hilton, A *Medieval Society*, 183.

Twenty-two of the surnames of the men and women from whom the abbey had acquired properties refer to places in the town (William of the Elm, William of the Dolehall); farmsteads, hamlets, villages or towns in the vicinity of Cirencester (Reginald of Kynegarshegge, William of Bisley, John of Baudynton, Margaret of Duntisbourne, Stephen of Campden, Walter of Cotes); and further afield (Robert Kent, William of Waleys). Occupational and vocational surnames (Walter the Woodward, Adam the Marshall, Henry the Blake, William the Tippere, William the Cornemongere, Robert of the Brewery, Robert the Vannere, John the Glover, William the Brewer, William Sheep, Gerard the Woolmonger and, perhaps, Richard the Wise and Adam the Sinecure) clearly refer to the kinds of specialist services that made the town what it was. In the late thirteenth and early fourteenth centuries, these men may have been what their 'surnames' implied.

Adam Brokenbury aimed to strangle the borough movement and reduce the commonalty to dependency at a time of civil war. Local barons like Maurice Fitzharding, lord Berkeley, and John Giffard of Brimpsfield were in rebellion against the king. Under cover of the dynastic struggle, small gangs led by minor gentry took advantage of the breakdown of law and order to war with each other and on the local populations, at a time when their incomes were declining for general economic reasons.[9] Bristol (with which Cirencester enjoyed constant relations) was in rebellion against the king from 1312 to 1316; within that rebellion was another, of 'populares' against the elite oligarchy of merchants. The aim was to set up a borough; conflict between the classes concerned the type of borough it was to be.[10] The Bristol insurrections ended when dearth became famine in 1316. Cirencester was undoubtedly well-informed about them. As the legitimacy of (belief in) Edward's capacity to govern without doing irreparable harm to the kingdom declined, the fragile institutions that depended on an efficient, sensible king also fell away, notably the law, such as it was. The rule then was every household and 'estate' for itself. All the hard cases and irreconcilable difficulties of the regions and localities that a steady and strong king's hand was required to arbitrate had to fall back on their own devices. The result, inevitably, was continuous informal trial by combat, endemic violence. Fuses shortened. People from all ranks were required, by law, to own weapons and to train themselves in their use. Who, finally, could put the strongest military force into the field? In this region in the fourteenth century the answer was usually a Maurice or a Thomas lord Berkeley. When the legitimacy of monarchy was in crisis, the Berkeleys, like all their reasonably competent greater and lesser contemporaries, looked to their own Estate.

9 S.L. Waugh, 'The Profits of Violence: the Minor Gentry in the Rebellion of 1321–2 in Gloucestershire and Herefordshire', *Speculum* 52 (1977), 843–69.

10 Samuel Seyer, *Memoirs Historical and Topographical of Bristol and its Neighbourhood* (Bristol 1821), 104, 141.

The abbot of Cirencester was an ally of the king, a much-needed one in a region where barons and knights were often at war with one king or another. In 1321, Edward II was at Cirencester Abbey, where he issued a safe-conduct to the rebel Sir Maurice Berkeley to visit the abbey for negotiations. When Berkeley arrived, Edward seized and sent him a prisoner to Wallingford Castle, where he later died.[11] Five years later Maurice's son, Thomas, was Edward's jailer at Berkeley Castle, where the king suffered a dismal imprisonment and, it was widely believed, a brutally undignified death.[12] Cirencester also had abiding ties with the 'hernesse' or 'hundred' of Berkeley, especially the clothmaking towns of Dursley and Wotton under Edge. If one event more than any other was the beginning of the end of Norman-Angevin England, the murder of Edward was it. The road from Berkeley to Gloucester, where Edward was taken for burial, is said to have been lined by the mourning populace of the region – another clue to abiding popular feelings with regard to the monarchy. The nobility was demonstrably not behaving lawfully, and was engaging in actions and behaviours that were patently inconsistent with the common good. This much was obvious. In hindsight, the epoch of feudal warriors was drawing to a close, but had yet to exhaust its capacity for destruction and oppression.

Doubts about the legitimacy of a king shook belief in the legitimacy of lesser lords. It is clear that throughout the last third of the thirteenth and into the early decades of the fourteenth century the abbey's 'hand' on Cirencester was far from 'dead'. Abbot Brokenbury died in 1320. The king issued an *Inspeximus* confirming that the abbey was entitled to take a 'reasonable tallage' (tax) whenever the king did so, thus confirming the double tax obligations of the tenants of the manor.[13] A licence of 1321 reveals that the ruthless acquisition of smallholdings continued.[14] Edward II needed all the allies he could get in a region where most of the powerful secular lords were his enemies. In 1322 an order to destroy Brimpsfield Castle, the stronghold of one of these families, the Giffards, was directed to the abbot, presumably on the assumption that the abbot was capable of carrying it out.

As we have seen, when their lordship was in any way challenged, abbots like Brokenbury governed their baileywicks personally, assuming the bailiff's duties, donning armour and leading men at arms into the households of recalcitrant tenants, arresting opponents, holding courts and supervising the collection of market dues, appointing officers of the peace and managing the jail. The jurisdiction of the manor, if it chose to exercise it, reached into all aspects of the lives of every inhabitant. Later abbots appointed prominent local men to serve as their bailiffs. Bailiffs were assisted by a clerk and a sergeant, again usually from the wealthiest inhabitants, later described by one of them

11 Baddeley, *A History*, 175.

12 Vita Sackville-West, *Berkeley Castle* (n.d.), 4, has a vivid description of the circumstances of the king's imprisonment.

13 Cal Close Rolls, Edw. II, 30 Mar. 1319.

14 Cal Pat Rolls, Edw. II, 19 Oct. 1321.

as 'the gentlemen of town and country'. In the sixteenth century the bailiff appointed constables, two 'wardsmen' for each street and officials responsible for the quality of bread, ale, leather and so on. The bailiffs of late medieval Cirencester were singularly powerful men. In this sense the constitution of Cirencester always had strong elements of 'rule by one', Aristotle's 'monarchy' or, its evil equivalent, 'tyranny'. To its lord, 'the fellowship of the town', whatever its exact composition, was merely the aggregate of inhabitants whose lives it was the right of the manor to rule. The entity referred to by a succession of jurors and petitioners as 'the fellowship', or 'the poor townspeople', had no institutional form. It embodied custom but, as we have seen, if the testimony of elders implied rights that reduced the abbey's hegemony, the abbey produced or obtained a written charter that proved it to be mistaken. Because it had no continuous institutional form, and no archival voice until the later sixteenth century, the movement of the 'poor people' has to be reconstructed piecemeal, out of fragments of evidence, lists, assessments, court records.

3

Classes of the commune before the Black Death

In late medieval England, as later, 'wealth in towns was distributed with extreme inequality'.[1] At Cirencester, the wealthy elite and the most substantial shopkeepers and tradesmen lived close to the market; the poorest lived in tenements, cottages and hovels stretched along the roads that led southwest out of the market-place towards Cricklade, Tetbury, Bristol and Bath, and west across the Wolds towards Gloucester. In a military assessment of 1522, 34 men in 'Chipping Street' (then more commonly known as Dyer Street), along which travellers from London entered the town, were assessed as holding £1,260 in goods and stock. Dyer Street was Cirencester's High Street; its residents were the wealthiest. Travellers entering the town from (or travelling to) Northleach, Burford, Oxford, Reading and London passed a great cross situated 'near the extremity of the borough, at the first stream of water', proceeding along Dyer Street to its opening into the still-spacious market-place in front of the church.[2] In 1522 the taxpayers of Dyer ward paid far more tax than those of Abbot Street (9 men, £120), Cricklade Street (9 men, £121), Gosditch Street (16 men, £293), St Cecily Street (4 men, £8), Castle Street (7 men, £152) and St Lawrence Street (6 men, £3).[3] The size of the place was such that no-one in the parish (more extensive than the town) lived more than ten minutes away from the centre. All roads led to and from the market and church. As long as this landscape is borne in mind, the commonalty of Cirencester can be imagined as a variant on the typical urban wealth hierarchy, a tall pyramid with a broad base consisting of people with few possessions or none at all.

Leaving aside the inns and taverns, the most substantial houses and the best streets were occupied by a heterogeneous class of independent craftsmen like dyers, butchers, perhaps a weaver or two, tailors and other petty merchants, and, in their midst, a few very wealthy individuals involved in inter-regional and (in the case of wool) international trade. Table 3.1 presents analysis of the

1 Christopher Dyer, *Standards of Living in the Later Middle Ages: Social Change in England c.1200–1520* (Cambridge 1989), 195.

2 Rudder, *History of the Town of Cirencester*, 117.

3 R.W. Hoyle (ed.), *The Military Survey of Gloucestershire, 1522* (Stroud 1993), 100–2.

men who paid Cirencester's share of Edward III's first national tax, in 1327. [4] It suggests that the commonalty of Cirencester can easily be made to fit into the three classes that contemporary urban clerks, somewhat unimaginatively, often called *minores*, *mediocres* and *majores*: the little people, the middles and the rich. What triggered solidarity between otherwise highly unequal individuals and classes was that none were remotely as rich and powerful as the abbot. The following calculations, based on the assessment of 1327, suggest that in the rapidly contracting economy of the early fourteenth century *minores* probably outnumbered the others by two or three to one.

The 1327 listing shows that 85 men of *Villa Cyrencestre* paid a total of just under £13 to the king's subsidy.

Table 3.1. Taxpayers in 1327

	Sum paid	No. of payers	(%)	Total paid	(%)
A	6–7d.	27	(31.76)	14s. 7d.	(6.28)
	8–18d.	34	(40)	32s. 8d.	(14.04)
B	2s.–5s. 4d.	16	(18.82)	34s. 1d.	(14.68)
C.	15s.–21s. 1d.	8	(9.42)	151s.	(65)
Totals		85	(100)	232s. 4d.	(100)

The contributions fall naturally into three broad classes. Beginning with the smallest amounts, 27 men paid 6d. or 7d. each and a further 34 paid a sum between 8d. and 2s. This lowest class, comprising 61 taxpayers, contributed from 6 to 18 pence, a total of 47s. 3d. A clear gap separates them from the 'middles': no-one paid any sum between 18d. and 2s. The 'middles' paid sums between 2s. and 5s. 4d. Between 'Nicho Coyfestare', the highest payer in the middle group, and Stephen Lanvale, who paid the lowest amount in the highest group, there is a gap of nearly ten shillings. The '*minores*' (72 percent of the taxed population) contributed 20 percent, the '*mediocres*' (19 percent) contributed 15 percent, and the '*majores*', comprising only 9 percent of all taxpayers, dwarfed the contributions of the other groups with 65 percent of the total.

The composition of the taxpaying community at Cirencester differed markedly from that of neighbouring villages and towns. Its lowest class of taxpayers (*minores*) was much more numerous, and its *majores* were much wealthier. At the wealthy Cotswold wool-town of Campden, for example, 27 households paid a total of 88s. 10d. Ten individuals were assessed at sums from 1s. (the lowest) to 1s. 11d.; ten more (including two women) paid a sum between 2s. and 5s.; six *majores* paid 5s. 8d. (2), 6s. 6d., 6s. 8d., 8s. and 18s. 6d. respectively.

4 Analysis based on *Gloucestershire Subsidy Roll, 1 Edward III, 1327* (privately printed, 1856): copy at GA. Two entries for the custodians of the hospitals of St John and St Laurence, 8d. and 7d. respectively, are excluded from the totals.

Relatively speaking, Campden had fewer *minores*, a larger group of 'middles', and a smaller and (except for one individual, Robert de Havele) less wealthy elite. The *minores* and the middles contributed more to the total (at least 50 percent, considerably more if those paying 5–6s. are counted as 'middles') in neighbouring market towns like Campden, Lechlade, Tetbury and Fairford than they did at Cirencester (35 percent). The wealth-structure of smaller towns was less polarized than that of a provincial capital like Cirencester.

Late medieval and early modern towns were 'transformers', 'conjunctures' of economic, cultural, religious and social 'circuits'. Early capitalism was the sum of these circuits, a system of sometimes integrated, sometimes fragmented 'higher' and 'lower' levels. The reason for its larger class of *minores* and its comparatively wealthier *majores* was that Cirencester was continuously connected into each 'level'. It was a very important local market, providing necessities and specialist services to its own residents, travellers and a local network consisting of about a hundred populous villages and market towns. A document of Edward II's reign listing the goods 'ordinarily brought to its market' gives an impression of the scope and variety of trade and craft activities. They included hemp, wool, woad, fleeces, linen, local cloth, Irish cloth, canvas, worsted, cloth with gold, silks, salt, butter, honey, bacon, lard, salmon from the River Severn, cod, conger eels, lampreys, herrings, wine, ale, oil, milk, metal goods like nails, horseshoes, pots and pans, hides and tanning materials, alum and copper, corn, bean-meal, pease, coal and wood-faggots, and livestock including sheep, pigs, cattle, geese, chickens and horses.[5]

The list implies an extensive network of middle-men who were most directly touched by the abbots' control of trade at the twice-weekly markets, the monthly fairs, animal trading and, most lucrative of all, the international wool trade. The abbots' manor of Cirencester was home to dozens and routinely visited by scores of small-scale merchants and traders, many of whom, from time to time, would have been semi-permanent 'sojourners' like those mentioned in 1209. Eight Cirencester merchants were assessed on their goods and chattels for a fifteenth in 1339.[6] Other visitors came from London, Bristol, Southampton, Flanders and, like Francesco Datini's agent, a junior member of the powerful Tornabuoni clan, Florence. He wrote in 1404 that the wool-market at Cirencester was 'considered the best' of all the Cotswold wool-marts. 'The best time to buy is around St John's day, for it is then that the Cotswold Fairs are held.' He was in no doubt that abbeys (not just Cirencester, but Winchcombe, Hailes, Gloucester, Kingswood and Malmesbury), not the local merchants, controlled this most lucrative of *Chondisgualdo* (Cotswold) commodity-trades.[7] The abbey was endowed by Henry I with a strong toehold

5 Baddeley, *A History*, 176, n. 14, qf. Cal Pat Rolls, a. 15 Edw. II.

6 Richard Jefferies, 'History of Cirencester', *Wilts and Gloucestershire Standard* (12 March–29 October 1870).

7 Iris Origo, *The Merchant of Prato: Francesco di Marco Datini* (Harmondsworth 1963), 70–1.

in a district that was ideally placed to benefit from any intensification of the traffic along the three national roads that crossed its market-place. By c.1200 the town had become a highly lucrative centre of the European wool trade, a position it still occupied two centuries later. Here were causes worth fighting for.

R.E. Glasscock's valuable survey and analysis of a subsidy collected seven years later, in 1334, provides a rough guide to Cirencester's place in these national and international 'circuits'.[8] The sums mentioned are taken to be an index of the amount of traffic a place attracted. In 1334, London (£733) was already in a class of its own, followed by a score or so of lesser and greater provincial capitals such as Bristol, Newcastle and Lincoln paying between £50 and £220. Cirencester (£25) belonged to a third class of towns paying sums between £20 and £49. It possessed less wealth, and perhaps fewer households, than Cambridge (£46 12s.), Nottingham (£37 1s.), Exeter (£36 12s. 4d.) and Colchester (£26 2s. 9d.), but more than county towns like Warwick (£21 9s. 8d.), Worcester (£20) and Bedford (£19 11s. 7d.). Its assessment was higher than three other towns that were routinely at odds with powerful local abbeys: Bury St Edmunds (£24), Abingdon (£17 18s. 7d.) and St Albans (£17 13s. 11d.). Glasscock assumes the returns 'should not unduly distort the *relative* distribution of moveable wealth' and ranks the Seven Hundreds of Cirencester as the wealthiest part of Gloucestershire and one of the wealthiest districts in England.[9] The town was considerably less well connected than Bristol (£220) and the county town, Gloucester (£54 1s.), but estimates of its local, regional and national functions increase if we take in the smaller towns that lay within its immediate sphere of influence, including Campden (£21), Painswick (£12 7s. 9d.), Fairford (£11 12s. 8d.), Winchcombe (£10 13s. 4d.), Lechlade (£11 12s. 8d.), Tetbury (£8 11s. 6d.) and Bisley (£4 19s. 4d.). Also very much parts of Cirencester's immediate marketing district were wealthy neighbouring villages like Down Ampney (£6 0s. 5d.), South Cerney (£9 16s. 3d.), Up Ampney (£10 11s. 4d.), Stratton and Daglinworth (£6 3s. 11d.) and Siddington (£8 2s. 6d.), and agricultural hamlets like Meyseyhampton (£4 0s. 6d.), Minety (£5 19s. 4d.), Harnhill/Driffield (£5 11s. 8d.), Cotes (£5 5s. 2d.), Duntisbourne (£3 15s. 8d.) and Baunton (£2 5s. 4d.).

In addition to its character as an integrated node of local, regional, national and international networks, early fourteenth-century Cirencester connected the developing clothmaking districts of central Gloucestershire and northern Wiltshire with London. Fortunes were made dyeing and finishing local cloth, some woven and fulled by tradesmen of the town, but also white cloths flowing in from the villages to the south and west, attracted by the strategic expertise of a succession of enterprising capitalist merchants. 'Rico Dyear' was one of seven 'sub-taxors' appointed by the tax commissioners for Gloucestershire in

8 R.E. Glasscock, *The Lay Subsidy of 1334* (London 1975).

9 *Ibid*, xxiii and map on xxvii.

1327, and therefore, presumably, one of the town's wealthiest inhabitants.[10] Nicho Dyear (2s. 4d.) and 'Willo Walkere (2s. 3d.) were among the middling taxpayers in 1327. This suggests the finishing end of the cloth industry was established and explains why 'Dyer Street' began to displace the older name for the town's thoroughfare, 'Chipping (market) Street'. In future the most successful woolmen and clothmen usually ended up purchasing a gentry estate; new men filled their places when they left. There was money to be made by conscientious, assiduous men with a little capital to invest in processing and trading in what was to become Gloucestershire's most famous product: woollen cloth. The legend that a poor weaver could, by his own efforts, become the wealthiest and most respected man in town, was based on the fact that in places like Cirencester, from the early fourteenth to the seventeenth centuries, it sometimes happened. Flows of finished cloth followed the Thames to Lechlade, Reading and London. Like the Thames, the traffic in packhorses and waggons gathered in size and force the further east it went. Cirencester was the gathering spot for an industry that was to be of increasing importance in the future. Merchants connected to the 'highest' levels of capitalism, involving international trade, were continuously represented in the town. As long as these networks continued, Cirencester had essential functions to perform. To perform all these functions it needed a resident population of a certain size, namely 2,000–2,500.

What proportion of Cirencester's householders did the 94 taxpayers represent?[11] Or to put it the other way, what proportion of households and individuals had no 'visible wealth' and were therefore not listed in the subsidies of 1327 and 1334? It has been estimated that in most of the small towns of the West Midlands at this time 40–60 percent of local populations were exempt from taxes on 'movable' or 'visible' wealth. Given that the wealthier, taxed households were more likely to include servants, apprentices and journeymen, they probably averaged at least five members, yielding a total of 470 individuals. Estimating the total populations of towns like Cirencester, where temporary 'sojourners', 'inmates' and 'passingers' always represented a fluctuating proportion of the total resident at any one time, is bound to be, at best, educated guesswork. My guess is that exemptions at Cirencester probably lay

10 'Richard le Dyere' was also one of the merchants appointed to represent the town at the Parliament of 1337: W.R. Williams, *Parliamentary History of the County of Gloucester…, 1213–1898* (1898), 3.

11 This figure adds the seven sub-taxers listed at the end, each of whom was taxed at a nominal 12d., presumably to compensate them for their efforts. That these seven were wealthy men is suggested by the fact that they included the three merchants 'elected' to parliament in 1337: Williams, *ibid*; given that the hospitals of St John and St Laurence had inhabitants, they too are included here.

towards the high end of the range for contemporary communities: say, sixty percent.[12] This gives a total population of about 1,200.

This figure probably underestimates the number of people resident or lodging in the town at any given time in the early decades of the fourteenth century. The wealthiest household in the town, the abbey, is not counted: in 1539 it employed 80 servants, some of whom had families. Commissioners sent to Cirencester in 1404 reported 490 households, roughly 2,205 inhabitants. If it followed national trends, there will have been more in 1327, not long after the famines and murrains of 1315–22 and twenty-three years before the Black Death. National population halved in the second half of the fourteenth century, but like other towns that became centres of clothmaking in the fourteenth century, Cirencester probably defied national trends.[13] In the sixteenth century, when parish registers and other sources permit more detailed analysis, Cirencester was unusually hard-hit by 'recessions' and mortality crises, yet always recovered very quickly.[14] Because of the opportunities it offered, the dead were swiftly replaced by immigrants. This was already so in 1327 but its optimum size probably increased in the fourteenth century as a result of the increasing presence of clothiers and weavers. If so, its average size in the thirteenth and fourteenth centuries was probably about 1,500 inhabitants, increasing to 2,000–2,500 by c.1400.[15]

To maintain its functions within national, regional and district networks the town needed a certain number of households, somewhere between 350 and 500. Numbers doubtless declined immediately after the catastrophic Black Death (when four abbots died within a twelve-year period), then grew through the vernacular revolution of the late fourteenth century, retained these levels through the fifteenth century to the tumultuous Reformation era and into the later decades of the reign of Queen Elizabeth I, when, in a time of greater national calamity than any other period since the Black Death, the town began a sustained period of growth, through the crisis years of 1577–1625, to the decades of the English Revolution.[16] We should continue to explore the relationship between a town's size and its functions in a bigger system: the 'economy', perhaps, the *regnum* of the crown, and a very influential word

12 Peter Franklin's excellent study of Thornbury, a large agrarian manor with a small market town in the southern Vale of Gloucester, gives the national variables and estimates that 63 percent of the 'peasants' at Thornbury were assessed: 'Gloucestershire's Medieval Taxpayers', www.localpopulationstudies.org.uk (np); Cirencester, by contrast, was an entirely urban, industrializing and mercantile borough, routinely topped up by immigrants.

13 R.H. Britnell, *Growth and Decline in Colchester, 1300–1525* (Cambridge 1986), 95, estimates that Colchester, roughly twice as populous as Cirencester, more than doubled in population between the Black Death (1349) and 1412–14. Similar calculations are not possible for Cirencester because the 1378–81 poll tax assessments are deficient.

14 See below, Chapter 10.

15 Hilton, *A Medieval Society*, 201.

16 See below, Chapter 10.

coined in the fourteenth century, 'commonweal'.[17] By the early fifteenth century local people all over England knew they were part of a greater society, and called it the 'commonweal/th'.

Bearing in mind that contemporaries were more concerned with considerations of precedence and order (what is the exact hierarchy, and where do I stand in it?) than with counting heads, the Cirencester subsidy of 1327 enumerated only the better-off forty percent. The broad base of the social pyramid was formed by the invisible sixty *per cent*, who paid nothing. Those paying 6d. and 7d., numbering 14 and 13 payers respectively, were proud enough to distinguish themselves from their more needy neighbours and 'passingers' by showing they did have possessions and could pay. The next largest (8) paid 9d., followed by five payers of 10d. and (after the first significant gap) five more who paid 2s. each. Above these groups, the list discriminates more precisely, most individuals paying a sum that is unique to them, a 'rung' or 'level' of their own on the taxation ladder: 11 individuals paying between 2s. and 5s. 4d.; the wealthiest payers are spread across 16 'rungs' and the top 14 had a specific rung to themselves. It looks as if assessors envisaged, or discovered, or both, a 'class' of moderately secure householders who shared more or less the same general standard of living, which, in the light of the fact that most of the population paid nothing, might be called, in a quite literal sense innocent of modern, marxist implications, the 'little bourgeoisie'. They were not wealthy, but neither were they 'necessitous', at least when the tax was assessed. The degree to which they were a self-conscious group of people – a class in the Marxist sense – is another question altogether. The wealthier men – the 'bourgeoisie' – were probably as prominent socially, as individuals, in terms of their influence and visible accoutrements, as they are in the list.

That the assessors had clear categories or classes of people in mind when they assessed individual contributions is suggested by the clear gaps that separate the *majores*, *mediocres* and *majores*. Another clue to contemporary class structuring emerges by cross-referencing surname types with taxation categories.

The emergence of surnames derived from place and occupation reflected the legal expectation that most people stayed where they were born, locationally and vocationally. As the name changes in manorial lists that go back to the twelfth century suggest, Cirencester *always* attracted outsiders. This was because it was a trading and manufacturing town, and as such exhibited a more extensive division of labour, hence the identification of people by occupation, a habit that was to continue into the future, long after surnames had become regularized.

17 P. Clark and J. Hosking, *Population Estimates of English Small Towns 1550–1851* (Leicester 1993), state that there were approximately 350 towns in England with 500–2,500 people in the seventeenth century. Cirencester had by that time been such a town for perhaps 400 years. The abstract category comprising all towns of a certain size does not explain the conditions that made them necessary.

Table 3.2. Surname types in 1327

Sum paid	Surname / Type			
	Place	Craft	Other	Total
6–7d.	9 (33%)	11 (41%)	7 (26%)	27 (100%)
8–18d.	12 (35%)	14 (41%)	8 (24%)	34 (100%)
2s.–5s. 4d.	10 (63%)	3 (19%)	3 (19%)	16 (100%)
15s.–21s. 1d.	7 (88%)	0 (0%)	1 (12%)	8 (100%)
Totals	38 (45%)	28 (32%)	19 (22%)	85 (100%)

Of the 85 taxpayers, 38 have 'place' and 28 'occupation' surnames (see Table 3.2). Crafts like Tailleur, Baker and Cotyler (Cutler) dominate the lower ranks. Twenty-five of the 28 craft surnames paid 18d. or less.[18] In contrast, only three craft names (Dyer, Walker and Chapman) occur among the higher payers, confirming the normal expectation that the people who made things were not as rich, and usually very much poorer, than those who engrossed, finished and traded them.

Ten of the eleven highest payers (5s. and up) had place (Dereham, Penyton, Crekkelade) or regional (Scot, Northerne, Waleys) identifications. It cannot be assumed that every man with a place-surname came from that place, and was thus a relatively recent immigrant. Yet at the very least, the preponderance of place-surnames shows that the system to which Cirencester belonged had recently gone through, and probably still was going through, a very mobile phase. Fourteen place-names refer to places in the region (Bristol, Hailes, Eyecote, Swell, Cricklade etc.). This is to be expected of a time when numbers were beginning to outstrip resources. Towns were places where, if anywhere, resources were concentrated. A strong, fluctuating yet unbroken stream of traffic flowed continuously through Cirencester. When a place was opened up by the death of an individual, or an epidemic created many openings, it was quickly filled by a candidate judged by communal osmosis to be admissible to what the elders of 1209 had called 'the fellowship of the town': this, at least, was the version of their constitution held most tenaciously by its commonalty from the twelfth to the seventeenth centuries.

The implication that at least 45 percent of the householders taxed in 1327 were immigrants is probably right. The proportion of its taxpayers with place-surnames is higher than any of the other 'big and growing towns' of the West Midlands at the time, with the single exception of Stratford-on-Avon, also undergoing rapid growth.[19] As a rule of thumb, the more strategic the town, the higher the flow of traffic; the higher the flow of traffic, the more susceptible to invasions of bacteria and viruses; the more susceptible to disease, the greater

18 The occupational surnames were: panelman, payn, dyer, carter, cutler, smyth, goldsmith, page, tailor, carpenter, baker, chapman, painter, muleward, walker, hooper.

19 Hilton, *A Medieval Society*, 184.

the opportunities to obtain a settlement at a place through which money and commodities flowed. The dream was that a little part of these flows would be diverted into the household of each citizen. The current of migrants flowed strongly through Cirencester because it was a regional capital, a strategic location in national – and international – networks.

Only a third of the lowest class of taxpayers – mainly craftsmen – had place- surnames; place-surnames increase as we ascend the hierarchy; the more wealthy a man was the more likely he was to have a place surname, and, by inference, to have brought his capital to the town from somewhere else. It was a place where profits were turned, and work was to be had. Later in the fourteenth century the legendary Dick Whittington (named after a village near Cheltenham) probably came through Cirencester on his way to fortune and fame in London. The capital of the Cotswolds was a scene of social as well as geographical mobility, and gave routine access to myths, legends and rumours of fame and fortune in the wider world.

Preponderance of place-names among the wealthiest inhabitants suggests a number of possibilities. We have assumed that only a small proportion of all the craftsmen at Cirencester were considered substantial enough to pay: no 'weavers', or anything implying the craft of weaving, occur in the list, and weavers, in later centuries, were generally among the poorer crafts. Similarly, there are no building trades (e.g. mason, tiler). These and other poorer trades, labourers, apprentices, journeymen and servants, were present but exempt from the tax. Craftworkers formed the lower and lower-middle levels of the wealth hierarchy. This, as we shall see, was the case in the late sixteenth and early seventeenth centuries, when the evidence is more complete. But what do the place-surnames that dominate the wealthier categories signify?

The only name implying a retailing or trading occupation is Luke Chapman; perhaps significantly, he is the wealthiest man in the occupation-name category, paying 3s. 1d. tax. It is certain that there were many dealers, retailers and merchants among the taxed population. The obvious conclusion is that for the most part they were given place-names. We cannot assume that craftsmen were never given place- or nick-names, but in view of the clustering of craft names at the bottom end of the list, and their complete absence at the top, it seems likely that the wealthier men were not, or were no longer, craftsmen. Very probably, most of the men assigned place-names were commodity-traders of one kind or another. The wealthiest category, with no occupational designations at all, named the big dealers, often wool-merchants. The 'middles' were probably what records tell us they were in the sixteenth and seventeenth centuries: innkeepers, butchers, vintners, tanners, clothiers and the like.

The size of the wealth elite is underestimated in Table 3.1 by the omission of the seven 'sub-taxers', who were appointed by the county commissioners to assess and collect the tax. As stated above, they include Rico Skarnynge, Johne Eyecote and Rico Dyeare, the three merchants appointed or elected to represent the commune in the Parliament of 1337. They paid a nominal 12d. Of those they assessed, beginning at the top, the wealthiest,

Johe Ceynestar (21s. 1d.), was not among the merchants assessed twelve years later and so had either died or moved elsewhere. Johne Goterest (20s. 3d.) may be the subject of the earliest brass memorial in the Lady chapel of the parish church; only a fragment survives, showing the merchant's feet resting on a barrel: he may have been a wine-merchant, supplying the abbey.[20] Walto Northerne paid 17s. in 1327; in 1339 Willo de Northerne, probably his heir, was the highest assessed local merchant, paying 40 marks 15s. Peter of Dereham (20s. 3d.; 25 marks 2s.) and Luc Chapman (3s. 1d.; 25 marks 2s.) also appear in both lists. It is possible to play with some of the nicknames. Willo Whythed is clear enough, and Rico Vole was perhaps a small man with a sharp nose. Was Thom. Bollewell, a sixpence man, perhaps a renowned stoolball player? The fine details are hazy and invite speculation. The general picture is what we are after. John Ceynestar was a rich, perhaps foreign, merchant, like Willo Kene (21s.), Peter of Dereham, Johne Goterest and Galfro. de Mersshton (20s. 3d. each), Johe Escote (18s. 2d.) – possibly an ancestor of the Estcourts, powerful gentry of the fifteenth to seventeenth centuries – Walto. Northerne (17s.) and Stepho. Lanvale (15s.). Peter of Dereham, along with Nicholas Coyfeste and John Meys, merchants, were assessed but unable to pay in 1339 as they had been robbed of 500 marks in merchandise at Southampton a few months earlier.[21] Clues to the vocations of such men are evident in the activities of Galfro de Mersshton, whose name Professor Hilton translates as Geoffrey of Marston, a small township in the North Wolds, not far from Chipping Campden.

Hilton came across Geoffrey, 'a burgess of Cirencester … in the records of Cirencester Abbey in 1306',[22] as signatory to a forward contract to purchase 100 marks' worth of 'good, dry and well-cleaned wool' from the priory manor of Barrington, at eleven and a half marks a sack. If Barrington manor failed to yield enough fine wool to fulfil the contract, 'the canons were to make up the value from other sources'. Local merchants like Geoffrey of Marston held an advantage over Italian and Flemish merchants who came only seasonally. To hold their position in a bullish market, they had to court the abbot and the canons. As Tuornobuoni, the Florentine Datini's English agent, pointed out to his impatient client in 1404, merchants had to take what the abbeys would give them. The latter could pick and choose their agents. It was as true in fourteenth-century England as it is in Australia, a region that is famous as a supplier of raw wool to the world's textile industries today, that the finest wool will find a buyer even in the most depressed market. Merchants with a line on bulk commodities like wool and cloth were likely to do well. This

20 W.C. Fallows, *The Brasses of Cirencester Parish Church* (Cirencester 1985), 4; Fallows dates the 'Goterest brass' to 1400 and suggests he was a member of a Bristol family, but a John Goterest was clearly resident at Cirencester in 1327.

21 Beecham, *A History*, 199.

22 Hilton, *A Medieval Society*, 180, for the quotes and information in this paragraph.

dominance of the commune by a dozen or so *relatively* well documented men will be a continuing theme of this book. Their relations with the rest of the inhabitants, as we shall see, depended on perceptions of their devotion to the commune as a whole.

4

The struggle continues, 1335–99

William of Hereward was elected abbot in 1335. On 3 January 1343 he was called before another commission of oyer and terminer to answer the complaint of John of Shardelow, John le Stouford, William le Thorpe and John le Roche, who sued the abbot in the king's courts 'for recovery of the kings rights usurped and withdrawn by the abbot of Ciceter'. The abbot seized and imprisoned them until they 'made very grievous fines with the abbot for their ransoms'. To secure freedom they paid up, but Abbot Hereward was not satisfied. The spokesmen for the commonalty complained that he 'daily procure(d) them to be indited of felonies and trespasses and in other ways the abbot strives maliciously to vex them who would sue for the king's right dare not for fear of him'.[1] The outcome of the case is not recorded, perhaps because it merged into a case involving larger claims for the status of the commonalty of Cirencester.

In 1343 a group described (once again) as 'the poor men of Cirencester' produced a copy of a charter by which, they claimed, Henry I had granted Cirencester 'the same privileges as the burgesses of Winchester'. Such men counted themselves 'poor' in 'estate', a term that implied possession of lands, wealth, status and institutional power: the leaders of the 'poor men of Cirencester' had wealth, but no formal institutional status and power. They claimed the original charter had been destroyed 'in 1292 (when) the abbot bribed the burgess who had custody of it, got possession of it and burned it.'[2] Twenty of the 'poor men' were called to Westminster to justify their claim that 'the town and manor had once been independent of one another'.[3] They charged the abbot and his predecessors 'with encroachments on the king's rights and their own'. This is essentially the same argument that runs through the twelfth- and thirteenth-century cases, and that had clearly been alive and kicking when Nicholas of Stratton was cudgelled to death earlier in the century. The 'poor men' of 1343 swore that 'since the reign of John' (strictly speaking, they should have said since those of Henry II and Richard I) the abbots had illegally taken possession of the patronage of the parish church, administered the two hospitals of St John and St Lawrence to their own advantage, and

1 Cal Pat Rolls, 5 Edw. III, 593.
2 *VCH Glos*, Vol. 2, 82.
3 Baddeley, *A History*, 176.

habitually disregarded a charter which, they claimed, had been granted to the town 'allowing it the same privileges as the burgesses of Winchester'.

The facts were not in dispute. The abbot certainly did exercise extraordinary powers and liberties in Cirencester and the Seven Hundreds. The townspeople questioned the legitimacy of the abbey's crushing dominion. A charter purchased by the abbey in 1343 confirmed an ascendancy as complete as it would ever be.[4] The king found that, as the 'poor men' naively asserted, the abbey did hold the rectory of the church of John the Baptist, with the chapels of Baudynton, [W]yggewolde and St Cecily, to their own use, as they put it, from the time of the foundation of the abbey, which, it was recorded, 'is before the memory of man'. The clause was important. It negated the people's argument, which, based on oral testimony, could not, therefore, reach 'beyond the memory of man', a feat only achieved by writing. By their own admission, the people had no writing: there *had been* a charter confirming their liberties, they claimed, but it had been burned by the abbot. Abbot Brokenbury's confident use of violence and bribery is a matter of record. Why wouldn't he have burned the people's charter, had it existed? Suspicion of written documents was a prominent characteristic of many of the popular movements of the time.

The abbot had writings that confirmed all of his claims, and his record *did* go back 'beyond the memory of man'. His abbey held the hospitals of St John and St Lawrence, the forest of Oakley, the manor (of Cirencester), the Seven Hundreds of Cirencester, with view of frankpledge, and, in case we forget, 'tallages whenever the king does'. For the artisans and traders this meant double taxes. The abbot was also confirmed in his liberty to license occupations and trades – or not, as the case may be; to charge fees at the two weekly markets, fifty-two weeks a year. The document leaves unsaid that Cirencester Abbey (though its abbots, officials, canons, clerks, servants and other employees would not have called it that) was a very considerable provincial territorial lord, the master of one of fourteenth- and fifteenth-century Europe's richest little provinces, roughly comprising the Seven Hundreds of Cirencester.

The charter roll entry explained why a new charter was considered necessary. For some time, it says, the abbot and convent had been 'impeached and disquieted, as well on the aforesaid matter [its liberties, as defined earlier] as on the allegation that a borough was being set up in Cicetre'. The commonalty had been 'murmuring' behind their back; false stories had been spread. The opposition, although its case had been rejected, was strong enough for its case to be set down in the record: a borough was being set up. Naturally, the abbot saw to it that neighbouring lords were made ready, should police action be necessary, and 'presentments were made in chancery and inquisitions and

[4] The next few paragraphs transcribe and develop Cal Charter Rolls V, 22, 20 Sep. 1343.

proceedings taken … and continued in other the kings places … whereon the abbot prayed the king for a remedy'. 'For a fine of £300 …' the king put an official seal on all that the abbot and his predecessors had taken, their many powers and acquisitions. The acquisitions continued. In 1346, the king licensed the abbot's purchases of another 49 messuages, 4 shops, 2 virgates, 7 acres, pasture for 2 cows and 2 parts of a messuage in Cirencester.[5] He also looked after his friends in the town, and in October 1346 made grants for life to Robert Cannynges and William of Weston, 'late Bailiff of the Pole' (i.e. the abbot's appointee), 2 messuages, 2 caracutes of land and 6 acres of meadow in Minety.

The missing people's charter may have been a forgery, yet the claim of the 'twenty poor men' of 1342–3 was essentially the same as that of the 'nineteen lawfull elders' 130 years earlier: a thread of popular memory connecting the charter – forged or not – to the time of which it wrote, linking the reign of Henry I to that of Richard I, and that of Richard's successor, John, to Edward II and Edward III. It referred to customs local people believed had once existed and were now usurped by an overweening magnate. It was a tenaciously maintained belief.

The 'twenty poor men' included John Cannynges, a member of one of the most powerful mercantile families in the western region, with bases at Cirencester and Bristol, where they were members of the governing oligarchy. Others were John Lucas, a goldsmith, a merchant called John of Cricklade, and the holder of one of the smaller local manors, John Erkenbald.[6] These men were not in any way 'poor' in relation to the rest of the townspeople. What gave the movement social depth was the abbots' rigorously pursued policy to make all the tenants on their manors, urban or rural, their subjects, and complainants' insistence that they represented *all* the 'poor people of the town'. This made Cirencester a place where the commonalty, which was highly stratified in terms of wealth and occupation, could unite against a clear and common enemy. John of Cricklade and John Lucas appeared in the 1327 subsidy list among the middle sort of merchants and craftsmen. The list sheds light on a political struggle that was probably grounded in 'everyday forms of resistance' that, whenever necessary, succeeding abbots countered with violence, whereupon the townspeople appealed to the king for justice and the king decided in the abbot's favour.

It is difficult to imagine a more complete constitutional hegemony. From very humble and insecure beginnings in 1117, generations of abbots and canons had increased their house's patrimony, up to the peak of its dominion in the late thirteenth and early fourteenth centuries. When, in those centuries, kings needed to know how stood the Seven Hundreds of Cirencester,

5 Cal Pat Rolls, 7 Edw. III, 40, 28 Jan. 1346.

6 Baddeley, A *History*, 177; Johne de Crekkelade and Johne Luccsone were assessed at 5s. and 1s. respectively in 1327.

they visited the abbey in person. They needed its support. In return, successive kings licensed (for a fee) the abbots' relentless encroachments on the customs and traditions of the people.

The turning-point came as soon as the abbey reached the zenith of its powers. Fifty years before the Black Death arrived from Southampton and Bristol, the abbots turned to violence. Through the fourteenth and into the early decades of the fifteenth century, they engaged in a relentless struggle to hold and extend their lordship, which gave them their dominant position in the extremely lucrative trade in very fine wool grown on the 'high, wild hills' of their domain, the Seven Hundreds. Their hegemony over this nice little corner of the European wool trade (fine wool sells in the worst slumps of trade) was probably achieved around the turn of the fifteenth century, when Marco Datini's agent informed his master that, as usual, the best fine wool was grown and sheared in the Cotswolds, and could be obtained from several sources. The abbot of Cirencester's wool, he wrote, was incomparably the best, and nothing could be done without his favour.

Tyranny produced its antithesis, a movement grounded in the stubborn insistence of the commonalty that the abbot's case was forged and illegitimate. Through the sources, stated or logically entailed by the abbey's own documentation, comes the opposition voice: Cirencester was once an independent community with only one, distant, lord. It governed itself, minded its own businesses, and came to the king's aid whenever it was called for. Cirencester was a borough, and its settled householders, the vast majority of them skilled craftsmen and traders, were citizens. The abbey was an unwanted imposition. Before it came, the people of Cirencester had been free. When it was gone, they would be free again.

Along with the clothiers' factors and agents came news from abroad, tales of truculent Florentines, rebels of Bruges and Antwerp. To master this international trade required sophisticated approaches to the gathering of information on the part of the abbots and their counsellors. Traders and their servants also told tales in the market-place, shops and pubs. In 1559, when the total population was at least as great as it had been before the Black Death, the town had 32 alehouses and 12 keepers of 'private inns without signs' that sold 'victuals' and at least two 'persons holding common inns, who vend provender for horses and provide other necessities'.[7] Word leaked out that not everywhere was the dignity of common townspeople 'before the memory of man'. In this sense we can say that the 'Renaissance' came to places like Cirencester not through rediscovered classical literature, but from stories told about contemporary politics in the most dynamic, industrial communities of Europe.

*

7 Beecham, *History of Cirencester*, 170.

Complaints of moral profligacy, corruption and degenerate behaviour on the part of the canons dominate the record in the second half of the fourteenth century. They need not be taken at face value, but they confirm the abbey's continuing unpopularity. Allegations of disorder were investigated in 1351, 1370, 1378 and 1381.[8] The depravations of plague in a town that was a vital part of national and international trade networks form an essential ingredient in a period of great general upheaval and turbulence. Four abbots died within a decade before the appointment of Nicholas Ampney, a local man by the sound of his name, in 1363.[9] In 1378 the almoner and the precentor were dismissed for gross maladministration and a treasurer was appointed by the bishop of Worcester to keep an eye on the abbey's fiscal activities. The exact circumstances are obscure.

The commonalty took the opportunity to press its claims once more; in 1369 a jury of knights was summoned to report to the king as to 'what customs and what services the men of Cirencester were accustomed to do in respect of lands in Cirencester in the time of Henry II and Richard I'. The jury reported that 'the abbot has recovered his seisin of the said service and customs according to the finding and all the men of Cirencestre are in his mercye'.[10] The reference to the abbot having 'recovered' his undisputed seigneury suggests that, in the turmoil following the first depravations of plague, he may well have lost it. One problem the abbey always had was that if its grip slackened the town simply reverted to running itself and keeping the profits. Abbeys were vigilant and ruthless because they had to be.

The judgement that the town was back 'in the mercye of the Abbot' was premature. The commonalty rose again four years after the Commons' Rebellion of 1381, attacked the abbey, broke in and did 'unheard of things to the abbot and canons, and threaten to do all the damage they could'.[11] The episode provided an occasion for rare ruling-class unity. Richard II ordered Thomas lord Berkeley and a posse of local knights, including John Beauchamp and Thomas Brugge (Brydges), to ride to Cirencester to 'make inquisition concerning insurrections'. The whole country was troubled by murmurings, threatened risings and riots at this time, but Lord Berkeley was specifically ordered 'to proceed only (against) such as were lately made in the town of Cicetre'.[12] A few years later, when Thomas Fitzharding helped Henry Bolingbroke dethrone Richard II, just as his grandfather and great-grandfather had helped dethrone Edward II, the Berkeleys danced to a different tune. They

8 *VCH Glos*, Vol. 2, 81.

9 William Hereward (abbot 1335–52), Ralph of Estcote (1352–7), William of Marteley (1358–61), William of Lineham (1361–3); Nicholas of Ampney was abbot 1363–93: Baddeley, *A History*, 198.

10 Cal Pat Rolls, 5 Edw. III, 14, 320, 10 Nov. 1369.

11 Cal Close Rolls, Ric. II, Vol. 2, 529; Cal Pat Rolls, Ric. II, Vol. 2, 93, 25 Feb. 1385; *VCH Glos*, Vol. 2, 82.

12 *Ibid*, 529; Baddeley, *A History*, 180.

were as jealous of their liberties, vis-à-vis their direct lord, the king, and their subjects the common people, as the common people were of their liberties as against those of the magnates.

Referring to similar anti-monastic risings at Bury St Edmunds, St Albans, Dunstable and Peterborough, David Knowles commented that

> the inhabitants of monastic boroughs exploited a rising (the Commons' Rebellion of 1381) in which they had no originating share in order to reiterate their old demands without any definite or thorough-going programme. The organized forces of conservatism were everywhere victorious.

Its continuity and consistency suggests, however, that the people's party at Cirencester did have a coherent programme, one that was reasserted at every opportunity, and was asserted again at Cirencester fifteen years later, as the next chapter will show. The timing of the monastic revolts, however, does suggest that townspeople were not instigators of the general insurrections of the (mainly) rural, though by no means always agricultural, population that came to be called the 'Peasants' Revolt'. It is noteworthy that the risings of English monastic boroughs coincided with general uprisings of the populace of industrial parts of continental Europe, and it was to these industrious regions that Cirencester looked for an important part of its trade. The international character of the popular movements of the late fourteenth century, like those of the early sixteenth century, is a reminder that lines of trade were also lines of communication.[13] Even so, at Cirencester the continuing field-of-force imposed a tight and repetitive plot on the unfolding epic. Something more fundamental had to happen for the plot to change.

13 Knowles, *The Religious Orders*, 269; Alastair Dunn, *The Peasants' Revolt: England's Failed Revolution of 1381* (Stroud 2004) is a useful recent account; for the continental context, see M. Mollat and P. Wolff, *The Popular Revolutions of the Late Middle Ages* (London 1973), esp. Ch. 2 and 4; Samuel K Cohn (trans. and annotated), *Popular Protest in Late Medieval Europe* (Manchester and New York 2004), esp. 261–374.

5

A turning-point: the generation of 1400

King (Henry IV): Kind Uncle York, the latest news we hear
Is that the rebels have consumed with fire
Our town of Ciceter in Gloucestershire;
But whether they be ta'en or slain we hear not ...
Northumberland: ... the next news is, I have to London sent
The heads of Oxford, Salisbury, Blunt, and Kent.
The manner of their taking may appear
At large discoursed in this paper here.

Shakespeare, *The Tragedy of King Richard II*, V, vi

The plot did change, momentarily, on 8 January 1400. The townspeople were presented with a rare opportunity to intervene decisively in the politics of the kingdom, using the occasion to pursue their long struggle. After the failure of the 'Epiphany Plot' to kill Henry of Lancaster and restore Richard of York to the throne, the Ricardian earls of Kent and Salisbury, accompanied by Sir Ralph Lumley, Sir Thomas Blount, Sir Benedict Sely and thirty other esquires, made their escape up the Thames Valley, arriving at Cirencester after dark. They took over the Ram Inn, abutting the market-place, where the landlord was William Tanner. None of the chroniclers tell us how the movement began, only that the lords and their retainers were quickly put under siege by 'an armed crowd of local villeins all armed with bows and sticks', led by John Cosyn, possibly the bailiff, and some local merchants, including Reginald (or Reynold) Spicer, a wealthy woolmonger whose memorial brass, dated 1442, describes him as 'a merchant of this town' and displays him with his four wives.[1]

Thomas Walsingham, chronicler of St Albans Abbey, left a detailed description of the episode. The inhabitants, apparently, were suspicious 'of [the earls'] display of arms' and, after making enquiries, were convinced 'that they were not telling the truth'. Seeing 'every way out' of the inn 'was blocked with beams and other great pieces of wood', the earls attempted to break out,

[1] The incident is described in Baddeley, A *History*, 186–7, from which the quotations in this and the next paragraph are taken. Spicer's brass, referred to by Baddeley, *ibid*, 188, n. 10, and in J.J. Simpson, 'The Wool Trade and the Woolmen of Gloucestershire', *Trans BGAS* 53 (1931), 90, is still there.

attacking the townspeople 'with lances and arrows'. The locals forced them back and

> began to shoot arrows at the lodging – some through the windows, some at the doors and gates – with the result that no place was safe for them, and not only were they unable to get out, they were not even able to look out. The ensuing battle lasted from the middle of the night until three o'clock the next day, when the earls eventually gave up, handed themselves over to the townspeople, begging not to be put to death before they had had an opportunity to speak to the king. They were accordingly led to the abbey, where they heard mass and were given breakfast for the day. During the afternoon, however, at about the hour of Vespers, a certain priest who was one of their followers started a fire in some houses in one of the streets of the town, in the hope that while the townspeople were trying to put them out the earls could seize the chance to escape. It was vain, however, for the townspeople anticipated such a ruse, abandoned the houses to the flames and rushed instead to the abbey to make sure that those whom they had spent so much effort in capturing should not be allowed to get away. By this time Thomas lord Berkeley had arrived and was preparing to take them to the king, which he would undoubtedly have done had the fire not been started in the town, but this wanton act so infuriated the townspeople, and indeed others who had begun to arrive from various parts of Gloucestershire and elsewhere, that no words could dissuade them from their determination to see the earls put to death. They even threatened lord Berkeley with death if he did not hand those traitors to the king over to them.
>
> Eventually, therefore, when the sun was setting, they were duly handed over, and the earls of Kent and Salisbury were beheaded at the hands of the people; by which act the Lord took his revenge on them with such punishment as their bad faith and lack of belief merits. For they were both unfaithful to their king, who had spared them, and, what is much worse, they were ungrateful to him who had shown them so much mercy.

Walsingham added for good measure that the noble rebels were Lollard sympathizers and 'despisers of holy images'.[2] A vernacular chronicler recorded that after the execution the townspeople stuck the heads on poles, 'and … carried them from Cirencester to Oxford, where they found king Henry lodging in the abbey of the Carmelites'. This chronicler was less inclined than Walsingham to take sides: the dukes and their men had

> faught manly; but at the laste they were overcome and take; and there thei smote of the Dukes hed of Surrey, and the Erles hed of Salusberye, & mony other moo; and there thay putte the quarters in sackys, and ther hedes on poles, born on hy, and so thei were brought through the cite of London vnto London brygge;

[2] C. Given Wilson (trans.), *Chronicles of the Revolution, 1397–1400* (Manchester 1993), 226–8; Walsingham's (d.1422) account is contemporary.

> and ther her heddes were sette vp an hy, & her quarters were sent to other gode tounes and cites, and set vp there...[3]

Walsingham wrote in Latin. At their best, late fourteenth-century Latin chronicles were intended for the education of rulers. They contributed what would later be called 'historical perspective' to the many forms of 'counsel' princes and lords were duty-bound to listen to, in order to govern justly and effectively. Chronicles were official memories. The vernacular account is less passionate or obviously biased than the Latin of Walsingham and his contemporary high churchmen. It does not denigrate the Ricardian nobles, or make wild accusations of heresy. It says the commonalty of Cirencester did this and this is what they did after they had done it. The perspective and prose of vernacular chronicles of the period of 'Middle' English is confident and matter-of-fact, and often extremely pithy. This birth and flowering of vernacular English was a sign that the English-speaking commonalty was starting to absorb its rulers: the Latin church and French nobility. French nobility rarely ventured into the town of Cirencester, though it often stayed at the abbey. French became less and less attractive to the nobility as a result of Edward III's wars.

More than anything that came before, the episode explored in this chapter was conducted in English, for an English auditory. It was important that stories of Cirencester's heroism could spread, in a common language. Because the episode was unusual (common people defeat armed nobles) it attracted attention, generating controversy and conflict within and beyond the town. Travellers were always passing through, swapping stories, carrying them on to new places. The chroniclers' accounts ascribe the fight and the victory to the townspeople generally, as if all were as one, and acted accordingly. Leaders are mentioned incidentally. The victory was achieved by a community acting as one. A large, very determined and well-organized assembly is implied by this defeat of armed feudal warriors, trained and hardened in the arts of war. The chroniclers make no reference to any outside assistance or encouragement.

Other sources, however, suggest the new king, recognizing Cirencester's strategic importance, had made preparations in advance. Another chronicler reported that the lords were led into the market-place by 'John Cosyn, Reginald Spicer, John Colman, Roger Carvill and Richard Small', where their heads were cut off to the acclamation of the crowd. The chroniclers' accounts implied the independent and spontaneous agency of the townspeople. Alone in the euphoric reception of this living symbol of popular support for Henry of Lancaster, Adam Usk spotted a constitutionally dangerous precedent – a sign of change that might, if not stamped out immediately, destroy the existing state altogether: the 'citizens' of Cirencester had an agenda of their own. A few

[3] Given Wilson, *Chronicles* 233–4; F.W.D. de Brie, *The Brut or the Chronicles of England* (London 1906), 361.

days later another Ricardian lord was 'most despicably beheaded by workmen at Bristol'.[4]

> All these acts were perpetrated solely by the violence of the common people [wrote Adam]. I fear that possession of the sword, which, although contrary to the natural order, was allowed to them in such circumstances, might at some future time embolden them to rise up in arms against the lords.[5]

These were a churchman's sentiments, at a time when popular feeling against church magnates was running high, and when vernacular religion ('Lollardy') was fashionable in the lower ranks of the nobility. Murmurings concerning the dispossession of the secular estates of the church were commonplace in the decades after the Commons' Rebellion of 1381; they surfaced in Parliament a few years later. The nobility, gentry and upper ranks of the commonalty – those with capital and rank – would benefit greatly from any redistribution of church lands. Church chroniclers and intellectuals naturally feared just such alliances of king, gentry and commonalty as were implied by Henry's coup. For magnates of the church, and supportive ideologues like Adam Usk and Thomas Walsingham, secular and religious elites should work together to maintain the subordination and obedience of the commonalty. Henry of Lancaster's populism was doubly threatening to the church hierarchy. Adam's judgement that 'these acts were perpetrated solely by the violence of the common people' and his warning that Henry's tactics 'might at some future time embolden [the commonalty] to rise up in arms against the lords' must be seen in this context.

Subsequent events, and what can be gleaned from the records about John Cosyn, possibly the town (i.e. the abbot's appointee as) bailiff in 1400, suggest that events were not quite as spontaneous, or disinterestedly enthusiastic for the Lancastrian cause, as the chroniclers implied. Cosyn was a minor squire with landholdings on the Cotswold plateau at Elkstone and Northcote. His first recorded association with the town is dated 1392, when Cosyn was listed with several other men of Cirencester, donors of seven houses worth £10, to salary a chaplain 'for celebrating divine service daily in the chapel of St Mary in the parish church, and to pray for their good estate, for their souls after death and the souls of their benefactors and others.'[6] As the next chapter will show, this makes Cosyn more than the ambitious esquire who appears elsewhere in the documentation. Consciously or not, he founded a new epoch in the religious history of the town. Cosyn's partners in the refinancing of St Mary's chantry left wills including bequests to pay for a good funeral procession and burial inside the church, or, in one case,

4 'Plebeiorum pagensium tumultu decapitai fuerent', C. Given Wilson (ed. and trans.), *The Chronicle of Adam of Usk* (Oxford 1991), 89–90.

5 *Ibid*, 90–1.

6 Cal Pat Rolls, 5 Ric. II, 173, 22 Sep. 1392.

the abbey.[7] Like at least one other of the four men who led the Ricardian earls to their execution in the market-place, Cosyn was no obvious member of the plebeian rank and file. Yet the sources are adamant that the actions of the townspeople were enthusiastically undertaken.

There is evidence that the new king knew Cosyn and made efforts to enlist his support. On 13 November 1399 – two months *before* the Epiphany Plot – Patent Rolls record a 'Grant for life to John Cosyn of Cirencester, whom the king has retained for life of ten pounds yearly' to be paid from the receipts of the royal manor of Merston Meny in Wiltshire.[8] Cosyn may have been the 'certain esquire from Cirencester, ... greatly skilled in arms', who sent a member of his household to attend the king's court at Christmas 1399, 'so that he could report back to him on the warlike deeds done in the jousts there'.[9] On 12 November, 1399, Cosyn was granted, likewise 'for life', the office of porter of the castle of St Briavels, which paid him 'sixpence a day from the castle and the Forest of Dean'.[10] Cosyn, it seems, was personally acquainted with Henry before the dramatic events of 8 January. The reward was not long in coming. A fortnight after the executions Cosyn was granted '100 marks yearly from the exchequer'. An entry in the rolls three days later spelt out that this was 'for his good service in manfully resisting at Cirencester, Thomas, late earl of Kent, and others who rose in insurrection against the king'.[11]

Who, then, was John Cosyn? The company he kept assigns him to 'a new rank of men situated between the knights and the commonalty'. His will of 1403 suggests he was an 'esquire', referring as it does to 'lands in Cirencester, Elkston and Winston' and 'my manor of Northcote'. Bequests to 'my servants at Cirencester, Elkstone and Northcote' suggest he lived at all three from time to time, and leased out the property at Winston. His chief counsellors were 'Sir Walter Kyrkeby my chaplain', who was left 20s., like a second chaplain, Sir John Yonge, and Richard Stanes, 'my serving man'.[12] Nigel Saul's excellent study of the emergence and exploits of men like Cosyn describes what might be called the epic phase in the evolution of the English country gentleman, the genesis of whom he places in the fourteenth century. In March 1403, John Cosyn and Richard Draper 'of Cirencester', in partner-

7 PCC Marche 2, 30 May 1402 Thomas Dyare; PCC Marche, 16 Dec. 1397 John Boys; PCC Marche 6, Nicholas Pointer Thurs before feast of St Alban 1403; E.A. Fuller, 'The Register of the Chapel of the Blessed Virgin Mary in the Parish Church of Cirencester', *Trans BGAS* 18 (1893–4), 320–31, writes that the earliest deeds relating to the St Mary Chapel date to the early thirteenth century.

8 Cal Pat Rolls, 1 Hen. IV, Vol. iii, 86; Cosyn was summonsed as a juror for the county on 3 June 1398: E.G. Kimball (ed.), 'Gloucestershire Peace Rolls', *Trans BGAS* 62 (1940), 162.

9 Given Wilson, *Chronicles*, 235

10 Cal Pat Rolls, 1 Hen. IV, 127.

11 Cal Pat Rolls, 1 Hen. IV, 182–3.

12 PCC Marche 4, 29 Mar. 1403 John Cosyn, Hockaday, Vol. 155.

ship with James Clifford of Frampton upon Severn and Anselm Guyse 'of Gloucestershire', stood guarantors of a hundred marks bonding one Richard Thomas of Elmore and John Peyntour of Northleach not to 'do or procure no hurt or harm to John atte Wood'.[13] The association with Clifford, especially in a bond for two known members of Clifford's gang, in a case in which Clifford is known to have been the prime mover, has wider significance that may cast more light on the events of early January 1400.

Clifford's career is 'without parallel in the annals of crime in fourteenth-century Gloucestershire': he was the only member of the Gloucestershire landowning class in the period actually to be indicted for murder. Clifford and, by association, Cosyn, belonged to a class that operated, throughout the fourteenth century, 'in a netherworld of frustrated ambitions and the daily reality of declining status'. His record suggests he may have been one of those armigerous gangsters whose

> chivalric code should not obscure an altogether more nasty and brutish everyday reality. A not inconsiderable number of these paladins [writes David Levine] were criminals who were pardoned in order to have them serve military ends. In the English forces which fought alongside Edward III in France and Scotland they seem to have been present in the hundreds. In 1339–40 there is documentary record of 850 such pardons; 'several hundreds' more were granted in 1346–7, 140 at Poitiers in 1356, and 260 a few years later (1360).

As we have seen, the Cirencester region was troubled for most of the century by 'the oversupply of trained fighters and the infrequent and unpredictable demand for their services'. Levine concludes that 'it was not surprising that rootless gangs of discharged fighters lived at interstitial points in the social structure'.[14]

This fits Clifford (and possibly Cosyn) like a glove. Bred to be a warrior, left with no foreign enemies to fight and plunder, and an insufficient and challenged estate, he turned his attentions to his more vulnerable neighbours. The first step was to identify estates not already, in some way, retained, attached or connected to a more powerful lord. Clifford was careful not to offend the Berkeleys and the Beauchamps, whose territorial spheres of interest met at the River Frome, which ran into the Severn through Clifford's little bailywick of Frampton upon Severn. Some of the Gloucestershire abbeys had more territory and retainers, but the leader of the Berkeley yeomen could always defeat a petty gangster like Clifford. Any potential source of income and estate that had the faintest whiff of a Berkeley or Beauchamp interest was out of bounds: except to each other. Time out of

13 CPR HIV, ii, 148; for another incident involving Clifford, see Kimball (ed.), 'Gloucestershire Peace Rolls', 165.

14 David Levine, *At the Dawn of Modernity* (London, 2001), 129, citing H.J. Hewitt, *The Organisation of War under Edward III, 1338–1362* (Manchester 1966), 30.

mind abbots of Cirencester, in times of riot, sent for help from the king, and the king sent a Maurice or a Thomas lord Berkeley (if he wasn't away with the king's armies in Wales, Scotland and France) to quell the troubles. 'Whether [Clifford] had an influential local patron is not known,' writes Saul. 'If he did, it was certainly not Thomas de Berkeley who had to be prevented from doing violence to him' (Cal Close Rolls, 1385–9, 672). He had a theoretically much more powerful lord. 'He was retained by both Richard II and Henry IV – from the latter he received the handsome fee of forty pounds.'[15]

His first enterprise came to the notice of the courts in 1363. It involved a claim to the Cotswold manor of Stowell. Clifford 'must have enforced his right, for the Cliffords subsequently appear in possession of it'. His rivals seem to have been retainers of the abbot. The case confirms other evidence suggesting that as soon as it was unable to employ violence wherever and whenever its *imperium* was challenged, the abbey began, quite literally, to lose ground to the pack of hungry contenders like Clifford and Cosyn. He got hold of Stowell and depopulated it.[16] Clifford's outright 'criminal career' came before the courts in 1385 'when he murdered one John Tailor at Saul, near Frampton'. Tailor's son appealed to King's Bench. 'Clifford produced a royal pardon and was acquitted by the justices of gaol delivery.' This outcome exactly fits Levine's bleak account of the lower ranks of fourteenth-century chivalry. In 1386 Clifford was involved in a campaign to expel William Fairoak from the profits of his church of Fretherne; for most of that time Clifford took by force the petty tithes and profits pertaining to the church. In 1396 a group of Clifford's neighbours offered surety that he would threaten no more harm to one John Wotton; and in 1399 he was accused of illegally occupying lands and rents in Frampton that had been taken into the king's keeping by the escheator.

In his later exploits Clifford collaborated with a neighbour, Anselm Guise of Elmore, who was married to Clifford's daughter, Catherine. Clifford wanted John atte Wood's farm in the Cotswolds for his son in law, Guise, and they conspired to secure a false inquest to indict Wood for felony. Wood was imprisoned for three and a half years. Clifford and Guise occupied his lands and still held them seven years later. Wood petitioned parliament for redress in 1402. He was murdered in 1406. In Kings Bench Clifford was convicted for having abetted and procured one Bartholemew Hunte *alias* Wyther, to murder John atte Wood at Gyldenacre in the parish of St Martin by the Mewes, Middlesex. He was pardoned and his son in law remained in possession of John atte Wood's farm. Saul observes that while he held none

[15] Nigel Saul, *Knights and Esquires: the Gloucestershire Gentry in the Fourteenth Century* (Oxford 1981), 176–7.

[16] *VCH*, Vol. 9, ed. Carol Davidson, A.J.C. Jurica and Elizabeth Williamson (London, 2001), 208–17; seven men of Stowell were assessed for the tax of 1327; 18 men paid the poll tax in 1381; in subsequent lists and taxes, only the lord was present.

of the main offices in the county, Clifford was elected once as a knight of the shire, representing Gloucestershire in the parliament that met at Coventry in October 1404. Clifford got away with murder – twice – because he was retained by succeeding kings.

The absence of references to Cosyns in the Cirencester records before 1392 and after John's death in 1403, and the fact that he was bailiff when the earls were executed, suggests he was a soldier, recruited by the abbot to assist in the administration and policing of the liberties of the town, i.e. the liberties of the abbot. Most likely, he was an old soldier, like Clifford. Once the soldiers got moving, the abbot was fit only to cook the prisoners' breakfast. He was not reading the politics very well. The depositions and reputed murders of Edward II and Richard II were crimes for which the whole kingdom would be punished. If the English crown could be won by violence, why couldn't any estate in England? In such a world, nothing was certain except that you had to manoeuvre and fight to gain, and fight to keep your gains. This was not a law-abiding culture. Law was whoever was powerful enough to coerce and persuade the others. It does not follow that many, even a majority of people were not law-abiding. Where lords took by combat, the commonalty appealed to law and custom. Short of rebellion, it was all they had. Murder was, then as now, a heinous crime, but if the murderer (or procurer of murder) was retained by a king or a powerful lord he would be pardoned, other things being equal. There was probably an understanding among the military classes that killing was what men like Clifford and Cosyn were bred to do.

We must weigh the effects of generations of warfare, or immediate readiness for warfare, on the assorted ranks of people, not only the kings, earls, barons, knights and esquires, but (increasingly the decisive force in English military victories) the bow/yeomen and their neighbours in the villages and market towns.[17] The ubiquity of courts, juries, judges of the King's Bench, an increasingly streamlined and efficient civil service, the emergence, in the century after Runnymede, of routinized parliaments, and parliamentary procedures – in short, the whole recorded history of Norman-Angevin constitutional history notwithstanding, none of it had quite penetrated the fabric of the ruling class, for which government was at 'the will of the nobility'. The commonalty wanted a law-abiding society, in which everyone up to the king was expected to abide by basic constitutional principles. Lords expected to *rule*. The advent of constitutionalism in England involved a victory for the commonalty over the lords. The popular movement lost all the battles, but won some campaigns and eventually won the war.

Cosyn's probable military leadership qualifies the Latin chronicler's statement that events at Cirencester were 'perpetrated *solely* by the violence of

[17] The arming of the commonalty is discussed in Rollison, 'The Armed Hand', in *A Commonwealth of the People*, 100–5.

the common people'. Defeat of armed Ricardian lords and their retainers could not have happened without the archers and stavemen of the town; they were led, and perhaps even persuaded to take the usurper's side, by some well-placed 'gentlemen'. If that was the case, however, the role of the rank and file, and its long struggle with the abbey, was not forgotten. Six weeks after the executions, on 25 February 1400/1, the king appointed a 'Commission to enquire into divers prepréstures, encroachments, insurrections and abuses committed by the abbot of Cirencester and his predecessors in the town of Cirencester and elsewhere in the County of Gloucestershire'. The townspeople had withdrawn customary services and boycotted the abbot's manorial and market courts, refusing to serve the customary harvest-works, which in some cases had already been commuted into sums of money. No-one had ever previously questioned the right of 'the king's fee-farmer' to the boon-works. Forms of feudal servitude had never been as unpopular as in the decades following the Commons' Rebellion of 1381.

The abbot took immediate steps to reassert his powers. On 28 February, the king issued an instruction to the escheator in Gloucestershire, 'for particular causes laid before the king and council, to take the town of Cirencestre into the king's hand';[18] from March until November royal officers (Cosyn?) ruled in the name of the king. Revealingly, the expenses of occupation were deducted from the revenues of the abbot.[19] The day he took the town under 'royal protection', Henry showed his continuing friendship for the commonalty by granting 'to the men of Cicestre… all the goods and chattels of the earl of Kent and the earl of Salisbury found there at the time of their arrest, except gold and silver in mass or money, vessels of gold or silver or gilt and jewells'.[20] A day later, among various grants out of the estate of the earl of Kent, is '36 pounds yearly rent which the said earl used to receive at the hands of the bailiffs and commonalty of Cirencester… mandate in pursuance to the bailiffs of Cirencester'.[21] This handed over tenancies, but to what legal body? In July the king further rewarded 'the men of Cirencester' with 'four does yearly in season' from the royal Forest of Brayden and 'a tun of wine yearly' in the port of Bristol. The ladies were not forgotten: Henry gallantly granted 'the women of the town' six bucks and a tun of wine.[22] This gave the king breathing space while he decided, not only how to deal with the populist expectations his victory had raised on a national scale, but (what it came down to) how to settle individual cases like that of the townspeople and the abbey of Cirencester.

The king *was* concerned with what had happened to the money, precious metals and jewels carried by the earls and their retainers. On 6 November

18 Cal Close Rolls, 1 Hen. IV, 28 Feb. 1400, 55.

19 J. Wylie, *History of England Under Henry the Fourth* (London 1884), Vol. 1, 100.

20 Cal Pat Rolls, 1 Hen. IV, 28 Feb. 1400, 55.

21 Cal Pat Rolls, 1 Hen. IV, 29 Feb. 1400, 223.

22 Cal Pat Rolls, 1 Hen. IV, 5 July 1401, 318.

he ordered John Rothwell, Richard Draper, John Ashley and John Wyking, all of Cirencester, to arrest William Tanner, landlord of the Ram Inn, and bring him to the king and council. Tanner was a local notable who married his daughter to the heir of a local gentry family.[23] He seems to have satisfied the council that he knew nothing of what had happened to the earls' treasury left in his inn. The king visited Cirencester two weeks later, in part perhaps to pursue the missing treasure in person. While there he issued a pardon to John Spalding of Cirencester, whom another townsman, Robert Cutler, had impleaded for a debt while Spalding had been fighting for the king in Wales.[24]

Henry's men made some progress in tracing the treasure, which seems to have been shared out among several townspeople. In June the following year Henry granted ten pounds of gold 'which John Schildesley of Cirencester took from certain coffers of Thomas, late earl of Kent and other rebels', and 'has hitherto concealed'. The inquiry continued: on 10 January 1403, a commission arrested 'John Cosyn, Richard Draper, Robert Cutler, John Spendelove, John Thryst, tanner, *alias* John Lovekin of Cirencester,' and several other men, and brought them to Westminster. By 13 June 1403, Cosyn was dead, but a record of that date suggests that some of these men had indeed been involved in the 'confiscation' of the earl's treasure. A few months later the king granted his kitchen servants £130 6s. 8d.

> from certain goods late of Thomas earl of Kent … forfeited to the king and concealed in the hands of Robert Cutler, John Spendelove, John Capron, John Thryst *alias* Lovekin, John Terling, Roger Corvile, Thomas Courser, all of Cirencester, and John Dotton of Salisbury, who incurred that sum for the same goods by default in the exchequer for not answering when warned by the sheriff of Gloucester.[25]

As for the strike of the townspeople, in April 1403 the king instructed twelve knights and gentlemen of the Shire of Gloucester to ride to Cirencester, to enquire into their withdrawal from the traditional services and dues of the manor. The lords' response was predictable. If allowed to stand, the townspeople's actions would 'do grievous harm and damage to all the king's lieges of the county'.[26] Villeins were villeins, even if they did have urban pretensions. Yet once he was satisfied face had been saved in the matter of the treasure, the king was content to ignore Lord Berkeley's predictable distaste for rent-strikes and revolting villeins. He still felt he needed popular support, and the

23 GA P86, CH 1.2 includes a marriage settlement dated 1403 between John George and Elizabeth, a daughter of William Tanner.

24 Cal Pat Rolls, 2 Hen. IV, 28 Nov. 1401.

25 Cal Pat Rolls, 2 Hen. IV, 233.

26 A translation of the document (*Inquisition ad quod damnum*, a. 4 Hen. IV, 13) is reproduced in Baddeley, *A History*, 190–1.

big reward came. On 4 July 1403, he issued a charter to constitute a Guild Merchant,

> with all its franchises, privileges, and the rest, with right to elect, on the morrow of Epiphany, at a certain spot within the town, a Master or Governor of the Gild, and all or any other officers they might deem necessary for the better governance of the said gild.[27]

The grant threatened liberties and rights granted to the abbots and confirmed by every king since Richard I. A Guild Merchant was most obviously of benefit to the small elite of wealthy merchants and (increasingly) manufacturers who ran the economy and (if later evidence is any indication) served as jurors and churchwardens. It entailed the right to use the town for the purposes of trade and, if they wished, to grant trading rights to others. On the face of it, this grant of a Guild Merchant does not seem likely to have benefited the rank and file. Government simply devolved from a single lord to an oligarchy of businessmen. This would indeed prove to have been the case, but it is likely that in 1403 memories and myths of the unity of the town having saved the king at a crucial point in his takeover had created a sense of unity. The grant forbade interference with the abbot's manorial rights, but since the abbots had been engaged for at least two centuries in actions to ensure that these included governance of commerce, a glaring contradiction was implied.[28] On 3 December 1403, the king affirmed his support by issuing a general pardon to the men of Cirencester 'for all treasons' and awarded the Guild Merchant a 'grant of all gold and silver and gilt and jewells taken from the rebels', or what, by then, was left of it.

The records are silent for the next two years. Subsequent events show the abbot and canons bided their time, waiting for circumstances to change. They knew the Guild Merchant was illegal. The first small hint of a fight-back came on 3 April 1406, when Reginald Spicer, Roger Carvile and John Terlynge, probably officials of the new Guild Merchant, and Alan Chaumbre of London, salter, were ordered to free Stephen Chamberlayne of Cirencester, imprisoned at the suit of John Rothwell.[29] Rothwell, like Spicer, was active in January 1400/1, a leader of the Guild Merchant movement and an active Lancastrian. The abbey was actively reviving its traditional claims and, in order to do so, applied pressure, piecemeal, to leading figures among the townspeople. On 30 May 1407, the king granted a

27 Trans. reproduced in Baddeley, *A History*, 194.

28 Fuller, 'The Manor and the Town', wrote that the king acted 'illegally' and 'had no right to make a present to the townsmen of any privileges contrary to (the abbot's) old manorial rights'.

29 Cal Close Rolls, 2 Hen. IV, 3 Apr. 1406.

> pardon to John Rothewell als Robyns of Cirencester, in consideration of the uneasiness sustained by him through divers persons on account of the love he has the king and for his late service at Cirencester against the rebels, for which he is indicted of divers felonies at the procurance of his enemies of the County of Gloucestershire.[30]

The abbot and his allies kept up the pressure; on 5 September the king confirmed his pardon of

> John Rothewell of Cirencester, webbe (weaver), in consideration of great enmities of divers persons against him on account of the love ... and his good services against the rebels for which at the procurance of his enemies of the county of Gloucestershire he is indicted of divers felonies.[31]

As a weaver, John Rothwell was a *mediocre*, representative or leader of a trade association lower down the ranks than wealthy merchants like Reginald Spycer and the clothier, William Nottingham. It is likely that the Cirencester Weavers' Guild began as an informal association of weavers and journeymen at this time and that Rothwell was one of its guiding lights.

On 28 November 1408, the abbot presented a selection of charters establishing the legality of his claim to the markets and fairs to the king's justices at Gloucester. The legality of the new trade oligarchy was under challenge.[32] On 27 April 1410 the abbot successfully prosecuted Robert Cutler for a debt of £32, and on 17 October 1411, another local man, Thomas Beck failed to attend court to answer the abbot of Cirencester 'touching a trespass and to answer the abbot & James Spilleman, his fellow canon, touching a trespass'.[33] The fightback was gathering force.

On 12 March 1412, the now dying king's officials sent commissioners to arrest several men suspected of leading the commonalty's resistance against the abbey: William Nottyngham, John Coston, Thomas Gage, John Lecke, John Greynden 'weaver', Richard Staines, William Kyng, William Bristowe *alias* Glovere and Henry Northcote. They were to be brought immediately before the king and council in Chancery.[34] On 11 July 1412, the earl of Kent's wife obtained permission to remove his bones from their grave outside the town and have them reburied at his own Mountgrace Abbey.[35] Confident the time had come to recover his estate and dignity, the abbot sent the king a copy of his charters of 10 November, 43 Edward III, and on 5 June

30 Cal Pat Rolls, 3 Hen. IV, 30 May 1407, 348.
31 Cal Pat Rolls, 3 Hen. IV, 5 Sep. 1408, 471.
32 Cal Pat Rolls, 3 Hen. IV, 28 Nov. 1408.
33 Cal Pat Rolls, 4 Hen. IV, 27 Apr. 1410; CPR, 4 Hen. IV, 17 Oct. 1411, 327.
34 Cal Pat Rolls, 4 Hen. IV, 12 Mar. 1412, 478.
35 Cal Pat Rolls, 4 Hen. IV, 11 July 1412, 416.

1413, they were confirmed.[36] Resistance continued, but it is possible that some of the leading men had seen the writing on the wall and were keeping in the background. On 12 March 1413, warrants were issued to arrest three weavers, William Bristowe, Thomas Broun and John Harding, and Thomas Adams, a glover, and bring them before the king.[37] The action now seemed to be coming from lower down the social scale. On 12 June 1413, Henry V sent a commission of oyer and terminer to Thomas, lord Berkeley, 'touching the bondmen and tenants in bondage of the abbot of Cirencester, who have leagued together to refuse their due customs and services'. There were two issues. Henry IV's award of the Guild Merchant probably persuaded the poorer townspeople, many of them tenants of the abbey, that they too could take advantage of the abbey's temporary weakness. The 'bondmen and tenants' had put the abbey under siege.[38]

State records allow us to trace the souring of royal beneficence towards the town and the apparent reversal of the gains of 1400–4. Henry V reverted to type. Single lords were easier to deal with than complicated, truculent urban commonalties. In 1410, under legal pressure from the abbot, and possibly from other regional magnates concerned at the implication that independent violence on the part of commoners might in certain circumstances be rewarded, Henry restored the abbey's franchise of the two main wool-fairs, the most lucrative occasions in the Cirencester calendar. This left only the small-goods trade in the ambit of the Guild Merchant. Henry died in 1413, and the abbot immediately asserted his right to claim market tallages on all goods, leading to a series of riots. Henry V's officials reviewed the case, annulled the Guild Merchant, and restored the abbot's liberties. The following year the abbot followed up his victory by charging a long list of named townsmen 'for withdrawing their services for thirteen years'. The king's justices found them guilty, but gave the abbot permission to pardon them should he wish to do so. In 1418, a Court of Chancery found that Henry IV's grant had, indeed, been 'contrary to the previous rights of the abbots'. The commonalty's struggle once again 'ended in the complete triumph of the monastery over the town'.[39]

The list of 'men of the town of Cirencester', pardoned in 1415 'for all treasons, insurrections, felonies, trespasses, inobediences, rebellions, negligences, misprisions, maintenances, contempts, councils, abetments, conventicles, confederacies, extortions, oppressions, offences, impeachments and other evil deeds' against the abbey, included 104 names.[40] Fourteen were explicitly assigned occupations, and fifteen more had occupational surnames. They

36 Cal Pat Rolls, 1 Hen. V, 27.

37 Cal Pat Rolls, 1 Hen. V, 24 Mar. 1413 as 12 Mar. 1412.

38 Cal. Pat Rolls, 1 Hen. V, 38, 12 June 1413.

39 *VCH Glos*, Vol. 2, 82; Baddeley, *A History*, 194–5; Beecham, *History of Cirencester*, 26–8.

40 Cal Pat Rolls, 1 Hen. V, 168, 15 Feb. 1414–15: 'Pardon to [104 names] …, men of the town of C for all treasons, insurrections, felonies, trespasses, inobediences, rebellions,

included nine weavers, three tailors, three glovers, two dyers, two curriers and single representatives of the trades or offices of carpenter, chapman, spurrier, ironmonger, woodward, baker, draper, smith, stillman and brazier. Such names clearly identified them as members of the commonalty in the class or 'third estate' (those who worked) sense. The surnames include a Malvern, Bristow and Nottingham; beyond these three, place-names had virtually disappeared. Surnames were now routinized: immigrants mostly brought firmly attached surnames with them and it was no longer necessary, except in special cases, to identify them by their place of origin. Only two, Thomas at the Well and William at the Mill, Weaver would fit comfortably in the listings of 1313–16, 1327 and 1334. The rest would not seem out of place in a nineteenth-century census. The 104 men shared a mere thirteen Christian names, John being easily the most common (41), followed by William (16), Thomas (12), Robert (9), Walter (6), Henry (6), Richard (6), and single cases of David, Stephen, Edward, Ralph and James. By contrast, the list encompassed no fewer than 100 different surnames, only four (Page, Snell, Smith and Forthey) occurring twice each. Surnames were institutionalized in the course of the fourteenth century. Henceforth the places and occupations of the commonalty would be given after surnames whenever it was felt necessary, as in John Smyth of Nibley or Tom Paine, Corsetmaker.

negligences, misprisions,, maintenances, contempts, councils, abetments, conventicles, confederacies, extortions, oppressions, offences, impeachments and other evil deeds'.

6

Highpoint of vernacular religion: building a church, 1400–1548

> And for good works, who seeth not that herein they went far beyond us … What memorable and famous buildings, what stately edifices of sundry kinds … What churches, chapels and other houses of prayer did they erect …![1]

Legend has it that while staying at the abbey 'in about 1380', the young Richard II and his wife paid a visit to the parish church. Richard's wife, Anne of Bohemia, expressed a wish that a chantry be set up 'at the east end of the north aisle of the nave', to pray for the souls of the kings of England and their friends.[2] True or false, it is recorded that on 18 November 1382 three pious burghers of the town, Robert Playn, John Boys and Nicholas Poynter, paid 40 marks into Richard's treasury for a licence to found a chantry dedicated to the Holy Trinity. They assigned 'the manor of Bagendon juxta Cirencester' and 'three acres of meadow at Bandynton, Gloucs.' to pay the salaries of 'two chaplains… to pray for the souls of the king's ancestors formerly kings of England, and for his welfare while he lives, one at the altar of Holy Trinity, the other at the altar of St Mary'. 'The altar of St Mary' referred to an older chapel, founded at the peak of medieval prosperity, around 1250, 'by all the parishioners of Cirencester to celebrate the divine service daily in honour of our Lord Jesus Christ and the most blessed Virgin Mary, on behalf of the whole parish'.[3] Special mention is made in the earliest documents of Richard Erkenbald, a freeholder, who may have been the 'proctor' at the town, the appointed leader of 'all the parishioners'.

Playn disappears without trace, but ten years later Boys and Poynter were joined by eleven more men – William Archebaud, John Cosyn, William

1 Philip Stubbes, A *Motive to Good Workes. Or Rather, to True Christianitie Indeede* (London 1593), 44–5, qf. Patrick Collinson, 'The Elizabethan Church and the New Religion', in Christopher Haigh (ed.), *The Reign of Elizabeth I* (Basingstoke 1987), 170.

2 Canon Rowland Hill, *Cirencester Parish Church – An Account of its History and Architecture* (Cheltenham 1985), 15.

3 Fuller, 'The Register of the Chapel of the Blessed Virgin Mary', *Trans BGAS* 18 (1893–4), 321.

Spendelove, Richard Poynter, Thomas Dyer, William Culpenne, Nicholas Seabourne, John Baker, Robert Sergeant, Philip Hardy and William Wodeford. They assigned the rents of 'seven messuages in Cirencester' to the maintenance of a 'chaplain to celebrate divine service in the chapel of St Mary … and pray for the said William and the others during their lives and for their friends after their deaths and for the kings of England'. [4] The second foundation put the souls of the founders first. The king and his descendants have become an afterthought. The popularity of the boy-king waned quite rapidly from the Commons' Rebellion (1381) on, and by 1392 there was much talk that Richard was a tyrant. The last time such things had been said of a king had been in 1327. Then, the tyrant had been deposed. There is no reason to suppose the commonalty of Cirencester (or elsewhere) was ever completely undisturbed by memories of that disturbing precedent. There is a hint in the chantry foundations of 1382 and 1392 of waning affection for Richard and perhaps for the monarchy itself. By the end of January 1400, everyone in England would know about Cirencester's mercurial loyalties.

There is also a hint that the wealthy elite, a small group of merchants and lords of small neighbouring manors, interrelated by marriage, was thinking more of its own souls than it was of the townspeople as a whole. St Mary's Chapel had been founded for the benefit of 'all the parishioners'. Holy Trinity and all the later fifteenth- and early sixteenth-century chantries and services that followed seem to make a sharper distinction between wealthy and prestigious individual founders and their immediate families, on the one hand, and 'all christians' and 'the poor', on the other.

Unlike Nicholas Poynter, who, in his will the same year, asked that his body be buried in the abbey, Cosyn wished to be buried in the parish church 'before the altar of St Thomas'. Trinity Chapel, set up by Poynter, Cosyn and the others but not completed until c.1430, was 'sometimes referred to incorrectly as St Thomas's chapel'. This is one of several ambiguities embodied in the Trinity Chapel that shed light on old historiographical conventions and ongoing scholarly debate. The Trinity chapel is a clue to the collective mind of the community that built it in four decades of such political upheaval that many historians have described what happened as a 'revolution'. This chapter shows that a religious revolution took place at Cirencester, begun (for want of similar evidence for earlier periods of church rebuilding and religious revival) in 1382, and continued by four, perhaps five new generations, up to 1548.[5] The abbots' recovery of their formal powers was a setback, but the failure of the Guild-Merchant movement established a pattern that represented a new

4 Cal Pat Rolls, 5 Ric. II, 173, 22 Sep. 1392.

5 This and the following based on GCL, 'Hockaday Abstracts', Vol. 155 (Cirencester 1400–1550), translations of PCC Marche 4, 29 Mar. 1403 John Cosyn; PCC Marche 6 Nicholas Pointer, Thurs before feast of St Alban 1403; PCC will, Gilbert Glasyer of C 1410 left 20s. 'to Abbot and convent'.

– or possibly revived – strategy that was centred, not on the abbot's manor, but the people's parish.

Cosyn expected to be buried 'in front of the altar of St Thomas'. Later reports associating Trinity Chapel with Thomas Beckett, murdered in Canterbury Cathedral by henchmen of Henry II, forever associated with power-struggles between church and king, religion and politics, the first and second 'estates', are probably significant. The altar of St Thomas stood 'at the east end of the Trinity chapel'. An ancient painting of the archbishop on its north wall was still visible in the 1770s, when Samuel Rudder saw it. Under the painting, 'in the rude orthography of the fourteenth or fifteenth century', were the following words:

> What man other woman worscip this holi seint Bisscop and mart[y]r every Sunday that bith in the yere wt a pat[ernoste]r and one ave [Maria] Othir ony almus geveth to a pore man or bring ony candill light laff or more he schall have v giftis graunt of god. The firste is he schall have reysonabil gode to his lyves end. The seconde is that his enimyes schall have no pouir to do hym no bodeley harme nor dysese. The iii is what reysonabil thynge that he will aske of god and that holy gent hyt schall be graunt. The iij that he schall be onbourdned of all his tribulacion and dysese. The v is that in his laste inde have schrift [confession] and housil [eucharist] and grete repentaunce and sacramente of an newntinge [extreme unction] and the[y] may come to that blysse that never hath ende.[6]

Worship the saint every Sunday in the year by saying the Lord's Prayer, a Hail Mary, give alms to 'a pore man' and light a candle to the shrine, and all a person could 'reysonabilly' hope for, in this and the afterlife, will come true. The inscription testifies to the extraordinary power Becket exercised in the minds of the laity. Trinity Chapel, for Cosyn's generation, was the most intimately sacred space in the church. That the inscription was in the people's tongue, at a time when Archbishop Arundel's reactionary 'constitutions' had pronounced use of the vernacular as an instrument of liturgy, preaching, teaching and writing books of religion as heresy, is a clue to the populist roots of the movement of the townspeople.[7]

Associated with this space were clear signs of connections with Richard II and later (more populist) dukes of York. Few events in Henry of Lancaster's coup more clearly symbolized the confusions of the age than what took place in Cirencester's market square in January 1400. At least one of the men who led the Ricardian earls to their execution, ten years earlier, had been a leading contributor to the fulfilment of Anne of Bohemia's wish for Cirencester to pray for the boy-king, his ancestors and his wife. It became evident that Richard II and his ancestors needed praying for. Most of the men of 1400,

6 'Copied exactly from the original' by Rudder, *History of the Town of Cirencester*, 292.

7 The national vernacular movement is discussed in Rollison, *A Commonwealth of the People*, Ch. 3, esp. 3.9.

including Cosyn, were enthusiastic in the cause of the king who deposed and would soon kill the old king. Thirty years later a new generation of burghers, in completing the work of the founders (Poynter, Cosyn, *et al.*), lost no opportunity 'of declaring where the loyalties of the founders lay'. They were, or became again, 'Yorkists'. As Rowland Hill observed many times during his incumbency at Cirencester (1962–78), 'at the apex of each window on both sides of the (Trinity) chapel is found the Yorkist badge of the falcon and fetterlock'.[8] Insurance, perhaps; Richard's deposition, being the second of a member of his family in less than a century, established a pattern. One deposition might be forgotten, in time, when the stories died down. Two made it a story less easily forgotten. If the last king had fallen, so could this one. The next generation of donors would keep alive the town's connections, direct and indirect, with the house of York, which began to adopt the populism previously associated with Henry of Lancaster in the second quarter of the fifteenth century, when the Trinity Chapel was built.

The deposition of tyrants was no mere theory in early fifteenth-century England. But in considering the mental worlds of that generation of the commonalty, it is necessary to know that the manifold divisions and struggles in late fourteenth- and fifteenth-century England were only *subsequently* subsumed into a contest between the royal houses of York and Lancaster. In 1382 the founders of the Trinity Chapel (and what it represented) were 'Yorkists' before the fact. The men responsible, ten years later, for refinancing the Mary chantry were merely monarchists.[9] They knew as well as anyone that kings could be overthrown. They were probably aware that in the past conflict between church and king had been brutal: the very widespread cult of St Thomas kept this memory alive. What lay behind the impassive monuments and memorials was a form of popular monarchism that was becoming unique to England. At Cirencester it was tempered by the knowledge that when the chips were down kings of England had always been willing to sell them out to their ambitious, wealthy lord. They preferred distant kings to local lords, but neither could be trusted to put the community interest before their own.

The second contradiction concerns religious authority and raises major issues in religious history. The Henrician Reformation and the massive

[8] Hill, *Cirencester Parish Church*, 15.

[9] It was reported to the Chantry commissioners in 1547 that 'Oure Lady chantrie' was 'founded by one Willm Orcheband and other who gave the land'; this seems to point to the 1392 group, in which 'William Archebald' is the first-named: Sir John Maclean, 'Chantry Certificates, Gloucestershire', *Trans BGAS* 8 (1883–4), 285; Fuller, 'Register of the Chapel', wrote that when the lady chapel was founded, in the thirteenth century, 'it was not a private family chantry… The chaplain [was] appointed by all the parishioners of Cirencester to celebrate the Divine Service daily in honour of Our Lord Jesus Christ and the most blessed Virgin Mary on behalf of the whole parish.' Special mention was made at that time, however, to one 'Richard Erkenbald', undoubtedly the ancestor of William, and probably the town's proctor at the time of the original foundation.

changes it set in train, the victory of protestantism, cast a deep shadow over the faith of the generations from c.1380 to c.1550. It is difficult to write about the religious lives of fifteenth-century English people without assuming what came next. This is unfortunate. As long ago as 1969, R.B. Manning's study of the Sussex archives led him to propose a 'three reformations' theory. The first, 'official' or Henrician reformation broke with Rome and erected royal supremacy in the English church for purely political reasons. The second, 'theological' reformation began under Henry VIII but really took off in the reign of Edward VI and continued into the middle of the seventeenth century. The third or 'popular' reformation, Manning argued, was when large numbers of people began assuming a protestant, as opposed to a merely anti-papal attitude.[10] A quarter of a century later Cambridge Regius Professor Patrick Collinson wrote that 'believers in a late reformation appear to be winning the argument'. Manning's three-stage model of what happened *after* Henry VIII's interventions closely fits the Cirencester case, as later chapters will show. This chapter focuses attention on an earlier, equally passionate and sustained religious movement that preceded and deeply affected what came next.

In a series of influential articles and books, Christopher Haigh and Eamon Duffy challenged the original protestant view that Reformation was necessary because the church was corrupt and irrelevant.[11] In this view it had to be torn down and replaced with something better. Another great Catholic historian, John Bossy, earlier put forward a moving account of a late medieval Catholicism with communal vision and relevance to the everyday lives of ordinary people.[12] Bossy, Haigh and Duffy, in different ways, describe a religion that was far from corrupt and distant from the needs of the people in their communities. If the accounts of these revisionists are right, it might be supposed that the 'Protestant Reformation' was what Thomas More, its earliest and most savage critic, said it was at the time: the work of a few disgruntled demagogues whose heretical opinions happened to fall in with the hubris of Henry VIII. The new view is that Protestantism was so unpopular it had to be imposed. My contention is that *both* these readings are correct. Communities pined for the old religion for at least a generation. In parish churches all over England the quality of religion declined. Revival began – in protestant forms – in the 1570s and 1580s. This is exactly what happened at Cirencester.

10 R.B. Manning, *Religion and Society in Elizabethan Sussex: A Study of the Enforcement of the Religious Settlement, 1558–1603* (Leicester 1969), xiv.

11 Christopher Haigh, *The English Reformation Revised*, ed. Haigh (Cambridge 1987); Haigh, *English Reformations: Religion, Politics, and Society under the Tudors* (Oxford 1993); Eamon Duffy, *The Stripping of the Altars* (Yale 1992); Duffy, *The Voices of Morebath: Reformation and Rebellion in an English Village* (New Haven and London 2001); Duffy, 'Religious Belief', in Rosemary Horrox and W. Mark Ormrod (eds), *A Social History of England* (Cambridge 2006).

12 John Bossy, *Christianity in the West 1400–1700* (Oxford 1985).

Do these revisions of English reformation historiography disprove the twin protestant myths: the medieval church was (1) corrupt, and (2) unpopular? The case of Cirencester suggests that both accounts, contradictory though they may seem, are true. The *institutional* church attacked by William Langland and others in the late fourteenth century, and by William Tyndale and his evangelical colleagues in the 1520s and 1530s, *was* corrupt. Now 'corruption' always implies something, some ideal or practice, in relation to which it is corrupt. 'The church', as represented at Cirencester by a wealthy, powerful and politically connected abbey, embodied contradictions that were too stark to be unnoticed. From the generation of William Langland and the anchorite Julian of Norwich (c.1350–1420) on, preachers represented Jesus the poor man, the carpenter who spent his life in companionship with common people, and who gave his life to redeem *all* people, as Julian emphatically put it.[13] Neither Jesus nor his disciples had 'estate', in the sense of institutionalized wealth and power. This simple image implied that Jesus had more in common with the artisans of Cirencester than the canons of St Mary's Abbey. This was the Jesus common people worshipped. The abbey's obsession with secular estate was corrupt in relation to the demonstrable vigour and vitality of the communally financed, managed and built religion that came, in the fifteenth century, to be centred on the parish church of St John the Baptist. Judged by the theological standards of vernacular reformers, from Langland and Julian to Tyndale, and the many different initiatives of the parochial elites of towns like Cirencester, the late medieval church was corrupt in its *estate*. Its religious authority was undermined by its practice of secular estate. As Eamon Duffy shows in his moving account of the Devon village of Morebath, local history is an excellent way to understand *popular* religion, remembering that in this context, 'popular' means 'of the people' rather than of great mitred lords like the abbot of Cirencester, cardinals, and counsellors to kings and popes.

Just as, in retrospect, we know the Reformation is coming, we know St Mary's Abbey is going to be dissolved. We have seen that the commonalty of Cirencester had been more or less continuously at odds with the abbey since its foundation. The last chapter showed that the instant it seemed possible to wrench trade and government out of the hands of the abbot, in January 1400, the commonalty acted and followed up its actions by withdrawing its labour and services. When the abbey began to reassert its dominion a few years later, the townspeople rose up and violently assaulted the abbey, *en masse*. In this light it may seem perverse to suggest that the commonalty did not wish to abolish or 'dissolve' the abbey, yet it is probably the truth. They wanted it to behave like a religious institution, not like a bullying, voracious lord. The hope that it could still, one day, become this, is evident

13 Andy Wood, *The 1549 Rebellions and the Making of Early Modern England* (Cambridge 2007), 181–2, notes the connection between the *universal* nature of the manumission of Calvary to the language of popular rebellion from the early fourteenth century until, most famously, Norfolk in 1549.

in Nicholas Poynter's desire to be buried in the then still physically dominant abbey church, and John Cosyn's generous bequest of 60s. 'to the abbot and convent of Cirencester'. The most auspicious item in Cosyn's will, however, would turn out to be his bequest of 40s. 'for the construction of a belfry of [Cirencester parish church]'.[14]

The founding of Trinity chantry marks the beginning of a movement in which, over several generations, the commonalty of Cirencester created one of the great English parish churches. The shell of the religious culture that, from 1382 to c.1530, inspired the building of the great tower and nave of the parish church of St John the Baptist, has survived, although its substance has long disappeared. John Cosyn's belfry would cost much more than his 40s. to build, and would not be completed until twelve years after his death. It would be another century before the parishioners added the magnificent nave. For over a century the sustained purpose of the townspeople was to make the building live up to, and be capable of accommodating, the busy and beautiful, communal religious culture that came out of the changes of 1382–1415. The best evidence of the movement, we shall now see, concerns what went on, continuously, inside the church. When John Beecham painted his celebrated scenes from the history of Cirencester in the mid-nineteenth century (see cover) the founders' 'belfry' had dominated the townscape for four centuries, and still does today. It is impossible to know if John Cosyn and his fellow-founders planned all of what came next, but it is certain that for the next century their legacy, the Trinity chantry, the tower and the Trinity Chapel (built by c.1430), would be the key institutions in the revival of a people's church.

The tower, built c.1402–15, is the still-living symbol of a great wave of vernacular confidence and pride, the beginnings of which preceded by a couple of decades the years of Henry IV's friendship and the abbey's (temporary) eclipse. By surviving the reversal of fortune and the restoration of the abbey's liberties that came with the new king, the tower, situated right next to the abbey church, yet standing between it and the other major place of communal association, the market-place, was the ultimate expression of now immemorial struggle with an overweening 'religious' lord. The structures of conflict had not yet changed, but one side, the commonalty, was getting stronger.

Yet 'revival' is a misleading term for the vernacular movement that produced the great 'wool' churches, not only at Cirencester and in the Cotswolds, but in many other parts of England (e.g. Norfolk) in the fifteenth century. Where the wool trade was concerned, the founders' wealth probably did come from the sheep's back (Cosyn owned property at Southampton, an important wool port). One sign of economic change is that clothworkers are prominent in the records of resistance to the abbey's fightback. They would be prominent in

14 In his will the previous year, another of the founders of 1392, Thomas Dyer, had left 20s. for the same purpose: Hockaday 155: PCC Marche 2, 30 May 1402 Thomas Dyare.

everything that went on at Cirencester for another two and a half centuries, until, after c.1650, the connection with England's first national industry ebbed away and was taken up, locally, by Stroud. The earliest copies of two Weavers' Guild charters, one for masters, the other for journeymen, date to the reign of Queen Elizabeth and only refer back to an earlier charter of Queen Mary. Yet the Weavers' Guilds almost certainly originated, formally or informally, in the generation of 1400, associated with the establishment of the Guild Merchant. Thirty years later the Weavers' Guild actively supported two local 'merchant-knights' in the employ of Richard, duke of York, Richard Dixton and William Prelatte. It is likely that when the Guild Merchant was declared illegal by Henry V, the Weavers' Guild took on some of its functions as the organizing hub of the commonalty in its resistance to manorial hegemony.

Not all 'weavers' were poor. Those who served as Masters of the Guild in the sixteenth century more closely resembled 'clothmen' and 'clothiers' like William Nottingham: they were weavers by trade, cloth traders by acquired vocation. In every generation, one or two 'poor' weavers eventually became rich by this route. Weavers, other clothworkers and many others probably donated smaller sums to the foundation and maintainance of the Trinity Chapel: not enough to be mentioned by name every time the mass priests sang the names of the more illustrious donors, but probably guaranteeing them honourable consideration among 'all Christian souls', at least for a time. When, following the struggles of the 'fellowship' in the early thirteenth century, the Mary Chapel was first founded, its chaplain had been explicitly 'appointed *by all the parishioners*' for masses to be said daily '*on behalf of the whole parish*', even though a local freeman, Richard Erkenbald, received 'special mention'. In subsequent generations, clothiers – men and (occasionally) women who engrossed, finished and traded in woollen cloth made in the town and neighbouring districts, not wool merchants – added many new chantries and offices and finally capped the movement by building Cirencester's magnificent nave a century later. The 'vernacular revival' at Cirencester may have been begun by wool merchants; as we shall see, it was completed by the capitalist clothiers who dominate the testamentary record in the second half of the fifteenth century. The wealthier inhabitants, whatever the sources of their capital, were expected to act for the whole community.

The will of John Cosyn was the first in a series of four or five generations of parish church-centred burgher wills. The series points to a sustained effort to make the parish church the unchallenged religious heart of a community: an example of what piety ought to be, not an imitation or creature of the abbey next door. The donations were small, but Cosyn's generation set an example that would be followed. Remember also that Cosyn had almost certainly made regular donations throughout the 1390s, and played a central role in preparing the way for what was left of the earls' treasure to be donated to the building of the tower. In his will he left 20s. each to 'Sir John Yonge, chaplain' and 'Walter Kyrkeby, my chaplain', and 20d. 'to every parish chaplain'. These may have been the earliest (part-time) incumbents specified by the deeds of the

Trinity and Mary chantries. 'Everyone celebrating continuously' at the parish church was left a shilling. Finally, almost as an afterthought, he left 20s. to 'the poor men and women of St John the Baptist': the poor of the parish.[15] They are small signs, significant only in that they seem to establish a pattern that is very familiar to historians of sixteenth-, seventeenth- and eighteenth-century English society. Except for the chaotic 1550s and 1560s, they were sustained.

Nicholas Poynter's was the last abbey-centred will. Where Cosyn confidently expected to be buried in front of the 'altar of St Thomas', in what would become Trinity Chapel, Poynter respectfully requested the abbot's permission to be buried in the still physically dominant abbey church. If not, his executors should fall back on the churchyard of St John. This does not speak for his reputation with the community. He left a mere 2s. to the parish church, but 40s. 'for tithes omitted' (i.e. not paid to the abbey, which owned the Rectory), 20s. to the abbot, 3s. 4d. to 'each canon not yet consecrated priest' and 'a large silver cup to the refectory office of the abbey'. A much larger sum (21 marks) was to be paid to 'a chaplain to celebrate for [his] soul for three years', presumably in the abbey church where his body, he hoped, would be buried. Poynter did not share Cosyn's explicitly parish church-centred world view. The rest of the series of fifteenth- and sixteenth-century will and chantry evidence, not unexpectedly in view of the church we see today, shows that the burghers' and craftworkers' largesse to the parish church lasted for another 150 years.[16]

From now on, church monuments testify to a secular boom, grounded in commerce and manufacturing, that was not dependent upon support from church or king. The brass of Reginald Spycer 'merchant of the town' (d.1442), a participant in the apprehension and execution of the rebels, and his four wives, is only one of many memorials to wealthy fifteenth-century wool and cloth merchants: Sir William Nottingham (d.1470) and his father, a clothier (d.1427); Robert Page (d.1440); Henry Garstang (d.1464); Chedworths, Avenings and Georges, are others. Robert Page and William Nottingham Snr were among the men pardoned in 1414 for rebellion against the abbey. Nottingham provided a link in the new chantry tradition by founding the Hospital of St Thomas in his will of 1427; his heir, eventually *Sir* William Nottingham, although no longer resident at Cirencester, founded a service in the Trinity Chapel in his will of 1470. Confirming the town's continuing presence in the wool trade, Sir Edmund Tame (d.1500), descendant of William Grevel of Chipping Campden, and John Tame, who moved to Fairford about 1480, continued his business at Cirencester and married a daughter of Sir Edward Grevel.[17]

15 Hockaday 155: PCC Marche 4, 29 Mar. 1403 John Cosyn.

16 Hockaday 155: PCC Marche 6, Nicholas Pointer Thurs. before feast of St Alban 1403.

17 Personal observation; Fallows, *Cirencester Brasses*; cf. J.J. Simpson, 'The Wool Trade

These were – or became – rich men by provincial standards. The men and women memorialized in masses and on brasses, in the Trinity and Mary chapels and by several new foundations of chantries and services, were wealthy businessmen, merchants and manufacturers. To what extent were such men members or leaders of the commonalty? The complex and highly stratified composition of the commonalty will be considered again in the next and later chapters. Structural fissures opened up after the dissolution of the abbey, as we shall also see. The testamentary and chantry evidence suggests that for most of the fifteenth century the elite, comprising rich merchants and the holders of small local manors, took its responsibilities for building, renovating and maintaining the calibre of worship at the parish church very seriously, albeit with the caveat that their names be remembered first. They were assisted from the outset by a craft of men generally less well-off, the Weavers' Guild, also associated with the erection of Trinity Chapel. Absence of evidence of disharmony among the townspeople during this 'epoch of the burghers' suggests that the new leaders mostly lived up to high community expectations. They held the 'fellowship' together.

Townspeople who wanted to satisfy themselves that this was so had only to go along to the parish church, admire (and participate in) the new building work and constant refurbishing, listen to the singing and masses, and check that the lights were all lit. In other words, to check that worship was alive and well. In a town like Cirencester (as elsewhere in England), false moves, perceived corruptions and injustices quickly turned into 'murmuring' that only went away if the fault was rectified. The wardens of the Trinity and Mary chapels seem to have led the way and kept the numerous chantries and services added elsewhere in the church up to the high standard of the founders.

The generation of wealthy burghers who financed its building are memorialized on the walls of the Trinity Chapel. Richard Dixton (d.1438) and William Prelatte (d.1462) are represented in full ceremonial armour, Prelatte with his two wives, Agnes and Joan. They may have made or inherited wealth accumulated in wool trading and clothmaking, but like Sir William Nottingham (d.1470) their status rose as they made their fortunes as receivers-general of the Gloucestershire estates of Richard, duke of York. Dixton, described in his will as 'squyer', ordered that his body be 'buried within the new chapell of the Trinitie at Ciscetre', to which he made several further bequests. He gave 'a cloth of silver and a black cloth of damask

and the Woolmen of Gloucestershire', *Trans BGAS* 53 (1931), 65–97; Sir William Nottingham was appointed chief steward to the bishop of Worcester in 1450 and remained steward to the bishop's Gloucestershire estates until shortly before his death. He was also a royal baron of the exchequer under Edward IV. Nottingham succeeded his fellow-townsman, Thomas Arnold, 'clothman alias woolman', as receiver-general for the bishop of Worcester's extensive regional estates. Arnold was the first layman to be appointed: E.B. Fryde, *Peasants and Landlords in Later Medieval England* (Stroud 1996), 91, 95, 98, 172, 181.

sengill and a gown of goldsmythes werk for to make vestments and a hundred gertiers'; twenty pounds for '3 prestes to synge for me duryng the space of a yere in the said church'; twenty pounds 'for my mynde day'; twenty pounds 'to prestes and clerkes for to do my service and exequies, and for almes for poore men' and another twenty pounds for the further embellishment of 'the new chapel aforesaid'. No less than a hundred pounds cash, gilt cloth and other small valuables went into the glorification of the new chapel. 'The two large flagons used at the communion' recorded by Samuel Rudder in the 1770s were probably gifted by Dixton – another patriarch of Cirencester church.[18]

Other bequests describe the extent of the connections he had brought to the Trinity Chapel and show Dixton to have been a very wealthy man: ten marks to the prioress of Usk (to which he seems to have retired); twenty pounds each to 'the grey freres' and 'the Freres Prechours of Gloucestre ... for three prestes ... to sing for my moder and me'; a gilt cup to the abbot of Tewkesbury 'and the like to the [abbeys] of Siscetre, Evesham, Bradestoke and Malmesburie'; ten marks 'to the abbot of Lanterny and his monkes' and twenty marks 'to the prior of Golcleve [Goldcliff, Monmouth] and his monkes. At a time when the monarchy of Lancastrian heir Henry VI was again becoming a subject of disquiet and murmuring, Dixton's patron was not forgotten. Each of the duke of York's '3 chapeleyns' received 20s.; the 'the yomen [i.e. serving-men] of my lordes chamber' and 'the officers of my lordes hall, pantrie, seler boterie and kechyn', twenty pounds each; 'John of the pantry', six marks; 'my lordes servants of his stable' received ten marks, and 'Richard of the wardrobe' got forty shillings and 'the fourth best hors that I have'. 'My Lorde of Yorke' was left '3 of my best hors, to be chosen either at Usk or at Wotton, and all my armour', and 'Edmond of Cornewayle' was left a small but expensive memorial in the form of 'an ersgendyll of silver'.[19]

Also remembered in brasses on the wall of the Trinity Chapel are the merchants Robert Page (d.1440), Reginald Spicer (d.1442), and their wives (Spicer had four). Although not as wealthy or high in status as Dixton or Prelatte, Page had prestigious connections: one of his executors was Sir Maurice Berkeley of Beverstone. He too was 'buried in the new chapel'. Page left a shilling to maintain 'each light in the parish church' and eight pence 'to every priest at my exequies'. Small bequests and donations like these would be the lifeblood of the parish church for the next hundred years. Page also made a bequest of forty shillings 'to maintenance and repair of the road at Eton near Cricklade about the bridge there'. After his pardon for resisting the abbey in 1414, Page had almost certainly passed on his cloth-trading interests to his sons, William and John, before he died. Family came first, of course. William and John received an additional fifty pounds each. The only bequest remotely

[18] Samuel Rudder, *A New History of Gloucestershire* (Cirencester 1779), 366, says 'given by Edward Dixon, esq.; in the year 1434'. See will of Richard Dixton.
[19] Hockaday 155: PCC Luffenham, 8 Aug. 1438 Will of Richard Dixton squyer.

connected to the abbey was twenty shillings 'to the high altar [of Cirencester parish church] for tithes forgetten'.[20]

If the successive founders of the Trinity chantry and chapel lit the flame and kept it burning in the first half of the fifteenth century, in the third quarter attention began to shift to the whole church, and, in the final quarter of the century, to the foundation of even more new services and chantries. Merchant Henry Garstang came to Cirencester from Lancashire, probably around 1420, and made a fortune. In his will of 1464 he asked to be buried 'in the wall next to the altar of St Edmund the Confessor' and ordered '1000 masses shall be said forthwith for my soul' in the parish church. Every light in the church received 20d. and every priest present at his funeral was given the same amount. Every parish priest received 2s. and the Chapel of St Edward the Confessor was given 'one primer to be chained in the said church'. Two chaplains, William Hampton and John Pratte, were left 'a gown of scarlet' and 'a gown of sanguine engreyned' respectively. Garstang left 'a pall of red cloth' to hang over the main altar of the parish church, and 'all the timber in the meadow next to the Fosse (Way)' was granted for repairing the parish church.[21]

These men now represented a movement affecting the whole region. The nave of Northleach parish church was rebuilt at this time. A great 'woolman' of that town, John Fortey, left 6s. 8d. 'apeece' for refurbishing the 'fabric of the naves of 120 churches round about Northleach …, that the parishiones of the said parishes may have me commended in their prayers'. Fortey was particularly generous to the poor, leaving £200 to buy and make linen and woollen clothes to be distributed to the neediest poor and 20s. each to '80 poor maidens towards their marriages.' A bequest of dowries for 'poor maidens' also features in the near contemporary will of John Tame of Fairford.[22] Fortey left 20s. each 'to the 4 orders of Friars at Gloucester' and 4d. 'to every prisoner at Gloucester Castle' but a resounding nothing to any abbeys and monasteries.[23] Fortey also left a small bequest to his relative John Fortey 'of Surcester, dyer'. The latter was not a member of the Trinity Guild, but nevertheless wealthy and generous enough to be 'buried before the High Cross'. There are signs at this time that the church itself was absorbing the social and religious prestige of all its individual chantries and services. Like Page before and most of those who followed, he made sure the building was maintained and the lights were

20 Hockaday 155: PCC Luffenham 27, 30 Mar. 1440 Robert Pagge; PCC Luffenham 30, Joan Spycer 6 Jan. 1445.

21 Hockaday 155: PCC Godyn 6, Henry Garstang 7 Sep. 1464; PCC Godyn 27, Robert Kyttes 20 Apr. 1469 is 90 percent religious bequests to the parish church.

22 Hockaday 155: PCC Moore 3, John Tame of Fairford 28 Jan. 1496, left £40 'to the marriage of 30 poor maidens within 4 miles of Fairford or else in the town of Cicetter'.

23 Hockaday 155: PCC Stokton 25 (Latin), 24 June 1458 John Fortey of Northleach Woolman.

kept burning, leaving a shilling for 'every light' and £6 13s. 4d. to 'the fabric of Cirencester parish church'.[24]

'Nottingham's service', established in the will of Sir William Nottingham (d.1470) left land and houses 'to maintain a priest to celebrate at the altar of St Michael in the parish church … to pray for his soul and all Christian souls, and also to relieve always four poor men weekly with 8d each …, and they from time to time to dwell in a house situate in Battlestreet …'[25] No vestry records survive to indicate who was responsible for looking after and administering the funds, and how the processes took place. Were they already institutionalized in practice but not codified? The exact foundations of a 'brotherhood of Jesus' with its own chapel are obscure, but Eamon Duffy writes that

> from the 1470s onwards, Jesus brotherhoods proliferated throughout England, dedicated to the maintenance of a regular celebration of the Mass of the Holy Name, often on a Friday, at an altar over which there might be its own Jesus image … Wherever it occurs, the Jesus Mass has all the hallmarks of a genuinely popular devotion. Yet the Mass of Jesus was also emphatically an observance seized on by elites in every community as a convenient expression, and perhaps an instrument, of their social dominance.[26]

This is an enduring theme: popular devotion is linked to social domination, implying that popular culture was reflexively deferent to established authority. Much depended on which Jesus – the carpenter or the emperor – was foremost in the minds of those who observed the images.

In his 1494 will Thomas Nele asked to be 'buried in the chapel of the brotherhood of Jesus in the parish church'. Nele was forgotten by 1547 when commissioners of the king conducted a survey of all English chantries. They were informed the founders of the brotherhood were 'not knowen'. What was known was that it was still supported by 'land put in feoffment' to 'keep and maintain singing at the altar of Jesu', and 'praying for the founders' souls and all Christian souls': founders forgotten, services continued. Not, in fact: the services had been converted 'about 6 or 7 years last past, since when the rent whereof has been employed upon the repair of the parish church'.[27] It is appropriate that the brief brotherhood of Jesus had become absorbed in the greater priority: the nave. Nele had connections with the abbey. It is not clear

24 Hockaday 155: PCC Wattys 22, John Forthey 16 Mar. 1475; PCC Godyn 27, Robert Kyttes 20 Apr. 1469 is 90 percent religious bequests to the parish church; PCC Logge 23, John Keke 27 Feb. 1485–6 was likewise buried before the high altar and left 4d. 'to each altar there'; PCC Logge 26, Richard Compton 30 July 1486, the will of a man who owned two small houses at Cirencester, left '20s. to repair parish church'.

25 Maclean, 'Chantry Certificates', 285.

26 Duffy, *Stripping of the Altars*, 115.

27 Maclean, 'Chantry Certificates', 286–7.

why he wished his body to be carried 'into their monastery of St Mary', but he left 6s. 8d. 'to four canons' to do the job, whereas 'every bearer of my body on the day of my burial' received slightly less, 12d. each. The high altar of the parish church (the abbot's domain) was left 3s. 4d., the other altars nothing. Finally, '13 poor folks shall be portioned out of my goods at the discretion of Joan my relict and W(illia)m my son my exec(utor)s'.[28]

These men were the leading employers of artisans and labourers. The amounts left to public and charitable works are consistent yet consistently small, relative to the total estates of the testators. It was important that they were consistent – every testator included them. Rich men were expected to be committed to the good of the community, centred on its religious life, which, in turn, was centred on the tower, nave and chapels of the church. Yet it is impossible not to notice how self- and kin-centred all the wills are. This, too, was expected. What assured the continuing prestige of the church and its administrators, the churchwardens, was that each generation of the wealthier sort, in their lives and in their wills, set aside just enough energy and finance to ensure that the common fund was always well-stocked. The degree of devotion to the common good probably varied from generation to generation. What made this a communal, trans-generational movement was that the effect (and affect) of the bequests was cumulative. The defining feature of the long fifteenth century at Cirencester was how long the impetus was maintained.

Adam Baker (d.1488), possibly a grandson of founder John Baker, almost made it into the chapel of the founders, requesting 'to be buried in the entrance near the door of the chapel of St Mary'. He shared the founders' ideal of a church in which singing and praying filled its space every day, perhaps even twenty-four hours a day. Baker left a shilling 'to the high altar' and five shillings 'for tithes forgot'. The altars of St Thomas (in front of which was Cosyn's tomb), St John and St Mary received 8d. each, those of St Laud, St Lawrence and St James and St Katherine 6d., 5d. for the 'High Rood' and 4d. to St Christopher.[29] His contemporary Robert Stone expected to be buried in the chapel of Holy Trinity. Like all benefactors, family came first. Stone left 'all my lands and tenements except one cottage in Hayworth, two oxen and my best gown' to his son John Stone. To his illegitimate son, John Stone tanner, he left a cottage in Hayworth, some lead, and forgave him '33s. 4d. he owes me'. Three priests, probably the incumbents associated with the Trinity and Mary chantries, received 20d. The high altar and Holy Trinity altar received 8d. each, the light of St Clement 20d. and 'every other light in the church, 2d'. It took a constant stream of such donations to keep the lights lit and constant music, singing and praying in every corner of the church. The priests, organ players, choirmasters and singers employed by a growing

28 Hockaday 155: PCC Vox 29, Thomas Nele 13 Dec. 1494.
29 Hockaday 155: PCC Milles 22, Adam Baker 1488.

list of chantries and offices all lived in the town, not the abbey. By 1500 the commonalty controlled everything except the high altar, now only one of many. Bequests to the poor, and to the maintenance of the roads leading to the town, were routine and, by now, often in money. Robert Stone's bequest was in kind: '16 pecks of corn to be distributed to the poor'.[30]

Many testators had favourite lights. Joan H[a]lle (who anticipated being buried somewhere 'in the parish church'), left 4d. to the 'lights of Holy Trinity John the Baptist and St Thomas the martyr', only 2d. each to 'every other light in the church'.[31] Thomas a Becket was a recurring favourite.[32] Some lights were probably kept alight twenty-four hours a day. Testatory and chantry records indicate that singing and masses were meant to be continuous. Patrick Collinson's notion that 'in Catholic ritual, eyes were exercised rather than ears' is probably wrong as a generalization and certainly wrong in the case of 'catholic' Cirencester. With two or even three chaplains to work shifts, successive patrons and governors of Trinity Chapel had no excuse ever to let the scented torches and candles burn out, or the audible singing to cease. In 1499 Richard Nelle, not high enough in wealth, status and reputation to be worthy of burial inside the church, contented himself with burial in the churchyard. Like all the testators we have considered, Nelle remained fixed on what went on inside. He left 6d. each towards keeping alight and replacing twelve lights, each with its own name: 'St John, Jesus, St Thomas, St Eligius, St James, St Christopher, St Clement, St Cuthbert, St George, St Mary, St Catherine, and Holy Cross'.[33] We may not agree with, or even fully understand its theories and practices, but it is evident that 'the old religion' was thriving at Cirencester – except that it was not that old. The lights of the founders, the generation of 1400, still burned in 1500, alongside the ten companions added by the generations that came after. Doubtless the eyes of many parishioners were drawn through the gloom, 'beyond the "rood" to the (high) altar', as Professor Collinson puts it; many were drawn to the church by the singing and music. The experience was multi-sensual, eyes were only part of it.[34] And it was not focused on the high altar, the province of the abbot. It was focused on the shrine of St Thomas in the Trinity Chapel.

The will of John Bennet, clothman, offers insight into the economic geography of Trinity Chapel, where, in 1490, he ordered his body to be buried. Until his death he and his wife lived at 'a messuage called Rodborough, with the watermill'. A mill in the chapelry of Rodborough, parish of Minchinhampton, hundred of Longtree, division of the Seven Hundreds of Cirencester, was the centre of his enterprise. It owed its growing importance as a centre of cloth production to its streams and its location 'on important local

30 Hockaday 155: PCC Dogett 15, Robert Stone 10 Oct. 1492.
31 Hockaday 155: PCC Horne 17, Joane Holle 15 June 1497.
32 Hockaday 155: PCC Horne 19, Walter Tylle 30 Apr. 1498.
33 Hockaday 155: PCC Horne 34, Richard Nelle 4 Apr. 1499 (24 June 1499).
34 Collinson, 'The Elizabethan Church and the New Religion', 171.

routes of communication'.[35] Weavers from neighbouring villages, hamlets and cottages on the extensive 'wastes' of the Stroudwater Valleys brought cloth to the watermill to be fulled and prepared for dyeing by the men who used 'all the shears called "sherman shiris" and "las handells"'. He leased the mill 'for a term of years with remainder to (my) kinsman Robert Davys'. His son John lived in a house Bennet owned in the weaving township of Kings Stanley, a few miles west. John Jnr also inherited 'a messuage in Ebbeley, and another in Strode in the parish of Bisley'. Bennet had connections throughout the Stroudwater Valleys, where most of the wool was spun and the cloth woven in hundreds of households – many of them 'squatters' on ill-managed 'waste' surrounding the old market town of Bisley – scattered through the valleys.

The 'limitation of Strode' (as one will put it) was a new town, a cluster of hamlets comprising mainly clothworking households grown up on the 'waste' of Bisley parish and concentrated on 'La Strode', the originally marshy confluence of the Slad Brook and the River Frome.[36] In centuries to come, Stroud would eclipse Cirencester as the central place of regional clothmaking, but not emphatically until after the civil wars. In Bennet's time, Cirencester, more specifically the Trinity Chapel of the parish church of St John the Baptist, was the most prestigious place of the territory of the clothiers and weavers living in the archipelagos of clothworking parishes of north Wiltshire and central Gloucestershire. John Blake, the last abbot, would soon make a belated effort to cash in on the now dominant economic activity of the region by building two fulling mills at Cirencester, still the logical place from which to transport finished cloth to London, and, therefore, a good place to dye and finish the cloth manufactured in the dispersed households of Cirencester's hinterlands. The town was already inhabited by dyers by, at the latest, the early fourteenth century, and it is likely that it remained a dyeing centre in the late fifteenth century. Bennet's will scanned the district. He left 6s. 8d. to 'Strode' chapelry, the same amount to 'the churches of Nunshampton (Minchinhampton) and Wodechester and the chapel … of Rodborough', lived at the mill in the valleys, but wanted his body buried in the Trinity Chapel at Cirencester. Bennet's will contains many fascinating details, but what is arresting is the strategic view of landscape he had absorbed in forty years a clothworker and clothier in one of many new industrial districts of fifteenth- and sixteenth-century England. His bequests encompassed a working landscape he knew like the back of his hand.[37]

Benet's widow Agnes lived for another seven years in the expectation that her body would eventually rest alongside her husband's in the 'chapel of Holy Trinity'. She seems to have moved into Cirencester when her husband died. At her funeral the lights burned on the high altar, in the chapel, and at the other

35 *VCH Gloucestershire*, Vol. 11, *The Stroud Valleys*, ed. N.M. Herbert, 'Minchinhampton', 184–90.

36 *Ibid*, 99–104.

37 Hockaday 155: PCC Horne, John Benet 15 July 1486.

ten or so altars scattered about the church. Agnes Bennet left five shillings to the high altar, *twenty* shillings to Trinity altar. Every other light received 20d. Her pall was followed by '20 poor men and twenty poor women' clothed in the '48 yards of cloth' she left 'to make them gowns'. 'Twelve torches of fair wax' were to burn through the 'dirige and all masses that shall be done for me as well within the abbey church of our lady of Ciceter as in the said parish church'. 'After my body is buried [the torches] shall be disposed to 12 poor churches round about the town.' Although Agnes made it perfectly clear where her heart lay, she expected the canons to acknowledge her passing too. She left some nice things to a dozen or so of her closest friends: a 'maser harnessed with silver with a print of Jesus in the middle annielled with blue'; a 'dozen of… best silver spoons', suggesting she had many more silver spoons that were not of the best; her 'beades of the best sort', a gown (among several of many colours) 'of violet colour purfilled with shanks', girdles, one 'with a blue cross and white harness' the other 'with a course of damask gold with a buckle and pendant of silver overgilt'; and 'a cup called *done horne* with a foot and a band of silver and gilt'.

After the funeral was over and the bequests were distributed, 'within 6 months after my decease', Agnes Bennet ordered to be purchased 'lands to the yearly value of 20s. or thereabouts …'

> to hold an obit yearly on the day God shall call me out of this world to his mercy, at the said altar, with 8 priests and 3 parish clerks and 2 children singers, having the 5 principal tapers of our lady burning upon mine hearse, paying to every priest 4d and to every clerk 2d and to every child 1d, for my soul and the souls of John Benet and Stephen Hewes; and they shall offer 1d to the priests lands and they shall dispose in alms on the same day to 5 poor men and 5 por women 1d apiece, in the worship of the 5 wounds of our Lord and the 5 joys of his most blessed Mother; and the bell called the Trinity bell and Jesus bell shall be at sundry times rung at the time of the said obit.

The memorial was to be conducted yearly, forever. To whom or what could such a task be entrusted? Who administered the Trinity Chapel with all its added functions and services? Agnes 'enfeoffed' two 'procurators of the altar of St Thomas the Martyr, and the wardens of the craft of weavers in the same town'. Any money left over was to be put 'toward the exhibition of a priest to sing at the said altar for the soules of Sir Willyam Notyngham and others, or toward the exhibition of some other priest singing there, founded on yearly conduct by the said procurators'. Yet Agnes worried that the authority of the Craft of Weavers might be fragile. 'If they fail in this trust,' she ordered, 'they shall forfeit to the churchmen of the said parish church 20s; to be bestowed on the reparation of the church.'[38] Here, the

[38] Hockaday 155: PCC Moore 7, Agnes Benet (late w. of Wm) 16 Jan. 1497–8 (13 Feb. 1500).

'churchmen' constituted an institution, a vestry of churchwardens (it is not clear how they were appointed in this period), that Agnes assumed would definitely continue. She was right. The parish and its vestry would survive the coming storms and emerge stronger than ever.

A year later (1498) another clothier, William Horne, asked for his body to be buried 'next to the altar of St Thomas'. Almost a century earlier, this had been the resting place of John Cosyn. By the late fifteenth century it seems to have been the altar of 'the craft of weavers', otherwise known, perhaps, as Trinity Altar. Because he symbolized resistance to kings, 'Thomas the Martyr', while a permanent popular favourite, was a risqué saint, especially in a chapel with so many ambiguous symbols of the contending dynasties in 'the wars of the roses'. Horne left money to maintain the same lights as his wife, who died before him, and paid for '100 masses [to] be celebrated on one day, or two days at farthest, for my soul and the souls of all my benefactors'.[39] Judging by the amount of money they set aside to pray for their souls, these men had a keen sense of how much they had sinned.

In 1501 clothier John Avening, 'to be buried in the chapel of St Katherine in an arch prepared by me', left 40s. for 'work on the new porch of the church'. Like his, the burgher wills of the next fifteen years continued to guarantee the chapels, chantries, services, altars, lights, masses, singing, bell-ringing and organ-playing.[40] By 1515 it was becoming clear that the old nave, built as it was three centuries earlier, could no longer accommodate what went on within it, or live up to the community's pride. 'Between 1515 and 1530 the nave was demolished and entirely rebuilt in the Late Perpendicular style.' [41] By this time there was enough money in the 'offices of the Trinity, Saint Katherine and Saint John' to give £4 2s. 11d. 'to be yearly bestowed in repairing and maintaining the body of the great church of Cirencester and one chapel called Trinity chapel'. Rowland Osmonde, 'buried between the chapels of the blessed virgin Mary and St Katherine', in 1517, left the hefty sum of £20 'for building of the church'. [42] Good progress was being made on the nave when, a year later, Robert Rycardes, clothman, left £20 towards 'the bilding of the midle ile, with such money as I have paide before hands'. This is a reminder that wills only cover what was given after a person was dead.

[39] Hockaday 155: PCC Horne 25, William Horne 17 July 1498 (18 Oct. 1498).

[40] Hockaday 155: PCC Moore 15, John Avenyng 4 Apr 1501, 24 Apr.; PCC Blamye 15, Richard Taunton of C Mercer 15 June 1502; PCC Holgrave 39, Latin Wm Bodynton 17 Apr. 1504; PCC Holgrave 24, 1505 Thos Wyneyard 11 Oct. 1504; PCC Holder 4, 31 May 1513 Sir Robert Morton knt 31 May 1513; the St Christopher service consisted of land enfeoffed by founders unknown to fund 'an organ player' whose job was also to 'maintain singing and playing in the... parish church': Maclean, 'Chantry Certificates', 286.

[41] Hill, *Cirencester Parish Church*, 22.

[42] Hockaday 155: PCC Holder 34, Rowland Osmonde 29 June 1517 Latin.

Where John Bennet had been connected to the Stroudwater Valleys, Rycardes had connections in the clothmaking districts of the Vale of Berkeley. He left £10 'to the church of Dursley' and a further £13 6s. 8d. for a 'priest-deacon' to make 'a suete of vestments and… releyve and helpe towardes his occupacion'. This may have been where Rycardes started as a 'clothman', but the unquestioned heart of his territory was Cirencester parish church. Beyond the generous donation towards work on the new nave, Rycardes left 'landes in the hundred of Berkeley… to find a priest perpetually at the awlter of St Anthony in Cirencester', chosen by his wife 'during her life'.

Rycardes wrote the will himself. He was 'sore seke at the makyng of this testament, and also lakked councell to make parfite the same'. Others knew his mind and he asked them to make sure that 'anything omitted that the preest ought to do shall be reformed and… put in a tabell or boke in the churche for perpetually remembraunce'.' By 'reformed', Rycardes meant 'formed into written words'. The 'tabell or boke' (which has not survived) was the first of many in which the accumulative constitutions of the parish would be committed to writing and carefully preserved.[43] Rycardes had clearly discussed this 'reform' with others. The priest was to be paid a further £8 'out of the profittes of my landes which I holde for terme of yeres in Frampton upon Severn, Hunlacy, and Northcote in (Glos), the yerely overplus beinge employed in the purchas of landes etc for the sure and continyall exhibition of the said preeste'. Most interestingly, he specified that the priest

> shall be a good singing man and have experince in synginge of playn songe and prikked songe and descant, and be bound to kepe the quere there daily the tyme of divine service as chauntry preestes within the same church be bound to doo. And he shall instruct from tyme to tyme 4 children in synging of playn and prikked songe for the mayntaynane of divine service there freely; the said children to be chosen by the churchwardens, with the advice of John, now Abbot of Cisseter, and his successors.

Here is the first written record of the church choir, whose boys must also have been expected to sing descants. Here too, perhaps, was a sign of a new kind of abbot, John Blake (elected 1522), whose authority was no longer the oppressive force it had been in earlier times. Throughout the fifteenth century tenants of the manor had been released from, or escaped, the immemorial boon-works: by 1540 all signs of the old system of bonded labour

[43] Hockaday 155: PCC Ayloffe 8, Robert Rycardes Clothman, 25 June 1518. Andy Wood notes the implication that at their inception the parish records were in English (personal communication). Rollison, A *Commonwealth of the People*, Ch. 3, evidences the argument that the shift in the language of government (from Latin to English) embodied a long 'revolution of commonalty'. Vernacular writing was an instrument of secular elites and, at the same time, a way in which local elites identified themselves with their communities as against the Latinate church.

had disappeared.[44] Little conflicts still arose, as when Blake built two fulling mills at Cirencester and leased them to men like Rycardes. The abbots were never able to dominate clothmaking in the way they had the wool trade. The clothmaking dispersed throughout Cirencester's hinterlands grew up on the margins of, or completely beyond their jurisdictions. Bisley, for example, was a crown manor, its administration neglected throughout the second half of the fifteenth century. By the time Blake succeeded to the mitre bestowed early in the century by Henry V, the 'clothmen' and 'clothiers' were indispensable in ways the middling cloth merchants had never been. Robert Rycardes thought John Blake was a good man to go to for advice. It's almost as if the commonalty and the burghers had finally created an abbey they could live with. If so, it was too late.

Four years after the first copies of William Tyndale's *New Testament* in English went on sale in London, and Sir Thomas More launched his long diatribe against the Lutherans, Henry Tapper, 'grocer' of Cirencester, left £10 in his will of February 1530, for 'building of the rood loft'. Tyndale favoured a tearing-down of the Church of Rome, bishops, monasteries and abbeys; he would not have encouraged the destruction of the great repositories of vernacular art he knew as a boy and young man. As he well knew, English vernacular piety took many forms. His caveat was that singing and services be in English. Robert Rycardes may well have met Tyndale and known his family, who lived near Dursley. Once the nave was complete, almost certainly by 1530, the rood loft was placed 'high up in the chancel arch' and on it was mounted a great wooden carving of 'the figure of Christ on the Cross with St John and the Virgin Mary on either side'. Tapper also left his daughter Alice £100 'to her mariage', but 'if she dies', as he assumed she might, the 'said £100 [was] to remain in the keeping of the treasurer of the parish church … he receiving for his labour from year to year 12d'. Family came first, the parish church second. This is the earliest mention of which I am aware of 'the treasurer of the parish church', an institution that would become central to the government of Cirencester, under a new religious dispensation, in the late sixteenth and early seventeenth centuries. Henry Tapper instructed him to spend £20 immediately on 'the highway at the Townes end at Ciceter from the sign of the lion unto the works of Master (Reginald) Spicer.' The founders were still remembered. For 'a solemn obit and anniversary for my soul *for ever more without end*', Tapper left the 'churchmen … yearly 10s 8d of the rent of a house in Chepin Strete' so that his 'anniversary shall be kept in the main body of the church with 12 priests there having for their attendance 4s'.[45] The motive was selfish but everyone could enjoy the singing.

44 Fuller, 'Guild Merchant', 318–19.

45 Hockaday 155: PCC Thower 2, Henry Tapper of C Grocer 25 Feb. 1530.

Robert Rycardes' wife remarried and was widowed again before she died in 1534. Her executor was 'cousin' Robert Strange, clothier. Strange dominated the town for thirty years after the abbey was dissolved, under a succession of absentee lords. Her bequest to William Purton of 'two looms now in his keeping' suggests that like many widows of clothiers and other businessmen, Mistress Rycardes continued to administer the business after her husband died. The bequest is also a sign that the leading clothiers in this part of England always tried to engross means of production, including many of the cottages in which the spinners and weavers worked and the tools they used. Continuing the now long-entrenched tradition of burgher pride that her last husband but one had exemplified, Elizabeth Toll (formerly Rycardes) left £10 'toward repairing of the new school house at Cirencester'. To 'the poor people in the almshouses and others dwelling in Ciceter' went 'my whole pile of wood standing between the great gate and the great barn'.[46]

The point, I think, is made. There are no signs, in the first third of the sixteenth century, of any weakening of the burgher-led, parish church-centred movement that took off in the first and second decades of the fifteenth century. Far from it, for there seems to have been a renewed interest, first with the foundations in c.1470 of William Nottingham's service and the brotherhood of Jesus, and again, after the turn of the century, the cloth-financed foundations of the services of Alice Avening, Robert Rycardes, John Jones and other bequests of 'obit rent'. There are no more chantries or services after the dissolution of St Mary's Abbey in December 1539, but the altars seem to have been maintained right up to their closure by Edward VI's chantry commissioners in 1548. Wills remained catholic until John Hooper visited Cirencester as part of his evangelical crack-down on the diocese in 1551–3, whereupon dedications revert to the neutral 'soul to God'.[47] We shall see in the next chapter that the members of the little oligarchy that governed the town for the absentee lords who became lords of the manor after the dissolution and maintained their grip until the 1570s, were what historian John Bossy has called 'survivalist catholic'. By that time, however, any communal solidarity represented by the great parish church was well and truly over – for the time being.

[46] Hockaday 155: PCC Elizabeth Toll Widow 31 July 1534.

[47] Hockaday 155: GPR no. 384, 4 May 1545 Thos Hall: Soul to God and hys blessed mother Mary; GPR 314 1545 John Glover 9 Sep.: Sole to heavenly company; Will of John Patchett 7 Mar. 1542 GPR 217 Vol. 2: Soul to god & to our ladye Saincte Marie; Alys Days widow 18 Dec. 1544 GPR 2 no. 2: Soul to god to the blyssyd Vyrgin Mary; Will John Taylor 16 May 1546 GPR 90 Vol. 4: S to G to his Mother our blessed lady; Will Thos Chaundler 2 June 1646 GPR 202 Vol. 3: Soule to G & hys mother Sanct Mare; GPR 1547 38 Vol. 4 John Hawle 14 May 1547: S to G & blessed Saint Mary; GPR 3 July 1548 John Solas Priest no. 39 Vol. 5: Soul to god nd blessed lady virgin; GPR 146 Will of Water Dygas Wever: Sowl to God; GPR 51 1 Apr. 1551 Jhon Dewce: S to G; GPR 70 John Turner 16 July 1551: S To G.

'Survivalist catholic' though they proved to be, the new 'oligarchs' led the way in unceremoniously tearing down the abbey buildings and carting off the fabric to build their own 'piles' at Chesterton and Baunton on the outskirts of town. They competed with each other to purchase abbey properties, including the 151 houses it had owned in the town. As for the abbey, there were undoubtedly monasteries and convents in England that had lived up to popular expectations from time to time. The abbey of St Mary may even have been one of them during the rule of the last abbot, John Blake (1522–39). Centuries of everyday hard-headed collections of dues, tolls, rents and the exercise of privileges, like the right to mill (and take a tithe of) every grain consumed in the town, never failed to raise hackles and undermine spiritual authority. The problem, always, was lordship, political and economic sovereignty. The contradiction between spiritual and material lordship was always bound to be the ground upon which many popular resistances to local religious magnates coalesced into a single, sustained cause. Like Langland's *Piers Plowman*, popular prejudice believed the church should lead by spiritual example, not rule by greedy accumulation, legalistic sleight of hand, armed thugs and the length of their purse. All the frictions generated by hegemonic corporations were potential occasions for the application of a golden rule: government was legitimate only when rulers and their subalterns put the community, and not their own selfish interests, first. The proverbial form of this communal ethic was attributed to Jesus: at its most pithy (and uncompromising): *love God and thy neighbour*. There were always plenty of people around, including a burgeoning number of preachers, to remind their social betters that this is what religion was supposed to be about.

The health of late medieval Catholicism, by contrast, lay in the fact that it was *popular*, 'of the people'. It might well be asked how 'popular', exactly, were the comparatively wealthy burghers whose ongoing collective legacy we have been considering in this chapter. Their relations with the rank and file of townspeople will be addressed more analytically in chapters dealing with a later period, when sources are more systematic. The short answer may be that Henry VIII's relentless taxation seriously affected the merchants' and manufacturers' capacity and willingness to maintain the role they had now performed for 150 years; his religious reforms (effectively, expropriations) probably sapped collective morale. The dissolution of the common enemy removed the keystone of collective solidarity, at least for a while. Factional beliefs and grievances were, for a time, no longer laid aside for an obvious common cause.

To conclude and sum up this episode: in spite of the restoration of the abbey's powers in 1414, fifteenth-century sources signal the beginning of the long decline in its relative status, ending more with a whimper than a bang in the dissolution of 1539, when the last abbot, John Blake, quietly retired to Fairford with a pension of £200. The seeds were sown in 1392, when a little coalition of merchants, tradesmen and squires transferred property 'to maintain chaplain for celebrating divine service daily in the chapel of St Mary in the parish church of Cirencester for their good estate, for their souls after death and the souls of their benefactors and others'. Over the next century there were many more coalitions, subsidizing building work, constructing new chapels, funding permanently praying and singing priests, paying for their robes, funding scholars to Oxford, ensuring masses were said and that there were always lights and singing somewhere in the church, funding sermons, relieving the poor and endowing poor maidens with dowries. A long list of items in the possession of the Mary Chapel in the mid-fifteenth century is indicative of the popular basis of the movement: they were the many modest 'votive offerings of the ordinary inhabitants'.[48]

After the quashing of the Guild Merchant the commonalty's attention shifted from the market to the parish church. Some of the mysteriously disappearing treasure confiscated from the aristocratic rebels financed the erection of the massive church tower, which, from its completion in the second decade of the fifteenth century, overshadowed the spire of the abbey church adjacent to it. The erection, in 1516–30, of 'the tallest (nave) of any Cotswold church, perhaps of any Perpendicular church anywhere', crowned this movement, and provides as dramatic a symbol of the powerful vernacular renaissance of the fifteenth century as it is possible to imagine.[49] Building was going on virtually continuously for 130 years. Then and henceforth the parish church, representing the aspirations of the urban community as against those of their lord, easily dominated the landscape. There is firm evidence that the builders intended the tower to be even more dominating than it is, for the original plan, evident in the masonry 'squinches' built across the corners of the tower, was to cap it with a spire.[50] This crowning humiliation may have been prevented by the abbey's recovery of its influence when Henry V came to the throne.

Because the most vigorous and intense religious activity of the age was communal, definitively local, it was also extremely varied. This chapter has presented one well-documented variant, place-specific, highly individual and distinctive, yet also representative. What sprang into being in the first quarter of the fifteenth century and collapsed in the 1550s was a visible, audible, visceral, beautiful communal religious culture, centred on an ardently loved and constantly renewed parish church. For over a century the parish church bodied forth the proud wealth of its leading townspeople and the solidarity of the 'inhabitants' (a term that, later evidence will show, encompassed a majority but by no means every person resident in the town at any given time). In the decades following the dissolution, 'survivalist' merchant-catholics continued to manage and govern the town, but after the dissolution of the chantries in 1548 and the brief yet systematic evangelical activities of a Zwinglian bishop of Gloucester, John Hooper, in 1551–3, the church and the parish began to

48 Fuller, 'The Register of the Chapel', 330.

49 David Verey, *Cotswold Churches* (London 1971), 74.

50 Hill, *Cirencester Parish Church*, 19.

fall apart. Within a few years the parish church became the locus of conflict, faction and sectarian divisions within the commonalty. Revivers of the Guild Merchant, sects, cabals and tavern theologians now routinely criticized and rejected what went on in the church. By the middle of the seventeenth century Cirencester would be home to many 'congregations': Presbyterians, Congregationalists, Baptists, Independents, Seekers, Quakers and even a reputed 'Ranter' or two. For this reason alone it is difficult to believe the complete absence of evidence of Lollards in fifteenth- and sixteenth-century Cirencester really means vernacular heretics, as defined by the Statute against Heretics in 1401 and Archbishop Thomas Arundel's 'constitutions' of 1409, were never to be found there. At Cirencester the common struggle with the abbey absorbed them, or the 'fellowship of the town' persuaded them to go somewhere else. But the inequality so evident in quantitative studies of the commonalty did not become paramount until after the old common enemy, the abbey, was dissolved.

Another change must be noted. During the fifteenth century an idea took hold in England that would eventually change the world. Raw materials produced locally should be worked into finished commodities locally, and then sold to foreigners. That way more money flowed into a community. Craftworkers, shopkeepers, smiths, carpenters, glaziers, shepherds, husbandmen, masons, shearers, combers, spinners, weavers, fullers, dyers and finishers could flourish. Their wives would die less often in childbirth, more of their children would survive into adulthood. Fewer would be swept away by routine epidemics of plague and a hundred more diseases. More money could be devoted to religious and charitable institutions. Churches could be rebuilt to stand as living symbols of the pride, enterprise and wealth of the communities that built them. As anyone who has seen it knows, Cirencester parish church is one of the great English parish churches, best approached on foot from any direction. Before the fifteenth century it had been dwarfed by the abbey. My contention here is that the community took over from the abbey in the century *before* the Henrician and Edwardian reformations. In the fifteenth century, the new tower, built by donations and bequests from good citizens like John Cosyn, made the parish church a supreme symbol of communal ambition.

The case of Cirencester refutes the Protestant myth that medieval Catholicism was entirely corrupt. Cirencester Abbey was pulled down quickly and efficiently, with no recorded tears. Its fabric contributed to a significant rebuilding of the town and surrounding manor houses in stone. The abbey consistently failed to convince the community that it was a *religious* institution and that it had the community's best interests at heart. The would-be citizens of Cirencester used *their* church to shame *the* church.

In 1547, two priests, Thomas Marshall, aged 43, and William Painter, a year younger, became the last in a continuous stream of priests serving and singing masses at the altars of Holy Trinity and St Mary, and (though this was never specified) performing the tasks of parish priests, according to their lights, in a town that always needed several. Over a century and a half, the duties of the 'chaplains' had become greatly simplified. The purpose of the Trinity chantry was simply 'to find and maintain two priests to celebrate and help sing divine service … and to pray for the founder's soul and all Christian souls'.[51] Connections with this vibrant, communal religious tradition, invented in the late fourteenth century, were finally cut in 1547–8.

51 J. Maclean, 'Chantry Certificates', 284.

7

Classes of the commune in 1522

The grossly unequal distribution of wealth, power and status is clear enough in the sources considered so far. Comparison of the assessment of 1327 with the national military survey of 1522 indicates that social structure, measured by systematic assessments of relative wealth, changed very little in the intervening period. The lists are comparable. Both exclude a large class of people considered too poor to be worth assessing. As R.W. Hoyle observes, 'it is clear that the 1522 return for the Cotswolds massively under records the names of men who in 1525 paid either 20s. in wages or 40s. in goods'.[1] Cirencester's listing has no-one paying less than £2. In the western parts of the county this category comprised up to 50 percent of the total. The Cirencester listing thus excluded at least half the households in the town, those dependent on wages or other forms of employment by the wealthier households. Like the listing of 1327, the assessment of 1522 probably offers a reliable indicator of the relative wealth of merchants, middling traders and craftworkers. Fewer men were assessed in 1522 than in 1327 (73 as against 85). It is possible that the total population was lower, but probably not much lower, for reasons given earlier. In 1522, 73 persons were assessed on a total of £1,962. Those assessed on £2–5 (22 or 30%) totalled £63 (3.2%); the next group, assessed on £5–59 (41 or 56%), totalled £641 (32.6%); persons assessed on £60–280 numbered 11 (15% of total assessed) and totalled £1,258 (64% of total). By comparing the data in the following tables it becomes clear that the groupings, in particular the small number of wealthy men, yield relativities very similar to those of 1327.

Table 7.1. Wealth distribution at Cirencester in 1522

A	£2–5	22	(29.7%)	£63	(3.2%)
B	£5–59	41	(55.4%)	£641	(32.6%)
C	£60–280	11	(14.86%)	£1,258	(64%)
Totals		74	(99.96)	£1,962	(99.8)

Note: 23 (31%) paid £5–20; 18 persons (24.6%) paid £20–59.

[1] Hoyle (ed.), *The Military Survey of Gloucestershire, 1522*, 'Introduction', xxiv; tables and analysis in this chapter are based on 'The town of Cirencester', *ibid*, 100–3 and 'the town of Tewkesbury', *ibid*, 160–6.

In 1522 as in 1327, the commonalty was dominated by a dozen or so wealthy merchants assessed on £200 or more. Throughout the fifteenth century and up to the time of the assessments of 1522, this elite, backed by (and intermarried with) capitalist clothiers of the Stroudwater Valleys and lords of neighbouring manors, had spearheaded a communal religious movement symbolically centred on the altar of St Thomas in the Trinity Chapel of the increasingly majestic church of St John the Baptist. Cirencester's merchant elite was smaller than that of neighbouring regional capitals (Bristol, Gloucester), but many of its individual members were as wealthy, as a result of their strategic involvement in the lucrative trades in wool and cloth. It is a measure of the relative commercial importance of Cirencester that none of the wealthy elite of Tewkesbury, a town of comparable significance across the north Cotswolds, at the confluence of the Avon and Severn valleys, was assessed at more than £160. On these figures Cirencester had a wealthier elite and a proportionately smaller group of 'middles' paying £5–59 (56% as against 65%). If we exclude Tewkesbury's nil-payers the percentages are as given in Table 7.2.

Table 7.2. Wealth distribution at Cirencester and Tewkesbury, 1522

Amount paid	Tewkesbury			Cirencester	
£60+	12	(4.4%)	(8.2%)	11	(15%)
£20–59	31	(11.6%)	(21%)	18	(24.6%)
£5–20	65	(24.3%)	(44.2%)	23	(31%)
40s.+	39	(14.6%)	(26.5%)	22	(30%)
Nil	120	(44.94%)	(Total 99.84%)		
Total	267			74	

Total 147 (100%)
£60+ 12 (8.2%)
£20–59 31 (21%)
£5–20 65 (44.2%)
£40s.+ 39 (26.5%)

The comparison shows that while nearly twice the number of men were assessed at Tewkesbury, Cirencester's wealthy elite was similar in size (11 against 12) but individually and collectively wealthier than its counterpart. The 'upper middles', assessed on possessions of £20–59 was roughly equal in size in both places (21% and 24.6%). The 'lower middles', assessed at £5–20, and probably comprising the better-established artisans and retailers, constituted a higher proportion at Tewkesbury (44.2% against 31%). Possessions assessed at 40s. probably included recently married artisans, retailers, market victuallers and a host of households with possessions that, however meagre, were observable and measurable. There is clear evidence that paying taxes was a mark of status later in the sixteenth century, and it is likely that this was the case earlier. It was the mark of 'independent inhabitancy' and may have led individuals at these lower levels to overestimate their ability to contribute to the (local and national) commonwealth for reasons of pride. At Tewkesbury that still left 120 households (44.9% of the total) with no possessions considered worth assessing. These figures are remarkably consistent with the wealth distributions suggested by later, more detailed sources, notably the hearth taxes of the 1660s and 1670s. Such continuities may conceal a multitude of differences and exceptions, but the pattern is hard to ignore.

Contemporary comparisons aside, continuities are striking. Like the industrious Essex communities studied by L.R. Poos, the social structure of Cirencester remained remarkably stable from the fourteenth to early seventeenth centuries.[2] Generation after generation, from the early fourteenth to eighteenth centuries, the inhabitants fell into four broad classes: the gentlemen of town and country; wealthy merchants; an amorphous class of relatively established artisan and retailer households; and a much larger and amorphous fourth class of people living permanently on or beyond the line between mundane poverty and outright 'necessytye'. The fourth class is least visible in the archives: it rarely appeared in tax assessments, left wills or had any possessions worth a parish inventory. It appears surprisingly rarely in the various court records because its defining characteristic was a lack or absence. Its members, being at best 'dependants', lacked credit. Reputation, an established household, temperance, productivity, respect, ability to pay taxes and therefore contribute to the common wealth, were attributes of 'independent inhabitancy'. The line between the top three classes and the fourth was between 'dependency' and 'independency'.

A few rich rentiers and merchants (at Cirencester, never more than a dozen or so interconnected households) continued to possess and control 60 to 70 percent of wealth, assessed in various ways. Most generations saw one or two of these merchant families move up, to London perhaps, but most visibly into the local gentry. Generation after generation, mercantile fortunes were invested in estates and manors, never more commonly than in the generations from the dissolution, which eventually released perhaps half the jurisdictions in the region on to the market, to the eve of the 'Great Rebellion' of the 1640s. The names of the men and families who acquired these estates figure largely in what follows. The unfolding impact of the unravelling of religious estates eventually led, in the last third of the sixteenth century, to the crystallization of a new, deeper and eventually divided ruling class.

At Cirencester a second class or category of middling agriculturalists, traders and artisans, never more than 30 to 40 percent of the total, had enough possessions and capital (clothing, tools, stores of food and wood, furniture and other household goods) to be considered respectably off by the

[2] L.R. Poos, *A Rural Society after the Black Death: Essex 1350–1525* (Cambridge 1991)

standards of the day. Their numbers and the linkage they formed with rank and file journeymen, apprentices and servants made them an abiding force in urban politics. The rank and file members of the Weavers' Company were of this sort, as were mercers, innkeepers, drapers, tanners, and the occasional wholesale tailor, glover and shoemaker.

In most generations one or two artisans and retailers moved into the elite to replace men who had moved on. 'Gentlemen of town and country' was the phrase used by a leader of communal reform in the later sixteenth century to designate the senior ruling classes of the town and its surrounding villages. They shared (and delegated) the key institutions of local governance with the elite merchants. Gentlemen of town and country were expected to be connected to sources of reliable information about national and international events affecting religion, commerce, law and governance, and to use this knowledge for the common weal of town and country.

This 'better part of the town', as Robert Strange would designate it, governed the church, market and streets by the appointment of trusted men from a second class of household, generally smaller-scale mercers, vintners and wholesale artisans employing apprentices, journeymen and servants. This subaltern class included the keepers of the largest inns, like William Tanner in the generation of 1400, wealthy sixteenth-century butchers like the Manns, and lesser clothiers. These wholesalers relied on a third class of 'independents', constituted by a hundred or so householding artisans and retailers. The fourth class – fluctuating from 40 to 60 percent – owned little more than the clothes they stood up in, the shoes on their feet and a rented room, and were more mobile: Sir Thomas Smith's 'fourth sort', 'rascability' or *proletarii*. The duty of the 'best part of town', with the assistance of the 'better sort' of the rest, was to harness the multitudinous labour of the 'fourth sort' to the 'common wealth'. In the sense that Cirencester always offered opportunities for an enterprising and fortunate apprentice or servant, individuals occasionally rose from the upper levels of the lowest class into the middles and even the elite. There is some evidence that the religious and political consciousness of rank and file artisans and husbandmen – their 'constitutional confidence', as it were – intensified in the later sixteenth and early seventeenth centuries. The 1570s and 1580s saw efforts to raise the morale and status of the rank and file inhabitants, a majority of whom were artisans, retailers and labourers.

The weakness of tax assessment data is that it reveals very little about consciousness. Evidence relating to the later sixteenth and seventeenth centuries will show that the commonalty of Cirencester was at its strongest and most effective (and affective) when the top three classes were unified. It looks as if efforts were made to make such an alliance work in the fifteenth century and, more certainly, from c.1570 to the outbreak of civil war in 1643. The structural basis of unity was that the members of the three classes enjoyed, albeit unequally, control of and access to society's resources. The increasingly articulate key to social harmony was the employment and relief of the fourth class. Generation after generation of townspeople discovered for themselves that the common weal depended on unity of purpose. The gentry of town and country needed the merchants and the merchants needed the artisans and retailers. Their household enterprises employed those who were not yet, no longer, or never would be capable of employing themselves. Although it is difficult to measure, it is likely that the most significant underlying movement of the sixteenth and seventeenth centuries was not structural. The four classes are reproduced in tax assessments of the fourteenth to eighteenth centuries. Cultural and material capital remained the monopoly of the top three classes. How they came to work together in the century before the civil wars of the 1640s is a major topic of Chapters 10 to 16. The other, more challenging, is to measure the presence and capacities of the fourth class, whom the greatest English constitutional writer of the sixteenth century, Sir Thomas Smith, christened *proletarii*.

The common denominator of the fourth class (or 'sort', as sixteenth-century authorities called it), the one that is largely absent from our sources, was what contemporaries called 'dependency'. The organic mode of production that prevailed at Cirencester, the Seven Hundreds and, indeed, through most parts of early sixteenth-century England, constantly generated 'dependants'. After the Black Death, a majority of this class was transitional: adolescents, young men and women employed as servants and apprentices in households where, if lucky, they would increase the skills and habits that would render them capable, in maturity, of relative independency. As long as the demand for labour exceeded supply, most labouring families were capable of achieving it as long as their health survived. What I will call 'independent inhabitancy' encompassed every household that conformed to such basic precepts as not being in receipt of wages or alms. Membership was determined by reputation and possessions, not 'property' in the modern sense. Landed property remained crucial in determining relativities of power and status, of course, but it is necessary to broaden our conceptions of 'capital' to encompass the importance of hard-won communal reputation in the achievement, in the eyes of the community, of independency. In other words, it was possible to be relatively 'poor' and (proudly) independent. Similarly, wealth and reputation did not invariably go together. A wealthy gentleman or merchant who worked only for himself, his household and his family and friends, indifferent to the communal weal, was badly thought of. Popular perception of a person's devotion to the common weal was the enduring variable. 'Class' measured by relative wealth was so entrenched that public opinion took it for granted. For much of our period it was regarded as God's will. The principle of common weal aimed to mitigate its effects by assigning mutually serving duties to every vocation, estate and class. The aim was not to remove class inequalities but to make them irrelevant.

Thirty-seven years later, the subsidy of 1 Elizabeth (1559/60) – see Table 7.3 – hints at a slight change: the gap between the middles and the wealthy elite had closed, or, to put it another way, there are more 'middles' and fewer, less wealthy, elite households. There are a number of possible reasons for this, one of which has been underlined by R.W. Hoyle in his analysis of mid-Tudor taxation: because of its dependence on the overall health of the English economy, its strategic location, Cirencester suffered as a result of the long economic recession of the middle decades of the sixteenth century, brought on by the rapacious taxations and confiscations of Henry VIII and enforced by a series of bad harvests and a national epidemic of 'sweating sickness' in the late 1550s.[3] Cirencester's surviving parish registers begin in 1560, so it is not possible to calculate the short-term effects of the epidemics of the 1550s on the town's total population.

Table 7.3. Wealth distribution in 1559–60 (Subsidy, 1 Elizabeth)

A	5s.	31	50%	155s.	24.7%
B	6–10s.	14	22.6%	126s. 2d.	20.1%
C	11–20s.	13	21%	202s.	32.2%
D	21–45s.	4	6.5%	145s.	23.1%
Totals	62			628s. 2d.	100.1%

The surnames of four of the leading payers to this subsidy, Christopher George (18s. 8d.), his brother John George (20s.), John Partridge (40s.) and Thomas Strange (45s.), lawyers, merchants and landowners, figure prominently in the better-documented governance of the commune in the later sixteen and seventeenth centuries.

3 R.W. Hoyle, 'Taxation and the Mid-Tudor Crisis', *Econ Hist Rev*, New Series, 51:4 (1998).

8

Surviving Reformation: the rule of Robert Strange, 1539–70

The manor of Cirencester left the church 'on the morning of 19 December 1539 and was taken into the hands of the Crown', where it remained for eight years. In July 1547 it was granted to Thomas, lord Seymour of Sudeley, who held it until his execution in March 1549.[1] It was then purchased by Sir Anthony Kingston, who died in 1556, another suspected traitor. Elizabeth I granted Abbey House to a more stable proprietor, her physician Richard Master, in June 1564. The aptly named Masters settled down, and were to prove an abiding presence in the turbulent politics of the town for the next two centuries. Thomas Seymour, Anthony Kingston and his successor as lord of the manor, Sir John Danvers, were courtiers. The Masters settled down to become 'gentlemen of town and country'. From the dissolution of the abbey until the 1570s, however, the manor and the parish were run by a small group of local men appointed by the bailiff of courtiers who were too preoccupied with national affairs to have a significant impact on local politics. The lordship of the abbots became, for practical purposes, a bourgeois oligarchy.

In the months following the fall of the abbey the 'custodianship of the site' was granted to a wine merchant named Richard Basing. Problems arose when the crown sold the 'Church Steplee and surplues houses of the late monastery' to a local knight, Sir Anthony Hungerford and his kinsman by marriage, Robert Strange, the late abbot's bailiff. In 1541 these men complained to the king that Basing 'doo dayly and wrongfully interupt and disturb your said supplicants to have and carye away the stones, timber and stuff of the said church steplee … contrary to all right equite and good concyence'.[2] It seems that Basing was only granted the abbot's manor house and grounds, not the abbey church, with its 'steeplee' (and all the valuable lead), or the 'surplus houses'. Hungerford and Strange were granted the right to demolish, carry away and sell their scrap. Whatever the exact circumstances, it is evident that the abbey was demolished remarkably quickly.

1 Reece and Catling, *Cirencester*, 15.

2 Richard Reece, 'The Abbey of St Mary, Cirencester', *Trans BGAS* 81 (1962), 198–202; the quote, from PRO E321 17/48, is cited on 201–2.

The records of its dispersal testify to the scale of the abbey's lordship. In 1545 John Pollard, 'the king's servant' and William Byrt, yeoman, made a request to purchase 152 messuages, 37 shops, 6 cottages, 27 gardens and other miscellaneous properties previously belonging to the abbey in the town of Cirencester.[3] Edward VI granted Thomas, lord Seymour the site of monastery and all the lands associated with the manor of Cirencester: 458 acres of arable, 27 acres of pasture and 46 acres of meadow attached to the Grange of Spiringate; the Almery Grange, consisting of 283 acres of arable, 7 acres of pasture 'called Hartes', 'Shepehouse close' and 'Pulchams Barn', 33.5 acres of meadow called Southam Almery Close, and other freeholds named Pullensbarn, Olmers Shepehouse, Newclose and Stratton Close. 'The profits of the liberty of the town' included 'outgoings of stalls & stallage with the profits of the 2 fairs' (£4); 'tolls or customs from carts called waynes entering and leaving the town (2s. 4d.); 'tolls on all kinds of good in the market' (20s.); 'rent and toll of resale of wool and leather sold at the fairs and markets' (£8); 'treasure trove with goods and chattels of felons, fugitives, suicides and wainage' (3s. 4d.); 'profits of 2 frankpledges, 24 halimotes and piepowder courts' (£19 6s. 8d.); the views of the hundreds of Crowthorne (30s.), Rapsgate (20s.), Brightwells Barrow (26s. 8d.), Bradley (£4) and Longtree (22s.). From this he had to deduct £6 13s. 4d. annual seneschal fee granted by the abbot to Sir Anthony Kingston for life; the same to the king for 'the office of bailiff of the Seven hundreds'; and 74s. 8d., 'the fee of Robert Strange, bailiff of the liberty of the town by an agreement with the late abbot and convent, conferred upon him yearly for life'.[4]

Strange was appointed bailiff by the last abbot, John Blake.[5] Like that proverbial tycoon of the dissolution, William Stumpe of North Nibley, who purchased the buildings of nearby Malmesbury Abbey and converted them into a weavers' factory, Strange had done well as a 'clothman', and was uniquely well placed to invest in opportunities arising from the selling-off of the abbey estate.[6] He used the stone fabric of the old abbey buildings to build himself a great house just off the market-place ('The Antelope'), another at Chesterton in the suburbs ('a very fair house, outhouses, barns, stables, gardens, orchards & backside, +300 acres'[7]), and in 1554 raised £586 to purchase the manor of Somerford Keynes (Wilts) from the crown, with an estate that included 'two watermills on the Thames'.

3 'Request to purchase by Willam Byrt & John Pollard': Hockaday 155, citing TNA Augm. Book 216.3, 6 Jan., 36 Hen VIII (1545), TNA Augm. of Parts for grants s70.

4 Hockaday 155, citing PRO Parts for Grants 1933 m12, 1 Edw. VI, Lands appointed to the Lord Seymour of the Kings Majestie.

5 Fuller, *ibid*, 340.

6 A document cited in Hockaday 155, Cirencester, dated 5 Oct. 1553, refers to 'Robert Straunge, Clothier'.

7 GA D4871, 'Strange Family'.

There is no evidence that he ever lived at Somerford Keynes, but his son and heir certainly did, 'breaking away from the commercial and civic traditions' that had made the family's fortune, in favour of a more genteel lifestyle.[8] The Stumpes and many other clothier-gentry families followed this proverbial English social pathway. Historically, the Stranges belong to a class of families that is particularly important in the history of this region from the fifteenth to the eighteenth centuries. They demonstrate, if demonstration is needed, that not all the middle-rank merchant families who moved into the breach created by the dissolution of religious estates were committed Protestants. Robert Strange was important because he took an already successful branch of a well-established mercantile family of the Bristol region (which in the Middle Ages included Cirencester) through a troubled period of change.

As for changes in the religion of the people, historians have used the religious formulae found in the prefaces to wills of the immediate post-Reformation decades to measure the onset of Protestantism. Cirencester wills of the 1540s and 1550s suggest their formulae should be used with caution. The traditional catholic formula, in which the testator bequeathed his or her 'sowle unto allmyghtie god and our blessed ladye sancta marie and to all the holye companie of heaven' continued to be used throughout the 1540s, until a few months after the arrival at Gloucester of the evangelical and extremely conscientious John Hooper, in 1549. From 1549 until 1555 (two years after Hooper had been removed) the more neutral, even perfunctory, 'sowle to allmyghtie god' appears.[9] In the mid-1550s a few minor eccentricities appear, suggesting confusion as to what the authoritative formula was. John Hawle, for example, left his 'sowle to allmyghtie god the lord and giver of all goodness'.[10] By 1557, six years into the reign of the catholic Queen Mary, wills gradually reverted to the catholic formula, with occasionally explicit references to the saints.[11] In all probability the vast majority of testators, many unable to write, most 'sick in body' at the time, were not responsible for the formulae used. Wills use the formulae that the clerics who wrote them judged to be acceptable at the time. They may tell us little or nothing about the convictions of the testators.[12]

8 GA D4871.

9 E.g. Thomas Fyfelde, GA GDR 1552/63; John Manbye, GDR 1554/67; the reference to the redeeming qualities of Christ's blood in Roger Teyll, GDR 1554/110, seems emphatically protestant, but such references are rare at this time.

10 GDR 1555/81.

11 E.g. the old bailiff, John George, GDR 1556/29, and Edmunde Hunte, GDR 1557/69, include reference to saints; Henry Tringham, GDR 1557/81; John Gurney, GDR 1557/166; Joane Titley, GDR 1557/150; John Lyttle, GDR 1557/145; John Dawbury, GDR 1557/165; and John Munde, GDR 1558/123, all use the formulaic 'sowle to almighty god and our blessed saint Mary and all the company of heaven'.

12 It may be significant that the will of one of the men who wrote the wills of these years, 'Thomas Perpynt, curate', GDR 1563/152, bequeathed 'my soulle to all mightye god and to all the heavenlie companye'; the reference is quite perfunctory and there is no explicit reference either to saints or to the Virgin Mary.

However, the wills of the 1550s do reflect the confusing religious changes that the town, like the rest of the country, was going through at the time. The secular rule of Robert Strange may have represented a reassuring continuity, at least for a few years.

We know him only from a dozen or so sources showing that he was a key figure in the political and religious life of the town up to the 1580s. He was probably a descendant of the Thomas Straunge who was pardoned in 1414 for his involvement in the Guild Merchant movement, and later served as the abbot's bailiff.[13] Another Robert Strange served as mayor of Bristol in 1474, 1482 and 1489, and died in 1491.[14] Connections between Bristol and Cirencester abounded: most significant Bristol merchants maintained agents at Cirencester, and vice versa; similarly with London, an even more important trade orientation in the sixteenth century than it had been earlier.[15] David Harris Sacks refers to 'well-known men of affairs' who became leaders, first, of Bristol, and then of London. We saw earlier that a member of the Canynges family was among the 'twenty poor men of Cirencester' in 1342. Sacks mentions George Monox, member of another family with a branch at Cirencester.[16] Wherever commodities were manufactured and marketing outlets existed, these families had connections.

There is little evidence of evangelical religion until the fifteen-sixties. Robert Strange and his brothers were what John Bossy, criticizing the use of the phrase 'old religion', called 'survivalists'. 'Being a predominantly social sentiment ("survivalist" catholicism) could persist only where there was a social institution to support it,' writes Bossy.[17] The dissolution of Cirencester Abbey did not mean the dissolution of the secular liberties it had engrossed. Throughout the sixteenth century these were administered on behalf of absentee lords by a small cabal of manorial managers centred on the bailiff and his relations by marriage, the locally prestigious Georges of Baunton. Strange associates all seem to have shared a belief in the 'survival' of the old ways. In 1551 Strange let 'The Antelope', his house at Cirencester, to another wealthy inhabitant, John Chapperlen.[18] Stranges and Chapperlens are emphatically linked with Catholic activity at Cirencester region later in the sixteenth and early seven-

13 Fuller, 'Guild Merchant', 50–1.

14 14 missing? Allow one line?

15 'Two great merchant families, Strange of Siston and Strange of Cirencester, had a common ancestor who was bailiff of Cirencester early in the reign of Henry VI and was an armigerous gentleman. He was the great-grandfather of Robert': GA D4871, 'Strange Family'.

16 D.H. Sacks, *The Widening Gate: Bristol and the Atlantic Economy 1450–1700* (University of California Press 1991), 30–1.

17 John Bossy, 'The Character of Elizabethan Catholicism', in T.H. Aston (ed.), *Crisis in Europe 1560–1660* (London 1965), 223.

18 GA D4871; GA D2957/(P98) 205A; the parish registers record that Chapperlen was buried on 2 April 1574; in his will, dated that year, Chapperlen describes himself as 'yoman'.

teenth centuries. We know from another source that in 1551 Cirencester parish church was still, for practical purposes, catholic. It probably remained so until 1570, as we shall see. A declining range of services continued as before, managed by the same people as before, but now for absentee lords. A committee of merchants and local gentlemen continued to run the administration and manage the affairs of the town, as they had most probably done for centuries under succeeding abbots. Robert Strange was the leader of the tight little oligarchy of local men who moved into the breach when Abbot John Blake retired to Fairford.[19]

Strange carved a gentleman's patrimony out of the fabric and estate of the dissolved abbey he had once served.[20] The Stranges were an old Cirencester family with long kinship connections in London and Bristol.[21] He used his knowledge of the manor and its records to make money, convert it into land, marry daughters into gentry and knightly families and acquire the status of a gentleman. The Stranges were by no means 'new rich', but Robert was able to take advantage of opportunities arising from the dissolution of St Mary's Abbey and take his own branch of the family into the gentry.[22]

We get a sense of the muscular style of Strange's government, when he was in his prime, from a Star Chamber case relating to years immediately following the dissolution of the abbey.[23] The bill was presented by one Robert Porte, Clerk, who believed that boss Strange owed him money. One day Porte was crossing the market-place from the church when he 'came unto one Robert Strainge Bayley of the town of Ciceter'. 'Then and there, openly in the street', Strange huffily explained, Porte 'demanded certayne money', a public act that the Strange entourage felt was not befitting dealings between 'gentell men'. Strange took offence, called Porte *knave priest* and threatened that if the priest continued in his demands, he (Strange) and his companion, Robert Ingram, would do him 'bodily harm and… kill him'. Ingram allegedly punched Porte on the nose (gave him a *blessed*). Henceforth Strange's gang took to 'lay[ing] in wayte for Richard Porte as he was coming to his house'. Witnesses confirmed that 'the said Richard Porte for feare of bodily hurt was fayne to leave the highwaie and bide by a back lane to his lodging'. Porte was a man of regular

19 Robert Strange reported to Privy Council that watch for vagabonds and disorderly persons had been kept in Cirencester and the Seven Hundreds; he was high sheriff for Gloucestershire in 1573: GA D4871, 'Strange Family'.

20 'Thomas Straunge for lands in Myntie. Release of tenement with lands called Scarletts in Myntie, with Thomas Straunge of Chesterton, Gent.' GA D205A (1.2).

21 'Anthony Straunge of London, Gent' is mentioned in the above deed, *ibid*; Robert Strange was mayor of Bristol in 1474, 1482 and 1489; 'there seems no reason to doubt that Robert was the son of a Cirencester man as Thomas Strange was living there in the early part of the fifteenth century': GA EN, R. Strange 1970; Fuller, 'Guild Merchant', 50–1.

22 For an account of the new post-dissolution gentry and nobility of the region, see below, Chapter 12.

23 TNA, Stac 2/19/38, 36 Henry VIII.

habits. One day on his way home (perhaps from the church) he spied Strange and another associate waiting for him in the market-place. Porte fled up an alley and ducked into a tavern run by Thomas Taylor. Also present was John Daubney 'of Ciceter … yeoman', who testified 'that he was drinking at the Inne of John Taylors when John Colne came in and said to the plaintiff [Porte] these words, "I wolde advis[e] you take the afterway homeward and go for youre owne safety."' Porte fled by the back door leading into 'a back lane sometimes called Gosse Ditch' just as Strange and his companion, one Grenewood, burst in through the front door. Strange and Grenewood were called before the justices to answer Porte's allegation that they had threatened and constantly harassed him by standing 'in the high road if … Porte should passe to his mancon house and if they did for what cause they did so'.

Strange was examined in November, 1544. He admitted owing Porte three pounds, confessed that he had been at Taylor's inn, but denied any harassment or threats. He admitted that 'on the first Monday in Lent last past (when) Porte passed by' he made some disparaging remarks to a companion, but suggested they were only words. He openly admitted 'reviling' Porte, in his view a creature beneath contempt who had brought charges against him 'only to put [him] to costys, charges and expenses'. It is possible but unproven that Porte was persecuted by Strange because, after his appointment as curate, he had displayed protestant leanings.

Strange was a well connected 'survivalist'. His brother, John Strange, had been a canon at the abbey; at the dissolution he was granted the old abbey rectory of Shipton Moyne, which he served until his death in 1566. There is 'good evidence that he preferred the old religion, but he did not allow the successive changes in the religious establishment to interrupt his own career'.[24] John Hooper suspected him to be an enemy of reform; during Hooper's brief, evangelical episcopate, some of his neighbours accused John Strange of continuing to live in sin with his housekeeper, rather than marrying her, as he was now entitled, indeed, in Hooper's eyes, obliged, to do.[25] Robert Strange the bailiff conformed successively to the orthodoxies of the abbots, Henry VIII, Edward VI, Mary and Elizabeth I, continuing to occupy 'the 14th seate, South the North Side' of the parish church, which 'antiently belonged to the family of Strainges', until his death in 1588.[26] His religious sympathies are not definitely known, but his past inevitably left him tangled in old loyalties, and in 1570 he was directly accused of being a 'papist'.

The 'papists' formed a tight-knit little group. Christopher George, the lord of the manor of Baunton, married Robert Strange's eldest daughter, Anna. His

24 'Strange Family Pedigree', GA D2930/3 (61); cf. also GDR PCC 37, Will of Richard Fowler of Cirencester, in which 2 calves were left 'to my cousin Parson Straunge'; GA D4871.

25 GA, GDR 6.15, 30–1: John Straunge v John Crippes Defamation; Office v John Straunge incontinency.

26 GA P86, CW4.1, 'Cirencester Seate Booke'.

brother, John George, was married to Elizabeth, Strange's youngest daughter by his first marriage.[27] John George's daughter, Elizabeth, was married to Edward Chapperlen, the son of the man to whom Robert Strange had leased 'The Antelope', in 1551.[28] Christopher George had a share of the tithes of the parish, and all of them, as manorial officials, would have a strong say in the appointment of rector and curates. In this sense, the interconnected cabal that governed the town for thirty years after the dissolution simply continued the habits of the burgher oligarchs who had built and maintained the parish church. Both of Robert Strange's brothers seem to have remained in the old faith.

Another Chapperlen, John, studied rhetoric at Cheltenham and Eton in the 1570s, 'read Catholic books and was finally converted by his cousin Thomas Strange, lately returned from Rome', in about 1590. Imprisoned under Elizabeth, he was released on the accession of James and returned to his family at Cirencester. The historian of the Counter-Reformation in Gloucestershire notes that when Chapperlen returned to Cirencester, 'his kinsman Thomas Strange again planned a joint escape.... His cousin and the Jesuits had sent him from Rome, and he desired to fight heresy and be an ecclesiastic.'[29] Chapperlen was probably a son of Edward Chapperleyn, and grandson of the man to whom Robert Strange leased 'The Antelope' in 1551. If so, he was Robert Strange's great-grandson, his mother being Elizabeth George, the daughter of a marriage between John George and Robert Strange's daughter Margaret.[30]

Except for the fact that he was from Cirencester, it has not been possible to trace Thomas Strange's family connections with certainty. His family must have been wealthy. When he became a Jesuit he made the Society of Jesus a gift of £2,000. The most likely explanation is that he was a son of Thomas Strange of Chesterton (the bailiff's cousin, thirty years his junior), whose wife first appears in a recusancy list dated 1577 as 'Mistress Strange of Chesterton'. John Sandys and Stephen Rowsham, two Catholics, were captured at the house of Bridget Strange at Cirencester and executed in 1586 or 1587.[31] A contemporary Catholic source described her as 'a most ancient and perfect catholic.... She hath been much and long chased into many shires for persecution, and yet liveth a most resolute Catholic where she can thrust her head, for her husband dare not keep her.'[32]

27 GA, 'Pedigree of Strange', D2930/3.

28 GA D4871.

29 Patrick McGrath, 'Gloucestershire and the Counter-Reformation in the Reign of Elizabeth', *Trans BGAS* 88 (1969–70), 21–2.

30 GRO D4871, 'Strange Family'.

31 McGrath, 'Gloucestershire and the Counter-Reformation', qf. Godfrey Anstruther, *The Seminary Priests: Elizabeth 1558–1603*, 296.

32 It is difficult to know what to make of the information that in 1625 'Mris George' of Ciceter' gave 5 pounds and 'Mris Strainge gave ten pounds' to the evangelical Calvinist Feoffees for Improriations, money used to purchase the presentation at Cirencester. Either

When he died in 1594, her husband, Thomas, left his sheep to his servants, and to his wife the now relatively meagre sum, after the inflation of the previous fifty years, of £40 per annum 'on condition that she gave up her obstinate refusal to attend church', which, on her own admission, she had refused to do for thirty years.[33] On this interpretation, Thomas Strange the Jesuit simply followed his mother's example – but not that of his father or grandfather, the old bailiff, who may well have been privately Catholic, but outwardly conformed to whatever regime ruled in church and state. Thomas was arrested after the Gunpowder Plot and held in prison until 1617.[34] However, by this time committed Romanists were a persecuted minority. Our concern for the moment is with the decades in which the transformation from catholic to protestant took place.

There is, then, enough circumstantial evidence to suggest that an aura of old religion clung to the little oligarchy of interconnected families who continued the everyday management of the town after the abbey went. In religion and social management they practised 'survivalism' through the reigns of Henry, Edward, Mary and continued to govern the key institutions of the market and the parish church into the first decade of the Elizabethan settlement. The key change brought about by the dissolution of Cirencester Abbey was that the lordship, with all the practical liberties it had engrossed over the centuries, was in the hands of new lords who, unlike the abbots, did not have the management of local affairs at their fingertips. Men like Robert Strange knew all the rules, and knew exactly where to lay their hands on some old document that established the legitimacy of this or that practice. He and his fellow oligarchs also knew which local estates once belonging to the abbey were worth purchasing; they had the money and credit to buy them. The abbey was gone, but the 'liberties' it had appropriated, and the system of government it had imposed on the town, had not been diffused very far.

the salesman failed to tell them what the money was for, or the matriarch survivalists changed their views after their husbands were dead. Isabel McBeath Calder, *Activities of the Puritan Faction of the Church of England 1625–33* (London 1957), 38.

33 McGrath, 'Counter-Reformation'.

34 *Ibid*; GA D4871, 'Strange Family'.

9

'The tyranny of infected members called papists': the Strange regime under challenge, c.1551–80

> there is more tyranie nowe in these daies used than ever there was.
>
> Robert Whiting, butcher of Cirencester, 1574[1]

Robert Strange's position as bailiff, and the network of connections set up by marriages of his daughters, was the strategic core of his political machine. We can assume on the basis of the past that opposition factions had a continuous if amorphous existence even when they generated no direct evidence. Cirencester was too small a place for everyone not to know who was communing with whom, and what the issues were. Had the evangelical Edward VI not died in 1553 and been replaced by the Catholic Mary, it is possible that Strange's control of the manor and, especially, the parish, would have been challenged earlier. Evangelical protestantism had paid its first visit to Cirencester in the person of Bishop John Hooper, in 1551, but the death of Edward VI and the accession of the Catholic Mary made him a heretic. He was burned at the stake under the walls of Gloucester Cathedral in 1555.[2]

In 1551–2, Hooper turned Gloucestershire inside-out and upside-down. In two extraordinarily busy years, he visited and made systematic enquiries into the state of the clergy, churchwardens and congregations of every one of the 350 or so parishes in his diocese. His records provide vivid and detailed illumination of a region of the commonwealth of England at a time of momentous, enduring change. John Hooper's visitation and court records

1 F.D. Price (ed.), *The Commission for Ecclesiastical Causes Within the Dioceses of Bristol and Gloucester*, BGAS Records Section (Gateshead 1973), 78.

2 Hooper was influenced by Zwingli through his residence at Zurich in the latter years of Henry VIII, and his continuing correspondence with Bullinger, Zwingli's successor; Norman Birnbaum, 'The Zwinglian Reformation in Zurich', *Past and Present* 15 (April 1959), 36–9, indicates the importance at Zurich of 'the Marital Court … in effect, a Morals Court' and observes that Zwingli's reforms ranged 'merchants, prosperous artisan masters' and 'simple journeymen against patricians'; his main allies at Zurich were the 'petty and middle bourgeois rising up into entrepreneurial roles'.

bear detailed witness to one of the most remarkable social experiments of the English Reformation. They make it possible to follow a great reformer's plans and movements on a day-to-day basis. They matter in this context because they not only framed and conditioned what came next across the whole of Cirencester's greater region to the west, they also refer directly to (and affected) every one of Gloucestershire's communities, not least the town that is the subject of this book.

As soon as he arrived at Gloucester in May 1551, an introductory 'Letter to the Clergy', composed in advance, was copied and sent out to every deanery of Gloucester diocese, for transmission to the parishes. Two kinds of ministers had nothing to fear from reformation, he wrote: 'the one, if they be of sound doctrine apt to teach and to exhort after knowledge, and able to withstand and confute the evill sayers'. The other 'if their life and maners be unculpable', meaning 'sober, modest, keeping hospitality, honest, religious, chaste, not dissolute, angry, nor given to much wine, no fighter, no covetous man, such as governeth well his own house, and giveth an example of vertue and honesty unto other'. The 'dignity and Maiesty of the Order of Priests and Pastors [had] fallen in decay', in Hooper's opinion. The days of priests who 'nourish and keepe a whore or Concubine at home in thy house, or els doth defile other mens beds', hunt with hawk and hounds, get drunk and be a 'haunter of Alehouses and Taverns, of Whores, Cards, Dice, and such like', were at an end. Hooper demanded a return to the exemplary 'Old Priests and Pastors of Christ's Church, [who] did by their truth and gravity subjugate, and bring under the hard necked, and stiff stubborne Ethnickes and cause them to have the same in fear.' Most if not all Gloucestershire districts had at least one notorious priest.

> Let every one of you therefore take good heede to approve your selves faithfull and wise Ministers of Christ, so that when I shall come to visit the Parishioners committed to my Cure and faith from God, and the Kings Maiesty ye be able not only to make answer unto me in that behalfe, but also unto our Lord Jesus Christ … a very streight revenger of his Church. Thus fare you well unto the day of my coming unto you.[3]

The letters were accompanied by three detailed 'interrogatories': one each for ministers, churchwardens and parishioners. By following up the letters with

3 GCL, Hockaday (General), Vol. 33 (1551). Hockaday transcribed it from a manuscript in the Roger Morrice collection at the Williams Library, Gordon Square, London, headed 'A true coppey of Bishop Hooper's Visitation Booke Made By him in AD 1551,1552'. Hockaday thinks it was originally part of GDR no. 5, a hundred pages of visitation records that were originally part of a bound volume, dismembered, thought Hockaday, 'before 1721', probably by Archdeacon Furney. The following account of Hooper's activities is based on my reconstruction of his day-to-day itinerary from Hockaday 33 (GCL) and the records of the ensuing consistory court meetings in the Gloucester Diocesan Registers.

a systematic visitation of all parts of his diocese, Hooper soon established that *anyone* – gentry, ministers, notables, 'better sort' and 'common people' – who failed to live out Hooper's detailed reconstruction of religious thought and practice would be called to answer to the bishop himself at the consistory court at Gloucester Cathedral. If they proved at all ignorant or recalcitrant, Hooper ordered them to perform humiliating public penance in their own parish church, local markets and central towns like Gloucester, Tewkesbury and Cirencester. No attempt to fill the gaping hole left by the dissolutions of monasteries and chantries, and the confusing changes of state policy, came near to matching the systematic overhaul Hooper set in motion.

Unlike the bishops who served the diocese for the next century, Hooper was no respecter of persons. If he found evidence that a gentleman had transgressed, he was summoned to answer the allegation in person, before the bishop. If Hooper was not satisfied, the gentleman was required to perform public repentance just like every common or garden adulterer, swearer of oaths and breaker of public morality and religious peace. This did not endear him to the gentry. No place escaped Hooper's attention. In the year following 1 June 1551, he personally visited every market town and deanery and most other significant centres of population or misdemeanors. In 1551–2 he presided over 511 consistory court cases involving men and women of all ranks. A third of the cases resulted in public penance orders. Processions of penitents became commonplace in the parish churches and markets of Gloucestershire.

Hooper visited Cirencester on Wednesday 10 and Thursday 11 June 1551. Awaiting him were the minister, William Phelpes, churchwardens John Gurney[4] and John Penyngton, and seven parishioners, William Stone,[5] John Fowler, Thomas Webbe,[6] John Saunders, John Walker,[7] John Rogers and John Keele. Also present were ministers, officials and parishioners from the district. The crowd of curious churchwardens and parishioners included 2 from Bagendon; 3 from North Cerney; 3 from Stratton; 3 from Daglingworth; 2 from Duntisbourne Abbots; 4 from Duntisbourne Militis; 4 from Northleach; 2 from Farmington; 2 from Hampnett; 2 from Chedworth; 2 from Rendcombe; 2 from Cotes; 2 from Siddington St Peter; 2 from Siddington Mary; 6 from South Cerney; 2 Driffield; 2 Harnhill; 2 Preston; 3 Ampney Mary; 1 Coln Denis; 1 Coln Rogers; 3 Compton Abdale; 2 Bibury; 4 Fairford; 6 Maiseyhampton; 2 Ampney Crucis; 2 Ampney Peter; 2 Down Ampney; 2 Quennington (no CW); 3 Hatherop; 2 Coln St Aldwyns; 2 Shurborne; 2 Kempsford; 4 Lechlade;

4 If this is the same John Gurney presented in 1563 for 'getting his servant with childe' (GDR 20.57 1563 Visitation), the churchwarden had experienced a fall from grace.

5 *Military Survey 1522*, Abbot Street, 40s.

6 Hockaday 155, 1545: 'Sergeant of the town'.

7 GDR 2a.45: Original Bond to John Hooper Bp of Worc in the sum of £100 by John Strange Clerk & John Walker of Cirncester clothier on his institution to the Rectory of Shipton Moyne).

2 Burthroppe; 2 Southroppe; 2 Eastleach; Painswick 8 yeonomi; Bisley 9 cw; Salperton 4 cw; Miserden 7 cw; Edgeworth 4 cw; Winston 4 cw; Cowley 4 cw; Elkston 6 cw; Brimpsfield 4 cw; Eastington 10 cw; Coberley 3. Robert Strange was not listed, but his sergeant, Thomas Webbe, was there, and Strange took a personal interest in at least one of the cases arising from Hooper's visitation. It concerned his brother John, lately canon of Cirencester Abbey and now rector of Shipton Moigne. On 27 June 1551, 'John Cryppes a witness sworn and examyned saieth [to Hooper] that he hath harde saye that Mr Straunge shuld lyve viciouslye withe oon Katherine Daw by the saying on Henrie Saverie and Thomas Sway and John Davisse.' A month later John Strange called upon four compurgators to exonerate him, but by then the damage was done.[8] No smoke without fire.

Hooper dined at Cirencester the day before his burning at Gloucester in 1555, and it is said that one, at least, of the townspeople was converted by his saintly demeanour.[9] Strange probably observed his arrival and departure from a discreet distance. Strange would remain a dominant force in town affairs until his death in 1588; this chapter will show that cracks began to appear in the 1560s. The Middle Ages would finally end at Cirencester with the deaths of Strange and his 'co-regent', Christopher George, son of Strange's predecessor and lord of the nearby manor of Baunton (d.1597). This chapter tells a tale of the slow death of the old and the emerging contradictions of the new.

By accident or design, Elizabeth I's restoration of a limited Protestant ascendancy meant that 'The machinery of the church', as Christopher Hill once put it, was 'now entirely at the disposal of the crown.' It 'offered itself as an instrument of government independent of Parliamentary control, and with a long tradition of prestige and authority behind it.' And yet, as Hill pointed out, 'if the church was to be of any use to the crown as an instrument of government its prestige must be restored and maintained'.[10] The fly in the ointment was that the diocese of Gloucester never recovered from Mary's removal and execution of Hooper, undoubtedly one of the most visionary and energetic of English reforming bishops. Hooper's successor, the catholic James Brooks, had the courage of his convictions: he later refused to conform to the Elizabethan settlement, and died in prison. His

8 Office v John Straunge incontinency, countered by John Straunge v John Crippes Defamation, 27 June 1551, GDR 6.15, 30–1.

9 Richard Jefferies, 'History of Cirencester', *Wilts and Gloucs Standard* (29 October 1870, citing 'Mr Froude's… history of this period' wrote that 'In the course of his journey [from the Fleet Prison in London to his execution at Gloucester, Hooper] stopped at one of the Inns… to dine', where he encountered 'a woman… who had always hated the truth and spoken all evil she could of him.' Upon meeting him 'she found that both in him and his creed there was more than she supposed… perceiving the cause of his coming she lamented his case with tears and showed him all the friendship she could'.

10 Christopher Hill, 'From Grindal to Laud', in Hill, *Religion and Politics in 17th Century England* (Brighton 1986), 64.

successor, Richard Cheyney, left diocesan government to a succession of avaricious, incompetent or corrupt chancellors, whose historical achievement was to feed grass-roots anticlericalism, and confirm criticism of prelatical religion with interest. The corruption and (under Bishop Goodman in the decades before the civil wars) waywardness of Gloucester diocese is notorious among historians: there is no reason to think it was not notorious at the time. It was one ingredient feeding a third, popular, wave of reformation. This involved the emergence, naming and gradual routinization of sects and strategies for reform from the local bottom up. Diocesan neglect and corruption became a factor in persuading the 'poor townsmen' of Cirencester, as they had been persuaded in the past, that they alone could make their town a Christian commonwealth.[11]

Hooper understood that effective church government depended on respect for the clergy, which meant rooting out notorious bad examples, like Roger Grene, rector of Stratton, who, in 1551, was accused by his parishioners of living an evil life, was admonished by Hooper and ordered to remove a certain woman from his company.[12] Grene kept his head down until Hooper went. In September 1574, parishioners reported that Grene was still 'oftentime overcome with drinke and the parsonage in great decay'.[13] Catholic contemporaries like John Baron of Siddington St Mary and Thomas Taylor of North Cerney were still telling their stoic parishioners in the 1570s that they 'had said mass and did trust to say mass again and that the gospel is not the word of God but doctrine of the church'. Hooper had been generally satisfied if a minister lived a decent life, did not actively defy Hooper's reforms, and lived with his neighbours in peace. He was much concerned with the doctrine of the dozens of Gloucestershire ministers who appeared in his courts in 1551–2, but they came to court in the first place because of the 'decent life' clause. Hooper did not invent the neighbourly abuse, scandals and rumours of sexual

[11] For the decay of Gloucester diocese, the work of F. Douglas Price remains both exemplary and indispensable: figures cited in Price, 'The Administration of Gloucester Diocese 1547–1579', B. Letters, Keble College, Oxford 1939, regarding cases in Gloucester Consistory Court are telling. In the period 1/6/51 to 1/6/52 Hooper heard 511 cases; in only 54 cases did the accused fail to appear and there were only 13 suspensions and exclusions (GDR 6.1–131); from 1/6/61 to 31/12/61 (Chancellor Powell) there were 328 cases, 177 failures to appear and 84 susp. and excl. (GDR 18.13–51); from 1/11/69 to 31/10/70 (Powell) 723 cases, 437 failures to appear, 225 susp. and excl. (GDR 26.5–149); from 27/3/77 to 11/7/79 (Powell) 285 cases, 205 failures to appear, 77 susp. and excl. (GDR 37.148–77). Price found that penance orders varied from 1 in 3 cases under Hooper to 1 in 40 under Powell (53). See also Price, 'Gloucester Diocese under Bishop Hooper', *Trans BGAS* 60 (1938), 51–151; Price, 'The Commission for Ecclesiastical Causes for the Dioceses of Bristol and Gloucester, 1574', *Trans BGAS* 59 (1937) shows clearly that the Commission for Ecclesiastical Causes was 'a body set up by the government for the express purpose of restoring order in an area where local ecclesiastical jurisdiction had broken down' (137).

[12] GA, GDR, 6.14, 6.25.

[13] Price, 'The Commission for Ecclesiastical Causes', 145.

incontinence, adultery and drunkenness that he found in many parishes and every district of his diocese. The intention was to raise communal standards. Had he been allowed to complete his mission, Hooper may well have created, on the scale of an English shire, the kind of communalist discipline that Calvin, Zwingli and Bullinger achieved in the compact, urban communities of Geneva and Zurich.

After Hooper, the Gloucester diocese became what the reformers had always said of the medieval church: indifferent to the everyday lives of ordinary people, incompetently administered, corrupt and unjust. Decay at the top had its grass-roots counterparts in the localities. In 1567 parishioners of Cirencester complained to the bishop that pastoral care was being neglected. The accumulated bequests and donations that once paid the wages of a dozen or more chantry priests had disappeared into the royal treasury twenty years earlier. Their provision of an organist and choirmaster may have lapsed too. The music and singing were silenced – not by communal hostility or indifference to such 'visible signs' as music, but by the sudden dissolution of their mode of production. The manorial cabal did little to fill the vacuum. The tithes of the high altar were sold off piecemeal and the impropriators, who included Christopher George and a local tradesman named Giles Selwyn, were cutting costs to make their investments pay. 'We have but one priest to serve that great cure,' parishioners complained, 'wheras it hath bene alwaies accustomed to have two priests and a deacon' serving the rectory alone.[14] Another depressing sign was that the roof of the chancel (the part of the church belonging to the manorial lord, now to the men to whom they had sold the tithes) was 'ruinous'. Parishioners complained to the bishop 'that for more than a year no one can sit there because the rain comes in'. On 28 July 1570, the bishop's chancellor admonished 'Selwyn, farmer, as he asserts of the rectry' and ordered him to repair the part of the church for which he was responsible.[15]

Giles Selwyn, is described in various records dating from 1557 to his death in 1597 as a 'yeoman', 'butcher', 'clothier' and – in his will – 'vintner'. Inherited status as a yeoman and trade, not craft, was Selwyn's *métier*. He was a middleman who turned his buying and selling skills to grain, vegetables, meat, cloth and wine. If anyone knew Cirencester's various sources and markets, he did. His fortune may have fluctuated: structurally, he belongs with the 'middling' taxpayers in the lists of 1327, 1522 and 1560. At the time of the sudden anti-catholic push in 1570, he was head of a family consisting of his wife Emmot and three daughters, Margaret (aged 9), Alice (4) and Elizabeth (6 months). A son, Giles, and two further daughters each died within weeks of their births in 1563, 1565 and 1569. He was substantial enough to have domestic servants, the death of one of whom is recorded in the burial registers for 1563.[16] Selwyn

14 GDR 20, 57.

15 GDR Vol. 26, 135.

16 Daughter Jone, bap 4/9/63, bur 19/9/64; s. Giles bap 25/8/65, bur 1/9/65; d. Elizabeth bap 1/3/68–9, bur 28/8/70: GA P86; in his will (GA GDR 1598/33), Selwyn commended

made no fewer than ten appearances in diocesan courts between 1557 and 1570.[17] One of these at least may relate to the 'poore people of Cirencester' (among whom Selwyn would certainly have included himself, at least for the purposes of appeals to the state) who were to complain to Privy Council about the 'papist' oligarchy in 1570. He may have purchased a share in the 'rectry' in order to challenge the cabal: he certainly represented the trade community. He appears again in the 1580s, as leader of an attempt by this 'middle sort' of retailers and craftworkers to revive the Guild Merchant.

Responsibility for enquiring into the activities of Giles Selwyn devolved on Thomas Powell, appointed chancellor by Richard Cheyney, in 1565. Unlike Hooper, Cheyney rarely sat himself as judge in the consistory court, and his appointee, Powell, instituted a regime marked by laxity and corruption in the form of commutations in exchange for money.[18] Unlike Hooper, they left the gentry to their own affairs and were willing to let offenders off the public acts of penitence upon which Hooper had always insisted, in exchange for fines.

We know only that Powell's judgement infuriated Selwyn. 'Openly and in full court (he) showed manifest contempt for the judge and his jurisdiction, saying that he could not get justice but injustice in (that) court.' He shouted 'that he would have lawe by them that knowe the lawe ... and that he would the judge were as true a subject as he the said Selwyne is.' He threatened 'that he would not tarrie till he sawe further authoritie'. Powell 'pronounced him manifestly contumacious, and... he was excommunicated in writing'.[19] It is tempting to cast him as a tribune of the middling sort of townspeople: we meet him again in the next chapter, leading the tradesmen and craftsmen in a revival of the Guild Merchant.[20]

The hold of the manorial cabal was weakening, perhaps because their forms of government were unable to deal with problems arising from a growing population, the epidemics and high mortality of the 1550s, and always unpredictable economic conditions.[21] The reference to 'deacons' in 1567 may be an early sign of Calvinist influences that emerged in the 1580s. The sources merely suggest fragmentation of governance into at least four documented factions: catholic, 'proto-Anglican', 'non-separatist Calvinist' and 'separatist-Anabaptist'. The leaking roof of the chancel was symptomatic of decay that affected villages and towns throughout Gloucester diocese. Another sign of the fragmentation of religious community emerges from a series of cases of 1569–74, at first before Chancellor Powell at the Gloucester Consistory Court,

his 'soule into the hands of almighty God my creator, maker, preserver, redeemer and sanctifier and my body to bee decently buryed in the church yeard'; he signed his will.

17 GDR Vol. 11, 34, 42, 47, 51 (1557); GDR B4/1/657 (1557); Vol. 16, 36 (1563), 333 (1566); Vol. 24, 508 (1569), 723 (1570); Vol. 9, 50 (1570).

18 Price, 'Commission for Ecclesiastical Causes'.

19 Hockaday, 'Cirencester 1570'; GA GDR Vol. 26, 139.

20 See below, Chapter 11.

21 See below, Chapter 10.

and then before the powerful gentlemen who served as the queen's commissioners for ecclesiastical causes in Gloucestershire.

The cases involved at least eighteen people who (for differing reasons) were loudly and publicly absenting themselves from church. Radical separatism is signified by two tradesmen, James Ireland and Thomas Bradford, who first appeared before the diocesan consistory court on 23 March 1569/70.[22] They objected to 'abominations' at the parish church, especially the wearing by the priest of 'the coope and the surplice'. Bradford stayed away because he could not 'be edyfied by a godly and learned man' there. Christopher Haigh casts Bradford as the leader of a 'conventicle at Cirencester'. Over the next five years the consistory court and commissioners for ecclesiastical causes in Gloucestershire interviewed, interrogated and imprisoned several other members, whose testimony suggests this was not a sect of leaders and followers. They include several more men and, perhaps most auspiciously, at least five remarkably courageous and articulate women.

Haigh mentions Alice (or Agnes) Long, who 'regarded the meeting as an alternative to church, and told the visitation commissioners that "they should not command her to any parish church, and that she would choose whether she will go"'.[23] Like Bradford and Ireland, Alice Long was a member of the 'sect of disorderly persons' reported to Privy Council in 1578 by four commissioners for ecclesiastical causes, Sir Giles Poole, Henry Poole, Richard Baynham and Richard Grene. Their practice was 'to assemble in a desolate place nere unto a wood side, appointing unto themselves a minister and a private order of service, according to their own fantasies'.

Two months later, in May 1570, the opposition factions were presented with a common enemy. A papal bull declaring the Queen of England an excommunicate heretic was nailed to the door of the bishop of London's palace. News reached Cirencester in as long as it took a horseman or carrier to make the journey; it presented an irresistible opportunity to attack the cabal. A party calling itself 'the poor townsmen' came together and petitioned Privy Council for relief from 'the tyranie of infected members called Papists as toller(at)ed have impoisoned a nomber of good subjects' in the town.[24] The 'chiefest' of men behind these 'execrable doings', they claimed, were 'Nicholas Phillipps common serjeant of the said towne… and servant to Sir Henry Jerningham…

22 What follows is from Price (ed.), *Commission for Ecclesiastical Causes for the Dioceses of Bristol and Gloucester, 1574*, 61–185.

23 Haigh, *The Plain Man's Pathways to Heaven: Kinds of Christianity in Post-Reformation England, 1570–1640* (Oxford 2007), 40, citing GA GDR 40, fo. 164–v; Bradford, Agnes Long and 'John Cox and his wyff' were reported by Bishop Cheyney in 1576: R.H. Clutterbuck, 'State Papers Respecting Bishop Cheyney and the Recusants of the Diocese of Gloucester', *Trans BGAS* 5 (1881), 235.

24 'Petition of the Inhabitants of Cirencester to the Privy Council', TNA, SPD Dom. Eliz., Vol. LXXI no. 30; transcribed in Hockaday 156: 'Cirencester', 1570. See also Price, 'Commission for Ecclesiastical Causes', 62.

as also Robert Straunge, Justice of the Pax, Christopher George Clarke of the Peace [and] other their adherents a great number': the heads and subalterns of the manorial cabal. The 'poor people' took particular exception to 'a sermon of late made by one Horton', who preached that 'the sacred word enclosed within the Bible [is] false and full of errors (as untruly translated), and therefore not mete amongst the common people to be reade or taught'. We saw earlier that Horton was not the only defiantly 'survivalist' catholic minister in the district. Roger Grene at Stratton may have been too intoxicated to notice, but John Baron at Siddington St Mary and Thomas Taylor of North Cerney may well have been preaching a similar message. 'Utterly detesting all such erroneous and execrable opinions as before their eyes is daily practiced,' certain of the 'poore townsmen' stood up in church and complained, only to be threatened with 'imprisonment of bodie, feare and death, and confiscation of theire goods, and called tumultuous rebels'.[25] The papal bull offered an opportunity to suggest that loyal 'common people' and 'poor townspeople' were being persecuted by rich, disloyal papists.

Strange's faction had probably controlled the vestry as well as the manor since 1548; Christopher George had a share in the tithes, but was not prosecuted for neglect of the chancel and pastoral care in the consistory court.[26] In the military metaphor that came so naturally to contemporaries when they spoke of social structures, the 'poor people' called the three big men who ruled the town '*captains* that are most pernicious in that commonwealth'. They urged the queen's privy counsellors 'to remove [and] weed out the said persons [... wicked and traitorous papists ...] from having any authoritie or to live amongst Christian people'. There was enough circumstantial evidence and, no doubt, common talk that they were catholics, to justify an enquiry, the responsibility for which was passed down the line to Bishop Cheyney, whose discretion could be relied on. The immediate result of the petition is not clear, but within months a blow was struck for the commonalty when Cirencester was made a parliamentary borough with the right to elect two MPs.[27] A struggle then ensued concerning the franchise: who had a right to a voice in the selection and election of candidates? By 1570 the achievements of the long fifteenth century were gone. The interregnum of 'survivalist' government by the Strange cabal was drawing to a close.

F. Douglas Price identified the Bradford–Ireland group ('puritans') with 'the poore townesmen' who complained about the papists in 1570,[28] but the sources indicate that several factions of wholesalers, craftworkers and tradesmen were brought together momentarily by a common desire to discredit the Strange regime. Giles Selwyn, for example, was never accused of belonging with intran-

25 The quotes are from the transcription in Hockaday 156.

26 'The answer of Christopher George Gent def. to the byll of Complainant of Richard Masters Esq. complt.', PRO Court of Requests 72/61; Hockaday, 'Cirencester 1578'.

27 Beecham, *History of Cirencester*, 171; see below, Chapter 7.

28 Price, 'Commission for Ecclesiastical Causes', 36.

sigent separatists like Bradford, Ireland and others, yet he was from the same class of petty traders and shopkeepers. Bradford was called into the consistory court again in 1572, charged with two other shopkeepers, William Whiting and Thomas Restall, that they 'let open their shoppes uppon the ymber dayes as though hit had not ben fyshe dayes'. They were butchers, but with quite different religious views, as would become clear.[29] A warning by the bishop to obey the rector and churchwardens by closing their businesses on holy days and Sundays was ignored, and a year later they were charged by Mr Aldsworth, the curate, with refusing to attend church and continuing to open their shops on 'fyshe dayes'. Restall and his associates made their point and went back to church, but Bradford and Whittinge refused to take 'a corporall othe upon the Evangelist' that they would mend their ways, and were imprisoned at Gloucester Castle.

The minister (it is not clear who appointed him, but he may have been installed as a sop to the complainants of 1570) offended at least two groups of parishioners, representing very different 'protestant' factions, united momentarily by common hostility to the Catholicism of the old regime and the contingent pretext of the pope's excommunication of the queen. The survivalists, led for decades by Robert Strange and his chief ally, Christopher George, were now a gentrified and increasingly discredited remnant. They still held the reins of market and police, but could not live forever. Aldsworth may, at first, have shared the martyred Hooper's radicalism with regard to 'visible signs'. Thomas Restall was a leading member of a group from what the next generation would call 'the better sort of inhabitants'. They were orthodox Elizabethans: God- and queen-fearing middle-of-the-road protestants, moderate and willing to compromise with the state and the now chastened oligarchy. They were offended by Aldsworth's insistence that communion bread and wine were only symbolically the flesh and blood of Christ. Now the church was officially recognized to be English, not foreign and overly Latinate, nothing more needed to change. Sturdy supporters of a moderate Elizabethan settlement, Restall, John George, John Morse, Thomas Monox and William Vyner were called before the ecclesiastical commissioners in November 1574, to explain their refusal to attend church. They complained 'that the minister will not minister the communion according to the booke of comen prayer and the injunctions'. Their centre of social gravity was higher than that of the conventiclers: Monox was described as 'gent' once, in a 1559 prosecution in the Hundred court for fighting a duel with John Marshall at nearby Culkerton.[30] Two years later he served as clerk in the market courts, and perhaps for the vestry.[31] The first reference to him in the parish register records the burial of his daughter, Ann, on 25 August 1562. A month later his daughter Elizabeth was baptized. Every two years from 1562

29 GCL RV 79.7, View of Frankpledge for Borough of Cirencester, 1560.

30 Beecham, *History of Cirencester*, 168.

31 GDR Vol. 17, 115, 148, 220, 261, 267, 277.

to 1572 his wife Joan gave birth to another child, who was religiously baptized at the parish church.[32] Restall, George, Morse, Monox and Vynor were back in their pews as soon as moderation was restored.

For them, the new curate Mr Aldsworth was taking reformation too far. Conformists of the 'better sort', they were sturdy contributors to local civic and religious life.[33] Their objections were taken seriously. The judge summoned Aldsworth to explain himself; he 'confess'd part therof' admitting that 'He ministred the communion with comen bread and… did not weare the surplesse for that he was licensed to do by the High Commission at London.' Aldsworth may have been trying to take up where Zwinglian John Hooper had been cut off fifteen years before. Monox, John George, Viner, Morse and Restall disliked Aldsworth's plain preaching style, lack of ceremonial and demystification of transubstantiation. The commissioners asked to see his licence. Aldsworth relented. By the end of November he had 'lately conformed, for the which (the parishioners) were glad and desired (his) lordship's favour for any offence passed'.[34] The moderates had their say, but as we shall see, circumstances were calling for sterner communal medicine.

Aldsworth was the second in a list of no fewer than eleven ministers who served the parish without being instituted as vicars or rectors from the death of the Catholic Phelps, in 1558, to the end of the century. The high turnover owed something to the fact that since the accession of Elizabeth I the rectory (which had belonged to the abbey, and then passed to the crown) was in the hands of absentee lay owners, like Christopher George, who viewed it as a means of controlling the vestry. Tithes, where they were applicable at all,[35] belonged to the wealthy families who had bought up most of the property belonging to the abbey in the decades following the dissolution. Several were conservative Catholics or (like Monox, Viner, Morse and Restall) 'Anglicans' who believed the key differences between the old church and the new concerned language and leadership. The pope was replaced by the monarch. The abbey was gone. Why change anything else? The wealthy businessmen and gentry who owned the rectory and the tithes had little interest in religious novelty, and might have thought it wise to employ men on short contracts so that they could be dismissed immediately if they caused trouble. Aldsworth lasted another two years, and was replaced by William Woodlande in 1576. He was followed by John Mortimer (1580), John Stone (1581), Nicholas Kekke

32 GA P86 IN 1/1: 19/9/65, 5/10/67, 19/9/65, 5/10/67 (bur 14/10/67), 16/6/69, 30/5/72; his wife 'Mistresse Joane Monox, Wydow' bur 18/2/1615.

33 'Willm Vinar' was listed as a juror in 1560: GCL RV 79.7; John Morse, sidesman at Tetbury parish church 1548 (GDR 4: 84); sidesman at Cirencester 1551 and 1559 (GDR 5: 24, 176).

34 GA GDR Vol. 31, 81–7; GDR 26, 137 (Morse).

35 'Most of the lands in the parish did belong to the abbey, for which reason they are exempted for payment of tithes, which would otherwise be £300 a year': Sir Robert Atkyns, *The Ancient and Present State of Gloucestershire* (Gloucester 1712), 342.

(1585) and Philip Jones (1586). We shall meet Jones, a fiery, class-obsessed preacher, in due course.

Aldsworth was persuaded to moderate his 'Presbyterian' iconoclasm. He was a few years ahead of his time. This reversal may have led to more pressure being applied to the Bradford–Ireland group, who regarded the new regime as little different from the old and absolutely refused to submit to its rules and rituals. They would not attend church, refused to have their children baptized, and insisted on their duty to keep their businesses open on Sundays and feast days. This must have caused quite a stir in the town, especially the paradoxical belief of this sect that it was their religious duty to conduct that most profane of activities, trade, on holy days. These were indeed what Christopher Hill termed 'the industrious sort of people' who believed their ministers should reflect their needs and beliefs.

Obstinate radicals like them had been burned as Lollards a century earlier. Thomas Bradford appeared again in the consistory court in 1570, when he explained that he refused to attend church because 'he cannot be edified by a godlie and learned man' there. Two years later he, James Ireland and others confessed to working on feast days and holy days; Bishop Cheyney admonished and let them go. In November 1573 they were still refusing to close their shops on holy days and to receive communion at the parish church. Their fellow sectarian, William Phelpes, told the commission in 1574 that he 'would have malefactors and papists excluded out of the church', suggesting that catholic influence, at least as Phelpes understood it, remained strong. Thomas Bradford repeated his reasons for not attending church and was sent back to jail: he 'saith for that the minister doth followe men's tradicion and do not minister to Gode's word'. Whiting refused the commission's order to baptize his children, on the grounds that the church font was 'a wicked and abominable trowe'. He 'arogantlie sayd that he would followe the quenes majesties lawes and her highnes proceedinges so far further as the same did agree to gods worde and not otherwyse'. 'He utterlye mislyketh to have godfathers and godmothers to the baptising of children.' The commissioners sent him back 'to (Gloucester) castell … for his unsemely wordes'.

His wife Elizabeth kept the torch lit: she refused to 'have her child christened for that it is superstitious and not agreeable to Godes word and that it was devised by Pope Pius'. She was in court that day with Joan Arnold, who affirmed she 'would not attend church for that the service of God is not ministred accordinge to the worde, and for that the minister doth bid holidaies and fasting daies'. Ann Bradford failed to turn up on this occasion and was excommunicated. She must have been arrested and sent to the castle, for she remained adamant at a meeting of the court on 21 December and was 'remanded' until 13 January. Elizabeth Whiting was not committed to join her husband in the cells at Gloucester Castle, perhaps because the court was reluctant to imprison a mother with a baby, and hoped she might be turned by an encounter with powerful Cotswold gentlemen. She was ordered 'to repaire to my lord Chandois, Sir Giles Poole and Sir John Tracie, for her enlargement'.

These men, the heaviest of the heavyweight gentry of Gloucestershire, had been called in to add secular force to the floundering diocesan authorities.[36] The commissioners had secular powers to interrogate and punish that were not available to the church courts.

In February a fourth woman, Ann Cole, and another Cirencester resident named John Butler were sworn 'before Sir [Giles] Poole, Richard Baynham Esq. and Richard Green' at the Poole house at Sapperton, 'concerning the christening of Whyttinge's child'. 'Finding greate obstinacy in the said Anne, it was therefore ordered that she be committed to the gaile of Cirencestre' until 10 March, when the gentlemen would interview her again. A month later she again refused to 'receyve the communion … because she is not worthy thereof for want of lerning to know what she doth receive until such time as God shall move her'.[37] Asked again on 15 April, Anne Cole 'sayd … she hathe declared that heretofore. And after many wordes by her uttering touching her opinion not worthy noting' the gentlemen gave her another month 'in consideracon her simplicitie … hopeing she will receive one this side the next court' in May.[38]

Sir Giles Poole met Elizabeth Whiting privately on several occasions on which she seemed to agree to have her child baptized, only to come up with an excuse for not having done so. In December 1574 Poole assigned responsibility for having Whiting's child baptized to 'the churchwardens, constables and two other of the substantiall inhabitaunts of Cicester'. When this failed 'the minister, churchwardens, constable and *five* parishioners were ordered to take the child themselves to be christened'.[39] Her husband remained in Gloucester jail, proving his obstinacy at another hearing in March 1575, when he told the commissioners 'there is more tyranie nowe in these daies used than ever there was'. The millenarian underpinnings of his belief were disclosed when he 'cried out with a loud voice and said that God would take vengeaunce uppon the majestrattes, rulers and governors of this realm and wuld rote out both prince and people for the mayntenaunce of idolatrie, supersticon and all other abomination and wickedness'. The gentlemen decided that the castle cells were too good for him. He was 'comited to the comon gaile of Gloucester, there to remayne until the said commissioners, or others there colleagues shall take further order for his enlargement'.[40] 'Enlargement', in this context, could very well mean whippings, or the rack.

A fortnight later later Giles Poole had Elizabeth Whiting brought to Sapperton, where he asked her again if her child had been baptized. He had,

36 Price (ed.), *Commission for Ecclesiastical Causes*, 64, 72, 77–8, 141–3; for decay of ecclesiastical authority see Price, 'Commission for Ecclesiastical Causes', 93–4, and for the decay of civil authority at this time, 93, n. 195.

37 Price (ed.), *Commission for Ecclesiastical Causes*, 77.

38 *Ibid*, 80.

39 *Ibid*, 134.

40 *Ibid*, 65, 78.

she said, but not at Cirencester. The child had been baptized 'by one Woodland, minister at Hawxbury, on the lord's day last, as she termed it'. Poole and his fellow commissioners were suspicious. Why would she have travelled across the wolds to the sprawling clothworker parish of Hawkesbury, when the job could be done just as well at Cirencester? Who, they asked, were the godparents? It became clear that all their coercion would not change her views. She said she 'utterly mislyked of and would not have [godparents] so termed, but cauled witnesses to the baptising'. As for the baptism, 'she was not present thereat', it 'being done by the procurement of the ministre contrarye to her husband's will'.[41] Asked why she still refused to take communion, she answered that 'she wyll not be tyed unto tymes and for other causes which she wold wyshe to be reformed'. Poole asked her again and she said 'she was content to receive at the handes of a minister that were a messenger sent from God, the evill being putt away and [the communion being administered only to] sanctes'.

The point made by these early 'dissenters' was that not even the most powerful men in the county would convince them if it went against the inner voice of conscience, something closely resembling the 'inner voice' of the later Quakers. Oddly patient with the women's recalcitrance, Poole ordered them to reform and return a month later.[42] There is even a hint that Poole found himself respecting these quietly defiant and 'simple' women.

Voices like theirs disappear from the sources – though probably not from the town – until, in the 1650s, we encounter the *Sufferings* of Quakers like Theophila Townsend.[43] Stereotyping them along later sectarian lines is reasonable – they probably founded the Anabaptist tradition that resurfaced in the 1630s and is well evidenced at Cirencester in the 1650s. At this time it may be more accurate to describe them as 'seekers' convinced that God, no respecter of persons, spoke exclusively to the private consciences of individual women and men. At the very least it must be said that this 'opinion' attracted some strong women.

Sir Giles Poole was a reputed 'cavalier'. A witness in a gentry divorce case heard before John Hooper in 1551–2 reported Alice Compton, wife of Walter Compton Esq., as saying 'she had lever kepe Sir Gieles Poole's hounds and hawks than to be Walter Compton's wife and that Walter Compton was a lusty child, but Sir Gieles Poole was a frowlicker'. Alice personally confessed 'she had received a bracelet with gold of the said Sir Gieles Poole' and another witness testified 'that he had hard oon Thomas Webb now departed, this depo-

41 *Ibid*, 37, 57–60, 74–6, 81–7; Price, 'Commission for Ecclesiastical Causes', 161ff.

42 Price, *Commission*, 80.

43 For Cirencester Quakers, see Rollison, *Local Origins*, Ch. 7; 'Theophila Townsend's testimony concerning the Life, Death and Sufferings of Amariah Drewet lately deceased', in *Some Testimonies of the Life, Death and Sufferings of Amariah Drewet of Cirencester in Gloucestershire, lately deceased* (London 1687), 8–9, conveys something of Townsend's confident voice.

nents fellowe in howsehold in the howse of the said Walter (Compton) saie as they were bothe in bed together and that his dame was a whore and that Sir Gieles Poole had to do with her'. He had also heard 'oon West', formerly servant to Walter and now to Poole, say as they went hunting that his dame was a 'whoor bitch'.[44] Poole may have been past 'frolicking' in the 1570s, but another distinguishing mark of Hooper's short spell as bishop had been a willingness to take on the gentry of the diocese, whom he expected to set a good example. Those who followed him were not so courageous, which may be why Poole's neighbour, Christopher George, was never summoned to answer the allegations concerning the neglect of the parish of Cirencester.

Post-Hooper officials of Gloucester diocese needed the support of the secular magnates to impose the Elizabethan settlement on recusants from the catholic right and the protestant left. The group of 16 men and women investigated by Poole and his fellow commissioners represent the first 'dissenters', the radical, often millenarian, stream of English protestantism that was never to be absent from the town and Seven Hundreds from the 1560s to the 1650s. A more moderate – non-separatist, presbyterian – congregationalism gradually became dominant at Cirencester after the 1580s. Yet religion remained a mercurial and unpredictable ingredient in a complex and shifting, even somewhat chaotic, field of force. One thing is certain: the 'dissenters' came from the middle ranks of the trade and craft community – as, indeed, did tradesmen who filled the minor positions in the government of the town – the Monoxes, Restalls, Viners and Morses – possibly ex-catholics, or subalterns of the survivalist manorial cabal, who applied the most conservative reading possible to the hazy requirements of the Elizabethan settlement. The new occupant of Abbey House, Thomas Master, seems to have become identified as a leader of this conformist branch of the bourgeoisie. Above them was the oligarchy, the powerful but ageing *bons bourgeois* Stranges, Chapperlens and Georges, with their survivalist traditions.

In Chapter 11 it will be suggested that the survivalists' last stand took place in the 1580s. In the wake of the movement to dislodge the 'papist' oligarchs following the papal bull of 1570, the Guild Merchant movement was revived under the leadership of Giles Selwyn. The issues may well have had something to do with national politics, in that the struggle clearly reappeared in the decade after the town had been granted the status of Parliamentary Borough, with what, in the eighteenth century, would be called a 'pot-walloper' franchise: 'the right to vote belonged to every householder who had lived in the town for at least six months and was not receiving alms'.[45] Strange's son, Michael, was now married to the daughter of a knight, Sir Anthony Hungerford, his partner in purchases of the old abbey buildings in the 1540s. Strange

44 GDR Walter Compton v Alice Compton his wife Divorce 12, 19, 28 Nov., 4, 7, 14, 23 Dec. 1551.

45 R.W. Jenkins, 'The Cirencester Contest', *Trans BGAS* 92 (1973), 158.

had been appointed as bailiff by the last abbot, and was reappointed by every succeeding lord up to the most recent, Sir John Danvers, who purchased the town in 1563, and with whom the queen lodged when she visited Cirencester in August 1592.[46] Danvers was a member of the earl of Essex's retinue, and was knighted by Essex in 1591. His son was executed in March 1601 for participating in the Essex rebellion.[47] The evidence suggests that Strange was very much the representative of the traditional manorial authority-structures that had maintained their grip on the town, by appointment of the Crown, since the Reformation – and, indeed, since the reign of Richard I.

From the late 1560s to the 1580s a gradually emerging 'party' of businessmen, artisans and retailers, some 'dissenters' and separatists, a majority not, challenged a 'papist' triumvirate. Divisions between survivalist *majores* like Strange and George, and *mediocres* like Selwyn and his supporters meant that, for whatever reasons, the customary duties of the 'better' and 'middle' sorts to work together for communal harmony were, demonstrably, not being fulfilled. In economic and demographic circumstances to be more fully explicated in due course, failure of pastoral care and local government created 'murmuring' among the resident population, threatening dissolution of good order into class struggle of the lower ranks of the commonalty against their employers. The gaps that had always existed between these 'layers' or 'levels' of the trade community were becoming ideological as well as material and political. In the midst of this religious fragmentation was an increasingly millenarian, prophetic element, a conviction that the troubled times through which the town was passing were signs that the *last daies* were imminent. Events at Cirencester in the late 1570s were to suggest they might be right.

46 'Her highness lodged at Sir John Danvers new House …', 'Queen Elizabeth's Progress in Gloucestershire', transcription of 'MS Book in the possession of the Corporation of Gloucester', *Gloucestershire Notes and Queries*, IV, 379.

47 Baddeley, *A History*, 239–40.

10

Phoenix arising: crises and growth, 1560–1660

Now the red pestilence strikes all trades in Rome
And occupations perish.
Shakespeare, *Coriolanus* III, i

Before considering what eventually replaced the Strange regime – the communal revival of the later sixteenth and first half of the seventeenth centuries – it is necessary to explore the economic and demographic contexts with which all the inhabitants of late sixteenth-century England had to deal as a matter of course. New sources now make it possible to reconstitute aspects of communal experience that can only be deduced from earlier sources. This chapter focuses on two apparently paradoxical themes, a relentless series of severe mortality crises in a context of long-term population growth. Mortality crises had always been part of urban experience. This chapter chronicles a continuing tradition of minor visitations and the incidence, in 1577–9, 1597 and possibly the 1550s and 1621–3, of mortality crises more acute than any since the Black Death. This biological regime impacted directly on religious sensibilities and communal administration and governance, for as Keith Wrightson writes, with reference to a devastating outbreak of the most feared disease of the age at Newcastle in 1636, in the eyes of contemporaries 'the ultimate cause of the plague was "God's wrathful displeasure … to the Communaltie, to the Kingdom, Citie or place where it is"'.[1]

In the second half of the sixteenth century, English population began to grow for the first time since the thirteenth century. The evidence suggests that, from 1570 to 1660, the Seven Hundreds hovered on the verge of ecological crisis comparable with that of 1250–1350, when war between the abbey and the townspeople had exploded into violence and murder. Evidence relating

[1] 'The dystopic vision of the plague served to lay bare and dramatize some of the deepest anxieties of the time': Wrightson, *Ralph Tailor's Summer: A Scrivener, his City and the Plague* (Yale 2011, forthcoming), Ch. 7, citing Robert Jenison, *Newcastle's Call*, 59–60; I am grateful to Keith Wrightson for allowing me to read *Ralph Tailor's Summer* in MS, and for permission to quote from it.

to Cirencester and its region supports the 'underlying crisis' model. In the national narrative, numbers did not collapse as they had done in the fourteenth century. As E.A. Wrigley puts it, early fourteenth-century England had been 'closer to a state of "bare subsistence" than at any other period in subsequent history'. National population halved in the fourteenth century and continued to decline in the fifteenth. In retrospect the collapse of the fourteenth and fifteenth centuries was 'a challenge [that] was met' – eventually. 'Five centuries later,' writes Wrigley, 'the country was partway through the period conventionally termed the industrial revolution. Population was sixty *per cent* higher than at the medieval peak' of c.1300, and population growth was faster than in any earlier period for which records survive.[2]

The turning-point in this 'recovery to economic (and demographic) growth' occurred on a national scale in the period from the Reformation to the civil wars. Historians have shown that, overall, population *and* resources grew in this period, but very unevenly in timing and location. The experience of the Seven Hundreds of Cirencester, likewise uneven in timing and location, was not, I shall suggest, untypical. In some ways it was archetypal. Contemporary survey and parish register data show that the population of Gloucestershire grew by 54 percent from 1563 to 1603 and by 72 percent from 1563 to 1650. From 1563 to 1603, growth was highest in manufacturing towns (+74%) and small rural parishes (+67%), lowest in market towns (+38%). Cirencester had always depended on immigration to revive its fortunes after mortality crises; we shall see that this was never truer than in the last third of the sixteenth century.[3] Migration from rural districts to rural industrial parishes seems to have accelerated a little later, from 1603 to 1650. By 1650 the clothing districts a few miles west of Cirencester held double their populations in 1563. By contrast, the rural parishes of the Seven Hundreds hardly grew at all in the five decades to 1650. Cirencester itself was like the industrial districts in that its population was 77 percent higher in 1650 than in 1563; it was like the rural villages of its hundred in that the new level of 3,000–3,500 inhabitants was reached by 1603. These two factors alone – continuing overall population growth and routine migration from villages to manufacturing towns and industrial districts – are sufficient to explain an urgent need for more effective local governance than appears to have been evident at Cirencester before c.1570. Also relevant to local government, as we shall see, was the constant insecurity of this growth.

About the middle of the sixteenth century, following a century of sustained growth, traditional markets for English cloth were destabilized by events on the continent.[4] Routinely mercurial and unreliable markets, however, did not

2 E.A. Wrigley, 'The Transition to an Advanced Organic Economy: Half a Millennium of English Agriculture', *Econ Hist Rev* 59:3 (August 2006), 438.

3 See below, Chapter 13.

4 Robert Brenner, *Merchants and Revolution: Commercial Change, Political Conflict and London's Vverseas Traders, 1550–1653* (Cambridge 1993), 4–5.

lead to a contraction of the populations of native manufacturing districts. On the contrary, their populations grew faster than anywhere. As noted above, the populations of Cirencester, Bisley and Longtree, the hundreds most committed to manufacturing for national and international markets, increased by 75 percent from 1563 to 1650. This meant 75 percent more individuals and households involved in some way in the production of woollen cloth for export; in practice 75 percent more inhabitants affected by booms and slumps in the 'vend of cloth'. The town grew by a similar margin. Succeeding chapters will show that the town went through something of a revolution in communal governance in this period, achieving a hard-won unity that would ultimately be destroyed by the complete inability of James I and Charles I to comprehend the nature of their kingdom and adjust their governance accordingly. The personalities, forms and achievements of this revolution cannot be fully understood without some knowledge of what might be thought of as the bass-line of a developing symphony: echoing crises of overproduction, periodic unemployment, intensified labour migration, dearth and disease that affected all classes but ultimately killed mainly the poor. Bear in mind that Cirencester had been through and risen out of many such crises in the previous three centuries. The flames that routinely scorched and burned this town were mortality crises associated with crises of production and trade; the ashes were the individuals and households who died in visitations of dearth and disease. The phoenix was immigration. What attracted immigrants of a sufficient number and quality to replace those who died or moved on? This chapter reconstitutes the demographic and economic conditions within which the governments of late sixteenth- and early seventeenth-century England had to operate.

Evidence abounds for the social 'discontentments' of c.1550–1660. Markets for cloth manufactured in villages and townships of north Wiltshire, the Stroudwater Valleys and the Vale of Berkeley were chronically unpredictable, and became more so in the 1570s. Markets for the best Stroudwater Scarlets usually held longest, which meant that the Stroudwater communities were not at first as badly affected as some of their neighbours by the looming crisis. In fact, a long secular growth cycle, of steadily expanding exports of manufactured goods in an epoch of demographic stasis, was at an end. By then a well-established regional capital of English clothmaking, Cirencester and the districts upon which it depended were especially affected by periodic crises of overproduction caused by growing population and intense unpredictability of markets. The prosperity of Cirencester and Stroudwater weavers depended on what was happening in Antwerp, Cologne and Amsterdam, or at Cadiz or the eastern Mediterranean, or, later, New England and Virginia. Over decades of slow but sustained population growth, more men, women and children of the region turned to some specialty in the conversion of wool into finished cloth. The poorer specialties (spinning, carding, fulling, eventually weaving) increased in numbers relative to households at the end where large fortunes (and losses) were made, the mercers, clothiers, clothmen and, above all, the men in possession of water-powered mills. There was a steady polarization of local society into wealthy clothiers and proliferating household units of production. Population increase in the clothworking districts meant increase in the number of individuals and households at the poor end of the industry.

Every region experienced symptoms of steady population growth differently. Young men and women were drawn from the villages towards the clothworking towns. It was an age of new 'projects', as the eminent agrarian historian, Joan Thirsk, showed. The Seven Hundreds were bitten by this bug, as were their neighbours. New commodities like tobacco later sustained large numbers of seasonal workers across the North Wolds at Winchcombe. Iron smelting in the Forest of Dean nourished new and self-confident communities in the late sixteenth and early seventeenth centuries, but only within its own orbits. Development, even within one English county, was very uneven. Cloth mattered particularly because it sustained whole districts containing many communities. If it collapsed (as it could) thousands of households, hundreds of hamlets, villages, manufacturing towns, regional capitals like Salisbury and Cirencester and cities like Bristol and London would be affected. My generation saw centuries-old mining communities slowly die when the pits closed.[5] There were times in the 1580s when it seemed as if a whole region could die. Let us first consider the population history.

The estimate for 1404 is impossible to check and that of 1563 (1,440), based on a contemporary estimate of 320 occupied households, appears anomalous. Uncertainties aside, it is clear enough that the long-term movement from c.1550 and c.1650 was expansion, from a late medieval base of 2,000–2,500 to 3,000–3,500 inhabitants: modest (slightly less than national growth, or that of the manufacturing districts) yet sturdy growth. In 1563 the regional economy was still recovering from the disintegration of northern European cloth markets in 1551–2. It is conceivable that the 'census' of 1563, however it was conducted, caught the town at a momentary low. In 1578–9, as we shall see, the town's population was reduced by nearly 900 (a third) in eighteen months. If a census had been held in mid-1579, there would have been many fewer residents than in 1551 (2,438) and 1603 (3,069). There are no registers of baptisms and burials to tell us if a comparable crisis occurred in the 1550s, causing temporary depopulation. As will become clear, Cirencester (by now even more a distant 'suburb' of London) was highly susceptible to sudden epidemics of death. It may have experienced one in the 1550s, the effects of which were registered in the low estimate of households in 1563. National trends are a poor indicator for towns like these, which always showed extraordinary powers of recovery as temporarily depopulated streets and households were rapidly filled by immigrants.

5 The comparison is not far-fetched; as A.J. and R.H. Tawney wrote in 'An Occupational Census of the Seventeenth Century', *Econ Hist Rev* 5:1 (1934–5), 46, 'Water power in the seventeenth century had in a small way the same influence in attracting and maintaining a relatively dense population as the coalfields were to acquire in the nineteenth.'

Table 10.1. Population estimates, 1404–1801[6]

Date	Unit	Number	Multiplier	Estimate
1404	Households	490	x 4.5	2,205
1547	'Howsling people'	1400	x 1.67	2,338
1551	Comm.	1,460	x 1.67	2,438
1563	HH	320	x 4.5	1,440
1603	Comm.	1,825+6+7	x 1.67	3,069
1608	A/B Men	355		
1650	Families	700	x 4.5	3,150
1671	HH	603	x 4.5	2,713
1676	Comm.	1745+155	x 1.67	3,173
1712	Inhabitants	4,000		4,000
1779	Inhabitants	3,878		3,878
1801	Inhabitants	4,130		4,130

It is an axiom of this book that Cirencester's size was a function of its traffic – with the villages and towns of north Wiltshire and the Seven Hundreds, with London, Bristol, Gloucester, the clothiers and tailors of Berkshire and boatmen of the Thames Valley, with the 'vend' (markets) of England and overseas. The vitality of the fifteenth-century elite memorialized in the chapels and nave suggests that the estimate of 1404 may accurately describe its equilibrium size (how many merchants? How many mercers, drapers, artisans, labourers, shepherds, innkeepers, alehouses, taverners, victuallers, tailors, smiths, bakers, musicians etc.?): 2,000–2,500. In 1547 chantry commissioners enquired how many 'howsling people' were served by the great parish church whose services they were in the business of ransacking: 1,400 communicants, confirmed inhabitants over the age of 16. Assuming a third of the population were unconfirmed children, the raw figure should be multiplied by 1.67, giving a total population of 2,338.

Four years later, in 1551, Bishop John Hooper visited the town to enquire into the ecclesiology, theology, qualifications, pastoral habits and moral tone of

6 Sources: 1547: Sir John Maclean, 'Chantry Certificates, Gloucestershire', *Trans BGAS* 8 (1883–4); 1551: James Gairdner, 'Bishop Hooper's Visitation of Gloucester', *Eng Hist Rev* 19 (1904); 1563: 'Furney MS B', BGAS Library, GCL; 1603: BL Harl. Mss 594–5, 'A Survey of the Diocese of Gloucester, 1603', trans. Alicia Percival, ed. W.J. Sheils, in *An Ecclesiastical Miscellany*, Pubs. of BGAS, Record Series, Vol. XI (1976), 68–102; 1608: John Smyth, *The Names and Surnames of all the Able and Sufficient Men in Body fit for his Majesty's Service in the Wars, in the Month of August, 1608, in the Sixth Year of the Reign of James the First*, ed. Sir John Maclean (Gloucester 1902); 1650: C.R. Elrington, 'The Survey of Church Livings in Gloucestershire', *Trans BGAS* 83 (1964); 1676: Compton Census 1676, 'Salt Ms 33', Staffordshire County Records Office (GA Photocopy 377); 1712: Sir Robert Atkyns, *The Ancient and Present State of Gloucestershire* (Gloucester 1712); 1779: Samuel Rudder, *A New History of Gloucestershire* (Cirencester 1779); 1801: 1801 Census.

the minister, churchwardens and parishioners. Hooper asked every minister in the diocese the same series of questions. Could he recite the Ten Commandments? Could he recite the Lord's Prayer, say where in scripture it was written down and who was its author? The 'survivalist' ex-canon in occupation of Cirencester Rectory could not recite the commandments but knew where to find them. He repeated the Lord's Prayer, could not say where in scripture it was written down, but did know who its author was.[7] If nothing else, the extraordinary flurry of private and public business associated with Hooper's short stay made everyone think a little harder. When Hooper asked Phelpes how many communicants there were in the parish of Cirencester the priest knew his inquisitor expected, not pedantry and cunning, but honesty and accuracy. He could answer accurately, because it drew upon information obtained every year at Easter, when priests used the solemnity of the occasion to collect a tithe. He reported exactly 1,460 communicants. Assuming again that at least a third of the population was under 16 and not yet a communicant, this translates into roughly 2,438 souls.

The survivalist catholic William Phelpes's replacement, Thomas Marshall, kept registers of baptisms, marriages and burials, beginning in September 1560.[8] In 1561 he (or his clerk) recorded 93 baptisms, an average of eight per month. In 1561 and 1562 there were 93 and 92 respectively. Burials were at 59 and 46 in 1561 and 1562 and then rose suddenly to 110 in 1563. July to December 1563 were months of high mortality, possibly a visitation of bubonic plague (started by the plague flea, which is active at temperatures of 68–78 degrees

7 'Bishop Hooper's Visitation of Gloucester', *Eng Hist Rev* 19 (1904), 98–122; for Phelps cf. 111. Inability to give the right answers did not mean a priest was ignorant. Of the 168 Gloucestershire incumbents who could not recite the Ten Commandments, not then a routine part of church ritual, 138 knew 'the very chapter of *Exodus* in which' they were written. 'And how far the failures may have been due to unfamiliarity with the English version, which was probably insisted on, is a matter for speculation': *ibid*, 99. Another document shows that Phelps had traditionalist doctrinal orientations ('William Phelps's Recantation' in Beecham, *History of Cirencester*, 285–6). This must have been later than the visitation of 1551. Phelpes was a former Austin canon (Baddeley, *History of Cirencester*, 296). In 1570 a man named William Phelpes was charged with others at the Commission for Ecclesiastical Causes with not attending church in accordance with the Act of Uniformity (Price, 161), but this cannot have been our man, who died before 13 Feb. 1559 (Baddeley, *History of Cirencester*, 296).

8 The following is based on aggregative analysis of Cirencester Parish Registers, GA P86, IN 1/1: baptisms 1560–81, marriages 1560–81 and 1585–1637, burials 1560–80 and 1585–1637; IN 1/2: baps 1637–1781, mars 1637–1776, burs 1637–1799. For the other parishes referred to in the following I used aggregations conducted by local historians in conjunction with the Cambridge Group's population project. I am grateful to the Group for allowing me to Xerox aggregation forms for Avening, Cam, Eastington, Fairford, Horsley, Minchinhampton, North Nibley, Stroud, Tetbury, Winchcombe and Wotton under Edge. I conducted my own analysis and prepared graphs from these forms. The lack of references to Stroud, Dursley and Tetbury, with Cirencester and Wotton the leading cloth towns, is due to the fact that their registers do not survive before 1620.

Fahrenheit, and dies below 45 degrees) in the hot summer months, turning to pneumonic plague, 'which is usually a winter disease spread by human breath and spittle in overcrowded and badly-ventilated conditions'.[9] Baptisms were low for the next four years, suggesting either that it took that long to replace the dead with immigrants, or that malnutrition-induced amenorrhea depressed conceptions: 76, 77, 76 and 61 respectively. The dip is not dramatic but was sustained and may mean that poverty and dearth were underlying causes. West of England clothiers complained in 1571 that the Merchant Adventurers were no longer placing orders with them, causing widespread unemployment in the local cloth industry.[10]

Table 10.2. Weddings, baptisms and burials, 1561–1709[11]

Years	Burials	Baptisms	Marriages	Burials as % of baptisms
1561–69	564	732	178	77
1570–79	1,181	757	282	156
1580, 86–89	516	386	169	133.7
1590–99	1,113	936	210	119
1600–09	824	889	224	92.7
1610–19	883	954	178	92.6
1620–29	835	883	162	94.6
1630–39	819	1,023	210	80
1640–49	1,123	1000	140	112.3
1650–59	789	1,015		77.7
1660–69	891	903	121	98.7
1670–79	892	920	144	97
1680–89	904	1,016	145	89
1690–99	891	941	224	95
1561–1709	12,225	12,355	2,387	99

The decadal averages recorded in Table 10.2 are misleading in that, while clearly supporting the overall population trends indicated in Table 10.1, they smooth out short periods of exceptional mortality. Assuming all infants were baptized soon after birth (not always the case) and working on a birth-rate of 30 per 1,000 inhabitants, an average of 79.9 baptisms per year in the

9 Andrew Appleby, *Famine in Tudor and Stuart England* (Liverpool 1978), 100–1.

10 R. Perry, 'The Gloucestershire Woollen Industry, 1100–1690', *Trans BGAS* 66 (1947), 101.

11 GCRO P86, IN 1/1 (baps 1560–81; 1585–1637; mars 1560–81, 1585–1637; burs 1560–80, 1585–1637); IN1/2: baps 1637–1781; mars 1637–1776; burs 1637–1799; the presence of Anabaptists from the 1570s means slight under-recording of baptisms: in 1615 and 1620, for example, seven and thirteen burials, respectively, are described as 'unbaptised'; burials of the children of eight named 'Anabaptists' are recorded in 1654–8.

1560s yields a population in 1570 of 2,663. As noted above, the figure of 320 households in 1563 may reflect a run of very bad years in the late 1550s and the recorded high mortality of late summer, autumn and early winter 1563. Following the crisis of 1563 baptisms (732) easily outstripped burials (564) in the nine years 1561–69.

Over the next four decades a healthy surplus of baptisms over burials turned into a considerable deficit. Burials (72) were relatively high in 1570 but baptisms (93) were still high enough to suggest that the fall-off in demand for West Country cloth, already impacting on the register-figures of Stroudwater and Vale of Berkeley parishes, had not yet affected Cirencester. Across the Cotswolds, in the Vale of Berkeley, the cloth village of North Nibley experienced a 'three-star' mortality crisis (burials double the nine-year moving average) in 1570. Its neighbouring market/clothing town, Wotton under Edge, experienced high mortality in 1571 and 1572. Demonstrating that the Stroudwater Valleys were not exempt, Minchinhampton was afflicted in 1571. Avening, sheltered in its valley between the weavers' village of Nailsworth and the wool stapling town of Tetbury, was in crisis in 1575. Eastington, a little clothing township on the lower reaches of the Stroud River, was struck in 1576. Mortality was at crisis levels once more at Wotton under Edge in 1577, 1578 and 1579. These were not crisis years nationally. The high mortality only affected clothmaking districts and was almost certainly caused by population growth, routine underemployment and the resulting poverty.[12]

At Cirencester there were 70 burials – not particularly high – but only the same number of baptisms in 1575. In 1576 baptisms (83) just edged above burials (82). Signs of serious trouble began in the records of May 1577, when 17 people were buried: double the monthly average. Ominously, 14 of the 16 who died were adults, including four married couples.

In June there were 27 burials (19 adults), three times the monthly average. They fell back to 15 in July, 11 in August (including the town sergeant, Christopher George's brother, 'John George Gent.') and 7 in September. The timing suggests an epidemic of bubonic plague: as the weather cooled the deaths decreased. In October they rose again to 20, a level sustained through November (21). The pattern does not conform to what might be expected of a transition from summer bubonic to winter pneumonic plague. If plague caused high burial rates in June and July, low figures in August and September suggest it had ended by then. Bubonic plague has to be present for pneumonic plague to take over as a killer in the cooler months. It can never be proved that unemployment, poverty and malnutrition made the local manufacturing workers and their neighbours susceptible to every virus and bacteria present in

12 Paul Slack, *The Impact of Plague in Tudor and Stuart England* (London 1985), Ch. 5, 'The Urban Impact', shows that while these were not bad years at Bristol and Exeter, Norwich, like Cirencester a cloth town, was very badly affected.

the environment, but the fact that these crises only affected clothmaking and trading settlements strongly suggests that this was the case.

Mortality continued at a rate classified by demographers as mild crisis[13] through the winter and spring of 1577–8, inching up from 10 burials in December to 20 in May: the impact of influenza-type diseases on chronically undernourished people seems likely. The quality of the harvest of May 1578 was irrelevant to people who had no money to buy supplies, and for the next nine months Cirencester's poorer quarters, where the roads from Bristol and the Vale of Berkeley, Stroudwater and north Wiltshire entered the town, were decimated. The list of burials suddenly lengthens in July 1578: 71 in all. August's list of 55 is slightly shorter but September's (107) and October's (98) seem to go on forever. Now the main businesses of the town were funerals and burying the dead. By November (49) the most vulnerable people were dead and the onset of winter weakened the impact of the warm weather diseases. The crisis gradually fell back through December (33 burials), January (23), February (21) and March (12).

Who died? General labourers, petty traders and craftworker households (and streets) were hit hardest. Not untypical was the household of Thomas Master, a weaver. He lost his daughter Agnes in January 1577/8. Another daughter, Elinor, was buried on 7 April. His wife, Joane, died on 5 May, followed by his sister Julyan (buried 14 May), son William (25 May) and daughter Alice (28 May). He survived this visitation, only to die in the next, in 1585. The household of his neighbour and fellow weaver, Thomas Chapman, was stricken in June. Chapman's eldest daughter Margaret (14) and her sister Lydia were buried on 12 July 1578. Four-year-old Sarah was buried on 22 July, the day before his son, Thomas, and two days before their mother, Dorothy, was lowered into her grave. Thomas himself was buried on 7 August, the last of his family. Clothworkers were by no means the only trade and rank to suffer. Thomas Mann, a substantial butcher, died in July 1577, and the case of John George, gent, has been noted. They were the only members of their families to die. The Chapmans were wiped out, and Thomas Master was left on his own to cope with the aftermath.

William Partridge, gent (lessee of a Mill at Stratton), Nicholas Stone, gent, a daughter of Christopher George, gent, Joan the wife of John Coxwell, gent (and clothier), and Thomas Farrington, the clerk responsible for entering the burials in the register, were among the dead of 1578–9. They had country houses to flee to, but stayed put. Every rank of local society suffered, but poorer households were more numerous, vulnerable and hardest hit. As well as the families of Chapman and Master, seven weavers or tuckers are scattered among the names of those who died. When there had been fewer of them, in the fifteenth century, weavers made good livings and sometimes enough capital to set up as clothiers. There was a handful of comfortably-off master weavers in

13 Burials 50 percent higher than the nine-year moving average.

the period 1560–1660, but perennially insecure journeymen and apprentices outnumbered them two or three to one.

Following a decade of market unpredictability, the full force of economic crisis struck Cirencester, the main commercial and clothmaking town of the region, in 1577, at a time when it was probably struggling to cope with immigrants looking for some kind of subsistence. After a year in which deaths inched up month-by-month, the poorer quarters of the town were visited, in the summer of 1578, by a plague of deaths from endemic and epidemic diseases. The national harvest of 1578 was abundant, but too late for the 350 men, women and children who, in a chronically weakened state, died during the winter of 1578–9. The following year Robert Strange complained 'there hathe ben lesse familiarity or societie or conference used among the inhabitants (of the town) than heretofore hath ben', blaming disturbances of 'the quiet government of the town' on the revival of the Guild Merchant issue. Declining communal sociability may have had more to do with the continuous funeral processions, priests too busy to do anything except conduct the funerals, and the fact that the graveyard, as W.G. Hoskins once said of Devon townships and villages at this time, 'looked like a ploughed field'.

We can only speculate about how it felt, not only to live through crises like these, but to maintain hope of living the biblical three-score years and ten in the expectation of having to survive maybe two or three crises of this sort in order to do so. Entries in the burial registers provide clues. Very few of those who died were viewed by the clerk as immigrants or persons passing through. Deaths of 'straingers' were routinely recorded in the registers after 1570. In the crisis months of 1577–9, a mere seven of the 642 burials that included some kind of classification can be included in this category, suggesting that the rest of those buried were seen as 'resiants'. The communal intensity of the crisis was not exaggerated by the burials of immigrants and sojourners. Quite the reverse, in fact: fewer persons described as strangers or sojourners occur in the crisis years than occur in the registers for the earlier 1570s, suggesting potential immigrants, other travellers and vagrants knew the town was in trouble and gave it a wide berth. Quite apart from the depressing affects of the constant funeral processions on community morale – an average of more than one a day, and on some days in the worst months, a dozen or more – economic life must have all but ceased, in a town that lived by its market and its artisans. As we have seen, a few families and households were completely wiped out. The tabulated data suggests that at least 120 households lost their male or female head, and 83 men who survived lost a wife. Hundreds of families lost children and young household servants.

Table 10.3. Categories of persons buried, May 1577 to January 1579

Category	Man	Woman	Wife	Wid	Dau	Son	Male serv.	Fem serv.	Poor	A child of	Total
May 1577	16 buried 10 men 4 wives										16
June 1577	27 buried 19 adults										27
July 1577	15 buried 8 adults 1 'adolescens'										15
Aug to Oct 1577	7	2	5	6	5	9	3	2	1		40
Nov 1577 to March 1578	10	2	9	7	13	15	4	6			66
Apr 1578	3		8	1	10	6	1	4	1		32
Jun 1578	2			2	5	7			1		17
Jul 1578	8	1	9	5	25	18	6	3	2		77
Aug/Sep 1578	27	2	21	7	45	42					144
October 1578	18	2	16	7	24	19	3			14	103
Nov 1578 to 30 Jan 1579	20	1	15	4	32	22 (2)			2	9	105
Totals	95	10	83	39	159	140	17	15	7	23	642

The crisis of 1577–9 carried off a third of the town's inhabitants. The curate for the period 1581–4, John Stone, took the 'new-writ' volume of register-entries for those years to Fairford, since when they have disappeared.[14] In 1586, when a certain Philip Jones was 'preacher of the Word at Cirencester', burials remained at a crisis level of 112 as against 101 baptisms. In 1587 there were 116 and in 1589 142 burials, against 74 and 78 baptisms respectively. One of the burials in 1588 was that of Robert Strange.

There are reports of riots. Robert Strange and his sergeant were harassed collecting manorial tolls in the market in the early 1580s. 'Dearth that bordered on famine' was the culprit in 1586, when justices and bailiffs of towns throughout Gloucestershire combined 'to abridge the liberty of buying grain, and malting was intirely prohibited'.[15] The Gloucestershire bench was instructed by Privy Council to investigate attacks by five or six hundred people

[14] Baddeley, *History of Cirencester*, 297.

[15] Rudder, *New History of Gloucestershire*: 'Tewkesbury'; Tewkesbury Borough Records ('Black Book'), GA.

on barques travelling down the Severn at Framilode, the mouth of Stroudwater, carrying barley and malt to Bristol. They reported the 'necessitie' of the clothworkers of the Stroudwater region. 'Divers of them justified' the raids on the ground that 'they were dryven to feed theire children with oates-dogges and roots of nettles with other like things they could come by'.[16]

Burials (114) exceeded baptisms (101) in 1591, were level-pegging from 1592–6, and then, in December 1596, began another terrible twelve months, when 291 people were buried. This time Cirencester's experience was not unusual. The great dying struck all regions of England. At Cirencester the sextons had already been overworked for two decades. Disease, famine and death stalked the clothworking districts throughout the last third of the sixteenth century, and even then had not finished their business.

The registers of Cirencester show a deficit (burials minus baptisms) of 1,079 between 1571 and 1600. Yet long-run data leave no doubt that the town *increased* its population in this period. An archdiocesan enquiry of 1603 reported 1,825 communicants, suggesting a total population of at least 3,048. Baptismal rates confirm the increase. In the 1560s an average of 79.9 infants were baptized each year. There was a slight fall to 75.7 a year in the 1570s. The record for the 1580s is incomplete, but the 1590s register an increase of 25 percent on the 1570s: 93.6 a year, suggesting a total population in 1600 of roughly 3,120, close to the figure obtained from the communicant census of 1603. In forty years with a baptism-burial deficit of 1,079, Cirencester's population *increased* by 28 percent. Over half (54%) of the inhabitants in 1600 were recent immigrants.

In retrospect it is clear that the 1570s, 1580s and 1590s were the worst decades. The crisis eased between 1600 and 1640 in the sense that there were no more catastrophic years to compare with the late 1570s or 1597. There were 'mortality crises' measured by the classification-system of modern demographic historians (burials double the moving average) in 1604, 1617, 1623, and lesser crises (50% higher) in 1612–13, 1629, 1637 and 1638. Nevertheless, baptisms were higher than burials in every decade, marking an improvement of some kind, albeit a marginal one. The four-decade surplus was only 388. Immigration must have continued, because the baptismal levels of the 1630s and the parliamentarian census of families in 1650 both confirm a total population by mid-century of about 3,500 souls. But the flood was stemmed, probably as a result of the introduction, also in the 1580s, of more vigilant and systematic administration in the town. The general crisis intensified the bureaucratic revolution ushered in by the Henrician Reformation, and imposed more effectively in Gloucester Diocese by Bishop Hooper.

This serial view of a century of extreme uncertainty leaves us with a paradox. The sources leave an indelible impression of underlying anxiety. Aggregated

16 Qf. Buchanan Sharp, *In Contempt of all Authority: Rural Artisans and Riot in the West of England, 1586–1660* (Berkeley 1980), 15.

parish register evidence undoubtedly shows many runs of good years, in which baptisms easily outstripped burials. Baptisms exceeded burials in 91 of the 100 years under observation, the exceptions being 1577–9, 1585–6, 1596–7 and 1621–3. The overall growth trend is unmistakable, both at Cirencester and throughout its region.

This growth needs explaining. It is difficult to reconcile with the details of the trend, which, together with other evidence, leave an indelible impression of an age of anxiety and uncertainty, punctuated by odd weeks, months and years in which it seemed (and was predicted that) the Last Days had finally come. The years from 1578 to the mid-1580s were such a time, 1596–7 was nearly as bad, and in 1621 Gloucestershire clothiers reported to the government that hundreds of clothworking families would die if markets were not found for their cloth. We must allow for exaggeration, but in the following two years many did die, and dozens of master-craftsmen and clothiers were ruined. Circumstances like these made the districts affected highly susceptible to millenarian messages, and receptive to preachers able to read signs of cosmic significance into the existing sorry state of the world.

Not one generation born in the century of crisis escaped experience of months and even years in which the traffic ground to an almost complete halt everywhere. Even if only one in every three years saw at least some artisan households in every village and town underemployed or unemployed, it was enough to ensure that anxiety levels were high, and symptoms like heavy drinking, violence and crime on the increase. We noted earlier that Elizabethan Cirencester was well-stocked with alehouses, taverns and inns. Clothworkers were often busy in years when grain harvests were deficient, the price of necessities rose, and profits were lost in the purchase of necessities.

Artisan households had ways of dealing with short- and medium-term uncertainty; master-craftsmen tried to purchase in large quantities when prices were low, but storage was a problem, and hostile neighbours a risk if the household's grain-store seemed indecently large in dearth years. Journeymen and apprentices at Cirencester had craft fellowships with clear rules defining minima of food and beer that had to be supplied by the master, regardless of price, but the rules did not govern what happened if the masters had no work and no supplies to feed extra hands. Several times between 1560 and 1620 the Weavers' Guild issued an order that no journeyman from outside the town was to be admitted to the Journeyman Weavers' Fellowship. This meant that if any journeyman did linger longer than a few days in the hope of picking up work and board for a week or so, he would be quickly moved on by the beadle, constable and wardsmen.[17]

[17] GA D.4590 2/1, Cirencester Weavers' Book: In 1614 'yt was agreed upon by the full concourse of the Wardens and Companie… that noe forraigne weaver or weavers shall sett upp any loombe or loombes within the Towne but shall paye to the Companie Tenn Pounds' (followed by 25 signatures and marks).

Hardship among the young and the least secure 'manuary' workers generated an electric current that coursed through every rank of their trades. In all trades turned-off apprentices and turned-away journeymen abused master-craftsmen, who immediately pressured the stewards of their fellowships to urge the merchants to open more markets. Murmuring and discontent intensified and in the worst times local customs and institutions may have all but collapsed. At Cirencester, as we have seen, the clerks continued to record the burials, marriages and baptisms in the darkest times. In such circumstances, a premium was placed on messages of hope.

11

Only the poor will be saved: the preacher and the manual workers

> The true wisedom of God … was not known of any of the Princes of the worlde, for had they knowen it, they would not have crucified the Lorde of glorie. And therefore albeit in number we be few, in estate poor, and in birth not Gentlemen, yet in the knowledge of God wee may be noble, in faith riche, and in the sight of God as precious as the honourable …
>
> Philip Jones, 1586

The protest of the 'poor townspeople' of 1570 against their 'papist captains' used national politics for local ends. A year later, in circumstances that are unclear, Cirencester became a parliamentary borough, with the right to elect two members of parliament. This event triggered old, unresolved questions concerning Cirencester's constitution and franchise.[1] Who, as H.R. French puts it, had a right to participate in the town's 'deliberations', in this case concerning the nomination and election of parliamentary representatives?[2] In an institutionalized borough like Bristol or Gloucester, such decisions were handled by the mayor, aldermen and the 'commonalty' of formally qualified burgesses. Cirencester was 'a parliamentary borough, but not a corporation'. The first instinct of the manorial cabal was to ensure that, at best, 'only the freeholders were electors' – owners, not tenants, and certainly not 'sojourners', 'inmates', 'passingers' and anyone in receipt of alms. This, it was hoped, would keep national politics out of the market-place and ensure only men favoured by the manor were elected.[3] In effect the lord of the manor governed the 'borough', and therefore enjoyed the right to nominate candidates and manage elections. Legally, Cirencester was still governed as it had been for centuries, by the bailiff of the manor, who enjoyed considerable patronage in the appointment, each year, of two constables, 14 wardsmen (two per street), two aletasters, two searchers of hides and tallows, two sealers of leather and two 'cardeners'.[4] The manor remained an important part of local

1 Discussed more fully below, Chapter 15.
2 French, *The Middle Sort of People in Provincial England* (Oxford 2007).
3 Rudder, *History of Cirencester*, 205; Atkyns, *Gloucestershire*, 347.
4 Fuller, 'The Manor and the Town', 342.

government at Cirencester in the eighteenth and nineteenth centuries, but no bailiff would ever again be as powerful as Robert Strange in the immediate aftermath of the Henrician and Edwardian state reformations. Events and movements of the final quarter of the sixteenth century concerned what would take the place of his regime. What came next?

First, out of the depths of the great dying of the late 1570s, a movement of artisans and retailers, led by the irrepressible Giles Selwyn, discovered that Henry V's annulment of the Guild Merchant had been erased or lost from the Exchequer Rolls, and set in motion a movement to resurrect it.[5] In the aftermath of the mortality crisis of 1577–9, crowds consisting mainly of smaller retailers and craftsmen, led by Selwyn, 'violently resisted the bailiff (Strange), the steward and other officers … in their duties … precisely in the old-time manner under the abbots of St Mary'.[6] According to Strange, Selwyn followed up these protests by collecting 'vast sums of money'. He 'persuaded the people of the town to give largely, promising that all, who thus contributed, should be incorporated into companies as, of mercers, tailors, shoemakers, tanners, etc., with power to make rules for trade, and to choose a master and other governors and officers to rule the town'.[7] An inquiry was instituted, and the octogenarian Robert Strange was called to give evidence for the manor.

Until recently, he testified, 'the bailiff and constable associated with the best part of the town … appointed by the lord of the manor … did govern and rule the town in good sort and civil manner'. This, incidentally, was the first recorded usage at Cirencester of a decidedly dichotomous 'language of sorts'.[8] Strange was being disingenuous, as we have seen. The authority of 'the best part of the town' (in his usage, himself, Christopher George and the appointees of the lord of the manor) to 'govern and rule' had been under challenge on various fronts for at least a decade. Strange testified that 'if there hathe ben anie lesse familiaritie or societie or conference used among the inhabitants than heretofore hath bene, yt hathe rysen by the occasion of Selwyn and his complices being disturbers of the quiet government of the town'.[9] Strange articulated the ideal: the 'quiet government of the town' rested on 'familiarity or society or conference among the inhabitants'. Today we call this 'civil society'. We have seen other reasons why 'the quiet government of the town' should have been 'disturbed' in the early 1580s.

5 *Ibid*; Selwyn is described as a yeoman in the GDR Records for 1583: Hockaday, 'Cirencester, 1583'; he was a beneficiary in the will of his brother William, a clothier who owned land at Siddington St Mary, on the outskirts of Cirencester: GDR PCC, 20 April 1556; a reference to a consistory court case in 1569 seems to imply that Selwyn was acting as one of the curates at the parish church: GDR Vol. 24, 508.

6 Fuller, 'The Manor and the Town', 340–2; Baddeley, *History of Cirencester*, 236.

7 Fuller, 'Manor and Town', citing PRO E178/8/22: 'Special Commissions, Elizabeth', 884–5, 959; PRO E112/15/46: Exchequer Bills and Answers, 24 Eliz. 46.

8 For further usages, see below, p. 205.

9 Fuller, 'Manor and Town', 342.

Strange's son in law, Christopher George, was next, arguing that the establishment of a Guild Merchant would benefit only 'those inhabitants of the town as mercers, drapers, tanners &c. (who) wold make the price of their wares at their owen pleasure'.[10] It was for dispassionate gentlemen like himself and Strange to regulate social life in the interests of the whole 'commonwealth' and 'countrey', not just the artisans and shopkeepers in the town. Only gentlemen stood aloof from particular interests and were fitted to govern. George was an educated man, an authority on the law. He kept rooms at the Middle Temple. Constitutional issues were being raised. The 'feet' were trying to take over the natural leadership of the 'head' and 'upper members' of the body politic. Strange was vulnerable to the charge of being a mere merchant who bought his branch of the family into the gentry within living memory. The Georges went back much further.

More than any, the Georges were an institution in the governance of the town and Seven Hundreds. They exemplified an ideal of local politics, a family who had been members of the elite, generation after generation, since the fourteenth century. They were conscious of this fact. In his 1556 will John George had passed to his 'eldest son … the greate pot of Brasse called *Sare* which hath gone from heire to heire by my ancestors wills before me, to him and to his heires for ever' and the 'greate Cuppe prell guilte with a cover and a crowne about him and a knapp on the top enamelled, to him and his heires for ever onely to goe with the pott from heire to heire'.[11] In his 1597 will, Christopher passed 'my greate brasse pot called SARE and my standing cup of silver called the George' to his eldest son, Richard.[12] An idea of temporal stewardship moderated and qualified the notion that possession of property was the basis of status and authority.

In the preamble to his will, Christopher George reiterated the duties of a gentleman of town and country. Having bequeathed his soul to God, it was his duty 'to employ and bestow his goods and possessions … and to distribute and leave them in such order and forme, as when God shall aske an account thereof'. He had received his vocation and estate from God. He was their 'bailiff and minister', not their lord, and it was his duty 'to use them to the honor and glory of God'. That taken care of, he turned to 'the necessary relief and comforte of my selfe and those I am naturally bownde to care for and minister helpe unto'. Having found his 'selfe by God's only goodness endowed with goodes and possessions farre above my … worthiness', it was his 'bownden dutye so to leave the order and disposition of them when I shall depart from this life … to the pleasing of Almighty God and to the satisfaction of the world'. It pleased God that 'the world' too was 'satisfied', that a gentleman did not leave a legacy of conflict and contesta-

10 *Ibid.*

11 GA P86 Ch. 1.4: 'My grate Grandfathers John Georges last will made 1556'.

12 GA P86 Ch.1.4: Will of Christopher George, 1597.

tion. 'I the said Christopher George therefore … commaunde my children and desire all my good fryndes and kynfolkes to be content with this my last testament … and to avoid all occasions of trouble.'[13]

Harmony hinged on what men like George felt was 'necessary' for the 'relief and comforte of my selfe' and, crucially, who, in the conventions of the day, a gentleman or rich tradesman was 'naturally bownde to care for and minister helpe unto'. The wills considered in this book leave the conventional priorities in no doubt. 'Kynfolkes' got the lion's share, usually followed by less generous bequests to 'all [the testator's] good fryndes' and last and very much least, the church and the deserving poor. It was a virtually unbreakable convention, in abeyance during the 'interregnum' of pastoral decay in the middle decades of the century, that there must be bequests to church, community and the poor, and they were often listed first. The convention was revived in the final third of the century, as the places left by death were filled by immigrants, as social *anomie* intensified and good order became increasingly difficult to maintain. Two other factors varied across time. First was the degree to which members of the elite felt obliged to serve and leave bequests to the poor and the parish. Second was the proportion of the population living in or on the borders of 'necessity'.

Christopher George thought only gentlemen or the sons of gentlemen were fitted to be masters and governors.[14] Guild government would leave the town at the mercy of traders and traffickers. Artisans and retailers would control the market for their own profit, not for the commonweal. Men of their sort could not afford the expenses of government. 'Having no land to the maintenance of the said guild… there wold be laid upon the inhabitants such taxation and impositions for (its) maintenance more than they [i.e. the Guild members and officers] are able to do or maintain.'[15] Revival of the Guild Merchant issue, following in the wake of the papist allegations, acquisition of the right to return members of parliament and the devastating mortality of the late 1570s, threatened to set 'the gentlemen of town and country' (as one of Strange's successors, John Coxwell, put it) against tradesmen, common 'mercers, drapers, tanners &c'. George repeated his point. Selwyn was supported by 'various clothiers, tanners and tailors of the town'. A chartered Guild Merchant would allow men like these 'to chose as they would the various officers of the town from among themselves, and so… be able to govern and control it, independently of [Sir John] Danvers or of any other manor-lord'.

13 *Ibid.*

14 'A representation … to Queen Elizabeth of three causes of decay and poverty', Bodleian Library, Rawlinson D23: 133, advised that commerce should be restricted to the sons of gentlemen; this would have raised the problem of how to regard 'gentlemen' like Robert Strange and John Coxwell, who were not sons of gentlemen.

15 Fuller, 'The Manor and the Town', 343.

A third witness for the manor, Thomas Marshall of Poulton, Wilts, confirmed it had always been 'lawful for anyone to bring anything to market without let or molestation of any of the inhabitants'.[16] A Guild Merchant was against the natural order and would create an institutional breach between the people of the country and the town.

Disenfranchised retailers and craftsmen had formed the rank and file of the movement to win ground from the manorial lords since the earliest documentation in the twelfth century. In this sense, Selwyn was only the latest in a long line of populist 'proctors'. The structure of the struggle, in which the crown farmed the manor to a lord for a fee, and the 'poor inhabitants' appealed to the crown, unsuccessfully, for an expansion of its liberties at the expense of the lord, imposed a rigorous continuity on Cirencester politics. Two new themes now complicated the field of forces. First, religion: the manorial party accused the trade party of Puritanism and the trade party accused the manorial of Catholicism. Second, the struggle acquired a new dimension from changes in the politics of parliamentarian representation.

From the late 1560s to the early 1580s the fellowship of the town was fracturing in ways that ranged successive factions of the business community, the wealthier merchants and lesser tradesmen, against an allegedly 'papist' oligarchy. Divisions between *majores* like Strange and George, and *mediocres* like Selwyn and his supporters meant that, for whatever reasons, the customary duties of the 'better' sorts ('the best part of the town', as Strange put it) to work together for communal harmony were, demonstrably, not being fulfilled. In a town experiencing rapid turnover, failure of pastoral care and local government created 'murmuring' among the poor majority, threatening dissolution of good order into class-struggle of the lower ranks of the commonalty against their employers. The gaps that had always existed between these 'layers' or 'levels' of the trade community were becoming ideological as well as material and political. In the midst of this religious polarization was an increasingly millenarian, prophetic element, a conviction that the troubled times through which the town was passing were signs that the *last daies* were imminent.

We now turn to a source that formulated a theology capable of consolidating this movement of the lesser artisans and retailers, a category that, potentially, included six or seven out of every ten households in the town, and no less than a third of those in the Seven Hundreds. Reaching and influencing this extremely amorphous and potentially fissiparous body or class involved appealing to conventional beliefs and prejudices. Successful public rhetoric involves the repetition of simple, indeed grossly simplistic, ideas. As E.J. Hobsbawm puts it, 'the ideas judged by generations of scholars and intellectuals to be "thinkers"' did not spread by reading as much as by 'a sort of osmosis whereby a few radically reduced and simplified concepts

16 *Ibid*, 342.

... somehow enter public or private discourse as recognized brand names'.[17] That is not to say the individuals to whom the rhetoric was intended to appeal were incapable of more refined, analytic and nuanced thought, only that it was necessary to draw up some clear demarcation lines. The preacher whose ideas concern us for the rest of this chapter divided society into two classes: rich and poor.

In 1586, in the midst of ongoing negotiations for a renewal of the Guild Merchant issue, one Philip Jones, 'preacher of the town of Cirencester', delivered a series of sermons, or lectures, on an immemorial, populist, potentially divisive Christian tradition.[18] Jesus was a carpenter. His companions, disciples and apostles were poor men and women. He set about the merchants in the temple and condemned the high priests. He owned nothing and lived in receipt of alms. He was poor. Creative genealogy notwithstanding, he was, by the standards of his own day and of Elizabethan England, low-born. He was not a king, lord, pope, gentleman or even priest. He was, Jones reminded his congregation, a 'manuary craftsman'.

We have seen that 'poor' was an elastic and ambivalent word. The rich men who led resistance to the abbots had often, in their petitions, styled themselves 'the poor men of Cirencester'. It is difficult to say exactly how 'the poor townspeople' who petitioned against the 'papist' manorial regime in 1570 was constituted. Jones was much more specific. 'The poor', in common parlance, included the haunters of alehouses and breakers of the 'walls of obedience'; they were not saved, not godly folk. 'Poor' had also been used for centuries to designate the townspeople ruled by the manor. The ordinary inhabitants of the town were 'poor' in estate, not equipped to defend their honour and estate, in court or armed combat, individually, but powerful collectively. Compared to chartered boroughs all over England, the inhabitants of Cirencester, whatever their material possessions, were *institutionally* 'poor'. A thousand funerals had made many of the inhabitants of

17 Hobsbawm, '"C" for Crisis', review of Richard Overy, *The Morbid Age: Britain Between the Wars* (London 2009), *London Review of Books*, 6 August 2009.

18 *Certaine Sermons preached of late at Ciceter in the countie of Glocester, upon a portion of the first Chapter of the Epistle of James: wherein the two several states, of the riche and poore man are compared and examined, the differences in quality, and duety betwixt them shewed... Penned at the earnest request of divers well affected inhabitants of the place: and now published as well for the use of others, as for the further profit of that particular congregation. By Philip Jones, Preacher of the word of God in the same Towne. Allowed by authoritie. Imprinted at London by T.D. for Thomas Butter 1588.* I am aware of two copies, one in the Gloucestershire Collection at the Gloucester City Library (GCL), the other at the Cambridge University Library. I would like to thank the GCL for allowing me to transcribe their copy, from which the citations in this paper are taken. The text contains three sermons, selected from what the author says was originally a series of six on the Epistle of James. The pages are not numbered. Unless otherwise indicated, all quotations that follow are from this source.

Cirencester ready to receive Jones's message that only the poor would be saved. So who were the 'poor'?

'By the poore man', he explained, 'I mean those upon whom it hath pleased God not to bestow so great a portion of riches as upon others for some secrete purpose of his wisedom.' To be poor was the most challenging of vocations. How was it possible to keep faith with religious and communal ideals when markets contracted and dried up and when disease and hunger ravaged families? A 'poore man' was 'no tall Cedar, no man of great office or authoritie in the common wealth'. He was not a gentleman of town and country, a bailiff, a treasurer of the parish, or a parliament man. Saints did not seek 'greate office or authoritie'. Jones's saint was not a gentleman or lord, a merchant or a clothier. Nor was he a proverbially virtuous tiller of the soil, a husbandman or ploughman. He was 'an artificer or handicraftes man, labouring diligently in his manuarie trade or science'.

This definition encompassed at least half the households of the town and a third of those in seven hundreds of Cirencester. Manufacturers of commodities for export now outnumbered every other vocation in town and 'rural' district. Yet even the practice of a 'manuarie trade or science' was not enough, for, as Jones explained, a 'saint … laboured … to releeve himselfe, and maintaine his familie thereby, demeaning himself honestly as a christian, and quietly like a subject in the feare of God, and according to the qualitie of his vocation'. Jones's ideal was an artisan with a wife and children, maintaining himself and his household/family by his trade, attending church and listening to lectures and sermons, reading or listening to another read the bible, contributing whenever possible to local and national taxes, no respecter of 'person(age)s', confident in the belief that God would reward him and his family if they tried to live godly lives and serve the commonweal.

'Such a one in scripture,' he concluded, 'I take to be a poore man.' Jones could not have been more specific about the target of his mission – not the country labourers who were to be the principle target of the SPCK a century later, the Kingswood colliers who first heard Wesley's message in 1739, or the urban proletariat of the classical industrial revolution, but the heterogeneous class of dispersed craftsmen and proto-industrial outworkers which, in many contemporary assessments, now constituted a sufficiently large and institutionalized proportion of the English workforce to constitute the hardest test of commonweal.[19]

[19] The British Library catalogue identifies 'Philip Jones, Preacher of the Word at Cirencester' as the author of two other printed works, one a news-sheet describing a sea-battle that took place in 1586 between a group of Turkey Company ships and a Spanish fleet near the island of Zante, in the eastern Mediterranean, the other a little booklet that looks suspiciously like an espionage manual, published in 1588: BL 683, h.5: Philip Jones, 'A true report of a worthie fight, performed in the voyage from Turkie, by five shippes of London, against eleven gallies, and two frigates of the King of Spaine …,

It is a very specific form of predestinarianism, designed to appeal to the small clothiers, weavers, dyers, tailors, shoemakers, blacksmiths, carpenters, glassmakers, papermakers, bookbinders and dozens of other manual craft-workers who made the town their home, or, as journeymen and apprentices, passed through it.[20] From them the idea would spread to the industrial towns and villages of north Wiltshire, the Stroudwater Valleys, the Vale of Berkeley, into Somerset, whence to the weavers villages of Dorset and Devon.[21] Jones's probable patron was a wealthy tailor, Philip Marner, whose memorial in the church identified him clearly as an 'articifer' in a 'manuary trade or science', his right hand reaching for his tailors' shears for eternity, a sign of encouragement to 'manuary trades' of the future. We meet Marner, a wealthy businessman who died shortly after Jones's revival, in Chapter 14.

The 'manuary trades' were hardest hit by the mortality crises that accompanied the wild swings of trade that made intense insecurity and uncertainty a way of life in the later decades of the reign of Elizabeth, and on into the reigns of the first two Stuart kings. What stands out is the ferocity of Jones's prophesying. 'Whosoever seeth this not, seeth nothing,' he warned: 'I see the date of that ancient prophecy of the Holy Apostle out, and expired, who long ago forsaw that in the last dayes there shall come perillous times.' No-one in the church could possibly have been unaware of what the phrase 'perilous times' referred to. More than a thousand corpses had been buried in the churchyard in the previous seven years.[22] Very few of the town's 600

Anno 1586', in Richard Hakluyt the Preacher, *The Voyages, Navigations, Traffiques and Discoveries of the English Nation* (London 1589–90), 227–31; Philip Jones, *Certaine brief and special instructions for Gentlemen, merchants, students, souldiers, marriners etc. Employed in service abroade or anie way occasioned to converse in the kingdoms and governments of forren princes* (London 1586); David Beers Quinn, 'Preface' to Beers Quinn and R.A. Skelton (eds), *Principall Navigations, Voyages and Discoveries of the English Nation* (Facsimile of 1589 edition, Cambridge 1965), xviii–xx, sees Jones's tract as 'advance publicity' for Hakluyt's *Voyages*, and uses it to date the publication to January 1589. Quinn seems to accept the BL attribution of these two pamphlets to the author of *Certaine Sermons*; allusions in the sermons to mariners' equipment and to familiarity with the geography of the Mediterranean lend support to the attribution. Roland Austin, 'Philip Jones of Cirencester', *Trans BGAS* 44 (1922), 153, presents an alternative view. For discussion of these pamphlets, and of the Hakluyt circle, see Rollison, *A Commonwealth of the People*, Ch. 7.

20 Occupations from analysis of Cirencester muster list prepared in 1608 by Thomas Archard for John Smyth of Nibley, secretary and steward to Henry, lord Berkeley, lord lieutenant of Gloucestershire: Berkeley Castle Muniments. I am grateful to David Smith, then Gloucestershire County Records Officer, for drawing my attention to this document, and for discussing with me other aspects of this treasure-trove for the social and constitutional history of the region from the fourteenth to seventeenth centuries.

21 Rollison, 'Discourse and Class Struggle: The Politics of Industry in Early Modern England', *Social History* 26:2 (May 2000).

22 Demography based on my aggregative analysis of Cirencester Parish Registers, GRO P86, IN 1/1: baps 1560–81, mars 1560–81 and 1585–1637, burs 1560–80 and 1585–1637;

households had been untouched by the worst years in living memory; some, as we saw in the last chapter, were wiped out. Many of Jones's congregations were immigrants trying to establish themselves. Death was utterly familiar to all of them. The power of apocalyptic preaching at this time was that in towns like Cirencester *everyone's* 'last daies' were imminent. Even that great survivor, Robert Strange, would have to meet his maker soon. Was it at Strange's pew that Jones glanced in moments when his condemnations reached vitriolic extremes? The 'poorer sort' would be 'safe from the raging storm' that heralded the Second Coming. They were like 'low shrubbes or bushes growing in the vallies under the winges, and defence of the hills'. The 'high-minded lovers of pleasure, the rich will be assaulted by every whirlwind ... open to every wind that bloweth'. The rich *could not* be saved.

Jones set this struggle between the productive poor and the parasitical rich, in a visionary, apocalyptic context. His sermons were also teaching exercises.[23] He was at pains to show his objectivity, at times adopting the persona of a dispassionate reporter and commentator. These were not merely opinions. Sign-posts evoking the voices of his sources are relentless: 'the Apostle speaketh ...; the Apostle doth heare say ...; consider the scripture speeches; as the prophet speakes ...; James singes another maner of songe ...; as James speaketh ...; the Evangelist Marke reporteth ...; the person of Jesus ...; comended by Christ ...; uttered by Christ ...; Christ indeed speaketh ...; the rich are expressly called thornes by Christ ...'. Jones assumed a 'preliterate' auditory; his authorities 'speak', rarely 'write'. He took up James's mission to 'enter into a course of schooling the poore man'. He explains his method and logic, and there are a few passages of mind-numbing pedantry, which may have been intended to validate his credentials as a scholar of the primary sources of the apostolic age. His words powerfully evoke the ethos of the 'prophesying' movement: he aimed to teach the lower-middling ranks of the commonalty, not so much how to read and interpret, but how to listen to the spoken words reported in Holy Scripture. Who are the faithful, who and what are their enemies? Upon the basis of what evidence, or testimony, can these questions be answered? How should the faithful respond to the threats that surround them?

IN 1/2: baps 1637–1781, mars 1637–1776, burs 1637–1799; cf. also Rollison, 'Exploding England: the Dialectics of Mobility and Settlement in Early Modern England', *Social History* 24:1 (January 1999).

23 For the broader religious context of this 'prophesying' movement, see Claire Cross, *The Royal Supremacy in the Elizabethan Church* (London 1969), 108 and docs on 192–7, 200, 201–5; Roger B. Manning, *Religion and Society in Elizabethan Sussex* (Leicester 1969); 'The official cessation of prophecying made little difference to what was now a settled pattern of provincial religious life, and one which was destined to outlive both the Tudors and their immediate Stuart successors ...': Patrick Collinson, *The Birthpangs of Protestant England* (London 1988); Collinson, 'Episcopy and Reform in England in the Later Sixteenth Century', Ch. 6 of *Godly People, Essays of English Protestantism and Puritanism* (London 1983), 175–83.

Jones taught that the books of the bible are direct lines to the original words of people whose lives could no longer be shared and observed, but who really lived, in a past that was not much different from the present. Scripture is testimony to events that once took place. Historical events, thus recorded, served to remind the living faithful that they were not the first to have been assailed by 'trials' and 'assaults'. What, he asked, is the proper state of mind, manner of behaviour, attitude towards social status – in short, way of life – of the faithful, in all times? This, he made clear, does not change. The state of mind and way of life of the faithful is the same in any age. It is inside but does not belong to history. History is what the faithful have to endure to show that they are faithful. Jones set out 'to shew and proove by testimonies and examples' that however much they suffered and were persecuted, they belonged to an unbroken tradition of people who had suffered and been persecuted for exactly the same faith.

And it was all happening *now*. 'The state of our own country… in this latter age', was as it had been in Christ's. The greatest enemies of the faithful were 'the riche', 'dubble-minded hypocrites' from whom the godly could expect, at best, ridicule, and at worst prosecution in the law-courts and even persecution unto death.

Hypocrisy – Jones explained that, in Greek, *hypocrisy* meant acting a part on a stage – was the primary vice of the rich and powerful, rulers and magistrates of mid-Elizabethan England. England was an *hypocracy*, in which bishops and magistrates paid lip service to religion but in truth were agents of evil. The faithful should therefore be wary of falling into the sin of 'respect for persons'. 'The cause of fayth and religion, doeth not hang upon the sleeves, and authoritye of men,' he warned. It did not 'consist in multitude nor in the degrees of persons … for multitude is no privilege for trueth, neither is gentility anie warrant for godliness'. As for great lords, even monarchs, 'the true wisedom of God … was not known of any of the Princes of the worlde, for had they knowen it, they would not have crucified the Lorde of glorie. And therefore albeit in number we be few, in estate poor, and in birth not Gentilmen, yet in the knowledge of God wee may be noble, in faith riche, and in the sight of God as precious as the honourable.' 'Gentilmen', 'princes' and all the conventional 'degrees of persons' were mere 'inventions and traditions of men'. Jones swept them aside, conveying his congregation back to the world of the earliest Christians. 'The time wherein Christ lived cannot resemble our time better': then as now, 'the mysteries of the kingdome of God, were hid from the wise and prudent, and men of understanding, and were opened to the simple, yea unto babes'. 'The great men, the princes, the Scribes, and the Pharisees, and the richer sort despised Christ, and counted the preaching foolishness, while the poore by his owne testimonie, and triall received the Gospell & were not offended in him.' In Jesus 'wee may see and finde the condicon of povertie sanctified unto us, and not onelie in him but in his Apostles also, who lefte and forsook al they had and folowed him'.

Scripture is spoken testimony: 'the Evangelist Marke reporte(d) the speech' of Jesus, 'who speaketh of such rich men, as in their wealth are idolators'. The rich 'are no better then greedie dogs, as the prophet speakes'. Consider 'the high degree of those that made a Mocke of Christ', in his own lifetime. Where once they persecuted Christ, now the 'rich apply themselves to the persecuting of him in his saints and members'. What the rich and powerful of his own day said of Christ, they say today of his faithful followers. 'Looke (say they) what a sort of beggarly, and poore fellowes doe follow him, such as have scarce a piece of silver in their purses, or of bread in their houses, they are his disciples, and are become great holy folkes, and wil shortly prove preachers, and proceed Doctors.' The rich are great 'respecters of persons'; their only measure of worth is wealth. Among themselves they said of Jesus, 'Who of us doe fancy him?'

> Doe not wee who bee gentlemen, rich men, rulers, and magistrates speake evill of the man: do not wee report the worst we can of him, amongst ourselves, and to strangers: doe not wee contemne his pulpit talk, make a jest of his thretenings, and preferre accusations, articles, and billes of enditements against him: there are none of us that doe love him, and therefore both hee, and they that heare him are deceived and accursed.

'Thus the Pharisees of our time deale with us.' The message was rammed home; the rich and powerful – 'the gentilmen' – were like 'the Jewes, whose hearts upon the hearing of Stephen's words brast for anger, and whose teth gnashed upon him: and such also, as were the Priests, and captayne of the Temple, and Saducees in Jerusalem'. The rich – secular magnates like Pontius Pilate and 'bishops' like the priests of the Temple – killed Christ.

A change was coming. 'Manie times we see great and mightie trees by violence of the wind overthrowen broken and pluckt up by the rootes.' The rich man 'is never satisfied: he is like unto the horseleech, who hath two daughters crying give! give!, he is like unto the barren womb and the grave which will never be full, and like to a man who hath the dropsie, who the more he drinketh … the more he doeth increase the drieness thereof'. The rich man's lust for wealth and power could not be satisfied. 'The covetous riche man, the more he hath, the more hee wanteth, and the more he aboundeth, the more he thinketh himself destitute, and therefore careth not what unlawful means hee useth to make his commoditie.'

Observe for yourselves, the rich care for nothing but 'prodigalitie, banquetting, covetousness, oppression, usurie, revengement'. They are a 'very plague of greediness, and of unsatiable avarice, which is the root of all evill'. They are 'wholly possessed with carnall greediness'. They follow 'only the things of the world, coveting to be rich in themselves' at the expense of the community, never holding back from 'unlawful practices, and ungodlie policies, to hale and pull corruptible pelfe into their hands'. To be rich is 'to be able to tell (count) much money, to produce good store of gold, to be able to buy, and builde, and by continuall purchase to ioyne land to land, house to house, and Lordshippe to Lordshippe, so to live, and dwell as princes of the earth'. In their actions rich men 'betray themselves to be no better then greedie dogs … which thinke that they have never enough'. Their greedy souls are rotten, poisoned and corrupted by their possessions. 'From this filthy fountayne springs the soul streames of their irreligious lives, their proud conceits, their voluptuous desires, their prophane epicurisme, their brutish forgetfulness of God, his honor, his word, and their own dueties every way.'

Jones's attack on 'rich men' was venomous. 'There are such amongst us,' he warned. 'The rich man hee is in minde troubled, in bodie businessed, in his thoughts distracted,' said Jones, resorting to sarcasm: the poor fellow has 'so manie farmes to visite, so many yoke of Oxen to looke into, so muche money to paye, and to receyve, and soe many thinges to doe'. No wonder 'he can spare no time to regard the state of his soule, nor spende an houre to provide his spirituall wealth, and welfare, by the hearing of the word of GOD', or that in his distraction he failed to hear 'the meanes of his salvation preached?' He barely has time to attend church, 'and if he doe by chance come to a sermon at any time, it were as good or rather better hee were absent: for although his bodie bee in the Churche, yet his wittes run uppon his business, and his senses are occupied about other matters, the voyce of the preacher is as an unperfect sounde to his eares'. Here he seems to be talking about absentees, men and women who knew what Jones represented and stayed away.

They *cannot* be saved. The evangelist 'Marke, reporteth of (Jesus's) speech how hardlie doe they that have riches enter into the kingdom of God'. 'The very possession of riches is such a pullbacke or rather plague unto a man… And yet (even) this is not al that ther is uttered by Christ' on the fate of the rich. Jesus 'proceede(d) further and affirmeth (it is) not only hard but impossible also that a riche man shoulde be saved'. Jones's 'hard words' were impossible to deny: they were uttered by the highest authority of all, the spoken word of God incarnate. If the rich were so corrupt, where did authority lie? 'The cause of fayth and religion, doeth not hang upon the sleeves, and authoritye of men,' he said. It does not 'consist in multitude nor in the degrees of persons'. Legitimacy is not a function of numbers, as in Aristotle's 'polity', nor is it related to prescribed rank, as in Aristocracy or Monarchy. Antichrist recruited his armies from all ranks: 'the people murmur, the kings of the earth band themselves, and the princes do assemble together, yet all this may be against the Lorde, and against his Christ, with purpose to cast off the yoke of his service, and to breake the band of their obedience. Multitude is no privilege for trueth, neither is gentility anie warrant for godliness.' The only authority was 'the eternal and immutable worde of God, which is the word of trueth, of life, of salvation, of reconciliation of the spirite, the onelie rule and direction of the faithful'.

Jones's anger against 'the rich' was palpable, indiscriminate and dangerous.

To 'the poor' he was gentler. Their resistance should be passive. They should take 'as it were, a *spiritual* view of that immortal inheritance and celestial possession, wherein they would be joined partner with all the faithfull of God'. What exactly did 'spiritual' mean? Anthropologists call this aspect of Jones's appeal 'introversionist' millenarianism. Was the 'partnership of the faithfull' an incorporeal, supernaturalist solidarity? Or did it mean a crowd or an army of poor people visited by the angry spirit of a vengeful God, surging through the countryside, raiding rich gentlemen, burning mansions, killing the wicked, preparing the way for the Second Coming the preacher taught was imminent? Was it like 1381, 1450, 1536 and 1549?

The poor had reason to 'fire their eyes'. To 'the brother of low degree the cross of povertie and want of common necessities is both very generall and very grievous'. This was no more than everyone knew, that want of common necessities was at the root of the crisis through which the town and its region were passing. Out there, 'riche men' were still collecting their dues, living 'in the breath of other men' and feasting heedlessly on the spoils. Signs of crisis were evident, every day, in the streets and taverns. There skulked another class of people who could not be saved: the tide of 'idle beggars and roguish companions'. Like 'the rich', they 'lived altogether upon the People'. They were 'common haunters of alehouses, unthriftes, spendals and drunkards, having scarce either pennies in their purses or coats to their backs'. They spent 'all the week long at tipling houses, having no regard for a civil behaviour, nor desire to purchase an honest and good report among men'. 'Unable to content themselves with theire poore condicon,' they 'doe breake the walles of obedience ... seeking to satisfye themselves by robbery, and oftentimes murther the consequence thereof'.

In a sense, Jones gave a theological answer to the gentlemen who spoke against a Guild Merchant. In the eyes of God, 'manuary workers' were worth all the 'rich ... gentilmen' put together. A body governed by 'the faithful' would be much more than a collective trading enterprise, it heralded a new Jerusalem. Yet he was no advocate of *bourgeois* social mobility, positively railing 'against a climbing humour, a bramble spirit, a disposition inclining to preheminence'. Instead, he appealed to the immemorial popular conviction that government should emerge from the people, 'purchase(d) by an honest and good report among men'. Here was another escape clause for the wealthy puritan merchants who were to take over and transform the government of the town, men like Philip Marner and John Coxwell: Tyndale's conception of 'elders' who were expected to emerge from the 'congregaycon' by dint of demonstrated virtue and capacity.[24] Communally observed merit, not wealth or birth, lay at the heart of this doctrine. A good monarch, magistrate, community treasurer or clothier was no more than the temporal steward of an estate, responsible for managing it in such a way as to ensure

24 Rollison, 'Tyndale and all his Sect', Ch. 4 in *Local Origins*.

the health, happiness and virtue of all those who depended on its enterprise and produce. His or her role was to ensure that the fruits of the earth, thus produced, were distributed to the faithful. Good 'rich men', *faithful* lords, used their authority to produce in order to give away. Such *wisedom* would ensure the respect and love of their neighbours. They were of, not above, the people. The 'climbing humour', the avaricious desire to accumulate 'land to land, house to house, and lordshipp to lordshipp', associated with the scramble for title, was another matter. 'Inclination to preheminence', he explained, was associated 'not with intent to do any common good to the country, but with purpose only to feed and satisfy the root of arrogancy and ambition, to command all men and be subject to none'. This had been the popular view for centuries: virtuous, godly authorities did what they did, not for personal gain, but for the 'common good of the country', the commonweal.

It is not surprising that Jones attracted enemies, perhaps from the survivalist rump of the manorial cabal. Ecclesiastical authorities went to some trouble to have him suppressed. On 19 October 1581, Jones was instituted to the rectory of Welford-on-Avon on the presentation of Lewis Grevell, heir to a family of great woolmasters. In 1584 he was called but failed to appear before the corrupt chancellor of Gloucester Diocese, William Blackleech. In his absence, Blackleech found him to be 'of suspected life; not a graduate, nor a (licensed) preacher'. In the circumstances, this means no more than that in Jones's absence, Blackleech accepted the word (and very likely the money) of the notables who brought the case against him.

On October 1586 Jones was again summoned to attend Blackleech's house to answer a detection that 'he came into this diocese without letters testimonial from the place of his ordination or of two justices… and served the cure and preached (at Cirencester) without licence of the Bishop (John Bullingham) or the Judge (Blackleech)'. This time Jones appeared and claimed that although he had 'not a licence under the seal of either the bishop or the judge' he did have 'the bishop's permission (*venia*)'. Blackleech ordered him to return later that day 'to answer certain (other) articles', but he did not return 'and was suspended from his office'.[25]

Jones the Preacher was somehow caught up in the turbulent politics of Gloucester Diocese at this time, perhaps on the side of Bishop John Bullingham in his struggle with Chancellor Blackleech.[26] Blackleech was perfectly capable of falsifying records, and Jones may have been suspended without knowing anything about the extra 'articles'. On 11 January 1586–7 he was again cited to appear to answer an allegation that 'he serveth the cure (at Cirencester) without license'. He failed to appear and the chan-

25 GCL: Hockaday Abstracts, 'Cirencester', 1586; Austin, 'Philip Jones of Cirencester'.

26 F.D. Price, 'Bishop Bullingham and Chancellor Blackleech: A Diocese Divided', *Trans BGAS* 91 (1972), 175–98.

cellor excommunicated him.[27] In March 1587 he was again called to appear in court to answer certain allegations, this time before Bishop Bullingham himself; he 'subscribed to the articles of religion and the bishop absolved him.

Three months later more specific allegations were heard against Jones, that 'he doth not followe the book of comen prayer in divers poyntes, he doth not reade the 11th and 12th verses of the lateny, (and that) he refused to baptise two children'. This was serious. It suggested Jones disagreed publicly with the Book of Common Prayer, denied the supremacy of the queen in the English church, and was most likely (it could be implied) an Anabaptist of some kind. The case was referred to the court of high commission.[28] Finally, in September 1587 Jones was a minor beneficiary in the will of a prominent 'gentleman tailor', Philip Marner. Among a long list of small bequests at the end of his will, Marner left cartloads of fire-wood to half a dozen poor artisans, and 'to Mr Jones the Preacher' he gave '20 shides of wood and my best blacke cloake'. The bequest may mean that Jones was poor enough to appreciate something to keep him warm. Marner expected Jones to be at his funeral, even to preach over his coffin. That it was Marner's *best* black cloak suggests Jones had powerful friends in the community, as well as powerful enemies beyond it.[29]

Jones's mission at Cirencester began before 1584, came to a head between October 1586 and November 1587. A case heard on 11 November 1587, described him as 'late curate', suggesting he had left town. In his absence, the town clerk, the new curate and two other men 'swore to depose what they knew in the matter of articles concerning the health of the soul and reformation of the excesses of Philip Jones'. In his pastoral care and his sermons, the complainants alleged, Jones 'used very slanderous and seditious words against the curate there and others'. Perhaps he had accused them of being 'rich'.

His sermons offer unique insight into the millenarian emotions that were caught up with, and added vigour and venom to, the more businesslike reforms of the generations between the prophesying movement and the civil wars. Jones was connected to powerful but unstable networks, of which, on the evidence of his sermons, he was likely to have been viewed as a somewhat unstable member. His benefice at Welford suggests he may have been a distant client of the earl of Leicester. 'Puritan' religious sentiment was common to this and the other major connection with affairs of state, via the Hakluyts. Excoriation of the rich and powerful was a common element in much of the preaching and propaganda that emanated from these networks in the 1580s, but it is likely that the more prudent leaders of the new reli-

27 GCL: Hockaday, 'Cirencester 1586'; GRO, GDR Vol. 59.

28 *Ibid.*, Vol. 60.

29 Marner's will: GA, GDR (1587).

gion would, by 1589, have considered Jones to have gone too far, taken one facet of the grand vision too seriously at the expense of the others.

In the fluid circumstances of the 1570s and 1580s labels may obscure the outstanding fact that the prophesyings of these decades represent a popular evangelical movement that was every bit as distressing to authorities opposed to empowering the poor and labouring classes in any way at all, as the Great Awakening was in Pennsylvania and New England in the 1720s. American historians have long recognized the direct links between the Great Awakening and the American Revolution. Historians of the English Revolution have sometimes been reluctant to concede that it had any long-term causes at all.

12

Gentlemen and commons of the Seven Hundreds

> Gloucestershire was a county in which independent small producers predominated, and on them its parliamentarianism rested.[1]

The most influential of Tudor-Stuart England's constitutional writers, Sir Thomas Smith, divided the English into two classes, rulers and subjects. The 'common wealth, or policie of England', he wrote, was 'governed, administered and maintained by three sortes of person'. The first of these 'governing sorts', or ruling classes, of course, was 'the monarch … in whose name and authoritie all things be administered'. Second were 'the gentlemen', whom Smith also divided into two distinct 'partes'. Highest in rank was 'the Baronie or estate of Lordes', consisting of barons 'and all that bee above the degree of baron': marquises, dukes, earls etc. Below these national magnates came a much larger class of gentlemen 'which be no Lords, as Knights, Esquires and simple gentlemen.' Henry French suggests that a 'concept of gentility' was 'accorded universal (if not always positive) recognition' in early modern England; the ideal gentleman embodied 'social distinction, political autonomy, intellectual authority and material independence'. 'Alone among social groups', writes French, 'gentlemen were the people who acted upon a national stage.'[2]

The third and lowest 'sort' of Smith's ruling class was 'the yeomanrie'. The local gentry ('second sort') and yeomen ('third sort') were responsible for putting 'policie' ordained by the senior ranks into practice in the districts and localities. As for the subjects, Smith consigned the remainder to an extremely various and capacious 'fourth sort of men which doe not rule', consisting of the '*capite censii proletarii* or *operae*, day labourers, poor husbandmen, yea marchantes or retailers which have no free land, copyholders, all artificers, as tailors, shoemakers, carpenters, brickmakers, brick-

1 Brian Manning, *The English People and the English Revolution* (Harmondsworth 1978), 261.

2 Smith, *De Republica*, Ch. 16–23; for a discussion of Smith's 'sorts', see Andy Wood, *Riot, Rebellion and Popular Politics in Early Modern England* (Basingstoke 2002), 29–30; French, *Middle Sort of People*, 202, 204.

layers, masons &c.' This, as we shall see, is the least satisfactory category, in Smith's rankings and in my tabulation of the inhabitants of the Seven Hundreds, in which (to conform with Smith's evaluation) all men with anything resembling a trade vocation are lumped together. Even though landed gentlemen and merchants (like Christopher George and Robert Strange) ruled the roost in communal affairs, a good many began their careers as 'marchantes or retailers which have no free land', even 'articifers'.[3]

Two new sources make it possible to list and enumerate the inhabitants of the Seven Hundreds (including the town) and, in doing so, to test contemporary accounts of the constitution. Registers of baptisms, marriages and burials at Cirencester survive for all but five years of the century 1560–1660. These are used in Chapter 13 to enumerate and explore the significance of immigration in this period. In the Autumn of 1608, John Smyth of Nibley, steward to the lord lieutenant of Gloucestershire, Henry lord Berkeley, instructed the lords of every manor in Gloucestershire to provide the names of 'the able and sufficient men in body fit for his majesty's service in the wars' resident within their jurisdiction. Original working lists for Cirencester survive, and Smyth later made a comprehensive fair copy of all the returns. The resulting compilation was edited by Sir John Maclean and published at Gloucester in 1902. In 1934, A.J. and R.H. Tawney showed the muster lists constitute an incomparably rich source of information about social and economic organization in the generation before the civil wars. On the basis of aggregative statistics and tables, the Tawneys outlined some 'limits within which hypothesis [about the social dynamics of early modern England] is profitable' and warned that only studies sensitive to variable local conditions can ascertain how true such hypotheses were. In the 1970s and 1980s John Wyatt checked and corrected the Tawneys' figures and calculations for the whole county, and showed that the musters are an even richer source than they had supposed.[4]

The document refers to an array (or physical inspection) of the men of every manor, tithing and hundred in Gloucestershire who were fit to serve as soldiers. Smyth's brief was to find out how many soldiers and weapons Gloucestershire could put into the field, and what their military quality

3 Smith, *De Republica*, Ch. 24.

4 John Smyth, *The Names and Surnames of all the Able and Sufficient Men in Body fit for his Majesty's Service in the Wars, in the Month of August, 1608, in the Sixth Year of the Reign of James the First*, ed. Sir John Maclean (Gloucester 1902); A.J. and R.H. Tawney, 'An Occupational Census of the Seventeenth Century', *Econ Hist Rev* 5:1 (1934–5); the late John Wyatt conducted extensive, systematic and excellent work on the musters in the 1960s and 1970s: see Wyatt, 'Men and Armour for Gloucestershire in 1608', *Gloucestershire Historical Studies* 4 (1970); Wyatt, 'Occupations and Physique in 1608', *GHS* 6 (1972); Wyatt, 'Trades and Occupations in Gloucester, Tewkesbury and Cirencester in 1608', *GHS* 7 (1973); Wyatt, 'How Reliable is Men and Armour?', *GHS* 9 (1978); Wyatt, 'Industry in Gloucestershire in 1608', *GHS* 10 (1979).

was. The original working lists for Cirencester were filled out on consecutive days, 28 and 29 September 1608. There are two lists for Instrope and Gosditch Streets and one each for the other five streets or wards (the terms were interchangeable at Cirencester).[5] Following a first listing of names only, perhaps from the wardsman's memory, or from house-to-house enquiry, the men attended a muster, at which the responsible official appended each man's occupation, a number indicating his age ('1' = 'about twenty', '2' = about forty' and '3' = 'between fifty and threescore') and letters designating stature ('p' representing 'the tallest stature fitt to make a pykeman', 'm' signifying 'middle stature fit to make a musketyer', 'ca' indicating 'lower stature fitt to serve with a Calyver' and 'py' meaning 'of the meanest stature either fitt for a pioneer, or of little other use'). The official – in this case probably the wardsman for each street – was required to mark 'tr' against the name of 'trayned soldiers' and 'subs', which 'sheweth that the said man then was a subsidy man'.[6] Where no additional data was recorded, it is assumed that the man in question was absent from the muster. For some reason subsidymen were not marked in the lists for the Seven Hundreds. For an early modern census, the muster lists of 1608 (see Table 12.1) provide a lot of information about a lot of men.

[5] I came across the original Cirencester listings (clearly working lists; henceforth 'Cirencester 1608') in the muniments of Berkeley Castle: I am grateful to David Smith, then Gloucestershire County Archivist, for loaning me a copy of his catalogue-in-progress, for obtaining permission for me to visit Berkeley Castle to consult the muniments, and for Xeroxing the Cirencester listings for me. They differ slightly in content from the printed version, e.g. in the MS lists 'Instrope Street' is called 'Instrop streete *alias* St Sysley streete', and there are two different lists for Gosditch Street, one titled 'Heare are the names of the able men dwelling in gosditch streate', which contains 17 more names than the other, clearly a later copy, probably in the same hand but much more neatly written and simply titled 'Gosditch Streat'. The list for 'Instrope Streete' is headed 'Cirencester 28/9' [the '9' being superimposed on the '8'] September 1608. Each street list is in a different hand.

[6] Maclean (ed.), 'The Burrowe of Cirencester', *Men and Armour*, 239–43; the procedure is deduced from the fact that the lists of names were written down first and occupations (usually after the name) and codes for age, stature and state of training (invariably above the name) were appended later. My guess is that the initial lists were compiled by the wardsmen, partly perhaps from memory but more likely from door to door, and the additional information was collected at the hundredal array, doubtless supervised by Smyth and Archard, perhaps the next day.

Table 12.1. The social and military formation of the Seven Hundreds, 1608

Hundred	Names	Tr.	Gent	Serv.	Yeo.	Husb.	Trad.	Lab.	Mill	Shep.	Inn.
Cirencester	353	27	5	36–23	2	9	222	43		3	3
		7.6	1.4	10.2							
				6.5							
Crowthorne	580	74	9	60–39	25	160	51	60	7	3	1
& Minety		12.8	1.6	10.3	4.3	27.5	8.8	10.3			
				6.7							
Brightwells	436	76	12	84–43	15	97	87	27	7	7	3
Barrow		17.4	2.7	19.2	3.4	22.2	20	6.2	1.6	1.6	.6
				9.9							
Rapsgate	269	33	4	36–18	2	143	52	11	2	-	1
				13.4							
		12.3	1.5	6.7	.7	53.2	19.3	4.1			
Bradley	450	39	15	98–55	17	66	54	56	3	9	3
		8.7	3.3	21.8	3.8	14.7	12	12.4			
				12.2							
Bisley	728	75	9	67–45	57	122	315	43	11+	1	1+
		10.3	1.2	9.2	7.8	16.8	43.3	5.9	1.5		
				6.1							
Longtree	820	43	7	60–34	12	116	437	42	4	5	8
		5.2	0.8	7.3	1.5	14.1	53.3	5.1			
				4.1							
Seven Hundreds	3,636	367	61	440–257	130	716	1218	282	34	28	20
%		10.1	1.7	12–7	3.6	19.7	33.3	7.8	.93	.7	.5

As Table 12.1 shows, the lists for the Seven Hundreds of Cirencester identify 3,636 men (excluding lords of manors) in 99 wards, manors and tithings.[7] In most cases the individual lists correspond to parishes and discrete settlements (villages like Baunton and Stratton on the outskirts of Cirencester, and market towns like Painswick, Bisley, Fairford and Lechlade). Including the lords of manors whose main residence was probably in or near the district, the lists name two barons, a dozen knights (and two knights' widows), 27 esquires, at least 61 gentlemen (excluding liminal categories like several obvious 'gentlemen clothiers' of Stroudwater and other merchants on the verge of gentility), 130 yeomen, over 700 husbandmen, 1,200-plus tradesmen of every variety, including clothworkers, 282 labourers, at least 34 millers, 20 innkeepers, 28 shepherds, a few apprentices (only mentioned as such on a few manors), and 440 servants. Except for the barons, knights and esquires, many of whom were listed as lords of manors, a few of them absentee, these figures clearly represent *minima*; they excluded men who were not able in body through illness, physical impediment and age, and, of

7 All the columns are self-explanatory except 'serv[ants]', in which the first figure denotes number of servants, the second the number of men with servants.

course, women and children. With allowances for these discrepancies, they represent a remarkable 'empirical' sample (the lists being compiled on the basis of observation) against which to test and qualify the most comprehensive near-contemporary accounts of the constitution of the English commonwealth by Sir Thomas Smith and Thomas Wilson.

In date and content, Thomas Wilson's adaptation of Smith's ranking system (1600) is about four decades closer to the context of the 1608 musters.[8] Where Smith came close to reducing rank to landed wealth, Wilson gave greater emphasis to the military dimension of the 'state of England'. Their ranking systems are almost identical, but Wilson emphasized the commonwealth's readiness and capacity to defend the territory. How quickly could every manor, township and borough transform itself into a platoon or regiment? English communities could take military formation quickly because, as Wilson saw it, social and military ranks were identical. When England was threatened, the monarch morphed into a commander in chief, as Elizabeth had done in 1588. Dukes, earls, viscounts and barons became chiefs of staff and generals, knights became colonels, esquires became majors, gentlemen became captains, yeomen became regimental and company sergeants-major and platoon leaders, husbandmen became corporals, and the multitudinous *proletarii* of landless artisans and labourers became the rank and file. From Wilson's perspective, musters like those of 1522 and 1608 articulated the constitution. Wilson warned that the loyalty of the 'third sort' (younger children of gentry and yeomen), so central to English constitutional practice since the late fourteenth century, could not be taken for granted. In arguments with the state, they were liable to side with their local commonwealths.[9]

How many soldiers could the Seven Hundreds put into the field? Column two in Table 12.1, enumerating men who were trained soldiers, shows that the average Seven Hundreds manor contained no less than four trained soldiers. All but 15 of the 99 jurisdictions had at least one man so designated. Cirencester had 27; the wealthiest ward, Dyer Street, had 10, and only one of the poorest and smallest wards, Instrope Street, had none. The communities of the Seven Hundreds so seldom failed to record a trained soldier that in such cases clerical error, failure to scribble 'tr.' against a name, might be suspected. Only in the clothworking communities of Bisley and Longtree hundreds were designated trained men relatively few and far between. Also noteworthy is that most places had (often several) men with calivers and/or muskets, which had completely displaced the longbows and crossbows that were the chief weapons of English armies up to the mid-sixteenth century. Guns were not as common as bows had been in some parts of Gloucester-

8 Smith is thought to have composed *De Republica Anglorum* in the early 1560s: Mary Dewar, *Sir Thomas Smith: A Tudor Intellectual in Office* (London 1964), 112–14.

9 See Thomas Wilson, *The State of England Anno Domini 1600*, ed. F.J. Fisher (London 1936); for a discussion of Wilson, see Rollison, *A Commonwealth of the People*, 417–23.

shire in 1522, but were present on most manors and almost as likely to be owned by a husbandman as by a gentleman. Some places, like Painswick, were trained and armed to the teeth.

The number and even spread of men who were trained soldiers is very significant. In 1642–3 it became a question of who the militias turned up to fight for, as George Brydges, lord Chandos of Sudeley, discovered to his cost when he tried to present the king's commission of array at Cirencester, in August of that year. Trained men were especially common in the villages closest to Cirencester: 74 of 580 men (12.8%) in Crowthorne and Minety and 76 of 436 (17.4%) in Brightwells Barrow. The successors of these men constituted the local core of the militia that was mobilized in the early months of the civil wars.

In what follows we must bear in mind this readiness for military mobilization. According to their designations, no more than 500 (13.75%) of the 3,636 men belonged to Smith's 'ruling sorts'. In Wilson's account, this was the (itself highly graduated) officer class. The remaining 3,136 servants, husbandmen, tradesmen and merchants, labourers, millers, shepherds and innkeepers (86.2%) were 'the fourth sort, who doe not rule'. Political and religious movements of the 1570s and 1580s targeted these 'other ranks'. Indeed, Philip Jones taught them they were God's chosen. We have to see the ranking systems of this epoch in several ways at the same time. Musters articulated their military functions.

Table 12.2 describes a town that clearly belonged to an 'advanced organic economy'. All but 29 of the 355 men mustered at Cirencester were assigned a specialist occupation. Of these, as Table 12.2 shows, 263 (74%) were direct producers of one kind or another, working with land (4.3%), grain (2.4%), meat (6%), animal hides (15%), wool (22.7%), wood (5.2%), stone (3%), glass (1%) and metals (4.3%). For such an important market centre, as the town certainly was, comparatively few local men worked in transport (4.3%) or in dealing of one kind or another (12.3%). On top of these we have a bailiff, five gentlemen and 43 labourers (13.2%). We know from other evidence that gentlemen were always more common than just the five listed as soldiers in 1608. Most surprisingly, there is not a single reference to any specialists in the preparation and sale of raw wool: no shearers, packers, loaders, staplers or woolcombers, and no-one specifically described as a merchant or 'cloathman'. The leading employer was clothmaking, which provided occupation for 92 of the mustered men (28%), of whom 42 (13%) were weavers. In terms of the occupations of its able-bodied men, it was larger version of the manufacturing townships of its hinterlands, places like Stroud, Painswick, Dursley and Wotton under Edge.[10] They were small district 'capitals'. Cirencester had double or triple their populations and some important concentrations, including some successful wholesale tailors and shoemakers. Its wealthiest men were much

10

richer than those of the smaller towns. Numerically, it was a town of many more or less independent artisans, retailers and labourers.

Table 12.1. Occupations at Cirencester in 1608

1. Agriculture			
Husbandmen	6		
Yeomen	2		
Gardener	3		
Shepherds	3	Total	14
2. Grain processing			
Baker	6 (1)		
Brewer	1	Total	7 (1)
3. Meat			
Butcher	17 (3)	Total	17 (3)
4. Animal hides			
Tanner	2 (1)		
Currier	1		
Shoemaker	20 (5)		
Glover	9 (1)		
Saddler	4 (4)		
Bookbinder	1		
Scrivener	1	Total	38 (11)
5. Cloth			
Cardmaking	4		
Weaver	42 (4)		
Dyer	1		
Tucker	1		
Clothier	5 (9)		
Draper	4		
Mercer	9 (1)		
Tailor	12 (1)		
Hatter	2	Total	80 (15)
6. Wood			
Sawyer	2		
Carpenter	3		
Joiner	6		
Cooper	3		
Wheelwright	2		
Hivemaker	1	Total	17
7. Stone			
Mason	6		
Slatter	2		

Tiler	1		
Pavier	1	Total	10
8. Glass			
Glazier	2 (1)	Total	2 (1)
9. Metals			
Smith (iron)	8 (1)		
Farrier (iron)	1		
Brazier (brass)	1		
Cutler (steel)	2		
Plumber (lead)	1	Total	13 (1)
10. Transport			
Carrier	2 (1)		
Carter	5		
Ostler	5		
Peddlar	1	Total	13 (1)
11. Alcohol, food, entertainment			
Vintner	1 (4)		
Innkeeper	3		
Tapster	2		
Victualler	1		
Carver	1		
Chamberlain	2		
Usher	1		
Musician	2		
Loiterer	1	Total	14 (4)
12. Shopkeepers			
Chandler	3		
Apothecary	1		
Barber	2	Total	6
13. Local official			
Bailiff	1		
14. Labourer	43		
15. Gentlemen	5 (10)		
16. Occupation not given	29		
Total names	355		
Direct producers	263 (74%)		
Distribution and dealing	57 (16%)		
Surplus extraction	6 (1.6%)		

(Figures in brackets indicate servants and sons)

Occupations included agriculture, grain processing, butchering, curing and working animal hides, making cloth, tailoring, working with wood, stone, glass and metals, transport, brewing and retailing alcohol, cooking takeaway food, playing music, providing entertainment, shopkeeping and general labouring. None of these are impossible to imagine in the Saxon market and minster town or the Roman provincial capital. E.A. Wrigley writes that 'during the quarter millennium before the nineteenth century the course of economic change (in England) must have been very different from that in her near neighbours'.[11] Continuous adaptation and development of water mills to the fulling and finishing of cloth was one important factor responsible for the transformation of this *countrey* into a mass producer of cloth. It still belonged to what Wrigley calls an 'organic' economy. It made commodities out of mostly locally produced (grown, dug, mined) raw materials. There is nothing in the list that Gloucestershire could not produce, from fine wool to steel produced in the new furnaces of the Forest of Dean. The difference here was the cloth industry. The workers recorded at Cirencester and throughout the clothworking districts of Gloucestershire and Wiltshire, were part of a densely but insecurely interconnected 'global' market.

What was the economic base of the officer class? Cirencester's population history up to 1640 suggests close and constant interaction between town and country.[12] Yet apart from its butchers, analysis of the occupational structure in 1608 reveals that townspeople had little to do with the trade in the raw materials that were sold in its markets and processed in its workshops. There were no wool staplers, wool drivers or millers. Grain, wool, meat, hides, stone, metals were brought to the town by outsiders who used local labourers for loading and unloading, but probably supplied most of their own labour too. Forty-three labourers does not seem too high for an important market centre like Cirencester. At this time, it seems, the wool was being sheared, packed and stapled elsewhere. Woolcombing and stapling (sorting) were almost certainly by-employments in the surrounding villages, as we know they were in the eighteenth century: occupations for the wives and children of husbandmen and labourers, the wool being distributed and the yarn collected, at this stage, by the clothiers. If, as the elections of 1640 were to make clear, Gloucestershire, politically, was divided into two camps, 'weavers and shepherds', Cirencester, occupationally, belonged to both.

Wool was produced in large quantities in the North Wolds. Twenty-nine townships and villages in the rural hundreds of Brightwells Barrow, Kiftsgate, Slaughter and Crowthorne and Minety mustered a total of 55 shepherds, in

11 E.A. Wrigley, 'Country and Town: the Primary, Secondary and Tertiary Peopling of England in the Early Modern Period', in Paul Slack and Ryk Ward (eds), *The Peopling of Britain: the Shaping of a Human Landscape* (Oxford 2002), 224; Wrigley, 'The Transition to an Advanced Organic Economy: Half a Millennium of English Agriculture', *Econ Hist Rev* 59:3 (August 2006).

12 See above, Chapter 10.

addition to three at Cirencester. Sixteen places record one shepherd, eight give two, one gives three, two (Naunton and Snowshill) four each, five came from Winchcombe, and the old Winchcombe Abbey manor of Sherborne recorded no fewer than nine. Sherborne was a famous shearing centre. Until 1539 the flocks belonging to the abbot of Winchcombe had been brought there every spring to be sheared and prepared for sale. The manor was sold in 1551 to Thomas Dutton.[13] His son, William Dutton, reputedly the wealthiest man in the county, was one of only five Gloucestershire landowners to contribute 40 pounds or more to the Subsidy of 1608, and the only one who was not a knight.[14] The muster for Sherborne lists one gentleman, 12 of 15 yeomen, 9 of 28 husbandmen and two of the shepherds in the Sherborne list as 'servants to William Dutton'. At first sight this suggests feudal pretensions, but what it probably implies is corporate mercantile organization: this was the core of Dutton's business. The high status of many of his 'servants' probably identifies them as his subordinate 'managers'.[15]

Sherborne was a prize asset. Straddling the road to Northleach, Burford, Oxford and London, the 'backside' of Sherborne overlooked the waterways in which, every year, thousands of sheep were washed in preparation for the shearing. The best and fastest shearers in England had gathered there for centuries, observed by factors from Florence, Bruges, wherever fine cloth was made, who watched the flocks arriving from the North Wolds, and eyed the batches that would best suit their purposes.[16] By 1608 styling yeomen and husbandmen as servants to the lord of the manor was old fashioned and falling out of use. It occurs in only five of the 400 places mustered in 1608, including Sapperton, where a 'gent', 15 husbandmen and nine yeomen were listed as 'servants to Sir Henry Poole, knight', the lord of the manor. Poole and Dutton were major parliamentarian families in that they constantly represented town and country from the 1580s on. Yet when their moment of decision came, from August 1642 to February 1643, they sided with the king.

The Sherborne listing also includes three millers and a loader: it was also a centre of distribution for grain and flour. This was unusual. Twenty-six villages in the relevant hundreds recorded millers in 1608, but only four mention more than one. Most Cotswold villages were self-sufficient in this regard. Those with several millers included Sir William Sandys' manor of Cranham, near Painswick, the crown manor of Lower Slaughter (sold to the London businessman William Whitmore in 1611); and Sherborne. References to loaders are rare and their presence probably indicates large-scale milling. They occur

13 Sir John Maclean, *Calendar of Sherborne Muniments* (1889), 14.

14 Atkyns, *Gloucestershire*, 21.

15 For 'Particulars of John Dutton's Estate' presented to the Committee for Compositions with Delinquents in November 1646, see *Historical and genealogical Memoirs of the Dutton Family* (privately printed 1899), 151–3 (GCL).

16 See R.H. Hilton, 'Winchcombe Abbey and the Manor of Sherborne', in H.P.R. Finberg, *Gloucestershire Studies* (London 1955).

on Edmund Chamberlen's manor of Maugersbury, part of Stow on the Wold; a carrier (again rare as a specialist occupation on the Wolds) is mentioned at Bourton on the Water, in the lordship of Grey Brydges, lord Chandos of Sudeley, the 'king of the Cotswolds'. Most of the 'senior officers' in this part of England opposed the policies of Charles I in the 1630s. Yet in 1642–3 they sided with the king.

Sir Henry Poole, lord of four manors (Duntisbourne Rous, Daglinworth, Coates and Sapperton) in 1608, was the scion of four generations of parliament men. We saw his father assisting the diocese in the matter or recusants in an earlier chapter. William's heir, John Dutton, led the country's resistance to crown impositions right up to August 1642. He was actively anti-court on every occasion for conflict. 'Resistance to the (so-called "free gift" of 1626) in the county was led by Dutton and Sir Henry Poole.'[17] Dutton paid tax on 59 hearths at his manor house in 1664.[18] Sapperton House was slightly smaller, paying on 30 in 1674, by which time it was in the possession of Sir Robert Atkyns.[19] Dutton opposed the Forced Loan of 1628. He tried to avoid composition for knighthood in 1630. He was 'the most notable opponent of Ship Money' and his resistance 'set an example for many others – gentry and yeomen alike'.[20] Some of them may have been the sons of men described in the 1608 muster lists as 'servant to William Dutton'. Usually, by this time, yeomen were nobody's servants. Yet Poole and John Dutton were at the king's court at Oxford when plans were made to take the parliamentarian bastion of Cirencester, executed by an army of 7,000 cavaliers, in February 1643.

If the enemies were commerce-tainted businessmen, insolent tradesmen, dirty craftworkers and labourers, the FitzHardings of Berkeley and the Brydges of Sudeley were never going to be anything but royalist, when, for each of them in their own times and places, 'the moment of decision' arrived. Berkeley Castle was an island of royalism in a sea of instinctive parliamentarians. Not so the territory of the lords Chandos, a country dominated by the Cotswold wool-magnates, and the Vale of Tewkesbury. 'In Cheltenham the lord of the manor (Dutton) was … a royalist,' writes Cheltenham's historian, 'and so were Conway Whithorn and John Stubbs of Charlton Kings. Henry Norwood of Leckhampton, William Lawrence of Shurdington, the Hicks family of Chipping Campden …' also supported the king.[21] The Tracys of Toddington and

17 L.J. Zweigman, 'The Role of the Gentleman in County Government and Society: the Gloucestershire Gentry, 1625–1649', Ph.D. thesis, McGill University (1987), 455.

18 TNA E179/246/16, 'Sherborne'; for an account of Sherborne House and Park, see Nicholas Kingsley, *The County Houses of Gloucestershire*, Vol. 1: *1500–1660* (Cheltenham 1989), 154–8.

19 Photocopy at GA D383, Bisley Hundred: 'Sapperton'; for Sapperton House, see Kingsley, *County Houses*, Vol. 1, 152–3.

20 Zweigman, 'The Role of the Gentleman in County Government and Society', 455, 456, 461, 473, 506.

21 Gwen Hart, *A History of Cheltenham* (Oxford 1965), 103.

their cousins of Stanway, the Chamberlens of Maugersbury, the Whitmores of Slaughter (also lords of the borough of Winchcombe), the Stratfords of Hawling and Swell, the Higfords of Dixton and the Grevills of Honeybourne, and all of the greater gentry of the region for whom we have any positive identification, supported the king. Can this be coincidence? What else did these men and estates have in common, besides their loyalty to Charles I?

During the sixteenth and early seventeenth century, such men had bought up the estates of the medieval magnates, most of them, in the Seven Hundreds, abbots. By the second half of the sixteenth century an expanded class of gentlemen had moved into political and economic space vacated by the dissolution. Had there been parliaments in the 1630s, Dutton, as a leader of the country opposition to the policies of Charles I, would have been elected as a member for the shire, or for Gloucester, or even perhaps Cirencester. New men like John Dutton had more in common with Philip Marner and John Cockswell[22] than with Grey Brydges or Henry, lord Berkeley. Yet when the moment of decision came to the region, in January 1643, Dutton was at Oxford with the king and his cousin, Ralph, was in Prince Rupert's army.

Contemporaries divided Gloucestershire east of the Severn into two socially and geographically distinct 'lands', of 'weavers and shepherds'.[23] Cirencester straddled both these worlds, but the wool trade was centred elsewhere. The rift between weavers and shepherds became explicit in elections for the Short Parliament in 1640, when one of the candidates compared it with the class-wars of medieval Florence between 'Guelphs and Ghobbellines'.[24]

Cirencester was the only place in Gloucestershire where these different political economies met regularly on a day-to-day basis. Great magnates like the Duttons and Brydges had little cause to visit the Stroudwater Valleys, or pass through the little cloth towns of the Vale of Berkeley. These places had grown up on the peripheries of Norman-Angevin domination. From a magnate point of view, they led nowhere. There were no men living there that the Cotswold magnates could regard as their equals: none, as far as my research indicates, could claim Norman-Angevin ancestry. Instead, they seethed with rude, 'masterless' men who did not particularly respect pretentious genteel display and manners, and were difficult to beat up if they were rude, or did not make the right gestures of deference, because it might start a riot. But there were other ways that the magnates could exercise their hostility to the manufacturing classes.

The increased scale of industrial activity in the sixteenth century expanded markets for food and raw materials. The rewards to established landlords spiralled. Occasions for dispute between the 'weavers' and 'shepherds' were routine. The conflict between manorial and trade factions in the town of

22 For Marner and Coxwell, see below, Chapter 14.

23 See Rollison, 'Weavers and Shepherds: the Elections of March 1640 as Social Drama', *Local Origins*, Ch. 6.4, 136–48.

24 *Ibid*, qf. 145.

Cirencester was part of a wider, regional class-conflict. There are distinct signs of class-hostility between the clothworking communities and the wool-magnates from 1560 on. G.D. Ramsey notes 'class jealousy subsisting between clothiers and country gentry in the West Country textile industry'. It became bitter in the 1560s, took legislative form in the 1570s.[25] Before 1560 'large clothiers ... sometimes sat in the Commons' representing the boroughs, 'but from the accession of Elizabeth onwards clothiers were rarely to be found in the House'.[26] In Gloucestershire, it must be added, clothiers were *never* elected. But the men who were elected were businessmen who, for all their royalism when the 'moment of decision' came, understood the threat posed by court policies of the 1630s.

An underlying field-of-force was appearing, involving tensions between the wool- and grain-magnates, and the other side, represented most obviously by the '200-plus clothier families who controlled the (manufacturing) and marketing of the cloth'.[27] They were the most obvious representatives of Gloucestershire's 'middle ranke', as John Corbet (somewhat misleadingly) described 'the only active men' for Parliament in 1645.[28] As the most important market centre in the region, Cirencester naturally experienced this adversarial conjuncture most intensely. In 1586 Philip Jones had criticized 'disdainful' magnates who engrossed 'land to land, house to house and lordship to lordship'. Locally, unpopular authorities like Robert Strange and Christopher George come to mind, but it would have been difficult to ignore the claims of Sir Giles Poole and William Dutton. One name came first in most lists where disdainful, aristocratic leadership was concerned: the Brydges, lords Chandos of Sudeley.

The 'senior officers' discussed in the foregoing paragraphs were those whom, parliamentarians complained, let their 'country' down when the warriors of the king invaded it in the winter of 1642–3. The rest of this chapter, and the next, is an anatomy of the ranks below this 'general staff'. Table 12.1 above enumerates and classifies vocations in the muster lists for the Seven Hundreds of Cirencester, Brightwells Barrow, Crowthorne and Minety, Bradley, Rapsgate, Bisley and Longtree. Columns 3–8 give the numbers of gentlemen, yeomen, husbandmen, artisans, labourers and servants listed under each place, with totals and averages for all the hundreds reproduced in that table.

Columns 3 and 5 show that while Smith's 'third sort' was not exactly thick on the ground, it was evenly spread across the district. Gentlemen constituted 1.7 percent and yeomen 3.6 percent of the total; 45 places list resident yeomen, 42 resident gentry. These were the colonels, majors, captains and lieutenants of the social order. Only 22 of the 99 lists contained no refer-

25 G.D. Ramsey, 'Distribution of Cloth Industry in 1561–2', *Econ Hist Rev* 57:227 (July 1942), 46.

26 *Ibid*, 47.

27 Perry, 'Gloucestershire Woollen Industry, 1100–1690', 113.

28 See below, Chapter 16.

ence to either gentlemen or yeomen. The upshot was that no-one in the Seven Hundreds lived more than a few miles from several gentlemen and yeomen. As for non-commissioned officers, husbandmen (tenant-farmers to 'officers') were absent from only ten places, yet were not nearly as common as peasant-society stereotypes would lead us to expect. They constituted only 20 percent of the mustered men and were unevenly distributed. Fifty-two percent of men from the thinly populated Cotswold plateau between Cirencester and the descent to Gloucester from Brimpsfield (Rapsgate Hundred), for example, were husbandmen, far more than the second highest in this category, Crowthorne and Minety Hundred, where the proportion of husbandmen was 27.5 percent and yeomen (4.3%) were present in slightly higher than average numbers. Husbandmen did well in the villages close to the town. The thin-soiled, windy plateau of Rapsgate was least attractive to (or productive of) gentlemen and yeomen. On the other hand, at least some men not described as husbandmen in the clothworking hundreds of Bisley and Longtree, where craftsmen (mostly clothworkers) constituted 43 percent and 53 percent respectively, aimed to hold enough land to sustain the household in market slumps and were therefore 'husbandmen' at least part of their time. Fast streams for fulling were not the only attraction of the Stroudwater Valleys. Dual economy, in which craft-workers also kept a few animals on the 'waste', and grew a little grain and some vegetables, was practised by every household that could afford it: it stacked the odds in favour of the household being able to maintain its relative independency through the cycles of 'weal and woe' described in the last chapter.

In their pioneering analysis of the muster lists, A.J. and R.H. Tawney addressed an ideal so important it was rarely necessary to name it, *independency*. It meant the capacity 'to live of one's own and not (like magnates and the undeserving poor) in the breath of other men'. 'Independent inhabitancy' entailed a further distinction: in all but the most radical of the constitutions put forward in the 1640s, employees were defined as 'dependent' and thus incapable of exercising an independent voice in local and national politics. The distinction between employers and employees was prominent in the propaganda of both sides before and during the early encounters of the civil wars, as will be shown in Chapter 16; it may not have infected discussions of the franchise until the Levellers raised it in the debates of the mid to late 1640s. How many of the men listed in 1608 were 'independent producers' and how many were 'employees'? The answer to that question, wrote the Tawneys, 'will determine whether, in the generation before the civil war, England is to be regarded as predominantly a society of peasant farmers, small masters and *travailleurs isoles*, or as containing large proletarian elements'.[29]

29 Tawneys, 'An Occupational Census', 47.

As the Tawneys realized, and as analysis of the Seven Hundreds of Cirencester shows unambiguously, local constitutions were extremely variable. Gentlemen, yeomen, husbandmen, small masters and 'proletarian elements' (labourers and servants) were present everywhere, but in very different mixtures and proportions. Allowing that 'the attempt to draw a sharp line between wage earners and independent producers is for the seventeenth century – and indeed much later – an anachronism', the Tawneys began by counting servants, apprentices and labourers. If large numbers of persons clearly employed in the service of others is an index of modernity, agriculture was easily the most 'modern' sector, with a county-wide percentage of employees (servants and labourers) of 59.1. The next highest, clothmaking, averaged a mere 4.8 percent. When knights, esquires and gentlemen (who employed 15.8% of the servants) are excluded, 'the relative number of employees found in other groups is almost negligible'. Across the whole county 'not less than one in four of the men returned were employees' in this narrow sense.

How many of the other 75 percent belonged to households that could, in times of crisis, 'live of their own'? The Tawneys concluded it was 'a system of family farms worked with the aid of relatives... and only to a small extent with hired labour'. If 'hired labour' is taken to include servants and labourers, it was more common in agriculture. In the Seven Hundreds, 846 husbandmen and yeomen rented or owned land. On the evidence of the lists, only a few of the larger freeholding yeomen and tenant-husbandmen held more than enough land to support an extended household, including a wife and children, servants in husbandry and even an apprentice. Yet even smallholding husbandmen were more secure in dearth years than landless households. To these potential 'independents' must be added most of the village gentry (with a single manor). This gives us close to 900 potentially independent inhabitants. Servants and labourers (both scarce in the cloth-working hundreds of Bisley and Longtree) come in at 682. As the Tawneys suggested, global figures like these 'indicate the limits within which hypothesis is profitable'.

In a considerable number of these households, wives and children manufactured a few items (notably woollen yarn for the local clothmakers) that could be sold at market; smallholding husbandmen hired themselves out as labourers to wealthier husbandmen, yeomen and gentlemen, as and when need and opportunity arose. Household was the key institution: everyone had to contribute to the household treasury as soon as they were old enough. The head of the household was its 'bailiff' or 'steward'. In agriculture most of the labour was 'done by men whose primary concern was with their own holdings, or by sons of "peasants" who expected to obtain one'.[30]

30 *Ibid*, 48.

In the clothmaking districts, represented in Table 12.1 by Bisley and Longtree hundreds and the town itself, the Tawneys pictured 'a multitude of one-man businesses, with a few large concerns employing less than half a dozen journeymen'. Men of craft or trade constituted the largest class of vocations in the Seven Hundreds: 1,218 men (33.3%). How many were 'independent producers'? As far as the largest category, textile artisans, is concerned, independency was qualified by the dependency of most households on clothiers. As we have seen throughout this book, 'it was commerce and finance which yielded the most substantial fortunes, and merchants, rather than [direct] manufacturers, who formed the aristocracy of the middle classes'.[31] The Tawneys calculated that, on average, each clothier found work for about nine weavers and about half that number of tuckers, fullers, dyers, shearers and other ancillary trades and occupations. Cirencester had its own organization, centred on the exclusive Weavers' and Journeymen Weavers' Guilds.

The lists for the clothworking hundreds of Bisley and Longtree look very different from those of the agrarian hundreds. The place of Cirencester and these two hundreds in the national cloth industry is suggested by a list of 353 'country clothiers' fined, in the twelve months from September 1561 to September 1562, for selling defective cloth to the merchants at Blackwell Hall. Sixty-six (18.7%) were from the clothworking districts of Gloucestershire, of whom more than half (34), including two widows, were from the hundreds of Cirencester, Bisley and Longtree.[32] These parts were more populous, the lists much longer and simpler than those for the rural hundreds considered above. Longtree Hundred included the oldest 'rural' cloth parishes in the region, 'Michell Hampton' (Minchinhampton) and 'Rodborowe'. They listed far fewer trained men (5.2%), and servants (7.3%) compared to averages of 10.1% and 12.1% for the whole Seven Hundreds. Bisley Hundred, including several manors associated with the unnamed chapelry of Stroud, was closer to the averages (averaging 10.3% trained men) but its numbers of yeomen, husbandmen, servants and trained men are distorted by unusually high figures for the exceptional township and parish of Painswick.[33]

In the hundreds of Bisley and Longtree, the cloth industry was already centred on mills owned (or leased) by great clothiers. There were still many small-scale clothiers, 'independents', finishing and marketing a few cloths made in their own and neighbouring households. Weavers and other ancillary workers were dependent on clothiers: many were, for most intents and purposes, 'employees of the clothier from which they received orders'. Yet

31 *Ibid*, 55.

32 Ramsay, 'Distribution of the Cloth Industry in 1561–2', 361–9.

33 Painswick recorded 161 men, of whom 30 were trained and 18 owned calivers or muskets; they included 2 gents, 18 yeomen, 33 husbandmen and 52 tradesmen: *Men and Armour*, 287–8.

as the Tawneys observed, 'they were not wage-earners in the same sense as the servants employed by them, [and] were sometimes themselves employers'.[34] Seventy of 164 men at Bisley, a sprawling manor with at least six fulling mills, four dyehouses and 14 'rack-rooms', gave clothmaking occupations.[35] This was clothier-country. Clothiers were capitalists, but the extent to which their neighbours considered them to be of high status depended on factors other than occupation and wealth. They were expected to employ and relieve the poor: the duty they owed to the commonwealth was similar to that of the minor gentry and yeomanry of the smaller, agricultural villages. When the inhabitants of their countries were endangered (e.g. by slumps, or an invading army) they were supposed to put their wealth and contacts at their disposal. They were not supposed to flee to a rural retreat when epidemics raged. Wealthy clothiers were would-be gentry. They had not only to be wealthy but to be trusted in their localities and countries.

Age and life-stage were crucial. The most independent weavers were adult heads of households. On the evidence of the lists, few had servants. Cirencester Weavers' Company records indicate that only about a third to a half of the town weavers were 'independent (household) masters', the others being members of the Journeyman Weavers' Company. The Weavers' Companies were revived and reformed in the 1550s, in response to (ultimately doomed) government attempts to ban clothmaking outside the towns. Their earliest written constitution is a copy of a document dated 1558, which, in turn, referred back to a 'fellowship' of 'antiquitie out of time and mynde belonging to the past and occupation of weavers in the towne of Ciciter'. Conditions for entry were restrictive. No weaver was allowed 'to sett up any such lombes, unless he... be worth five poundes in moveable or unmoveable substance, or hath lands to the yerely value of twentye shillings'. If they met this condition, 'all forreners and oute comers ... shall have such freedoms as though they had been prenticed in the said towne'. 'No journeyman or other tenants ... not heere before prentice in the same towne shall worke' without the company's licence, nor was any man to 'take a prentice without the licence of the master or wardens'. 'If any journeyman or prentice be dysobedient to his or their master' the offender was brought before the fellowship, wardens and master, enquired into, and if found guilty, 'scourged'.[36]

Members attending annual general meetings were listed each year. In 1588, thirteen masters met to affirm their constitution and elect officials. In 1598, 23 masters attended, but in 1600 and 1601 only 5 fellows paid their dues and 7 defaulted, suggesting that at this time there were only 12 master

34 Tawneys, 'An Occupational Census', 48–9.

35 *Ibid*, 43.

36 GA D4590 1.2, 'The charter of King Philip and Queen Mary, 18 May Anno Regni 4', renewed as 'The charter of Queen Elizabeth, 8 February 1558' (dated 'AD 1576' with 'began 1558' in Elizabethan hand).

weavers at work in the town, and that the fellowship was factionalized or apathetic or both. The crisis did not last long. Three years later 25 masters signed or made their marks: the average attendance from 1603 to 1618. In 1610 the guild tightened restrictions on entry: the gaps left by those who died in 1597 were, by then, completely filled. Only men who could add to what the town produced would be allowed entry for the time being. Five of 22 men who attended in 1619 signed an agreement to add to the company stock, the rest signed with marks. On this evidence, the proverbial literacy of weavers does not seem to have reproduced itself at Cirencester. Nor did matters change much in the next two decades. Only five of 19 signed a similar document in 1646.[37]

The Weavers of Cirencester were a special breed, different from their country cousins in the small scale of their organizations and their contacts with the London mercantile community. Cirencester weavers specialized when necessary, but were capable of producing many types of cloth and therefore of responding quickly to the needs of local mercers, drapers and clothiers. The company institutionalized two-tier membership, as indicated in 'The Customs and constitutions of the Journeymen Weavers', signed or marked by 35 men. The journeymen had their own master and regular meetings. Every year 'two of the most discrete and wysest men of weavers being journeymen (were) to be freely chosen and appointed as two stewards'. It was felt necessary to state that 'the journeymen of Ciceter shall kepe a decent order in their hall or meeting place'. Routine tensions between masters and journeymen are implied in the rule 'that they speke no hastie expressions and words before the Stewards and Warden… and one to speke after another'. They were not to haunt alehouses, and if any journeyman knew of another journeyman or apprentice who was what the document calls a 'pykar' or 'stealer', he was to 'report him to the stewards'.[38] No journeyman could teach any apprentice, or employ other journeymen 'like a master'.

It is assumed the workshop was usually the household of a master. The existence of a separately constituted fellowship of journeymen institutionalized the key divide and suggests journeymen's interests could not be subsumed in those of the masters. At times they 'clubbed', acted collectively in their own interests, when the masters failed to look after them. If the muster lists are any indication, few journeyman weavers actually lived in the houses of their masters. As was definitely the case in the urban centres during the eighteenth century, they went to work at the master's house in the morning and returned to their lodgings at night. It is likely the distinction between weavers and journeymen was nothing like as

37 GA D4590 2/1, 'Weavers Company Book'; Richard Jefferies, 'Cirencester Weavers Company: A Review of its Records', *Wilts and Gloucestershire Standard* (29 Dec. 1917 and 12 Jan. 1918), GCL 10600/3.

38 GA D4590 1/3, 'Customs and constitutions of the Journeyman Weavers'.

sharp in the burgeoning industrial districts beyond Sapperton to the west, the Stroudwater Valleys, dominated by the country clothiers.

The muster lists distinguish clothiers from weavers, but do not distinguish established master weavers from journeymen, let alone offer any indication of how many of the journeymen could reasonably hope or expect, one day, to set themselves up as independent householders. At least fifty percent of Cirencester's weavers were journeymen; it is likely a slightly smaller proportion of those listed in the manors of Bisley and Longtree hundreds were young journeymen aiming to work their way up to the status of an 'independent' householder, married with children who would be expected to earn a few pennies as soon as they were old enough, an apprentice to learn mastery of the trade and (given connections to a reliable clothier or clothman with connections to London merchants with access to reasonably stable markets) even a journeyman or two. One difference between the guild-centred urban workers and the rural districts was that mass production – of white cloth, or the usually marketable Stroudwater Scarlets – was the order of the day. The clothiers and weavers of the rural industrial districts specialized. The goal was to produce dozens and hundreds of units of uniform type and quality for export. The merchants of London, Antwerp and Cologne needed to be able to rely on uniformity and quality.

Getting established as a master weaver involved a secure tenancy, ownership of a loom, substance enough to breed and feed a family, take on an apprentice and, whenever possible, hire another loom to employ a journeyman. Equipment like 'the lome that standyth next the dore' of the widow of Thomas Wyther 'of the Limitation of Strode', 'with a payre off shuttells', and the late Thomas Butley's 'brode loome with thappertenances' worth twenty shillings, were ubiquitous in the Stroudwater Valleys.[39] Production capacity was not limited to the number of people described in 1608 as 'weavers' and other clothworking occupations. The households of many yeomen, husbandmen and other trade households turned out unfinished cloth in slack times of the agricultural year, and were self-sufficient enough to be able to wait until a clothier had orders to fill. It was all about capital, credit and connections. An assiduous journeyman upon whom *fortuna* smiled might, eventually, accumulate both. Tales of rags to riches were more common in the industrial districts of early modern England than they were in agricultural production. I don't know of any cases of men who rose from husbandman to gentleman in less than three generations.

Over the whole district 12 percent of the listed inhabitants were servants and a mere 7 percent of the men employed one or more servants. Servants were present in all but a handful of manors. The age-classifications strongly

[39] Hockaday 359: Inventory of the goodes of Thomas Butley of Stroode taken 10 October 1587; GA, GPR 305, Vol. 2; Will of Thomas Wyther of the Limitaycon of Strode, 20 Jan. 1544/5.

indicate that service, like apprenticeship in trade and manufacturing, was, for most youngsters at any rate, a liminal stage of several years between leaving home and saving enough to set up an independent household as a husbandman or labourer. At Cirencester, 23 men employed 36 servants, of whom no less than 30 were 'about twenty'. The rural hundred of Crowthorne and Minety, where 39 men employed 60 servants, has slightly more in the 'about forty' (19) and 'about fifty' (3) categories, but the youngest age group (35) is still much the largest. When they married and set up households, servants either invested savings (or a small inheritance) on some copyhold land and became husbandmen, made the transition to wage-labour, or, most commonly, a pragmatic mixture of both. Permanent service was a more specialist (and exceptional) affair; servants in the fifty-plus category were largely restricted to households like that of Sir Henry Poole, at Sapperton. Service for life to a wealthy knight was a career option; service with a yeoman, husbandman or rural craftsman was for young men and women who were expected, in time, to make the institutionalized moves to the much-coveted independency that full adulthood entailed: a rented cottage or tenement, marriage, children, neighbourly service to the community. Service was, for most men and women, a liminal stage between childhood and marriage. That was the ideal, and if the ages of male servants listed in 1608 are a reliable indicator, it still worked out in reality – for some.

At the grass roots, Wilson's adaptation of Smith's constitution rested on communities containing junior officers (gentlemen), and non-commissioned officers (yeomen, husbandmen and master craftsmen). They, and labourers, were much less prominent in Bisley and Longtree, where the core business was manufacturing cloth for export. This meant a domination of *artisani*, the most ambiguous and heterogeneous member of Smith's 'fourth sort'. Clothiers, finishers, dyers, weavers and broadweavers, tuckers and millwrights, alongside other clusterings of occupations more characteristic of market towns, signal a very different constitutional formation. Smith's first and second 'sorts' are conspicuously absent: nine of 13 lists for Bisley, eight of 14 for Longtree, have no resident gentlemen. Lords, where they existed at all, were absentee, like Thomas, lord Windsor, lord of the manors of 'Michelhampton' and Avening. The few resident gentlemen listed fewer servants. Only two gentlemen of Longtree and Bisley hundreds had more than one. Henry Bridges of Avening, a relative of Lord Chandos of Sudeley, was accompanied to the muster by no fewer than 12 servants, 11 of them 'about forty'; 16servants and nine 'husbandmen servants' worked Sir Henry Poole's manor of Sapperton, a short walk from Cirencester. Poole was an executor of the 1610 will of puritan elder John Coxwell, whom we meet in Chapter 14.

Painswick's 30 trained men, 18 yeomen and 33 husbandmen (five with servants) boosted Bisley's totals. Here, on the face of it, traditional order coexisted with the new: three clothiers (no servants), 33 weavers, ten tuckers and a millwright aligned Painswick with the dominant 'fourth sort' of neighbouring Stroud.[40] The local yeomen did well producing food, hides and wool for their market-dependent artisan neighbours. Most if not all of the greater clothiers of Bisley and Longtree hundreds, like William Trotman, who attended the Rodborough musters wearing his armour, accompanied by five strapping young servants, or his neighbour William Chapman with six, were sons or grandsons of men of yeoman rank. William Trotman's grandfather left yeoman independency (a substantial working farm, some capital) to several of his sons out of the profits of a cloth mill in the Vale of Berkeley. William's uncle, John, was an elder of the parish of Cam, in the Vale of Berkeley. A generation later men like Trotman and Chapman were styled 'gent'; they differed from traditional yeomen and gentry, not in being 'hands on' (for most gentlemen and yeoman of the region were that), but in the character (and problematics) of their communities, their fluid capital and credit networks and the larger contexts within which, necessarily, they operated.

If half of the 1,218 tradesmen and craftsmen are assumed to have been independent householders, and the independent household (i.e. the head *and* the parts) is assumed to be the pivotal unit of sentiment, production and consumption, the total number of 'independent producers' in the Seven Hundreds was 1,516, or 41 percent of the total. The calculations are impressionistic, but it was roughly this 'class' of people (overwhelmingly but not entirely exclusively male) that contemporary parish clerks had in mind when they referred to 'inhabitants'. To these we can add many of the labourers who had left service in order to set up their own households. Like anyone else, labourers' wives and children were expected to contribute to the common pot in order to avoid the shame of having to appeal to the Vestry for assistance. Tax minimization was generally an activity of the wealthy. For more borderline 'inhabitants', those who expected to have a voice, at least, in parochial deliberations, contributing their sixpence to local and national taxes was often a matter of hard-won pride.

My impression is that 'independence' was a quality of nuclear families and households, never, in reality, of 'producers', who were, by definition, *interdependent* with many other households. As John Corbet defined it in 1645, 'independency' meant not 'living in the breath of other men'. Even though most of them rented their one-hearth houses and owned few possessions, pious, responsible, hardworking husbandmen, artisans, labourers and shepherds with hardworking wives and children qualified for independency (at Cirencester they had a voice in parliamentary elections) if they maintained themselves respectably. On Corbet's (probably conventional) definition, a healthy commonwealth restricted dependency to childhood

40 Clothmaking at Painswick was clearly aligned with the neighbouring township of Stroud, a 'settlement which grew up [in the late Middle Ages] by the Frome in an outlying part of Over Lypiatt, but at the centre of local routes of communication': N.M. Herbert, 'Stroud', in *VCH* 11, 99–104.

and youth: magnates and the 'undeserving poor' never grew up to become full, i.e. independent, members of the commonwealth. Two classes were becoming the rhetorical enemies of a prosperous commonwealth of independent households: wealthy magnate rentiers and the 'undeserving' poor. The challenge in the 1580s was to incorporate the 'manuary workers' who, as we saw in the last chapter, always formed the bulk of the population, and who, at that time, were particularly restive.

13

Immigrants

Only the wanderer
Knows England's graces,
Or can anew see clear
Familiar faces.[1]

Cirencester's customs incorporated guarded but necessary hospitality to strangers. 'Passingers' – people passing through – were welcome. The town *needed* immigrants to maintain the number of inhabitants required to perform its traditional functions. Every death, of a gentleman-merchant, yeoman-clothier, artisan, butcher, shepherd, bookbinder, papermaker, even of its one, symbolic, 'loyterer', was an opening to be filled. If Cirencester's weavers failed to keep up their numbers, or the quality of the cloth and knowledge of markets, the clothiers of Painswick, Stroud and Bisley would soon take their place. Recollect the custom declared by the twelfth-century elders:

> that if a stranger coming hither slept in Cirencester on midsummer night, and afterwards stayed there till the king or his fee-farmer had his corn reaped, then, whosoever he might be, whether freeman or bondman, male or female, he (*sic*) must do three bederipes to the king, or to his fee-farmer, for the fellowship that is of the town, which the said man had used and had enjoyed up till that day.

Travellers, sojourners and immigrants are constants in Cirencester's history, from the testimony of the elders of the town in 1209 to the 'passingers' recorded in the vestry minutes and parish registers of the late sixteenth and early seventeenth centuries. Evidence illustrating what might be termed the *quotidian* mobility of relatively settled inhabitants of the town's hinterlands is indirect. A collection of depositions relating to the case of William Tawney, a baker of Stow on the Wold, arrested at Cirencester in early June 1638, on suspicion of having murdered his sister in law, Christian Wheeler, probably illustrates what was considered fairly

1 Ivor Gurney, 'Song', in Ivor Gurney, *Selected Poems*, ed. P.J. Cavanagh (Oxford 1990), 3.

normal for a man of his occupation.[2] Tawney was brought before Justices William Morton and Edward Hungerford Esq. and asked to account for his whereabouts since Wheeler was last seen alive (on the evening of Thursday, 24 May) at the house Tawney (a widower), his child, Wheeler, his mother and another couple, Christian Blisse and her husband, shared at Stow. Wheeler and Tawney had recently spent eighteen weeks together in isolation at the 'pesthouse at Stow', where Wheeler's brother and father had died. There were rumours that Tawney had made Wheeler pregnant and had given her a 'drench, drink or potion … for the destroying of her childe' and had said, after their release, that he 'would be rid of the said Christian'. Tawney's mother had not missed Wheeler on Friday morning because 'she thought … Christian was gone to London for that shee had been in London about a fortnight before and heard her say shee would go to London again'.

After his arrest, Tawney gave the justices two slightly different accounts of his movements since Wheeler's disappearance. In both depositions he testified that he had gone to bed at 10 o'clock on Thursday and arisen at '3 or 4' the next morning, gone into the fields to hitch his horse (which was in the habit of getting loose in the cornfields) and returned to bake bread. That afternoon he rode to Bourton on the Water, where he thought Wheeler might have gone to sell bread, and returned home that evening. He remained home on Saturday and rose early on Sunday morning, when he rode to Toddington 'to collect a debt of £10 owed to his mother' by her tenant there, one 'Mr. Langston'. From Toddington he rode to Winchcombe, went to the market, stayed until 4 pm, then went to a place called 'Coldharbour' to visit his aunt. On Monday morning he rode to Naunton 'and from there to Compton in the hole (*sic*) to collect 10s. owed him for bread and so to Harnhill to enquire for his aunt, but found her not', whereupon he rode to Cirencester, 'at the Bull [Inn] where he lay Sunday' at night and stayed all day on Monday, sold his horse, met his aunt's daughter and 'rode before her to Coldharbour where he stayed for seven nights'. The implication was that Tawney's energetic travels were not at all unusual for an enterprising baker whose mother counted at least one gentleman as her tenant, and who routinely sold his bread at markets all over the North Wolds: he had a reason for being in all the places he visited.

From the 1560s on, Cirencester parish registers record another level of mobility, the flotsam of a tide of jobless, hungry people: 'William a stranger',

2 The following is based on 'The examination of William Tauny of Stow baker arrested upon suspition of murder taken before me Edwarde Hungerforde Esq. the 7 day of June 1638 at Windrush'; 'The examination of William Tawney of Stow, Baker, touching the murder of Christian Wheeler late of Stow, spinster, taken by William Morton, one of His Majesties Justices of the Peace (n.d.)'; 'the examination of [widow Tawney] before William Morton JP [illeg.] June 1638'; and examinations of William Hag, Christian Blisse, Elinor Hanpacke and Isobell Baker, all of Stow: GA D45, 'Whitmore of Lower Slaughter', Hundred of Slaughter Presentments, recognizances etc., 1638.

'Jeffery Davis a stranger', 'a stranger', 'John Hill a stranger', 'Joan Balbright a young woman', 'a poor man, a stranger', 'Margery a poore woman', 'Agnes a poor child' and 'John Pratt a poor man' all died on the way through. At any given moment in its recorded history, the town had attracted and selected suitable replacements for those who died, and moved on as many of those considered unsuitable as it could. Every generation experienced greater and lesser mortality crises, and in every generation, the population history suggests, the town reconstructed itself with remarkable rapidity. After 1577–9, through the death-haunted 1580s, and again after the great dying of 1597, the surviving inhabitants were replenished by immigrants, until, by 1600, over half the inhabitants were newcomers. The ones we know about are the minority who stayed long enough to get their names recorded. Among them are the names (or no-names) of the poorest level of traveler, including the names of several children travelling alone.

There are signs of crumbling courtship procedures among the poor. The first direct reference to a 'bastard' occurs in May 1579, but at least twelve baptisms in the 1570s mention only a mother's name, without designation as a widow or reference to a father. From 1570 until 1598 there were 38 such references, almost certainly indicating illegitimacy. From 1598 to 1620, 47 bastards are mentioned in the lists of baptisms. Keith Wrightson's description of this period as one 'of unusual instability and insecurity in the courtships of the poor' is supported by the Cirencester registers. 'Fewer opportunities existed for the poor to marry and set up independent families,' he writes.[3] At the heart of it was one brutal reality. 'Death,' wrote the social historian W.G. Hoskins, on the basis of his examination of Devonshire parish registers, 'must have been as common a sight as on a battlefield'.

Prenuptial pregnancy was common, meaning no more than that many courting couples began sexual activity before they married. However, Cirencester was not an entirely typical early modern community. People passed through all the time. Besides poor 'strangers' and travellers unfortunate enough to die on the way through, my calculations suggest that 1,699 people must have arrived and stayed in the last two decades of the sixteenth century. It is not possible to calculate the 'total flow' from which these immigrants were diverted, but it must have been considerable. After 1598 the churchwardens and manorial officials clearly made an effort to record 'reputed fathers' in the registers. Where no information could be gained, and the woman was local, they promised recent immigrants like the journeyman weavers Richard Jones and Humfrey Long they could stay if they married a 'fallen' woman. Elizabeth Collins's bastard son was baptized in December 1598. She married Richard Jones in May 1601. Elizabeth Cobbe's bastard son Robert was baptized in March 1599. She married Humfrey Long

3 Keith Wrightson, *English Society, 1580–1680* (London 1982), 146.

two years later. In many cases the fathers died before they could get married, or had to move on in search of work.

Few of the 353 men listed and classified by the wardsmen in 1608, can have heard Philip Jones preach in the aftermath of the holocaust of 1578–79, though some may have been introduced to his ideas by word of mouth and via his little book. The twenty years following its publication saw a massive turnover in population. By cross-referencing the names on the muster list with the parish register indexes it is possible to say with reasonable certainty that over half (222) of the men listed in 1608 had come to the town since 1586. Only 74 (19.2%) were definitely born there. The continuities we have observed in communal politics were maintained by 'permanently settled' (invariably wealthier) families. Most but not all the vestry officials in the 1610s were baptized at Cirencester. There were two other forces for continuity: first, its functions, the type of town it was and its connections with many regions, the kingdom, the nation and the commonwealth; secondly, and much more difficult to document, was social memory: basic precepts and ideas, passed from one generation to the next, relating to a specific, named place-based community that routinely received migrants, and, in times like these, depended upon them.

We should not presume that migrant workers were invariably 'pushed' to leave the places they came from by dour economic circumstances. Economic realities always featured in the thinking of men and, increasingly in the seventeenth and eighteenth centuries, women, who had to earn a living, wherever they went. Other motivators cannot be excluded: curiosity, ambition, alertness to useful information, a desire to see more of the world, a desire to hear fiery sermons, observe strange places and discover different traditions among people very like themselves. The great poet and traveller Laurie Lee (from Slad, near Stroud) is unique, like W.H. Davies, the tramp-poet and author of *Diary of a Supertramp*, who came from Nailsworth; yet they are also exceptional representatives of a wandering, adventurous *type*; it would be rash to assume that such people did not exist in every generation. We too easily forget that *Homo sapiens* was a traveller for hundreds of thousands of years before the coming of agriculture. Travellers sometimes know better than settled folk that it is wise to avoid getting one's name written down by some arm of the state: in this case, a constable, beadle or churchwarden. The rule is approach local authorities with caution. Get a job, blend in, observe, decide whether this is a place a migrant, pulled by a sense of adventure as well as the need to earn a living, might like to stay a bit longer. A place like Cirencester had to make itself attractive to migrants. As the elders of the twelfth century knew, migrants were its life-blood. Its nearly fifty street-ale sellers and victuallers, alehouses, taverns with signs and without, and inns, suggest busy streets, thriving trade, and plenty of those reprobates, the undeserving poor, haunting alehouses and being disrespectful to their elders and betters.

In the aftermath of crises like that of 1577–9, when communal recovery was more important than fine discrimination, the community still had to maintain a semblance of communal harmony. There was a high premium on responsive, careful, committed and innovative forms of local government. We know nothing of the informal, day-to-day experiments in governmentality practised in the past, by Nicholas the Proctor in the contracting economy of the early fourteenth century, John Cosyn and the generation of 1400, and the builders of the church in the fifteenth century. For the generations of c.1570–1660 there is more: a few more fragments to piece together the condition, religion and government of a town in what Christopher Hill called 'pre-revolutionary England'. Towns like Cirencester (London is the archetype) naturally replenished themselves with the same types of people – they hoped for those to whom Philip Jones had addressed himself, independent householders with enough capital to set themselves up, yet, like Cirencester, they also attracted poorer sorts of migrants such as those mentioned a few paragraphs ago. We saw earlier that whatever the lords might say, to be granted the fellowship of the town meant to be accepted by the community. The extreme conditions of the late sixteenth century may have entailed a relaxation of standards, but there were enough survivors to keep the old customs and standards alive. Thus while the 1608 muster list is no guide to the exact personnel twenty years earlier, it is a superbly detailed guide to the importance to Cirencester of the class of people Jones defined in 1588. Here, the emphasis is on migrants.

Cirencester was a great regional market. In the fifteenth and sixteenth centuries it had become a manufacturing town, the 'funnel' through which much of the cloth produced in the Stroudwater Valleys and the Vale of Berkeley was processed and passed on to the merchants, up the Thames Valley, in London. Along the River Churn's channel, through old abbey lands, was a string of fulling mills, two of them commissioned sixty years earlier by John Blake, the last of the abbots. The lists of men and occupations in 1608 describe an extensive yet still traditional division of labour. Many trades were represented, but the weavers were the most numerous and best organized, with their own 'company' in existence since the fifteenth century. 'If any master weaver of the said company shall not at St Katherine's Eve tyde … be at dinner together with the Wardens of the Company,' reads a document of 1618, '… he shall forfeit 3s. 4d. to be paid for the use of the said Company'. The company owned land and had a 'hall', in which there hung a bell to summon its members to meetings, ceremonies and annual feasts like that of St Katherine's Eve. Each year the wardens appointed a beadle to see that the company's rules were kept, and a 'key-keeper' responsible for the hall and the records kept in the great chest.

The records of the Cirencester Weavers' Company suggest that the wave of immigration lasted from the 1580s until about 1610. In 1614 'yt was greed uppon by the full concourse of the wardens and companie … that noe forraigne weavers shall sett upp any loombe or loombes within the town but shall pay to the use of the companie tenn pounds' – a hefty and, for most weavers, prohibitive entry fine.[4] The 'Customes and Constitution of old Antiquite out of tyme and mynde belonginge unto the Craft and occupations of weavers beinge Journeymen' was signed or marked, possibly in 1559, but almost certainly around 1600, by 35 men. The agreement of their masters, 'the craft and occupation of (master) weavers', in 1614 was signed by 25 men, including several wealthy clothiers and a greater number of men simply designated, in 1608, as 'weaver'. Another hint that the tide of in-migration was turning is the fact that at least 18 of the men who attended the journeymen's meeting had been resident in 1608. By contrast, as many as two-thirds of the weavers who attended the 1608 muster had migrated to the town since 1586. Let it be noted that the journeymen and the weavers' guilds were important and integrated instruments of local government. Some of the master weavers were also members of the increasingly important vestry, and clothiers often served as churchwardens and tithingmen. Steady, enterprising local government was needed when, in 1614, after three or four decades of constant immigration, it was necessary to call a halt – for the time being.

The Company of Weavers consisted of those recognized by their peers as *masters*. This meant the unchallenged head of a family and household with apprentices and, from time to time, journeymen. Preference was given in the award of apprenticeships to the sons of local families, and local journeymen were preferred in principle. From 1578 to 1610 there were never nearly enough local candidates. Philip Jones seemed to embrace journeymen and master craftsmen when he described the elect ('the poore') as 'an articifer or handicraftes man' who lived by his 'manuarie trade or science … to releeve himself'. The last clause, however, granted full membership only to those who 'maintaine(d their) familie(s) thereby'. This was an important, and a conventional, distinction. Full membership, be it of the Cirencester Weavers' Company or the commonwealth of England, was open exclusively to the heads of families and households, independent, mature survivors. Master weavers were members of the aristocracy of labour at Cirencester, alongside their (less numerous) peers: master shoemakers, tanners, cutlers, tailors, musicians and other trades. They were often but not always 'elders' in the literal sense. Ten of the master weavers who attended the 1614 meeting appear in the second age category of the 1608 muster list, 'about forty', and three were 'about fifty'. Only two were 'about twenty'. The unchallenged

4 GCRO D4590 2 (1): 'Register Book for the whole company of weavers inhabiting the towne of Cirencester … for the year 1580'; D4590 1(2), 'The charter of King Philip and Queen Mary, 18 May *anno regni* 4' and 'The charter of Queen Elizabeth 8 February *anno regni* 18 (1576)' on which 'began 1558' is written in an Elizabethan hand; D 4590 1(3), 'Customs and constitutions of the Journeyman Weavers … by voluntary agreement'; 'Cirencester Weavers Company: A Review of its Records', *Wilts and Gloucestershire Standard* (29 Dec. 1917 & 12 Jan. 1918), GCL 10600/3.

leader of the commonalty in 1614, John Coxwell, may even have been a centenarian.

The commonalty at Cirencester was as polarized, wealth-wise, as it had always been: a small core of successful merchants, most of them over 50 and several well over 60, supplemented by perhaps fifty householders 'of the better sorte of the parrishe', among whom the 'about twenty' and 'about forty' age-groups predominated. These 50 households belonged to a larger class of maybe 150 or so households that occasionally employed apprentices, journeymen and labourers. Because of the repeated mortality crises of the 1570s, 1580s and 1590s, there was certainly a larger pool of young householders who might become 'better sorte', lenders not borrowers, payers of rates and taxes, and not 'haunters of alehouses', a 'sluggard' like eleventh-century Robert, or 1608's Thomas Crosse, who attended the St Lawrence Street muster with his father and uncle (both labourers), and was listed as a 'loyterer'. A year later, perhaps after words were spoken about his loitering, he married Elizabeth Gurney. Only a few, or a few hundred metres separated their households from those of 'better sorte' like Robert George esquire, John Coxwell esquire, Robert George gent, Jeffrey Bathe gent, John Mortymer gent, Rowland Freeman mercer, William Turbill mercer, George Fereby mercer, John Hooper dyer, William Hopkins dyer and John Iles shoemaker, Thomas Stone gent, John Channler chandler, Robert Alexander mercer. [5] Yet they were separated by an almost unbridgeable social space. Artisans very occasionally climbed every rank of this unofficial yet cast-iron social hierarchy. Coxwell may be the legendary case of his generation; he did not make it until he was in his fifties, and did not become the best of the better sort until his eighth, ninth and tenth decades. There may have been some, but I do not know any true histories of labourers moving from rags to riches.

The manorial records of the mid-sixteenth century and the vestry records of the early seventeenth century suggest that in these decades the town came to be ruled, for practical purposes, by a slightly larger oligarchy than the 'triumvirate' (Robert Strange, Christopher George and Thomas Marshall) singled out by the anti-papists of 1570.[6] This emergent elite consisted of gentlemen (old and landed like the Georges, some merchants like John Coxwell), merchants (mostly mercers), dyers (owners or renters of mills) and a few unusually successful craftsmen. Their wealth and connections (often marriage connections) put them in a different category from

5 The vestry 'Orders' of 10 April 1615 use 'better sorte' in this way three times in the first two Orders: GA, P86 VE 2/1, 'Minutes, 1613–1886'. Cirencester usages support Keith Wrightson's finding that 'the language of sorts' was enjoying increasing currency in the later sixteenth and early seventeenth centuries: 'Sorts of People in Tudor and Stuart England', in Jonathan Barry and Christopher Brooks (eds), *The Middling Sort of People: Culture, Society and Politics in England, 1550–1800* (Basingstoke 1994), 32; the occupations of the men listed are from *Men and Armour*.

6 GA, P86 VE 2/1, 'Minutes, 1613–1886'.

the shopkeepers, petty traders and craftsmen who filled the next category: in good times a hundred or so households with enough 'capital' (a store of grain and wood, and maybe a garden), enough work and a good enough diet to stand a chance of surviving lean times and even 'times of woe' like 1577–9 and 1596–7.

Another 200 or so households, most of them living in cramped one- or two-hearth rented accommodation in a 'tenement' in one of the lesser streets, could sometimes afford to pay the various dues and taxes that were required for membership of 'the fellowship of the town' but often not. That left something up to 200 'households' who, for taxation purposes, possessed nothing. These 'lower classes' would always include young working people with prospects, travelling with or without a trade, working as a clerk (if literate) or a labourer, taking whatever came up and then moving on. The muster of 1608 captured quite a few young men like this. They stayed around long enough to get caught by that particular state net (the muster of 1608) at this particular place, and then moved on. From the elders of the twelfth to those of the seventeenth and eighteenth centuries, 'the fellowship of the town' incorporated immigrants as a matter of course. All they had to do was to pay legally established dues to the king or his appointee (the abbot), and establish themselves in the eyes of the elders. We need not concern ourselves with the strict legality of this claim, which was rejected by King John's justices. What matters for our purposes was that the young men, immigrants and elders of Cirencester in the early twelfth century took for granted that immigrants had, routinely, to be incorporated into 'the fellowship of the town'.

The parish registers for the period 1560–1660 demonstrate that it had to be so. As with London, Cirencester could not maintain its services without a constant stream of immigrants. Analysis of the registers in conjunction with other census-type sources showed that at least half of the inhabitants in c.1600 must have been recent immigrants, replacing those who died in the series of mortality crises that struck the town from the late 1570s to the late 1590s. By cross-checking the muster list of 1608 with the parish register indexes, it is possible to be exact to the point of providing the names and addresses of the 222 mustered men who had filled the void left by the dead. One of these men was John Munden.

Like Philip Marner, Munden was a tailor, 'one of those whose business it is to make clothes': this was the occupation assigned in 1608 to John Munden, householder of the now parliamentary borough of Cirencester.[7] Like nearly twenty thousand other 'able and sufficyent men in body fitt for

7 *OED*, 'Tailor'; 'The names and surnames of all the able and sufficyent men in body fitt for his Ma'ties service in the warres in the Division of the Seven hundred … viewed by the Right Honourable Henry lord Berkeley Lord Lieutenant of the said County … in the month of August, 1608', *Men and Armour* ('The Burrowe of Cirencester', 239–43; for Munden, see 243).

his Majesties service in the warres', Munden was caught in the county-wide net cast by the musters of 1608. In every manor under his jurisdiction, Lord Berkeley, as lord lieutenant of the county, 'viewed' the relatively fit, willing and loyal men, those who, should occasion require, would fight in the king's wars. Where these wars might be, and who they might be against, were not specified. Munden appears with 21 other men in the list for Instrope Street, or 'Ward'.

His companions from Instrope Street were men in the prime of life. As we saw, they were classed in three age-groups: 'about twenty', 'about forty' and 'betweene fyfty and threescore'. Of the 353 men named in the lists for the seven streets or wards of Cirencester, only 12 (3.4%) were in the oldest category. The town had a terrible demographic record in the last third of the sixteenth century. Only the fittest (or luckiest) survived. Those who died were quickly replaced by immigrants from elsewhere. The men from Instrope Street were all in the 'about twenty' (45%) or 'about forty' (55%) groups. John Munden was 'about twenty'.

Judging by the occupations represented, Instrope was not a select 'ward', 'street' and 'tithing'. It was one of three streets leading away from the market square and the parish church, towards the road out of town towards Bisley and Stroud and the clothworking districts of central Gloucestershire. Of the 22 men, 18 had arrived since 1600. The remaining four arrived in the late 1580s or 1590s. This conclusion, while not absolutely watertight because of the missing registers in the early 1580s, is drawn from parish register evidence. Thus, for example, there are no references in the baptism, marriage and burial records for one man, Robert Hibbard, beerbrewer, nor for anyone of that surname between 1560, when the Cirencester registers begin, and 1630. This could mean many things: he was a bachelor; he was born and married somewhere else, bore children somewhere else, and raised his family, none of whom died or were married in the town; he wasn't around for long. I conclude he was an immigrant. He probably moved on to serve another brewer somewhere else.

At the other end of the scale, the earliest surname reference for William George, labourer, is the man of that name who married Margaret Rogers in 1571. That put him into the very oldest category in 1608. Our William George, however, was classified as 'about twenty'. There were several George families in the town throughout the sixteenth century, but I have not found a baptism of the 1580s under that name. A certain 'Hugh George' was baptized in November 1586, so would have been almost 22 in August 1608 – 'about twenty', Smyth's designation for our William George. Although I suspect William George was local-born, I mark him as uncertain. There is no record of him ever having married and had a family. He died, still a young man, in 1613.

Combined with other contemporary sources, viewed microscopically, the muster lists merge to yield a portrait of an extensive English region more vivid than any other contemporary source, especially when viewed with the aid of Christopher Saxton's maps. Of each man, we know his place of settlement, occupation, approximate age and height, and in what military capacity (pikeman, musketeer, caliverman or pioneer) he was thought fit to serve. Although it is a static, obviously biased source (there are no women or children), it is an excellent place to start. John Munden was about twenty, of middle height, fit to be a musketeer. If rebellion ever came to Cirencester again, as it had in 1400, the footsoldiers would be firing guns, not longbows. (Twenty-seven [7.6%] of the Cirencester listing were designated 'trained' soldiers.) In 1522 the longbow and stave were universal. By 1608 staves were still in common use, but shot was replacing the arrow.

Munden was the only tailor in the street. Nine (43%) of the others from Instrope Street were labourers. There would be plenty of work for them, most of the time. A gradual rebuilding, using Cotswold limestone to replace wattle and daub, was in its early stages; when the money was flowing into the town there would be work for the masons, carpenters, plasterers and tilers working on houses in the town or in the surrounding villages, where there was also seasonal farm work.[8] A lot of men of different occupations were probably still part-time shearers. The powerful gentry – relatively thick on the ground in this region, in spite of John Corbet's assertion to the contrary in 1645 - were building, or rebuilding, their power houses in the surrounding countryside. There was always money to be earned loading, unloading, shifting goods, helping to erect stalls in the market, the busiest 'central place' of its region. Trade and demand for the specialist crafts and manufactures represented at Cirencester – and labourers were skilled men too, in case it needs saying – fluctuated. The town was the capital of a small but internationally regarded region, producer, in earlier centuries, of the very finest wool in Christendom, producer, from the fifteenth to the late eighteenth centuries, of some of its most ambitious clothiers, dyers and mercers. Labourers in particular have suffered from the 'Hodge' stereotype, which pictured them as sturdy but shambling, passive, forelock-tugging yokels: Richard Jefferies' lasting contribution to English sociology in the 1870s. We cannot assume that labourers were politically passive. We know too little (almost nothing) about individual labourers before the nineteenth century. They belonged to the class that provided the rank and file of England's armies. Royalists and parliamentarians would need them for their armies.

At Cirencester, if they were householders not receiving relief of any sort, they were entitled to vote in parliamentary elections. Forty-three labourers attended the Cirencester muster in 1608, a high proportion of them from the poorer St Lawrence, Instrope and Cricklade wards. This was the largest occupational category, one more than the next-highest, weavers (42). After

8 'The later sixteenth century seems to have marked a change from extensive use of timber to a greater use of stone': Reece and Catling, *Cirencester: Development and Buildings*, 15.

them came shoemakers (20), followed by John Munden's group, the tailors (12). We should not assume these to have been homogeneous groups. The weavers had a guild; nothing is known about organizations of labourers, formal and informal. Had they at any time or for any reason been capable of united action, they would have posed a considerable force.

The musters were held in September, early autumn. Nicholas Poore, shepherd of Instrope Street, was at home with his wife, Elizabeth. He probably spent weeks on end away on the Cotswold pastures looking after the sheep of one of the powerful gentry, or the combined flocks of gentry, yeomen and husbandmen pastoralists of the district.[9] He was in the same age and height brackets as Munden, also a newcomer to the town. His wife was expecting a baby. Their daughter, Elizabeth, was baptized at the parish church on 27 January 1608/9, and buried two days later. They went on to raise four sons and a daughter, all of whom were still alive in 1623, when the family seems to have left the town, escapees from the high mortality that year. At any rate, they are not recorded among its victims.

Poore's presence represents one of the routine interactions between the town and its surrounding countryside. William Pirrie, a carrier, probably travelled long-distance runs to Bristol and London, where it would not be difficult to get a return load. He was about forty, and at the time of the muster he and his wife had two small sons, baptized at the parish church in 1605 and 1607. Pirrie was in Cirencester for about ten years. He and his family disappear from the registers after the baptism of their first daughter, Joan, in September 1614. Carrying was a mobile profession. Richard Little, peddler, also about forty, was a member of an equally mobile trade. His name occurs only once, registering his marriage to Elizabeth Bowley in April 1608. He probably never settled anywhere for long. Carriers and chapmen had been passing through Cirencester for centuries.

Tailors travelled during the 'journeying' stage of their craft. It was part of their training. They went from place to place picking up work where they could, learning how things were done in different places, how fashions and customs varied. Some never lost the itch to move, but most aimed to achieve the mature stage of their craft, to be an independent master-craftsman. This meant setting up an independent household. Marriage and children were not strictly necessary, but it was more difficult for a childless bachelor to claim equality with the elders of the craft and trade communities. This meant getting established and settling down somewhere. If they found somewhere that appealed to them, or met a girl and wished to settle down, they often stayed.

9 A shepherd of Holyrood Ampney, Richard Flux, said in 1641 that he was unable to testify regarding the minister's capacity to preach because, 'being a shepherd' he was 'not in church once in a month or two': GA D8, Z1, 'Benedict Grace Papers'.

John Munden was just beginning this 'householder' or 'master-craftsman' phase of his craft cycle. The first reference to him in the parish registers records his marriage to Elizabeth Sanders, on 13 June 1607. Fifty-three weeks later their son, John, was baptized. He died and was buried nine days later. According to the parish registers no other children were baptized in Cirencester, and only one, another John, was buried there in 1616. There may have been intermittent periods living elsewhere and children born elsewhere. He may have been a member of the Anabaptist congregation for a while. Elizabeth must have died, for in his will dated January 1632/3, he left most of his goods to his wife Mary. To his daughter, Elinor, he left the considerable sum of £10, 'at marriage or aged 21' and sufficient household goods, including pots, pans, pewter platters, an 'oak standing bedstead', and 'one silver spoon', to set up her own household.[10] I have not been able to trace the burial of his first wife, his second marriage or the baptism of his daughter, and can only speculate about periods away from the town in the years between 1608 and 1633. Whatever they were, his inventory and will show that he was well settled at Cirencester when he died, aged in his fifties.

At the time of Munden's death officials acting for the Diocese of Gloucester conducted an inventory of his household goods, for probate purposes. The inventory takes us inside his household at the time of his death. He probably no longer lived in Instrope Street, and these sources give some insight to the material comforts a craftsman of his sort could, if reasonably successful, attain.

Munden's house, including the cellar, was of three stories and contained eight rooms; whether of timber and plaster, or Cotswold limestone is uncertain. Judging by the weight of bed-coverings and rugs in Munden's inventory, it was a cold house, possibly stone, at this time becoming the vernacular building material for houses of any lasting substance in this region. In the stable and 'backside' were plants and a woodpile worth £2. He kept a small kitchen garden, and wood supply. John Smyth wrote elsewhere that a good wood supply was an absolutely minimum requirement for life in the Cotswolds. Cirencester, on the eastern watershed, was on the edge of the limestone plateau, sheltered, but damper because of its position at the confluence of the Daglingworth and Churn streams, feeders of the Thames. It was on the borders between the Cotswolds, Shakespeare's 'high, wild hills', and a district described by John Aubrey as 'durty, claey country'.

As post-Restoration tax-collectors classified households like his, Munden's was probably a 2–3, and possibly even a 4–5 hearth household. He was a master-craftsman in a substantial but small way of business, an independent household head, very much of the class described by John Corbet fifteen years later as 'middle ranke'. In Corbet's terms, Munden 'lived of his own,

10 GA, GDR, Munden, 1633/66.

and not in the breath of other men'. He was the very epitome of the class Philip Jones the preacher nominated as God's elect.

What his words and thoughts on these political and religious matters would have been, we can only guess. He simply bequeathed his 'soul to almighty god', but by 1633, profusions of religious sentiment were becoming unfashionable. Munden did not write his own will, but left 'my bible' to daughter Elinor and signed with the well-formed initials 'JM'. That he left the bible to his daughter and not his wife may mean the latter could read and the former could not. The rest of his goods, with some small exceptions, reveal practical substance without luxury, independence and simple common sense. His cellar contained 'three hogsheads and five small barrels, (and) other implements' worth £1. This was the beer-cellar, the household's drink supply. In the 'backside' he had stores of malt and barley worth £20, surely in excess of his own household needs, unless, that is, he was running a little factory, and/or a kind of boarding house. The number of beds in the house – in every room except those that look as if they were work-rooms – indicates that he could easily have lodged an apprentice, a journeyman or two, and even some lodgers. There was bacon hanging in his kitchen, and he was fattening up 'five store piggs' in the yard. On this evidence, the household might, on a very simple but mixed and healthy diet, be able to retreat into its own resources for up to twelve months; capital, if necessary, to survive a siege. During epidemics, its members could retreat inside until mortality abated. During dearths, as long as they did not last for longer than a year, they could avoid the market until prices fell. During slumps in trade, whatever their causes, the household could tighten its belt and wait for orders to start coming in again.

Munden took on and laid off journeymen in response to fluctuations in demand for his services. Journeymen were meant to go from place to place, following the work and learning more about their trade in anticipation of the time when they would become master-craftsmen themselves. Tensions could arise between these two levels of the trade, the young men and the independent men, when there were sustained recessions of demand. If they came to maturity in a time of economic recovery and expansion, they could get themselves established, as had Munden. An infinite number of variables could intervene: an apprentice or journeyman who got a reputation for truculence, or insolence, might find it difficult to get settled, and would eventually move on. A journeyman who proved too good at what he did might look like potential competition. This would matter if work was tight. If a man's journeying stage coincided with what contemporaries called 'slumps', he might never achieve independence. Sooner or later, in sustained 'depressions', there were rumblings against immigrants, the people who, in better times, would be welcomed and would settle. The civil wars came at the end of a sharp, two-decade long recession, in the middle of which Munden died. His household goods reflect this.

A room on the ground floor called 'the lettis room' suggests that Munden did a lot of work with fur, and was thus at the luxury end of the trade. The term 'lettis' denoted 'a kind of whitish-grey fur', but 'the application of the name… varied at different times'.[11] Munden probably worked with any kind of fur, according to supplies of raw materials and fashions in coats, trimmings and 'lettis bonnets', which were in fashion throughout his lifetime.[12] During the early stages of the English colonization of North America, fur supplies suddenly boomed. Items made from fur may have fallen in price and come within the range of lesser middle-rank households. The scale and substance of Munden's household, and, indeed, the fact that after settling there in 1607 he made it his home, suggests that he had done quite well meeting the requirements of the gentry and yeoman households of the surrounding countryside, and his contemporaries in the town.

The hall, which opened into the street, was probably used for meeting and measuring customers. It was comparatively bare, with no rugs or carpets, but a fireplace and implements to work it. It contained two frame tables, a cupboard and two chairs. Leading directly off it on the ground floor fronting the street, the 'parlour' was stuffed with beds and bedding materials: Munden's own 'high bedstead' with 'hangings', a 'truckle bedstead, one bolster bed and two flockbeds', also another frame table, four joined stools, a form, a dozen cushions, 'and the table and presse'. Heavy curtains hung across the windows. The parlour must have been quite a large room. The 'chamber' above it contained 'two flockbeds, two ruggs, one bedstead with a flock mattress, one coverlet and one blanket, two bolsters, and three joined stools': sleeping accommodation for three apprentices or journeymen or both, perhaps. Next to it, the room over the 'lettis room' contained a feather bed, two bolsters, two more rugs and a blanket, a round table, a chest and a coffer and three joined stools.

The room over the kitchen had sleeping facilities for three more people, and the chamber over the hall could sleep one. It is tempting to conclude that as well as providing accommodation for the odd servant, apprentice, and journeymen, Munden ran a cheap boarding house. A chest of linen downstairs, worth £3 10s., is compatible with such a presumption. The kitchen too was set up to feed numbers, with its 'three great kettles and brass pans, two spits and 27 pieces of pewter, 5 salt and malt mills' and other kitchen implements, including six candlesticks and 'two silver spoons'.

The first impression, that this is a surprisingly large and substantial house for a tailor, is qualified by evidence of crowded living, and a very basic lifestyle. It is only when we come to consider the value of his 'wearing apparel', which included, carefully noted, 'his purple sash', that we get some sense of anything beyond a substantial sufficiency. In his dress, Munden was an advertisement for himself, the sash a flash of colour in the streets, the market-

11 *OED* 'Lettice'.

12 All references to lettis bonnets cited in the *OED* occurred in the period 1599–1624.

place and the church (if he went there, and he would be expected to). His clothes were worth £6, a sum rarely achieved in contemporary inventories of other craftsmen and petty traders, or yeomen from the villages. What kind of a tailor would he be, who did not dress well? His funeral costs were high – £5 6s. 8d. – although how much of this was in ostentation, and how much distributed to mourners and the poor, is not recorded in his will. Three men owed him a total of £18, the largest debt, £12, being that of a Henry Munden, presumably a relative. His will mentions a brother, Thomas, to whom he left 'my best doublet and hose'. The total value of his inventory was £74 6s. 8d., a sum that places him well within the ranks of the 'middling' town trades and craftworkers.

From the time of his arrival in Cirencester shortly after the turn of the century, until his death thirty years later, like many other men who had migrated there at around the same time to replace those who died in the disease and starvation years 1578–97, John Munden had attained the life of a substantial tradesman. Judging by his possessions, he spent his time and money accumulating necessities and basic comforts. There is not much in his inventory, beyond the purple sash and valuable personal wardrobe, to catch the imagination. We can glean a portrait of his household, but not his mental furniture. It is a dowdy, cluttered picture that emerges, a false impression perhaps, because we are told nothing of the colours of his rugs, carpets, bed-hangings and coverlets, curtains and clothes.

It is Munden's status as a successful immigrant craftworker that makes him typical of the town's abiding social milieu. It was probably true of Roman *Corinium*, and was certainly true of the town at the beginning of its documented social history, in the twelfth and thirteenth centuries, that its population was constantly topped up by immigrant workers, some of whom, like John Munden, did quite well.

Also typical, however, were 'poor strangers' whose 'settlement' occurred at Cirencester merely by dint of the accident of happening to die there, and the majority of immigrants, the labourers, weavers, shoemakers and other 'lesser' trades who were more vulnerable to a mercurial economy and epidemiological regime. Many of them married, stayed for a few years marked by the births (and very often deaths) of one or two children, and then disappear from the Cirencester registers, signifying that they had, in all probability, gone somewhere else in search of stability and sufficiency.[13]

This 'class', 'rank' or 'quality' of householder can be identified with the men who had paid the smallest and middling amounts to the tax of 1327, were affected most intensely by mortality crises of all types, and who lived in one- or two-hearth households in partitioned tenements, cottages, or hovels

[13] The first study to draw attention to the tendency of the poorest 30 percent to disappear from the essential source of reconstitution studies, local parish registers, was Keith Wrightson and David Levine, *Poverty and Piety in an English Village: Terling, 1525–1700* (New York 1979).

on the edge of town. The class straddled the dividing line defined by Philip Jones, between the respectable 'manuary craftsman' and the idle haunter of alehouses and other places of ill-repute Jones unequivocally condemned. Many examples would serve to illustrate its membership. Michael Dubber, a victualler, had arrived at Cirencester with his wife, Margery, around the turn of the century. The first event relating to him records his wife's burial in August 1602; the second describes him as the reputed father of 'Charitie Pitman's bastard child' who died unbaptized in May the following year. By this time he had married again, and between December 1603 and December 1612, he and his wife Grace produced four daughters and two sons, only one of whom had died before the family disappears from the registers. He probably did quite well out of his victualling stall in the market. Philip Jones would not have approved of him and he would have been hard-put to ever be considered 'better sorte'.

Nor would Jones have approved of the Cirencester-born Thomas Cross, son of labourer Leonard Cross, and described in the muster list for Cricklade Street as a 'loyterer'. Robert Griffith, in 1608 working as a cutler from his house in Dyer Street,[14] William Litten, a blacksmith in Castle Street,[15] and Nathaniel Lewis, a glover in Dollar Street,[16] are examples of men who established themselves. Others, like Robert Fletcher the barber, John Manery a shoemaker, Robert Munford a weaver, and 51 other men, appear in the muster list and disappear elsewhere. They were short-term immigrants who never established themselves.

Among the rarer trades was John Parke, a bookbinder, who arrived before October 1596, when his daughter Joan was baptized, and found enough work in the town for it to be worth his while to remain for another fifteen years. Up to 6 January 1611, no fewer than nine of his children were baptized, only two of whom died before he moved on, perhaps in search of a bigger town and clientele. William Minety, a 40-year-old musician, came to work at Cirencester before March 1600, when his son Raynald was baptized. He was about forty, and living in Castle Street at the time of the muster. His wife, Edith, was buried in 1606, and four months later he was married again, to Joan Wright. Meanwhile, his son, also William and also a musician, lived

14 Arrived before 12 January 1596; aged about 40 in 1608; six children baptized up to 19 July 1610, none buried. Son Robert married Sarah Raynford at Cirencester 1621, and produced seven children, of whom four died in infancy. Robert Senior buried April 1632.

15 Arr. Cirencester with family before first event 4 January 1587, son baptized; three more baptisms before wife, Elinor, buried 12 June 1601. Son, also William, took over smithy soon after, married and had seven children baptized 1604–21. William Litten Snr (the original immigrant) buried 19 June 1613; his son buried 13 April 1621, aged about 40.

16 First record muster list, a tall man aged about 20; married Margaret Maslen 11 August 1612; six children baptized between February 1613 and 23 January 1631, when the family disappears from the registers.

around the corner in Castle Street with his wife and one child, baptized in September 1602. William Minety Senior was buried at Cirencester in September 1618, five months after the death of his wife. The Minetys, and other musicians they employed from time to time, may have done quite well busking in the market-place and at the fairs, in the inns and taverns, and on special occasions in the houses of the wealthier inhabitants of the town and in the surrounding countryside.[17] The presence of men and occupations like these were among the qualities that made Cirencester a special place. George Spragot, a scrivener who lived a few doors up from John Parke's bookbinding shop in Castle Street, was another.

Notice should also be made of inkeepers like William Hayle and Thomas Powle in Cricklade Street, and John Chambers in Gosditch Street. Listed alongside Chambers's name are a 'Chamberlain', two tapsters, four ostlers and two carters: this was clearly a large hostelry, and a favourite stopping-place for travellers. Whether they brewed their own beer, or obtained it from a beerbrewer in Instrope Street, is not known.

Except in times of extreme stress – famine, disease, moments of complete breakdown of law and order – mobility in and between districts, regions, provinces and the nation, between the 'four kingdoms' of England, Scotland, Wales and Ireland, and between the Atlantic Isles and the continent, defined the field of forces within which towns like Cirencester operated. Karl Marx saw these as the centuries when the English peasantry was dispossessed of the land and houses it had occupied since time out of mind. Marx had a very passing interest in kings and lords, his view being that what happened to England from the thirteenth to nineteenth centuries had to do with underlying and often unrecognized historical processes. The dispossession of the immemorial peasantry came to a head in the reign of Henry VIII. Marx argued that the 'free' (proletarian) labour force of 'the bourgeois mode of production' sprang into existence 'in the generations of (Sir John) Fortescue and (Sir Thomas) More': Fortescue and More were among Marx's British Library sources. On the basis of the legislation of his (and his three children's) reigns, a strong case can be made for the proposition that Henry VIII's chancellors, Wolsey and Cromwell, in particular, instituted an ultimately revolutionary new regime of labour discipline, including savage legislation against the flotsam and jetsam of all the traffic of labour, vagrants and vagabonds. If peasants are settled and proletarians mobile, thirteenth- to seventeenth-century England was somewhere between the two. As we have seen, towns like Cirencester depended on a certain amount of routine migration.

Yet theories of the origin of capitalism imply that the preindustrial world was much more settled and sedentary than the worlds of industrial capitalism. Peasant-based civilizations are said to be grounded in autarkic, 'cellular',

17 A 'John Long, Musician,' was buried on 14 July 1614.

local communities; capitalism is global and mobile. Local studies like this one show this immobile 'world we have lost' (as Peter Laslett once put it) exaggerates the settled and ignores or marginalizes the mobility. Not by any stretch of the imagination did Cirencester resemble a community of peasants. The townspeople were well-informed about national and international affairs; they had to be, engaged as they were in national and international trade-circuits upon which the very existence of their town depended. Towns like Cirencester were connectors and distributors, ensuring that no news likely to be of use to interests in the region failed to be passed on. All sorts of traffic converged there: it was a town with resident musicians, preachers connected to the most up-to-date theories concerning the difficulties through which towns like Cirencester so frequently passed, scriveners, bookbinders, apothecaries and some of the most enterprising capitalists anywhere in England, including London. It was effectively a suburb of London.

14

The revival of the parish

Research on the lower, local levels of government suggests that, constitutionally, late sixteenth-century England differed from its neighbours, in Britain and on the continent, in that a sophisticated and dedicated culture of governance was present, and practised, in localities all over the country.[1] How it was structured and practised varied greatly, but at certain key periods of English history one institution, the parish, came to the fore. This had happened at Cirencester before the period that concerns us now: the parish had been the magnetic centre of communal life throughout the fifteenth century. There are also signs of an even earlier parish revival in the prosperous thirteenth century, centred on the Guild of St Mary. The parish-centred movement that replaced the Strange ascendancy at Cirencester, associated with 'puritanism', revived and recycled an old institution, the townspeople's enduring alternative to the hegemony of the manor.[2]

Of all institutions of early modern England, the parish alone enjoyed religious *and* secular legitimacy and concerned the government of all the inhabitants. Parish constitutions varied greatly across and between districts, regions and the nation as a whole. They can be classified according to Aristotle's system. Some were ruled by a single big man, classically a gentleman who owned the parish and the right to appoint priests. A second category is

1 Steve Hindle, *The State and Social Change in Early Modern England, 1550–1640* (London 2000) is authoritative, based on many community reconstitutions in different parts of England; Keith Wrightson, 'The Politics of the Parish in Early Modern England', in P. Griffiths, A. Fox and S. Hindle (eds), *The Experience of Authority in Early Modern England* (London 1996), 10–46; Beat Kumin, 'The Fear of Intrusion: Communal Resilience in Early Modern England', in William G. Naphy and Penny Roberts (eds), *Fear in Early Modern Society* (Manchester 1997), 118–19, writes that 'For England … it has recently been emphasized that the strengthening of central powers derived not only from institutional change and legislative programmes, but just as much from impulses by humble local government bodies.'

2 But note the slipperiness of the term 'puritanism'; Noel Malcolm, *Aspects of Hobbes* (Oxford 2002), 66, usefully points out that it is not the same as 'zeal, seriousness, ethical strictness or practical piety (unless, for example, we are willing to describe Laud as a Puritan).… Any attempt to define, or at least delineate, the nature of Puritanism must surely start with attitudes towards rites, observances, church government and the nature and sources of spiritual authority.'

rule by a few: oligarchies consisting of a few dominant and/or public-spirited households, classically yeomen. The third category is rule by a majority or even, in some instances, all the 'inhabitants'. Examples of and mixtures of all three were to be found in one or another of the parishes of the Seven Hundreds. Regardless of form, what made constitutions good or bad was the degree to which the ruling part was seen to serve the whole community. Cirencester's constitution was a mixture. Historically, its constitution shifted 'from one to another (mixture of good and bad forms) and back again'.[3] The Strange 'tyranny', as the petitioners of 1570 described it, was, by 1600, replaced by an oligarchy of gentlemen and businessmen (usually both) in a context of popular participation.

That institutions of the parish were the most likely resort of communities desirous of communal solidarity is not surprising. Churches were usually the oldest continuously occupied, and the most impressive, buildings in the parishes, surrounded by the graves of the dead generations and other sacred symbols like the 'rood' in the churchyard of Holyrood Ampney. Regardless of its constitution, the parish was a continuing, potentially *popular* ('of the people') institution. The fact that Cirencester was a one-parish town, symbolized by its dominant parish church, embodied the possibility that a place manifestly riven by innumerable gross inequalities could live at peace, be prosperous, act as one united *community*. Robert Strange's response to state reforms of religion, locally, had been to let sleeping dogs lie by not enforcing Sunday attendance, thereby relieving more rigorous souls of being forced to watch the decay and the chaos of ecclesiologies and theologies that went on inside the mighty church of St John the Baptist, in the reigns of Henry VIII, Edward VI, Mary and into the first decade of Elizabeth. Failures to attend were not reported to the relevant authorities until the Strange ascendancy began to weaken.

Underlying these unpredictable confusions was a pre-eminently practical problem. The dissolution of its chantries meant the funds administered by the parish treasurers and churchwardens for maintaining the church and relieving the poor dwindled to virtually nothing. The wealthy stopped leaving bequests to the parish. By 1570 the institution that had served Cirencester so well in the long fifteenth century was in ruins. Robert Strange hung on to as much authority as he could until he died, in 1588. His fellow consul, Christopher George, died ten years later.

A new generation of patriarchs rebuilt communal governance out of the dying ashes of the Strange regime. The men who assumed the leadership of parish and region in the late sixteenth and early seventeenth

[3] Such a classification avoids anachronism; Tudor–Stuart intellectuals were trained to study constitutions using the system derived from Aristotle's *Politics*. The most celebrated anatomy of the constitution of Tudor–Stuart England, then and now, is Sir Thomas Smith, *De Republica* (the quotation is from Part 1, Ch. 14, 200). Like his master, Smith warned that in real life constitutions were unique mixtures of the three basic types.

centuries, like their predecessors, were rentiers and businessmen. Part of this context was that 'English agriculture had as its setting a commercial, increasingly individualistic society, in process of an industrialisation that was more than merely local,' as R.H. Tawney put it. 'Fixed incomes falling, and profits rising, who could question that the way of salvation was to contract interests as a *rentier*, and expand them as an entrepreneur.'[4] The purchasing of rural estates and lordships was, of course, the immemorial practice of men of Cirencester who made fortunes out of the manufacture and marketing of local commodities. Conversely, established lords of country manors, counselled by the latest generation of Cirencester merchants, invested in trade. Stimulated by an urgent need to restore cohesion to communal life, they also invested, once again, in the parish.

As far as communal governance is concerned, the most significant change was that, beginning roughly in the 1580s, it gradually became *de rigueur*, once again, for 'the gentlemen of town and country' (i.e. the wealthiest townspeople and neighbouring country gentlemen) to leave significant bequests to the church and the parish. Unlike their predecessors in the fifteenth century, however, they did not found chantries and obits. The new revival was grounded in bequests for establishing and maintaining three related initiatives: preaching, investment in employment schemes and relief of the poor. How was order to be maintained? No-one doubted these were 'times of woe'. Constant expectation of the death of markets, unemployment, dearth, disease, constant replacement of dead inhabitants with suitable immigrants, the flow of those who failed to gain the assent of 'the fellowship of the town', passionate religious division, and an awakening constitutional crisis concerning the prerogatives of king and parliament, of how England ought to be governed and by whom: the question was how to turn the times around and restore 'times of *weal*'. Study of a town and country as richly documented as the town and the Seven Hundreds offers an opportunity to explore the English Revolution from the grass-roots up: what, if anything, changed in just one of England's provincial '*countreys*'. At Cirencester, this and the next chapter will show, three themes dominate the period from the 1580s to 1640: preaching, economic stimulus by careful (and socially 'deep') investment of parish funds, and growing solidarity with parliaments that shared their religious and secular vision of a godly, enterprising commonwealth. The parish was one of the two institutions that spearheaded the unfolding social revolution that exploded in the 1640s. The other, Parliament, will be considered in the next chapter.

The scale of the parish revival is revealed by lists of bequests left to the parish from 1587 to 1645. In 1587 the churchwardens administered bequests worth a mere £3 6s. 8d. per annum: the rents of two houses left to the parish

4 R.H. Tawney, 'The Rise of the Gentry, 1558–1640', *Econ Hist Rev*, 1st series, 11 (1941), 184.

by Alice Avening and John Weobley in 1498. By 1630 the vestry collected rents from 13 houses and was responsible for allocating £420 per annum, which further bequests had increased to £661 in 1645.[5] How these funds were managed and allocated will be considered in due course. The first task is to show how this extraordinary expansion of the parish treasury came about. The better-documented parish revival of the late sixteenth and early seventeenth centuries may also shed light on the earlier revivals of the thirteenth and fifteenth centuries.

We saw in Chapters 9–11 that the 1570s and 1580s saw the emergence of various collective actions by Philip Jones's 'manuary householders'. The parish revival that emerged in its wake marshalled the insecurities of such households and redirected them. Great efforts were made to demonstrate that their enemies were not local employers and merchants. The elite's contacts sometimes failed: they were expected to keep the manuary households in work as long as it took. If they made windfall profits when markets opened up again, it could be said they deserved reward for having supported the commonwealth in times of woe. They were expected to live in the town and not retreat to country estates when times were bad. In sustained slumps they blamed monopolistic London merchant companies with influence at court. In terms of constitutional change, a cynic might say that rule by one mighty religious lord was succeeded by rule by a tiny elite of wealthy businessmen and landlords. Tyranny was replaced by oligarchy. But it had become clear in the 1580s that the manuary workers who constituted the many less wealthy producers also expected to be consulted where the government of the commune was concerned.

What did not change was that a few wealthy men continued to occupy the leading positions in communal government. In the past the town had always worked best when its capitalist elite not only enriched itself and its closest friends, but fed enough of their wealth and energy back into the community to convince the inhabitants they had the community's 'poor' inhabitants' interests at heart. What made a town of 3,000 inhabitants different from a village of 250 was that class structures swallowed up in personal relationships in smaller places were magnified and enacted in towns. Towns were always potential theatres of class-struggle. Local merchants like Philip Marner and John Coxwell, the leaders of the parish revival of the late sixteenth and early seventeenth centuries, ran the risk that their neighbours would see them as 'caterpillars', as a Quaker of Siddington St Mary described the 'rich' of the 1650s. They had to distinguish themselves from another stereotype of popular culture, represented in this region by the 'kings of the Cotswolds', the Brydges lords Chandos of Sudeley: wealthy hunting *lords* with castles, mansions and parks, scores of tenanted farms and dozens of servants and retainers, who cared nothing for their country and gave nothing back to the commonwealth.

[5] Calculated from lists in Vestry Minutes, GA P86, VE 2/1; see also Rudder, *History of Cirencester*, 326–7.

English puritans were shaped by a need to be the opposite of men like Henry, lord Berkeley, who 'havocked his estate' in a vain quest for glory in the circumstances described in Chapter 10. The crime of such men was not that they were rich and powerful, but that they appeared to put their own glory before that of their country. They gave nothing to the community. They 'lived in the breath of other men'. This stereotype of magnate nobility, the senior members of Smith's 'second sort', was immensely influential in the later years of Elizabeth I (d.1603), James I and, most intensely, Charles I. To achieve their ends, wealthy parish statesmen like Philip Marner and John Coxwell had to convince the inhabitants they were not 'rich men' like these.

At the other extreme, godly commonwealth was threatened by 'spendalls' and 'unthriftes', unwelcome 'passingers', 'inmates' and 'sojourners' whose churches were alehouses, had no morals, produced noisy, ill-mannered, illegitimate children, did no work and 'lived altogether on the people', as Philip Jones put it. The new men were non-separatist 'puritans'. Looking back on the events of the 1640s, Thomas Hobbes (1588–1680), was convinced that rich Calvinist merchants were the chief instruments of the English Revolution. Debate ever since has circled around the role of 'puritans' and 'puritanism'. In 1570 Bishop Cheyney of Gloucester classed 'Brownists, Familists and Traskites &c' as 'commonlie called puritans'. [6] Whether by 'commonlie' he meant churchmen and statesmen alone, or the people of his region generally, or both, is not clear, but it proves the term was in use, definitely in Bristol and very possibly in 'rural' parts too. As this chapter will show, 'precisian', another contemporary usage, is perhaps more accurate in the sense that believers tended to be rather 'precise' in their views of who were and were not 'God's elect', and also, notably, in their projects for reforming society. Both terms generalized a great upswelling of religious and social reform that undoubtedly happened, and that culminated in the civil wars.

The first clue to the revival is a brass memorial on the wall of the church near the entrance to the Trinity Chapel, to 'Philip Marner who died in the year 1587'. Marner, apparently a bachelor who could therefore devote his entire fortune to the good of the community, was seen by his contemporaries and successors as the seminal figure in communal affairs, setting an example to his own and the generation that followed his. When, in 1611, the churchwardens purchased a book in which to record their 'constitution' and yearly accounts, the first entry was a lengthy abstract of Marner's will of 1587. Although he described himself in his will, and was probably seen by his contemporaries as, a 'gent', Marner was a wholesale tailor, probably specializing in leather, respected locally and routinely in contact with trade communities elsewhere, and in London.[7] His memorial is different in style from anything earlier: the figure,

6 Clutterbuck, 'State Papers respecting Bishop Cheyney and the Recusants of the Diocese of Gloucester'.

7 Direct connection with the London retail market and overseas trade is indicated by a bequest 'unto John Bennet, sonne in lawe to *my cosen Mr Stiche of London Draper if the*

dressed in a long cloak over a doublet, reveals efforts to achieve a likeness that Marner's contemporaries would be able to recognize. Looking up from his right foot is a little dog. Marner's head is represented as turning towards, and the right hand appears to be reaching for, a large pair of scissors cut into the plate alongside the head, an obvious symbol of Marner's dedication to his vocation. This was an important detail, clearly representing the theology preached by Philip Jones, to whom Marner left twenty bundles of firewood and his 'best black cloak', and whose sermons or lectures Marner almost certainly initiated and financed. The representation is more animated than the opaque, uniform medieval memorials referred to in Chapter 6, from which individual personality is completely absent.

The change in style is significant. The emergent protestant 'congregationalism' of the last third of the sixteenth century placed great pressure on individual personality in two senses. Firstly, of course, the individual's relationship with God required no mediator: every individual had, ultimately, to answer *personally* to God. Secondly, much greater emphasis was placed on harmony between the inner and social lives of individuals, so much so that many commentators have suggested that the new vocational theology is responsible, among other things, for the emergence of a modern 'sense of self', the root of modern, capitalist, individualism.[8] The key to it was a fully worked-out vocational theology.

Marner's memorial signifies – and was seen by his successors as signifying – a movement, a new spirit and the seeds of a more interventionist and evangelical style of communal governance. Another pioneer of this movement was Marner's executor and 'well beloved Friend', John Coxwell, one of the town's wealthiest gentleman-merchants. Coxwell was treasurer of the parish church from the declining years of the old bailiff, Robert Strange (d.1587), until his own death, apparently aged 101, in 1617. In an effort to ameliorate the local effects of the general crisis, Marner and Coxwell united the independent, taxpaying households of the town by making the parish church the central place of a vibrant, evangelical religious vision. They may have supported the efforts of the middling traders and craft workers to revive the Guild Merchant in the 1580s. If so, they quickly realized that, given the collective control they and their closest associates actually exercised over the means of production and trade, and over the potentially powerful institutions of the parish, the Guild

saide John lyve to come from beyond the seas, my best salte with a cover, being parcel gilt, and if the said John Bennet shall deceyse… then I geve the said salte to my said cossen Stiche': Will of Philip Marner, GCRO, GDR 1587/160. William Styche of the parish of St John the Evangelist was assessed for a national subsidy in 1582 at £8: R.G. Lang (ed.) *Two Tudor Subsidy Rolls for the City of London* (1993), 163; I have not been able to identify anyone with the name 'Stiche' in the parish registers, but one 'Robte Stich' served as a churchwarden at Cirencester in 1635–6.

8 Examination of Marner's brass based on personal observation; see also Fallowes, *Brasses of Cirencester Parish Church*, 19–20.

Merchant issue not only offended the old elite (Strange, Christopher George, Thomas Marshall), it was anachronistic and unnecessary. New approaches were called for. Marner's will is important because it embodied a new approach to communal management.

When Marner wrote out his will, 'in the 19th year of oure Sovereign Ladye Elizabeth', he belonged to the last and by now rapidly diminishing generation to have been born in a catholic society.[9] His conviction that after his death he would one day 'rise again in the generall resurrection to lyve forever with God's Angells and Saints in Celestiall Blysse ymmortallie' hints at what might be termed the 'secularization of the saints' involved in the transformation of Catholicism into Calvinism. Marner conducted his business and became a wealthy man when Calvin's influence was growing: once again, Bishop Cheyney identified Calvinism as an enemy of Elizabethan settlement in this region in the late 1560s. Its personal and social disciplines were obviously relevant to the 'trials' of the age. One visionary tenet of all the more radical forms of Protestantism, including popular (i.e. simplified) Calvinism, was that there existed a large class of *living* 'saints', with a mission from God to lead and transform society. All shades of Christianity as it was practised in England shared a millenarian belief in the Second Coming. It was second nature to read the world for signs that the Last Days were imminent in events they witnessed around them. Men like Marner felt their mission more acutely because they had the power to put it to good use. In his mind was a synthesis of medieval angels and mid-Tudor Calvinist saints. This 'company' of the Elect was the community at the end of the universe. Marner was an English catholic Calvinist the last time it was possible to be all three at the same time.

The new saints were not long-dead martyrs but living reformers. Like the old saints they would join the company of heaven, but for different reasons. 'First, and above all other thynges', Marner 'humblye commend[ed his] sowle unto allmychtie God my Creator, and to his blessed Sonne oure Lord Jesus Chryste my Savyour and Redeemer, by whose onlye Passyon and Deathe and mercye I constantly beleeve that I have and shall have full pardon and remyssyon of my synnes.' New men like Marner and Coxwell did not rely on clerks to write their wills for them. Their studious lack of concern with *where* they were buried, a marked change from the mentality of the fifteenth-century elite, reflected the faith that wherever it was they would rise again in the 'general resurrection'. In keeping with the new order, Marner bequeathed his body 'to the earthe to be buried in such place and Decente sorte, as to my Executor and Overseers shall be thoughte meet for my estate and degree'. Men like Marner were not enemies of traditional patterns of 'estate and degree', as long as those it privileged were perceptibly devoted to the godly commonweal.

Marner's will suggests that he had been on friendly enough terms with the old manorial regime: Robert Strange's relative, Thomas, Strange's son in law

9 Marner's will: GA, GDR 1587/160.

Christopher George, and Mr George Master, now resident at Abbey House, each received cash bequests and small mementoes.[10] This, too, would be an enduring theme: a desire on the part of local reformers not to offend powerful (or even humble) neighbours any more than could be helped. The aim was to co-opt them. Marner's successor John Coxwell, who put his ideas of communal improvement into practice in the decades following Marner's death, also made every effort to remain on good terms with the 'powerful gentry' of the town's environs, notably Sir Henry Poole. The ultimate task is to explain why such efforts fell apart in the early 1640s.

They were, definitively, practical men. The bequests that were considered to be of greatest importance to the people responsible for the erection of Marner's memorial were recorded in its inscription:

> In Lent by will a Sermon he devised
> And Yerely Preacher with a noble prized
> Seven nobles he did give the poor for to defend,
> And £80 to xvi men did lend
> In Ciceter, Burford, Abington and Tetburie
> Ever to them a stock Yerly

Preach the word, employ and relieve the deserving poor and invest money in small businesses. With regard to the latter, Marner instructed his executors (the same men) to 'delyver and paye unto the said John Coxwell, Henry Poole and John Stacye Fourscore pounds of Lawfull monie' to be invested as follows:

> One £20 thereof shall be lent from yere to yere, and … *for ever* unto suche foure men of trade and occupation in Cirencester for their ayde yerely without paying anything for the same.… And at the end of that yere my wyll and meaning is that the same £20 shall be loaned out to foure other younge men of the saide towne of some trade or occupation for one other yere without anythinge to be paid.

That in his lifetime Marner had been active on a more than merely parochial level is suggested by the fact that he bequeathed the same sums for the same purposes to the cloth towns of Burford, Abingdon and Tetbury. Marner clearly anticipated that this experiment in communal capitalism

[10] 'Item I geve and bequethe to *my good friend Xpofer George* Esquier ten pounds in money & my best goblett.… Item I geve and bequeathe unto *Thomas Strainge gent* my greate chest above in my chamber and chayer in my parlour, and to his wyfe *Mrs Bridgett Strainge* I give an oulde ryoll (?) of gold.… Item I give unto *Robarte Strainge Esquier* an olde spurr ryoll in golde.… Item I give unto *Mr George Master* one double ducket of goulde.… Item I geve unto *Humphrey Brydges* one of my greatest silver spoones and one of my best brasse candlesticks, my medie gown, and one double duckett of golde': Marner's will, GA, GDR 1587/160.

would continue for ever, and left detailed instructions concerning the selection of replacements for dead feoffees.[11] Every year £5 was to be given to four deserving tradesmen in each of these towns to invest as they saw fit. It was a more substantial sum than any of the poorer sort of craftsmen and traders would ever have to their name: enough, perhaps, if they were lucky with the year the loan was made to them, to establish them as settled, godly householders. Administered as it would be by the godly elite, it provided an incentive for poor craft householders to live godly lives.

The idea evidently proved successful enough for others to follow Marner's example. In his 1613 will a local merchant, Henry Hill, left a further £30 to be lent out to tradesmen without interest.[12] John Coxwell, in his 1610 will, left £100 'to be delivered unto the treasurers of the parish church of Ciceter and the churchwardens of the same and the anncyent men of the same town to use as hereafter followeth':

> That they shall deliver the whole sum to ten men of trade in the same town as clothmen, mercers, drapers, showmakers, chaundlers, butchers and hosiers, hatters, tanners and gardeners, and anie of these to have it for one whole year paying for the same £5/5/0 … them to pay the same at yeare end, and then another 10 occupiers to have it … and so to continue in the same maner for ever … and for this £5/5/0 which is to be had of them … it is to be devided [as follows] … 40/- to the poore on Saturday before Passion Sunday in Lente; and for the 40/- yt remayneth … it shall be given to a godly man to give 2 sermons at Chrysteyde or in Lente as the Treasurers and Churchwardens shall think most meet. And the odd 5/- to the honest men to drink for their pains taken in distributing money to the poor.[13]

Bequests like these were the 'small thinges' that brought into being what Gloucester radical John Corbet called 'the grande designes' that inspired many of the region's 'middle rankes' to propose alternatives to rule by kings, bishops and magnates. Just such a 'grand design' was committed to paper, early in the reign of James I, in the form of a parliamentary bill proposing to institutionalize, in all the counties of England, social relations of production that had prevailed in the Seven Hundreds of Cirencester for nearly two centuries. The bill was never presented; its importance is that it reveals how the most lucid minds of the English business community were thinking

11 'And further my will is that when it shall please Allmygtye God to call to his mercye oute of this transitory world anye one of the said John Cockswell Henry Poole and John Stacye that then such of them as shall be survyvyng shall in tyme convenyent enfeoffe some other persons … and theire heirs or assigns … and that from tyme to tyem then after when any one of the feoffees shall deceyse the other two survyving shall make or cawse (another person) …': GA, GDR Marner, 1587/60.

12 Rudder, *History of Cirencester*, 326–7.

13 GA, D 269B F1 'John Coxwell Sen. His last will and testament' (dated 1 February 1610).

about economic and social organization in the century before the English Revolution. The formulators of the bill surveyed England for examples of best practice in the encouragement of manufacturing, which, in their view, held the key to national prosperity. The example that caught their eye was from Devon; they may also have had in mind another local company designed by Robert Cecil to inculcate industrious habits in the working people of Hatfield (Herts), with legal assistance from his neighbour, Sir Francis Bacon.[14] In fact few provinces better exemplified efficient social relations of production than Cirencester's.

Like Marner's and Coxwell's bequests of seed capital, the bill was one of a number of 'experiments', in this case a kind of master-plan, 'designed to bring within the company system classes – in some cases the landed gentry with capital to invest, in others the rural producers – which hitherto had remained outside'. The aim was to 'incorporate ... speculative capitalists and skilled manufacturers'. The draft Bill outlined a systematic programme to achieve these ends everywhere in England. According to its preface, 'the general conceaved opinion of the vulger sort hath ben and still is that wee stand no need of any manner of foraigne commodetyes'. This prejudice 'bredd a greate discouragement of all industry, especially to rayse Commodetyes for Transportation, and thereby abandoninge all Commerce and Traffique as alsoe use of shippinge'.[15] To counter these prejudices the bill proposed to appoint commissioners:

> To enquire, heare, examine and informe themselves, by all fitte wayes and meanes, whither each County, City or Towne Corporate doth yearly afford soe much manufacture and commodety, raysed by the industry, laboure and invention of that particular people by theire ymployment, vendible and vented by being Transported to foraigne nations, as doth any way equalize and balance the foraigne commodetyes dispended in such County, City or Towne Corporate, yea or no. If yea, to certifye in and by what Commodetyes; if not, then to certifye, upon mature Consideration first had, what materials every such county doth or may afford and what manufacture and what manner of profitable and useful ymployment may most aptly and fittley, in such commissioners opinion, be established and used for setting on work the poore men, weomen and children.[16]

The language is precociously modern: 'examine and informe', 'fitte wayes and meanes', 'industry', 'ymployment', 'nations', 'profitable and useful ymployment' and, last but not least, 'men, weomen and children'. Being poor and having to work reduced common 'men, weomen and children' to a single capacity: to be useful by producing the commodities that were to

14 F.J. Fisher, 'Some Experiments in Company Organization in the Early Seventeenth Century', *Econ Hist Rev* 4:2 (April 1933), 177–94.

15 *Ibid*, 181, 190.

16 *Ibid*, 190, qf. TNA SPD James I, Vol. XX, No. 32.

make the whole commonwealth prosperous. Where workers were concerned, gender was subordinate to economy. In multiple-occupational – and profitable – regions like this, it was assumed that every member of even the least household would strive to maintain a semblance of collective independency. Where they failed it created a stain on the character of the household head and reduced the godly harmony of the commune.

In the event that a county was found to have an unfavourable balance of trade, local commissioners were to be identified and appointed. Members of 'the Company or Corporation of that county', thus constituted, would then be 'rated and taxed' whatever sum was thought necessary to finance a four-year plan. 'Every yeare one equall fourth parte' was to be used 'in taking of [local] commodetyes from off the hands of such as doe worke them.' Local overseers of the poor would use parish rates to set up poor households in some branch of textiles. Wool spun by poor women and children would then be distributed by the company to 'skilled artisans', whose 'finished wares' were to be bought back by the company 'at reasonable prices'. The county companies had responsibility for searching and sealing the 'commodetyes' by quality and, as noted above, transporting them to 'foraigne' markets.

In essence, the bill aimed to institutionalize a system that had been operating in the Seven Hundreds of Cirencester since the early fifteenth century, but had fallen into chaos following the dissolution of the monasteries. Where they dominated, religious houses had organized social relations of production. As we have seen, they were often perceived as having done so for their own estate alone, at the expense of commonalty and commonwealth. The lynch-pins of many estates, some scattered, some very consolidated, were suddenly removed. No sooner had the abbey buildings been stripped of their wine, gold, silver, jewels, chests, robes, ornaments, icons, barns, roofs and fabric, long before its '200 servants' had found alternative secure employment and the redistribution of its estate had settled down in new formations: it immediately became obvious that, for all their unpopularity, the abbots had held this little commonwealth together, if only by hatred and resentment. In fact it was more than this. At their best, the abbots of Cirencester had been in *command.* Some places in England were less affected by the dissolution than others. Those most heavily affected, like Cirencester, Abingdon, Bury St Edmunds and all the other places where monasteries had dominated, found themselves in a position of having to create new command structures. This was the case at Cirencester and in five of the Seven Hundreds after 1539.

What, or who, was to take the mitred abbot's place? At Cirencester, a perceptibly new command structure does not begin to emerge from and impose itself on the primary sources until the 1580s. Professor Fisher's Jacobean 'experiments' in the formation of 'county companies' were sophisticated outcomes of three generations of experiments designed to fill the gaps where the old command structures had been. Robert Strange held the fort for nearly fifty years, but his generation's self-evident material voraciousness, spiritual emptiness, pastoral indifference and sheer age eventually undermined it. By the late 1560s, rebel 'projects' have emerged on all fronts: Brownists, Familists, Anabaptists, Congregationalists of many kinds, some of whom believed that the dissolution of the monasteries was, and should only be seen as, the prelude to the dissolution of all existing 'traditions of men' and their replacement by priesthoods of all believers.

Such experiments were 'economic' in the modern sense, but were rather more at the time. It is essential to any understanding of the popularity of sermons and lectures in this period to realize that they communicated visions of cosmic transformation, spiritual and material progress, that were grounded not in economy (how material things are produced and distributed) but theology (theories of first and last things, what we are in God's eyes, how God wants us to behave). Connecting capital and raw materials with manufacturing was a practical pivot of larger schemes. Men like the charismatic Philip Marner and John Coxwell were self-identified instruments of a larger movement to forge a new synthesis of all the parts and members of their communities. They wanted to create nothing less than a prosperous, pious and harmonious commonwealth such as the world had never seen. Much as we globally warmed twenty-first-century denizens of wealthy modern nations may regret the movement these generations forged – 'capitalism', the ransacking of the world's resources, the death of thousands of species and hundreds of human cultures, the burning forests and so on – no historical account that fails to acknowledge that these elders of capitalism were inspired can get close to understanding how the world came to be the ways it is today. Religion played a central role in the birth of capitalism, which was, in its infancy, driven by a profoundly millenarian force.

The visionary bill never went before Parliament, probably because something like the system it advocated was already operating in many places. Observation demonstrated that different versions of the grand design, harnessing economic life to devout religion and best practice in governance, were already being developed, or actually in place. Where it was not happening, local magnates and gentry were so opposed to manufacturing and all it represented ('dirty villages up to the knees in mud', as James Wolfe described the Stroudwater Valleys in the 1740s), that unless such powerful opponents were removed, the project would be impossible to implement there.[17] The sources take us into the worlds of this seminal, modern, national 'development project'. The traditional rulers of England feared this movement was overwhelming them. From the 1580s to the 1650s their fears were justified. And in the long run, aristocracies and monarchies, where they survived at all, would eventually be disarmed and converted into soap operas for the masses.

17 Beckles Wilson (ed.), *Life and Letters of James Wolfe* (New York 1909).

Philip Marner's 'trusted friend', John Coxwell, was reputedly the wealthiest man in town.[18] He would have been one the first to have been appointed a 'commissioner' and paid-up member of a hypothetical 'Company' of the Seven Hundreds of Cirencester. In effect, he ensured that the parish of Cirencester became a flourishing 'department' of such a 'company'. Like his older contemporary Robert Strange, he had survived all the crises described in Chapter 10, and continued to accumulate wealth after the sustained contraction of foreign markets for English cloth after c.1550. He did not flee the epidemic of 1577–9: it took his wife, Joane. He exemplified the social mobility enjoyed by many socially conscientious capitalist clothiers of his era. Born in 1516, 'John Cockswell, treasurer of the parish church' was buried 101 years later, reputedly after a fall from his horse on St John's Bridge, Lechlade, in November 1617.[19] He was not a native of Cirencester and almost certainly came to the town as a young man, perhaps as an apprentice or 'servant' to William Partridge, whose daughter, Joan, he married.[20] Partridge was another clothier who, in later life, moved his family into the gentry.[21] His son or grandson, John Partridge Esq., was lord of three local manors in 1608 (Ampney St Mary, North Cerney and Side) and another of his heirs, Anthony Partridge, was lord of the manors of Wishinger and Miserden, in Bisley Hundred.[22]

Partridge almost certainly came to Cirencester shortly after the dissolution of the abbey, to rent one or two of the abbey mills in a strategically placed town. In a court case concerned with the blocking up of the millstream in 1584, Robert Strange referred to 'Mr Partridge's mill otherwise known as Clerks Mill'. 'Margaret Partridge Widow' gave evidence that 'her husband was tenant to [the new mill and Langleys Mill]' and testified that 'she knew four flockmills under the rush of St Mary's Mill and a gygg mill'.[23] Partridge died during the crisis of 1577–9, leaving a 'decidedly Protestant will'.[24] Two years earlier, in January 1575, Sir Giles Poole had ordered Christopher George, William Partridge and John Coxwell to 'make their repair to the house of [Elizabeth] Whitting', and take her child to be baptized at the parish church.[25] They were probably churchwardens, but no lists survive

18 He was assessed at £16 for the Subsidy of 5 James I; compare this with Sir Henry Poole of Sapperton, the highest assessed in the Seven Hundreds at £50: Atkyns, *Gloucestershire*, 21–2.

19 GA 269 B/f. 117 records birth date as 1516; for burial, see GCRO P86, Nov. 1617.

20 GA D4871; for the Partridge genealogy, see Sir John Maclean and W.C. Heane, *The Visitation of the County of Gloucester in 1623* (London 1885), 120.

21 William Partridge (1490–1578) purchased the manor of Wishanger, Miserden parish, in 1563–4: *VCH* 11, 51.

22 *Men and Armour*, 249.

23 GA D674b, L1, 'Heads of Evidence about the Mill Stream'.

24 Caroline Litzenberger, *The English Reformation and the Laity: Gloucestershire 1540–1580* (Cambridge 1997), 151, n.90.

25 Price (ed.), *Commission for Ecclesiastical Causes*; for Whitting, see above, Chapter 9.

until 1610 against which to check this. Partridge and Coxwell were non-separatist 'puritans'; George was not.[26] Another of Partridge's sons in law, Thomas Restall, had been in trouble a few years earlier for opening his shop on Sundays and not attending the parish church.[27] As for his business, flock-mills were for shredding cloth for use in papermaking and gigg mills were used for raising the knap on lengths of cloth. It is not clear which of these Partridge's mills were used for; either or both were potentially profitable options and the leasing of a mill was often the key step made by successful merchant-clothiers on the road to gentility. Partridge was probably related to a kin coalition of moderately wealthy clothiers from Kings Stanley and Leonard Stanley in the Vale of Gloucester.[28]

There are no Cockswells or Coxwells in the *Military Survey* of 1522, so either his relatives were too poor to be assessed or (most likely) he originally came from outside the county. The first reference to his father in law residing at Cirencester is in the inventory of abbey tenements of 1545, where it is recorded that William Partridge rented 'two messuages lying together next Swynbruge in Abbot Street'.[29] This became Coxwell's house (mentioned in his will): shortly after his death in 1617, Abbot Street was renamed 'Coxwell Street', in recognition of his services to the community.

John Coxwell had six daughters and three sons. The first mention of him in the local records is as a juror of the manor, in 1560.[30] His daughter, Mary, was baptized at the parish church on 16 August 1562.[31] In 1577 a 'John Cox and his wife' were named by Bishop Cheyney among those who, according 'to the common fame and beleefe of their neighbours', were refusing to attend church. [32] Also accused was one Agnes Long. Coxwell left several bequests to members of the Long family. His daughter Elizabeth was married to Richard Long; both are named as receiving bequests, alongside Mary Long, perhaps his granddaughter.[33] Given that Coxwell's will was Calvinist, it is entirely possible that his was one of the many moves against the survivalist regime at the parish church in the 1560s and 1570s. Sir Giles

26 'First I commend and gyve my sowle unto the most holy and blessed Trinitie three persons in one God who in the personne of the sonne becoming man hath redeemed my sowle with his most precious bloude.... And my bodie to be buryed in the chapel of St Katherine in the p[ar]ish where my grandfather Thomas George, my good father and mother and my late good wife doe lye and are buryed …': GA, P86 Ch. 1.4, 'Will of Xpopher George' (1597).

27 Maclean and Heane,*Visitation of 1623*, 120, records marriage of Margaret Partridge to Thomas Restall; for Restall, see above, Chapter 9.

28 Military Survey 1522, 187, 192.

29 Hockaday 155: 1545.

30 GCL RV 79.7, 'View of Frankpledge 1560'.

31 GA P86, IN 1/1.

32 Clutterbuck, 'State Papers Respecting Bishop Cheyney and the Recusants of the Diocese of Gloucester', 235.

33 D 269B F1: 'John Coxwell Sen. His last will and testament'.

Poole may have ordered him (and his father in law) to see that Elizabeth Whitting's infant was baptized in order to test where he stood with regard to the more radical dissenters.

He made his money in the Cirencester woollen cloth industry and lived in Abbot Street, later called Coxwell Street. The fact that he purchased Ablington Manor, near Bibury, from Arthur Basset for £346 13s. 4d. in 1574, a year after the birth of his eldest son, Nathaniel, suggests that, like many country clothiers and merchants of his generation, he always intended to use his wealth to move his family into the gentry. 'John Coxhall of Cirencester, Gent' contributed £25 'to the defence of this country at the time of the Spanish invasion in 1588', as did his neighbour Robert Partridge, son and heir of William, and Sir Giles Poole.[34] He began rebuilding the manor house in 1590; in 1608 six Ablington men were described as 'servants to John Coxwell, gent'.[35] A seventh man, John Symms, rented one of Coxwell's ten houses in Cirencester and was described in 1608 as 'servant to John Coxet'. Nathaniel was educated at University College, Oxford, and the Middle Temple. He was married in 1596 to Susannah, daughter of Edward Long, who paid £400 for the privilege; in return, Coxwell settled Ablington on the married couple. Coxwell was an extraordinarily assiduous accumulator of tenements and parcels of land: his will lists ten houses at Cirencester, the rectory and tithes of Siddington, and further properties at Frampton, Bisley, Stroud, Minchinhampton, Baunton, Stratton, Preston, Chesterton, Barton and Spiringate.[36] His tenants at Cirencester included Thomas Hopkins, a baker, Harry King, clothier, Thomas Lloyd, mercer, two weavers, Robert Braine and Roger Vaughn, and his servant, John Symms.[37] Given his activities on behalf of the parish, old John probably lived most of the time at Cirencester, but his second son, Samuel, was born at Ablington in 1587. Like the Strange family a generation earlier, the Coxwells moved up, leaving space to be filled in the town elite. John Coxwell's activities illustrate a key theme in the period we are considering here: the intense involvement of the local gentry in civic life, their devotion, not only to the amassing of property and profit, but also to the commonweal. The movement may have been driven by the felt need of new wealth to demonstrate the ideal qualities required of gentlemen.

Wherever he had stood on these matters in 1570, Coxwell died a convinced Calvinist:

> I doe assuredly beleyve, [he wrote in his will] that after death I shall rise again to everlasting life by Jesus Christ my onelie saviour who hath shed his precious blood for thy sinnes to appease the wrath of God his father and is risen again

34 *Gloucestershire Notes and Queries*, Vol. 1, item CCCCXXXV, 441.
35 *Men and Armour*, 258.
36 GA D269B/T1.
37 Will: D 269B F1; *Men and Armour*, 241.

> for my Justification and is sit on the right hand of God and maketh intercession for his elect and I trust that by him I shall after this life I shalbe received into the company of good obedient people there to praise and magnifie him for ever.

Coxwell was not a man to let others speak for him (or punctuate his prose): 'I the said John Cockswell,' he wrote, 'have written this my last will with my own hand.' As with his predecessor Philip Marner, his place of burial was a matter of indifference: 'and my bodie to the Earth from whence it was taken and to be buryed in such convenient order as my executors shall think'.[38] Wherever it was, a lifetime of what he saw as service to the commonwealth of Cirencester left him 'assured' that, as a member of the 'elect', Jesus would 'intercede' for him and he would spend the rest of eternity in 'the company of good, obedient people' and, of course, God.

Professor Fisher's observation that the 'experiments' of Coxwell's lifetime represent a systematic effort to connect capital with the production of commodities for export was only part of the truth. In some ways the most urgent task at the time was to relieve tensions between capitalists and skilled manufacturing workers by uniting them against a common enemy. The communal 'investment funds' of Philip Marner and John Coxwell addressed this problem directly, in a documented context. One of the outstanding features of the various movements of resistance to the survivalist manorial cabal from the late 1560s to the late 1580s was the active role played by middling tradesmen and craftsmen, householders below the elite of wealthy merchants like Partridge and Coxwell, those who had composed the second and third ranks of taxpayers since the third decade of the fourteenth century and probably earlier: quite literally, the project aimed to unite the *bons bourgeoisie* of merchants like Coxwell with the *petite bourgeoisie* led, from the 1560s to 1580s, by Giles Selwyn. The Calvinist vocationalism of men like Marner and Coxwell aimed to discipline the somewhat anarchic turbulence of the artisans and small tradesmen within a common vision, united by a common theology.

The new religious mentality was to be furthered by preachers. In his will of 1610, Coxwell left 'forty shillings per annum for the having of a godlie preacher in Ciceter for the exercise every Friday continually… so long as the parish holdeth sure that the gentlemen of the towne and countrie will give to a godlie man their charitable gyfte to furnishe him for his paynes', and another forty shillings to 'be given to a godly man to give 2 sermons at Chrysteyde or in Lente as the Treasurers and Churchwardens shall think most meet'.[39] Here, in few words, Coxwell enunciated his view of consensual government by 'the better sort': 'godlie preacher', 'the parish' (vestry), 'the gentlemen of the towne and countrie'.

38 Will: GA D 269B F1.

39 GA D 269B F1: 'John Coxwell Sen. His last will and testament'.

Once again, Coxwell was following the precedent set by Philip Marner. Instead of mass priests, the elite left bequests to preachers.[40] Marner left the rents of two houses in Dollar and Abbot Streets, with gardens and furniture, to pay for 'a Godlye sermon to be made in the parish Churche of Cirncester … yearly uppon the first Fryday in cleane Lent *forever*'. As their bequests to 'good friends' and their executors' names affirm, both men envisaged parish governance as the spearhead of an alliance between 'the gentlemen of town and country' bequeathing and managing a constantly expanding communal fund aimed at supporting suitable artisans, employing the able-bodied poor and relieving the deserving. It was understood, for example, that country gentlemen would benefit from lectures and sermons at Cirencester, especially on a Friday, one of the town's two market days. Like Marner, Coxwell was remembered for his efforts to restore standards of parish governance not encountered since the early sixteenth century.

The new vestry book, commissioned c.1610, includes an abstract of Philip Marner's will and a list of lands and money left for the churchwardens to administer. The earliest minute, titled 'remembrances what thyngs have been agreed upon', refers to a meeting of 11 July 1613. The outgoing churchwardens, a mercer and a wholesale shoemaker, 'delyvered [their accounts] up into the hands of Mr John Coxwell, one of the treasurers'. Coxwell's fellow-treasurer was Robert George, brother of Richard, Christopher George's heir: a powerful duumvirate. Two years later, on 10 April 1615, a minute lists 'orders agreed upon' by

> Robart George esquire, John Coxwell esquire, Treasurers of the same parish church, Robert George gent (Christopher's nephew), William Searle gent, Rowland Freeman (mercer), William Turbyll (occupation not given in 1608), now churchwardens, Thomas Stone gent, John Channler (chandler), Robert Alexander (mercer), John Iles (shoemaker), and many others of the better sorte of the saide parish.[41]

Following Marner's plan and with the support of the Georges of Baunton and the Pooles of Sapperton, Coxwell put Cirencester's affairs on to a good business footing. The first 'order' concerned collections 'for loss bye fire or other matter of charitable devotion'. They were to be 'made knowen [and delivered] unto the treasurers and six others of the better sorte of the parish'. The second item ordered that 'before he give in his accompte to

40 Further bequests for sermons were included in the wills of Giles Fettiplace (1607: 20s. for a sermon on 5 November every year 'for ever'), Jeffrey Bath (1618: 6s. 8d. for a sermon on Ascension Day), the London businessman Sir Thomas Roe (1637: £2) and John Monox (1639): Rudder, *History of Cirencester*, 307.

41 GA P86, VE 2/1; occupations from *Men and Armour*; Robert George Gent, son of Christopher's younger brother, John, was the father of John George, MP for Cirencester 1626–61, for whom see below, Chapter 14.

the parryshe' every outgoing churchwarden 'shall first shew the same to the Treasurers or to one of them and two other of the better sorte of the pishioners'. Their audit was to take 'a delyberate view of the accompte ... to avoide all confeucyon and dyslyke that otherwise may happen to aryse'. Order 4 concerned pew order. 'The minister and six other persons of the better sorte of the pishe' were to consider every application in the light of 'whether the same person be fytt to be rancked with the other tha[t] were in the seate before'. Order 5 laid down that anyone who wanted to hear a peal of the bells must pay 'three shillings for every peale'. There was to be no ringing 'after eight o'clocke of the night nor before four of the clock in the morninge'. Clearly these men (all of whom lived within a hundred metres of the belfry) were early risers.[42]

The treasurers, churchwardens, select vestrymen and the 'better sort of parishioners' were also to inspect the church fabric and furniture, present 'decays and abuses', see to it that repairs were properly carried out and, if satisfactory, paid for. 'Provysion' was made in 1613 for 'better cheasts and boxes for keeping of the goods and evidences of the church'. Many of them were 'rotten and dustye' after almost half a century of neglect. Every year one treasurer and one churchwarden were to visit every tenement owned by the parish to ensure it was being kept in good repair. If a tenant failed to pay the rent at Michaelmas, he or she was to be given twenty days to pay, after which time 'the lease [was] to be void'.

The death of 'John Coxwell Esquire, treasurer of the parish church' was recorded in the burial register in November 1617. Perhaps out of respect no-one was formally appointed that year, whereafter Christopher's younger son, Robert George Esq., took on the task alone, except for one brief experiment with an assistant in 1619, until 1622. The minutes indicate concern that a consistently high standard of integrity be applied to the management of parish lands and moneys. 'Briefs of all accomptes' were to be 'registered' for audit by the treasurer and a meeting of the 'better sort'. Lecturers and preachers were appointed to the positions paid for by the 'better sort', bequests and collections for the poor were to be invested in tools and raw materials so that the poor 'may be sett either to carding, spynning or some other laboure according to their age and habilitye'. Marner's twenty pounds were to be turned over every year; Coxwell's will added a further hundred to be distributed to and collected from the beneficiaries at the end of their allotted year. A beadle was appointed to oversee public order and cleanliness. Among his duties, he was to 'take specyall care for the restraining and punishing of such as in a rude manner do fowle and defile the streets to the greate annoyance of the Inhabitants and passingers'.

The ideology that underpinned the parish revival is summed up by a later memorial in the parish church. 'Here lieth buried ye Body of

42 *Ibid.*

HODGKINSON PAINE,' the inscription reads (etched in a neat village hand). Paine was a 'Clothier, who died ye 3d of Feb 1642'. He was 'killed with [the town's red and white, probably emblazoned with the phoenix] colours in his hand', cut down 'at the water-mills on the left hand of Giffard's house' by royalist musketeers.[43] The memorial explains the vocation for which he had died (and which parliamentarians eminently represented):

> The Poore's Supplie his life & calling grac't
> 'till warre's made rent & PAINE from poore displac't.
> But what made poore unfortunate PAINE blest,
> By warre they lost their PAINE, yet found noe rest
> He looseing quiet by Warre yet gained ease,
> By it PAINE's life began, and paine did cease;
> And from ye troubles here him God did sever,
> By death to life, by Warre to peace for ever.

What the gentlemen of town and country had in common with a common clothier like Paine, and the master-craftsmen and shopkeepers, was they were all employers of labour. The vocation that united them, as Paine's eulogist (probably his wife, Elizabeth) stated, was 'the poore's supplie'.[44] As we have seen in succeeding chapters of the town's history, what gave relatively wealthy men prestige and legitimacy, at least in their own eyes, was their dedication to 'the poor townspeople'. What changed in the generations of John Coxwell and Hodgkinson Paine was that their ideology, challenged and sharpened by king and court's reassertion of traditional conceptions of degree, became a national movement.

[43] Inscription transcribed from the original; for an account of Paine's death, see *A particular relation of the Action Before Cyrencester … Taken on Candlemass Day 1642 by Part of His Majesties Army under the Conduct of … Prince Rupert* (Oxford 1642/3), EEBO, 11–12.

[44] For Elizabeth Paine's memorial, see below, Chapter 16 p. 243.

15

'More than freeholders ought to have voices': parliamentarianism in one 'countrey', 1571–1640

> … at that time it was the usuall mistake of particular associations to confine every enterprise to their own counties, and divide the common-wealth into so many kingdoms.[1]

The contemporary term '*countrey*', so important to the identity of seventeenth- and eighteenth-century English people, referred to a form of collective identity that was in part a corollary of the steadily increasing importance, from the early fourteenth century, of the House of Commons. Unlike the more mutually opaque *pays* of its larger and more populous neighbour, France, the identities of English *countreys* were formed, not only out of routine interactions, specific and distinctive accents, customs, economies and ecologies, but also from regular engagement, as parliamentary electorates, with national policy and government. The task here is to show why that feeling intensified in the decades leading to civil war.

In the outlying villages and market towns of the Seven Hundreds of Cirencester, as in every English shire, only freeholders holding land worth at least forty shillings per annum had 'voices' in parliamentary elections. This chapter will suggest that, in the fifty years before the civil wars, about one in five to six households of the 'shire' part of the Seven Hundreds were entitled to a 'voice' in the election of knights of the shire. If the issues interested them, they were active and aware enough to be willing to travel all day to whichever town was nominated for them to cast their voices at a poll. Cirencester became a borough in 1571 and its 'leveller' franchise was confirmed by Parliament in 1624. It will also be seen that town and country practised a form of 'deferential voting': they usually elected trusted local knights, esquires and, more occasionally, lesser gentlemen. The important question was, did the candidate have the wherewithal and reputation for integrity to speak for their country or town in the Parliament of the nation.

1 John Corbet, 'A true and impartiall History of the military government of the citie of Gloucester from the beginning of the civil war' (London 1647): BL Thomason 64: E.402 (4), 118.

Powerful gentry like the Pooles, Duttons, Estcourts and Berkeleys were also seen as representing their 'affinities', or relatives, most of whom, in this region, lived close by. It was, however, crucial that they be seen as being *of and for their 'countreys'*.

The theme of this chapter complements the last in that representation in Parliament, from 1571 to the elections for the Short Parliament in 1640, had a central role in the formation of the 'widespread sense of independence' that J.H. Plumb saw as characteristic of the constituencies of the later seventeenth and eighteenth centuries; in this region it nourished the divisions between court and 'countries' that exploded in the early 1640s. This movement, as Plumb wrote of it in the later period, 'was based on the position of the gentry and provincial merchants in local government',[2] but its elitism was strongly moderated, before the consensus fell apart in the civil wars, by the capacity of the elite to convince the middling yeomen, husbandmen, tradesmen and manual workers of town and country that they belonged to, and could be trusted to work for, a commonwealth that included all the inhabitants of town and country except the 'undeserving poor' and a few great magnates. This 'parliamentarian dimension' was part of a movement premised, like the parish revival, on the idea that their commonwealth depended on good relations between an expanded 'better sort' or 'middle rank' of large and small employers, a few rich, capitalist landlords and their more numerous employees. Hodgkinson Paine's memorial testified to the crucial valorization of the employer function that is evident in the propaganda of both sides during the civil wars. The legitimacy of the employer class, great and small, rested on a reputation for investing their capital in the labour of their neighbours even when 'foreign' markets for their commodities dried up. The duty of this 'better sort' was to employ and govern all 'lesser sorts' of people, always, of course, in the interests of their communities and the commonwealth in general.

At Cirencester, the parliamentarian dimension of the new communalism was complemented by the fact that every householder was entitled to a 'voice' in parliamentary elections. Interconnections between town and country (and between town and country and the mercantile, political and religious communities in London and Westminster) were manifold, intense and routine. Every village had men entitled to a voice in shire elections, a sense of engagement in national affairs, and connection with the House of Commons. The roots of this highly consequential movement were in local government, where, from the 1580s, duty to commonweal meant investing communal capital in the lesser sorts: employing them to make commodities for piece-rates, lending money to little businesses, subsidizing apprenticeships, provision of tools and raw materials, marketing local commodities,

2 J.H. Plumb, *The Growth of Political Stability in England, 1675–1725* (Harmondsworth 1967), 33.

ensuring undesirables were moved on, the able-bodied had work, evangelizing and policing the social and religious lives of their communities. Theologically grounded in a personalized relationship with God, the favoured social institutions were preaching, the parish, and, increasingly, parliamentary elections.

By these means, English 'countries' gradually overcame the institutional effects of reformation. Albeit at the expense of the poorest, most migrant class (and the great courtly magnates), communes like Cirencester caught up and kept pace with intensifying labour mobility, social inequality and economic instability by means of evangelical religion and firm economic management, backed by an increasingly lucid, 'progressive' ideology, emergent 'parliamentarianism', and the reform and management of what we have seen became, at this time, the chief institution of local governance, the parish. This 'new communalism' took time to emerge, but was largely in place by the 1620s. By then it defined itself in relation to what it was not: 'undeserving' poor and magnates who contributed nothing to the commonwealth and lived 'in the breath of other men'. To repeat the point, two institutions were of critical importance in the formation of the highly politicized *countrey* that sided with parliament in February 1643: the parish and the House of Commons.

This explains why, when the moments of decision (Crown *or* Parliament?) came for all ranks of regional society, from August 1642 to February 1643, the town and its '*countrey*' was universally expected to be, and was, parliamentarian in its allegiance. Explaining why that fragile consensus (as it turned out to be) fell apart after February 1643 is a much simpler matter than showing, from many archival fragments, how it was created and by whom. A parliamentarian witness to the defeat of February 1643 summed up thus: 'Our greatest enemies from the first have been our owne countreymen.' The gentry and (to a lesser extent) Presbyterian merchants in fact lost their enthusiasm for the parliamentarian cause quite rapidly after 1643, when national divisions displaced them and local consensus fell apart. This chapter is concerned with delineating the emergence of the unit of allegiance and identity – a parliamentarian *countrey* – to which John White (the witness) alluded in his explanation of defeat. Being a godly country commonwealth became central to the political identity of the Seven Hundreds of Cirencester in the fifty or so years before the outbreak of civil war.

National policies, especially trade monopolies and taxation, affected different countries differently. Beyond subsistence, the 'common wealth' of Cirencester and the Seven Hundreds (distributed with gross inequality, yet nevertheless raising the acceptable standards of prosperity of all except the poorest classes) depended on the export of fine wool, many varieties of cloth, and finished commodities like articles of clothing in cloth, leather and fur, and shoes. The ebbs and flows of national and international markets were directly and routinely affected by government policies, especially the question of mercantile monopolists with influence at court. The relationship between political constituencies – shires and boroughs – and *countreys* was not exact. Gloucestershire, for example, embraced several ecologically and culturally different *countreys*, which, it was assumed, necessarily responded differently to external stimuli like parliamentary elections, taxes and, in the event, war between crown and parliament. The moods and responses of constituencies changed over time. We can only surmise how different parts of the Seven Hundreds had responded to Edward III's need to tax wool producers to pay for his imperial schemes of the 1330s. Not until the late sixteenth and early seventeenth centuries is there nearly enough evidence to begin formulating fruitful and systematic hypotheses about local political identities.

In England as a whole the 'commonalty', understood here as the word was used at London and other fully incorporated boroughs, to denote every householder entitled to a voice in local and/or parliamentary elections, grew considerably in the sixteenth century. By a variety of causes 'which happened in the former part of the sixteenth century, power, the insepa-rable attendant upon property, became more vested in the hands of the Commonalty', as an eighteenth-century commentator on the *Reports* of Sir John Glanville, speaker of the Short Parliament, put it.[3] Inflation caused the number of qualified freeholders in the shires to increase, to which must be added 'an encrease of near 200 members' in the House of Commons, representing just over half that number of new urban constituencies.[4] One of these was Cirencester, created in 1571.[5] In the reigns bracketed by Henry VIII and Charles II, Parliament and its electorates became increas-ingly busier in pursuit of their 'prerogatives', steadily insisting on their inde-pendent jurisdictions vis à vis those of the king and his courts. As Quentin Skinner has affirmed, the respective prerogatives of crown and Parliament were more hotly debated under the Stuarts than ever before. Under James I and Charles I the inhabitants of Cirencester and the Seven Hundreds came to see the House of Commons as the institution of government that most clearly understood and was trusted to speak for them and pursue policies that served their needs. This engagement with Parliament complemented the parochial initiatives and local senses of community discussed in Chapter 14.

3 Introduction to John Glanville, *Reports of Certain Cases Determined and Adjudged by the Commons in Parliament in the 21st and 22nd years of the Reign of King James the First* (London 1775), i; Glanville had local connections: he was married (in 1615) to Winifred, a daughter of William Bourchier of Barnsley, near Bibury, and lived at Broad Hinton, Wilts: see Alexander Grosart, 'Introduction' to *The Voyage to Cadiz in 1625, being A Journal Written by John Glanville*, ed. Grosart, Camden Society, New Series, XXXII (London 1883), xxix.

4 *Ibid*, vi.

5 *Ibid*, cvii.

There is no direct data relating to the number of voters in the Seven Hundreds (i.e. the shire constituency) at any election except that of February 1623/4. The following calculations of the size, composition and inclinations of the parliamentary constituencies of the Seven Hundreds in the period before the civil wars project figures in Sir Robert Atkyns' *Ancient and Present State of Gloucestershire*, first printed at Gloucester in 1712 and referring to early eighteenth-century polls, into the period 1570–1640. Atkyns' figures probably represent a reliable guide to the proportion of freeholder to non-freeholder households a century earlier, at the end of the long reign of Elizabeth I and the beginning of that of James I. Earlier evidence is not available, but it is reasonable to assume the great inflation of the sixteenth century roughly doubled the number of forty-shilling freeholders. The effects of inflation were probably somewhat counteracted by the routine contractions described in Chapter 10, which fed a tendency for wealthier freeholders to engross farms and lands at the expense of their smallholding neighbours. We have seen that village population growth slowed in the first half of the seventeenth century. The absolute number of freeholders probably reached a peak in the early decades of the seventeenth century. Proportions of freeholders to total households may even have decreased thereafter. If so, Atkyns' figures offer a guide to the formally qualified electorate of late Elizabethan and early Stuart Parliaments.

Aggregating Atkyns' figures for all of its parishes (excluding those of the parliamentary boroughs of Gloucester and Cirencester) gives a shire-wide average of one freeholder for every 4.7 households. Table 15.1 shows that averages for the six 'rural' hundreds of Cirencester ranged from a high ratio of 1:4.8 in Crowthorne and Minety (Cirencester's immediate hinterlands) to a low of 1:6.7 in the most populous and industry-based of the six 'rural' hundreds, Bisley. Of a total of 5,068 households resident in villages and towns of the Seven Hundreds, excluding the borough, 882 were freeholders. This yields an average of one freeholder for every 5.7 householders, slightly fewer than the shire as a whole. As Table 15.1 shows, poll-books of the early nineteenth century suggest that after 1712, while absolute numbers of freeholders rose as a result of resumed population growth in the two industrial hundreds (Bisley and Longtree), the overall ratio of freeholders to householders diminished considerably, to an average of one to every eight households. It is entirely possible that the electorate of the Seven Hundreds was greater at the time of the two elections of 1640, and possibly by the 1620s, than at any other time before the Reform Acts of the nineteenth century.

These figures record the proportion of legally franchised to unenfranchised households, not their character, opinions and interests, or the degree to which they constituted a relatively unified 'bloc' or 'class'. Nor do they tell us anything about relations between freeholders and the populous 'fourth sort of men', who, as Sir Thomas Smith pronounced, 'do not rule'.

Table 15.1. Freeholders of six rural hundreds in 1712 and 1801[6]

	Freeholders		Households		HH per FH		+/-
Hundred	**1712**	**1800**	**1712**	**1801**	**1712**	**1801**	
C&M	108	42	521	519	4.8	12.4	+7.6
BB	110	71	540	743	4.9	10.5	+5.6
Bradley	88	56	514	679	5.8	12.1	+6.3
R'sgate	82	106	401	532	4.9	5	+0.1
Bisley	244	275	1624	2183	6.7	7.9	+1.2
L'tree	250	373	1468	2760	5.9	7.4	+1.5
Totals	882	923	5068	7416	5.7	8	+2.3

It must be noted that regardless of the expansion of electorates, freeholders always elected wealthy gentlemen, and usually returned prominent *local* gentlemen. Esquires and, more usually, knights, feature largely in lists of candidates and members. The point that needs emphasizing is the election of *local* gentlemen. This point will be taken up in relation to the borough. Other than that, evidence of how elections were conducted, according to what precepts and expectations, is limited to disputed shire and borough elections in 1624. A shire poll was held in February of that year at Painswick, roughly equidistant from Berkeley, Gloucester, Cheltenham and Cirencester. Cirencester's powerful neighbour, John Dutton of Sherbourne, received unanimous acclamation as first member. 'But some doubt was conceived, whether Mr (Robert) Poyntz (of Iron Acton) or Sir Thomas Estcourt (of Shipton Moigne, near Tetbury) had the more voices' as second member. A poll was called for and the gathered freeholders were directed into Painswick church, to swear an oath and be counted. Before they were polled, Estcourt informed them that 'he did not desire the place for himself and prayed to be spared'. In spite of this oaths were sworn, a poll taken and the count revealed Estcourt 'had above a hundred freeholders more'.

This does not tell us how many freeholders turned up; that Estcourt got a hundred votes more than Poyntz suggests several hundred may have taken their oaths and given their voices, individually, for one or the other candidate. The question arose whether Sir Thomas (or anyone) could be elected 'against his own consent', and it was referred to the Commons Committee for Privileges and Returns, who considered it after Parliament sat, some weeks later. It looks as if Estcourt may have meant it when he said he was perfectly happy for Poyntz to take his place, but the committee would have none of it, taking the opportunity to state a high principle. 'No man, being lawfully chosen,' it determined, 'can refuse the place.'

6 1712: aggregated from the parish totals in Atkyns, *Gloucestershire*; 1801 aggregates from Thomas Rudge, *The History of the County of Gloucester* (2 vols, Gloucester 1803).

> For the county and commonwealth have such an interest in every man that when by lawful election, he is appointed to this public service, he cannot, by any unwillingness, or refusal of his own, make himself incapable; for that were to prefer the will, or contentment, of a private man, before the desire and satisfaction of the whole country, and a ready way to put by the sufficientest men, who are commonly those who least endeavour place.[7]

Parliament embodied a supreme public duty that must take precedence over 'the will, or contentment' of any 'private man'. Parliament embodied the English commonweal, namely that 'the county and commonwealth have such an interest in every man' that it takes precedence over every lesser interest. Seldom has the communal identity of England's early modern *countreys* been so bluntly expressed. Society came first, and Parliament embodied society.

Another principle prominent in the minds of the members of the Commons committee was stated with regard to a dispute concerning John Pym's election as the second burgess for the nearby borough of Chippenham, Wilts. Their judgement was that 'the most indifferency [impartiality] ... is when [burgesses] are made by the greatest number of voices that reasonably may be had'. They determined that elections at Chippenham were to include not only the bailiff and the twelve 'incorporated burgesses', but also the men who gave their voices in local elections, a 'commonalty' of 32 men designated as 'freemen'. Pym (who was a member of the committee) had won the bailiff and burgess voices by 7–5, but every one of the 32 freemen gave their voices for Sir Francis Popham: an indication, incidentally, of systemic differences between the elite and the 'commonalty', at least at Chippenham. They being the greater number of those whose voices should be taken by custom, Pym's opponent, Sir Francis Popham, was declared elected.[8] As Pym had also been lawfully elected as MP for Tavistock, in Devon, the decision made no difference to the composition of the House: the committee nevertheless took the opportunity to state what they regarded as an important principle that they would later apply to the franchise at Cirencester. As Derek Hirst writes, 'The extension of the urban franchises… was primarily a political weapon aimed at the elimination of aristocratic or other unwanted influence.'[9] The committee assumed that oligarchies were more corruptible than popular franchises; the more voices, the more likely they were to elect men whose interests lay with their now firmly protestant countries rather than with kings and courts whose religious and political inclinations were at odds with those of the House of Commons.[10]

[7] Glanville, *Reports*, 108, 111.

[8] *Ibid*, 50–62.

[9] Derek Hirst, *The Representative of the People: Voters and Voting in England under the Stuarts* (Cambridge 1975), 75.

[10] Ever since he was appointed to the throne, James I had insisted that 'parliamentary

If my hypothesis, that Parliament became central to communal identity in this period, is correct, we might expect it to have been evidenced by increased participation in elections. In pure numbers, this was undoubtedly the case in the Seven Hundreds. The number of householders entitled to a voice in parliamentary elections was *greatly* increased by the formation of a parliamentary borough at Cirencester in 1571. To complete these calculations we must estimate the number of 'voices' or 'voters' entitled to vote for the borough in the dozen or so elections from 1571, when it was granted the right to return two members, to late 1640.

Once again, the only direct evidence concerns the elections of February 1623/4. The same House of Commons Committee for Privileges and Elections, chaired by John Glanville (later speaker of the Short Parliament of 1640), also investigated a dispute that had arisen at Cirencester. At the election of February 1624, 'Mr (Henry) Poole was clearly elected for one of the [Cirencester] burgesses … by most voices, without contradiction.' Poole (an executor of John Coxwell's will and son of an executor of Philip Marner's) belonged to one of the wealthiest and most extended gentry kin-coalitions in the region. He was a native of the country and, since 1615, lord of Cirencester manor. 'In the next place Sir William Master had the greatest number of voices of the inhabitants present and so was declared by the bailiff.' Master was the grandson of Queen Elizabeth's physician, Richard Master, to whom she had assigned Abbey House in the 1570s: another local gentleman, as was customary. The returns anticipated elections of the later seventeenth and eighteenth centuries, which usually returned the two lords of the moieties of the old Abbey manor. The defeated candidate, Sir Maurice Berkeley of Rendcombe, also local, but too closely associated with the courtly Berkeleys of Berkeley, questioned the rules concerning 'how the election should be made, whether by the voice of all the inhabitants, or else only by the freeholders'. 'The undersheriff', who had taken it upon himself to organize the election, gave as his opinion that only freeholders should participate. Sir Maurice demanded 'that the freeholders might be determined by the poll, thereby to discern clearly who had the most voices of the freeholders only'.[11]

The initial expectation was that inhabitants who were not freeholders were accustomed to participating in elections: as a result of the undersher-

privileges were derived from royal grace'; one of the issues in the elections of 1623/4 was the power of the duke of Buckingham and the treatment of Prince Charles when he visited Spain to negotiate a marriage settlement; it was assumed that a parliament that truly represented public opinion (and not the ability of the king, Buckingham or any other powerful man to purchase a seat for a rotten borough) would be vehemently anti-catholic and anti-Buckingham: Robert E. Ruigh, *The Parliament of 1624: Politics and Foreign Policy* (Harvard 1971), 11 and passim.

11 'The Case Concerning the Election of one of the Burgesses for the Borough of Cirencester', in Glanville, *Reports*, 105–6.

iff's decision, 'some of the inhabitants went away unpolled ... the assembly being adjourned to the church, the freeholders were there all polled by the undersheriff, in the presence of the bailiff, an oath being first administered to every elector to declare whether he was a freeholder or not, before his voice was admitted'. Again Sir William Master was elected 'by five more voices' than were polled for Sir Maurice Berkeley.[12] The result seemed clear enough, but someone, it is not clear whom, petitioned the Committee for Privileges and Elections to determine the question of the franchise, which may have arisen before. The committee included some illustrious names – besides Glanville, most were knights like Sir Edward Coke, Sir Dudley Digges, Sir Robert Hatton, Sir Heneage Finch and Sir Nathaniel Rich – but 'Mr Pym' was a member, as was a neighbour of Cirencester's Wiltshire hinterlands, Sir Henry Poole, Member for Oxfordshire, whose local knowledge (and that of his cousin, Henry Poole of Sapperton, elected at Cirencester) would no doubt have contributed to their deliberations.[13]

The committee determined that the undersheriff had no jurisdiction and could only act as 'clerk or minister [to the bailiff] and not in the quality of sheriff'; his administration of an oath 'was an unlawfull act: for such an oath is only to be given in the county court... in case for choosing Knights of the Shire and not in case of choosing burgesses within a borough'. 'The polling, or numbering, of the freeholders only was [also] an unlawful and void act, they not being the sole electors.' They discovered that nowhere was it written down 'who should be electors and who not', and so it was necessary to 'have recourse to common-right':

> Which, to this purpose, was held to be, that more than the freeholders only ought to have voices in the election; namely, *all men, inhabitants, householders, resiants within the borough*.[14]

The committee concluded, against the courtly Berkeley affinity, that 'Sir William Master was well elected by the greater number of the due electors, namely of the inhabitants, householders, resiants'. The oaths and numbering of the borough's dozen or so freeholders 'was meer surplusage and idle'.[15] As at Chippenham, their decision did not change the result. It did confirm (and record) the principle, first stated by the elders of the early thirteenth century, that 'the fellowship of the town' encompassed 'all men, inhabitants, householders, resiants within the borough'. These terms did not include all who lived there, but it included the great majority.

The right of every resident householder to a voice in parliamentary elections was never again challenged, but the question of who qualified as a

12 *Ibid*, 106–7.

13 'Introduction' to *ibid*, viii.

14 *Ibid*, 108–9.

15 *Ibid*, 111.

'resiant' continued to be an issue. It was not until 1690 that the House of Commons formally 'resolved that the inhabitants of the borough of Cirencester, being inmates, have no right', but as Henry French emphasizes, 'status as one of the "inhabitants"' of English communities at this time 'signified more than the single geographical fact of residing there'. It meant 'recognition that the individual possessed a material stake' in the commune and 'was entitled to be represented within it, participate in its deliberations, and pay towards their implementation.'[16] In 1712 Sir Robert Atkyns reported that out of a total of 810 households, 700 'voices' (86%) had been counted in a recent election. In 1792 it was determined that 'no person can be deemed a householder, who does not possess an exclusive right to the use of an outward door of the building'. As Samuel Rudder put it, 'the original right to an exclusive use [of such a door], is, then, the point of discrimination between the householder on the one hand, and the inmate on the other'.[17] Representatives of over 75 trades and occupations and no fewer than 74 labourers are listed in the earliest extant poll-book of the eighteenth century. Disputes of the later seventeenth and the eighteenth century refined but did not change the decision of 1624. The meaning of 'resiant' was clarified, formally, to exclude lodgers, 'passingers' (as the vestry of the 1610s called temporary residents and persons passing through) and anyone in receipt of alms. They formalized long-standing qualifications for residency (including the possession of a door that opened onto a street), but numbers remained high. The traditional return of local gentlemen continued. Surviving poll-books for later elections indicate that Atkyns was not exaggerating. Two facts stand out: (1) Cirencester enjoyed a 'leveller franchise', and (2) except for the elections of 1604, when, first, Richard Marten and, to replace him, Edward Jones, London lawyers, were elected, leading local gentlemen received the acclamation.[18]

16 Implying that it is legitimate, in this case, to extend the usage in French, *The Middle Sort of People in Provincial England, 1600–1750*, 27, where he is referring explicitly to the 'imagined community' of the parish, to formal communities in general.

17 Atkyns, 'Cirencester'; Rudder, *History of Cirencester*, 207; Rudder added that 'paupers, inmates and lodgers are excluded … because [they] are most exposed to seduction'. But 'they are infinitely less culpable than more independent and better informed individuals, who pretend to be admirers of our excellent constitution, whilst they press electors to consider on which of the contending parties their [personal] interest lies.… This is an argument not more frequent than base.… To act, or advise to act on such foul, selfish, and corrupt principles, is as derogatory to the true spirit of our law and of our constitution, as to vote for money' [emphasis original].

18 1571: Thomas Poole Gent; 1572: Thomas Poole and Thomas Strange; 1584: Thomas Poole and William Estcourt; 1586 and 1588: Charles Danvers and George Masters; 1592: Oliver St John and Henry Ferrys; 1597: James Wroughton and Henry Powle; 1601: Richard Browne Esq. and Richard George Esq.; 1603: Richard Marten and Arnold Oldisworth; 1614: Lord Newborough and Thomas Roe; 1620: Sir Thomas Roe and Thomas Nicholas Esq.; 1623/4: William Masters and Henry Poole Esq.; 1625: Miles Sandys and Henry

In the absence of direct evidence it is impossible to know for sure why this middling and lower-rank electorate always acclaimed gentlemen and usually acclaimed local lords. My hypothesis is that in this period, as a result of the highly motivated alliance of local gentry, leading merchants and the 'better sort' of tradesmen, electorates were motivated by *communal* (broadly, the 'commonwealth' of towns, countries and the nation as represented by Parliament) rather than factional, hierarchical or individualist ideas. Communes like Cirencester and *countreys* like the Seven Hundreds supported each other, not primarily because of deference to rank, but because they were 'fellow countrymen' whom they trusted to represent the common good of their commune or *countrey*. Deference was a factor, but it was not unconditional. Abundant evidence for this region supports Henry French's judgement that the 'concept of gentility' was 'accorded universal (if not always positive) recognition'. It embodied 'social distinction, political autonomy, intellectual authority and [the decisive quality] material independence'.[19]

It was obvious that, given their residence and support for local initiatives in day-to-day governance, men like Henry Poole and John George were capable of representing their communities in the highest court in the land. John George (the nephew and heir of Richard, lord of Baunton manor) epitomized the ideal type: he lived in Dyer Street, his father, Robert, had assisted John Coxwell as treasurer of the parish and taken over his duties when he died, knew the town and district intimately and had assiduously contributed to the reform and management of parish and manor. He supported Congregationalist reforms of the parish and knew from experience that episcopal governance, in Gloucestershire at least, was a non-starter. His family had been directly associated with the government of the town for centuries and, although they had gained from the dissolution, their gains were small compared with those of magnates like Henry Poole and John Dutton and 'disloyal' barons like the Berkeleys and the Brydges of Sudeley. In marked contrast to his grandfather, Christopher George, he was a moderate puritan. He was the ideal representative for the borough, and was acclaimed to represent it in 1625, 1628, 1640 and 1641. He led the defence of the town in 1642–3, but only wished for an acknowledgement of

Poole Esq.; 1625/6: Sir Neville Poole and John George; 1628: Sir Giles Estcourt and John George Esq.; 1640: Henry Poole Esq. and John George; 1641: Theobald Gorges and John George. See Browne Willis, *Notitia Parliamentaria: or, an history of the counties, cities and boroughs, containing an account of the first returns and incorporations … that send Members to Parliament* (London 1750), 81, 91, 102, 111, 121, 130, 149, 160, 170, 179, 190, 210, 221, 232, 242; for biographies of these members, see Williams, *Parliamentary History of the County of Gloucester, … 1213–1898*; for eighteenth-century elections, see *A View of the Cirencester Contest … by a friend of the Old Interest* (G. Hill, Cirencester 1754) and *The Poll of the Borough of Cirencester Taken … 1768* (Samuel Rudder, Cirencester 1768); R.W. Jenkins, 'The Cirencester Contest', *Trans BGAS* 92 (1973) adds invaluable context to the later disputed elections.

19 French, *The Middle Sort*, 202.

communal autonomy and parliamentary prerogatives, not the *defeat* of the king. Accordingly, he was removed from the House in 1645 and replaced by the parliamentary general, Sir Thomas Fairfax.[20] By then circumstances had changed irrevocably. The hard-won alliance between the gentlemen and commonalties of town and country that had been constructed between 1570 and 1640 disintegrated and the interests of the countries fell by the wayside in the national struggle between Crown and Parliament. How that happened is the subject of the next chapter.

The final, decisive, act in the construction of a puritan commune occurred when connections between the reformed parish and the puritan 'new merchants' in London were consolidated by the intervention of the notoriously Calvinist Feoffees for Impropriations. In 1627 the Feoffees purchased 'the Rectory Impropriate of Ciceter' for £350.[21] Based at St Antholmes, London, inspired by the puritan theologian John Preston and organized by John White, MP for Dorchester and, later, chairman of the Long Parliament's House Committee on Religion (which also took an interest in the affairs of the Seven Hundreds, as we shall see), the aim of the Feoffees was 'to provide pulpits for Calvinist clergyment' in strategic towns.[22] 'Meane places they doe not ayme at,' wrote an opponent in 1633, but 'London, Hertford, Ciceter, Shrewsbury, Dunwich, and good borough townes.'[23] Several of its members shared interests in the New England Company and its successor the Massachusetts Bay Company.[24] Archbishop Laud regarded the Feoffees as 'a cunning way to overthrow the church government'. Court propagandist Peter Heylin preached vehemently against them, and their activities were referred to the king's attorney general, William Noy. A royal decree suspending their activities in 1633 reported that 'at Ciceter… they consult[ed] how Mr Burgess the present incumbent may be removed, and to procure the consent of the Bishop of Gloucester for that purpose.' Burgess was 'altogether unwilling to be gone' until he was 'offered the next Easter Book and £30 in money'.[25] In 1627 Burgess was paid off and Alexander Gregory, a man of 'a notorious inconformity' who had been 'hunted from one diocese to another' and sentenced by the High Commission, was appointed in his place.[26]

Some of the money was collected locally. The most generous local contributors were aged widows of the now entirely defunct old regime.

20 Browne Willis, *Notitia Parliamentaria*, 242.

21 Calder, *Activities of the Puritan Faction of the Church of England 1625–33*, 38; Ethyn W. Kirby, 'The Lay Feoffees: a Study in Militant Puritanism', *Journal of Modern History* XIV (March 1942), 22.

22 Kirby, 'Lay Feoffees', 1, 12.

23 *Ibid*, 23; Calder, *Activities*, 53.

24 Kirby, 'Lay Feoffees', 6.

25 Calder, *Activities*, 55.

26 Heylyn, *Cyprianus Anglicus*, I, III, 200, qf. Kirby, 'Lay Feoffees', 23.

The contribution of hitherto notoriously catholic 'Mris [Bridget] Strange', daughter in law of the old bailiff, who 'gave £10', is very difficult to explain, unless we see her erstwhile Catholicism as the stubborn response of a strong-willed and public-spirited woman to the 'politic religion' and neglect of pastoral care that had characterized the rule of her 'survivalist' father in law and estranged, now dead, husband. Her neighbour 'Mris George of Ciceter', probably the widowed mother of John George, gave £5.[27] It is tempting to suggest that these *grand-dames* of the old regime, almost old enough to remember what the commune had been before their husbands took on its governance, admired the pastoral reforms conducted by the generations of their children and grandchildren and gave what they could to support them. London merchant Sir William Whitmore, recent purchaser of the Cotswold lordships of Winchcombe and Slaughter, contributed generously to the purchase of Bridgenorth but not to that of Cirencester, which was too close to home. Whitmore's bailiff was still trying to deal with the blanket rent-strike that followed his master's efforts to increase the rental of the 'borough' of Winchcombe.

Little is known of the details of Alexander Gregory's activities at Cirencester after his arrival in 1627, except that Peter Heylyn saw him as chiefly responsible for the town's dramatic resistance to the king in 1642–3. The same can be said for the puritan preachers who were installed by parishioners at Stroud, Painswick and Minchinhampton at this time. Joseph Woodward, appointed minister of Dursley, a clothing township in the Vale of Berkeley, in 1645, probably followed Gregory's example. It was said that Dursley 'became one of the most wealthy and best trading towns in the neighbourhood' under Woodward's guidance. 'His presence in the streets [made] the guilty to hide themselves in corners.... For his house being distant from the church, everyone got their families ready as he came by, and stood in their doors, and so fell in with those that followed.' Woodward taught Dursley's children to read at a school in the church, gave lectures every Tuesday and Thursday, and was troubled by 'sectaries' who came to the fore at Dursley, as they did to an even greater extent at Cirencester, in the 1640s and 1650s.[28] Like its author, Woodward, Gregory signed the presbyterian *Gloucestershire Ministers' Testimony* in 1648 and a year later burst out his unqualified dismay at the king's execution in the parish register: 'O! England what didst thee do the 30th of this month.'[29] The revolution of which Gregory had once been a conscious instrument had gone too far.

One final episode adds insight to relations between local parishes and Westminster, and between the inhabitants of those parishes and their lords.

27 Calder, *Activities*, 11.

28 Woodward's story is told in Joseph Stratford, *Great and Good Men of Gloucestershire* (Gloucester 1867), 55–68; context in Rollison, *Local Origins*, 37–9.

29 Joseph Woodward, *Gloucestershire Ministers Testimony* (London 1648); GCRO P86 1/2, entry dated 31 January 1649.

The case of the parishioners of Holyrood Ampney *versus* their Arminian rector, Benedict Grace, was one of hundreds sent to the Long Parliament's Grand Committee for Religion in the winter of 1640–1. The Ampneys were three villages, each a parish, strung out above the Ampney Brook a few miles west of Cirencester on the way to Fairford. In each case the village had an English name, the parish a Latin version. Grace's parish 'Holyrood Ampney' (in Latin, 'Crucis') was the largest, with 2,660 acres and about 60 families (270 individuals). Ampney St Mary, or 'Ashbrook' was a small parish, encompassing 533 acres, a parish church and about a dozen families. Ampney St Peter, or 'Easington' (2,541 acres) served 32 families. Seventy-five men attended the musters of 1608 from the three villages. They comprised gentlemen and their tenants: three gentlemen, no yeomen, 24 husbandmen (18 from Holyrood), eight tradesmen, eight labourers, ten servants and a higher than average number of trained soldiers (18, or 24%).

Forty households were assessed at Ampney Crucis for the hearth tax of 1671. The younger Robert Pleydell's Ampney House was still a modest mansion in a park next to the church, with ten hearths, including 'a handsome mantelpiece built by [the elder] Robert Pleydell in 1625'.[30] Pleydell was an officer in the defence of Cirencester in the siege of 1640 but lost enthusiasm for the cause after c.1645. Next in size in 1671 was the seven-hearth household occupied in 1608 by the Lloyd family, children and grandchildren of George Lloyd, whose freestone monument in the church portrayed his gentleman's arms, a wife, and 16 children.[31] Of the remaining 38, ten (25%) were non-liable on grounds of poverty. Twenty-two of the villagers lived in one-hearth housing, ten in two, five in three and one with four.[32] Robert Pleydell sent five servants (three aged about 20, two about 40) to the musters of 1608; John Lloyd Gent sent two, as did two husbandmen, Edward Kirby, and John Rodway, each with enough land and sheep to feed the extra labour. The rest worked for themselves, each other, and for their landlord, Robert Pleydell. In the Subsidy of 5 James I, Pleydell was assessed on £10, compared with John Coxwell's £16, William Dutton's £40 and Sir Henry Poole's £50.[33] He was a 'village gentleman', one of those who assisted in the defence of Cirencester in February 1643.

Apart from an absence of yeomen, the social structure of Ampney Crucis was similar to that of about half the parishes in the Seven Hundreds. The lord of the manor was resident, as was another local gentry family, the Lloyds. Most if not all of the inhabitants were their tenants: husbandmen, husbandmen-craftsmen and labourers with enough land to keep a family

30 'Transactions in the Fairford District', *Trans BGAS* 22 (1899), 25.

31 *Men and Armour*, 249–50; Hearth Tax: GRO D83; 'Transactions in Fairford', 24; 'George Lloyd of Ampney Crucis' was used as an arbitrator by the Commission for Ecclesiastical Causes in 1575: Price, 'Commission for Ecclesiastical Causes', 119.

32 GA D383, Crowthorne & Minety.

33 Atkyns, *Gloucestershire*, 21–2.

in a good year and a few sheep in the flocks looked after by three local shepherds. During his troubles, Benedict Grace asked one of the shepherds, Richard Flux, to sign a 'certificate' attesting that he was assiduous in his Sunday services. Flux made his mark but later testified that 'he did not reade' Grace's certificate, only told Grace that he might have said any number of prayers 'for ought he knew being a shepherd and not in church once in a month or two'.[34] It appears that Richard Flux could read but not write and was not keen to take sides in the struggle between parson and squire, crown and parliament. He looked after their sheep and let the others get on with it. But he was an 'inhabitant', and as such, worthy of being consulted.

The Pleydells were new-wave (post-Reformation) gentry, purchasers of dissolved abbey estates. Erastian Robert Pleydell Esq., lord in 1641, undoubtedly led the movement to get rid of Arminian Grace. Only two letters relating to the case survive, but were undoubtedly part of a continuous correspondence by which, via Pleydell, the inhabitants were kept informed (or told what they needed to know) about events in London.

The king appointed Benedict Grace to the rectory of Ampney Crucis at a time when conflict over religious and ecclesiastical sovereignty was especially bitter. What took place at Ampney Crucis reflected the greater national struggle. The Stuarts believed their right to govern was divine. Religious as well as secular authority was theirs alone to bestow. Religious authority radiated from above. In congregational theologies, church governance radiated from the greater commonwealth and the communities, or *countreys*, of which it was the sum. Congregational theologies tended to confirm Cirencester's historical experience. The quality of the congregation, consisting of the inhabitants, determined how well or how badly it was governed. Without the localities there would be no priests, bishops, lords and kings. They knew best how to govern themselves. They *had to* govern themselves. The Stuarts never understood this entrenched fact of English provincial life. The very broad congregational movement of the later sixteenth and first half of the seventeenth centuries was grounded in long experience. They knew that whatever the pretensions of higher lords, the peace and prosperity of localities depended upon their inhabitants, rich and poor.

Grace came to Holyrood Ampney with an evangelical mission. His first act was to move the altar from the centre of the people's nave to the king's chancel at the east end, without, it appears, consulting the congregation. When they refused to process submissively to the relocated altar, Grace 'denye[d] the Sacrament to such as will not come up to the railes'. Following what was probably a week or two of hasty confrontations, Pleydell and 60 other parishioners signed and marked a 'petition' accusing Grace of being 'furiously violent in conversation' and 'going armed with a rapier, dagger

34 GA, Benedict Webb Documents.

[and] javelin to and from church'.[35] He took the king's £50 a year, plus all the other fees that went with the job, and lived the life of 'a common drunkard, [who] in his drunkenness hath abused himselfe and others'. It was said 'he [mumbles] and hurries over prayers', 'sayeth them at unseemly times', and 'maliciously absented himself at burials to vex his neighbours'. Violent in word and deed, Grace was a veritable 'striker abroade' who 'without provocation hath beaten and wounded divers at home of his parishioners'. Although it would have been inappropriate to say so in a petition, if any of this was true, it reflected on the judgement of the presenter, in this case, the king and his chief religious counsellor, Archbishop Laud.

The parishioners' petition of December 1640 was signed (19) or marked (41) by 52 men and eight women, six of them widows. The signatures of Robert Pleydell, his brother William and his son John head the list, followed by William Forden, possibly one of the more substantial husbandmen, the mark (a shaky 'E') of Elizabeth Lloyd and the signature of her husband, Henry Lloyd, probably the Stuart son or grandson of the Elizabethan yeoman-gentleman of the parish, 'George Lloyd', sturdily entombed in the nave. The fact that below the gentry only 29 of 61 petitioners had names listed in 1608 suggests that turnover of husbandman tenancies had been quite considerable in the intervening thirty years. On 22 February, John White, president of Parliament's 'Grand Committee for Religion', sent word that he would hear the testimonies of 'Pleydell and the inhabitants' and of Benedict Grace the following 15 May.

Grace made his way up to Westminster, where he presented the committee with half a dozen not very impressive 'certificates' to the effect that 'he preached and read when he was able'. None of his certificators (including Richard Flux the shepherd, referred to earlier) seem to have read what Grace put before them to sign; each of them later added a caveat that if the documents contained anything more than extremely tepid agreement, they 'renounceth it'. The impression they give is that they were less passionately engaged than the priest and the lord of the manor, and would have preferred not to offend either. Pleydell was their landlord. Importantly, he went to the trouble of consulting them by seeking their signatures and marks. Some, perhaps all, probably were deeply offended at Grace's arrogant moving of the altar.

On his way home from meeting the committee in London, Grace lodged at the sign of the Red Lion, near Henley Bridge. A few pints of ale loosened his tongue. 'He took occasion to speak very scandalously touching the finding of the Parliament against the late lord Strafford, affirming they had maliciously put him to death and adding "pray God they doe not soon wish

35 The case is chronicled in GA, D8, Box 4/5, 1–18; D8/Z1, including a copy of H.R. Heatley, 'Annals of Ampney Crucis: Amenities of Social Life in 1640', *Wilts Standard* (28 July 1912), has accurate transcriptions of most of the documents.

him alyve agayne".'[36] A few days later, John George happened to spend a night at the Red Lion on his way to attend Parliament in London. On learning he was an MP for Cirencester, the innkeeper told George about Grace's possibly seditious and certainly anti-parliamentarian words and behaviour a few days earlier. The innkeeper said that, being also a constable, he had arrested Grace for his unseemly words and taken him to see a magistrate. The magistrate not being home, the innkeeper extracted a promise that the minister would go off quietly and seek lodgings, and leave first thing the next morning. Grace took the long way home. He 'went typpling from place to place' enlarging to the inhabitants of Henley on the great virtues of Archbishop Laud and uttering scandalous calumnies against parliaments.

The next day Grace rode home, where he was told Pleydell had a warrant to arrest him. Grace fled back to London. The evidence tails off and leaves unanswered the question of why Grace, after an absence of possibly three years, returned in 1646, and remained vicar in 1650. He was then ejected (again?) but returned after the Restoration and continued to enjoy his salary and fees until his death in 1670: another 'survivor'. Conservative independents like Pleydell and John George (expelled from the parliament in 1645) were unhappy with the radical turns taken after war broke out. Like most moderate 'presbyterians', they only ever supported the impeachment of the king's evil advisers and the maintenance of godly parochial disciplines. Like Alexander Gregory at Cirencester, they came to fear the many streams of plebeian independency that the civil wars had let loose.

36 John George to Robert Pleydell, 16 May 1641, Benedict Grace Papers.

16

Moments of decision: August 1642 to February 1643

The moment of decision for most men came when they were faced with Parliament's Militia Ordinance or the Royal Commission of Array, each of which commanded their military service.[1]

'Our troubles began about August last', explained 'one who was present [at the] taking of Cicester':

> on Thursday, February 2, 1642/3, by seven thousand of ... Cavaliers, under the command of Prince Rupert, Prince Maurice, the Earls of Northampton, Carnarvon, Denbigh and Cleveland, the Lord Digby, Lord Andevour, Lord Wentworth, Lord Taffe, Lord Dillon, Lieutenant-General Wilmot, Sir John Byron, Colonell Gerrard, Colonel Kyrke, Colonell Dutton, Captain Legge, and divers others.[2]

The symbolism of the list was lost on no-one. The lords came to Cirencester to do more than take a town. Eminences of the kingdom of Charles I came to assert the ascendency of the king's court over a rebellious, parliamentarian, commonalty that, for the time being, included most of the local gentry.

'Our greatest enemies from the first have been our owne countreymen,' he explained. The 'moment of decision' had come six months earlier, on 11 August 1642. George Brydges, sixth lord Chandos of Sudeley, the king's

1 Alan G.R. Smith, *The Emergence of a Nation State: The Commonwealth of England 1529–1660* (New York 1984), 292.

2 *A relation of the taking of Ciceter in the county of Glocester, on Thursday, Febru. 2, 1642, by seven thousand of the cavaliers, under the command of prince Rupert, prince Maurice, the earls of Northampton, Carnarvon, Denbigh, and Cleveland, the lord Digby, lord Andevour, lord Wentworth, lord Taffe, lord Dillon, lieutenant-general Wilmot, sir John Byron, colonel Gerrard, colonel Kyrke, colonel Dutton, and captain Legge, and divers others. Sent to a friend in London, by one who was present at, and some days after the taking of it. Published because of many false reports that were in print concerning that businesse. Printed at London, February 20 1642/3*: BL, Thomason Tracts 16: E90 (7); hereafter A *Relation*: the page numbering in what follows is mine, the original being unnumbered.

lieutenant in Gloucestershire, sent out messengers summoning the leading men of Gloucestershire to a meeting 'at the sign of the Ram', Cirencester.[3] This was the inn at which, 242 years earlier, the Ricardian earls had been surrounded and captured, prior to their execution in the market-place to the acclamation of the crowd. In 1400 the townspeople had intervened decisively in a struggle between two rivals for the throne. In August 1642, talk all over England was about the very 'prerogatives' of lordship and monarchy. The Long Parliament had sat since November 1640; the king's closest secular and religious counsellors (Strafford and Laud) had been impeached and executed; the printing presses spewed ever more controversy into the unpredictable maelstrom of public opinion; mass protests and uprisings had spread from the streets of London into the provinces.[4] Brydges was not exaggerating when he wrote that 'The whole kingdom (is) labouring at this time under one comon distemper.' The time had come for the gentry to act. Events were 'now brought to that height as delays are daungerous'. We cannot 'be safe but that there needes some advice, what way may best conduce to oure owne preservations'. Who did Chandos mean by 'we'? Who was threatened by whom? This was a letter to the class that had ruled the county 'since time out of mind': Smith's second and third 'sort'. It was a moment for ruling-class solidarity.

Chandos 'desired there may be a present meeting to consider and resolve amongst ourselves, what is fitt to be acted by us according as occasion shalbee offered, that wee bee not found tardy in our service, neither to our kinge, country or ourselves'. He continued:

> And because I suppose Cirencester the most equal place of distance from every man's residence I doe wish the meeting may be there at the sign of the Ram, where I will bee godwilling upon Munday next by ten of the clock in the morning, hoping to find every man willing and ready to bee assistants as far as in us lieth to putt an end to these distractions, which doe threaten us with comon destruction.[5]

Since his ancestor, Sir John Brydges of Minety, carved his domain from the dissolved abbey of Winchcombe in the 1540s, the Brydges had become 'kings of the Cotswolds' in something resembling the style exercised in the Vale by the medieval Berkeleys. Their domain on the north-western Cotswold Edge, with its castle overlooking the ancient royal borough of Winchcombe, was

3 GA D2510/18: Chandos-John Smyth of Nibley, 11 August 1642.

4 See Manning, *The English People and the English Revolution*; James Holstun, *Ehud's Dagger: Class Struggle and the English Revolution* (London and New York 2000); David Cressy, *England on Edge: Crisis and Revolution 1640–1642* (Oxford 2006), esp. 292–3, 320–9.

5 Chandos-John Smyth of Nibley, 11 August 1642, GA D2510/18; Anthony Fletcher, *The Outbreak of the English Civil War* (New York and London 1981), 364, describes Chandos's summons as 'disingenuous'.

a microcosm of the absolutist kingdom as conceived and developed by the Tudors and Stuarts.

He could account only for his own district. How would the several districts in his jurisdiction respond if they had to *choose* between the prerogatives of crown and parliament? The only surviving copy of Brydges' summons was sent to John Smyth of Nibley. Brydges wanted to know for whom the Berkeley yeomanry would fight. He knew that if Smyth of Nibley spoke on the question, the whole Vale from Gloucester to Bristol (including its lords and gentry) would listen.

Brydges' choice of venue was inflammatory. Cirencester had been garrisoned for Parliament.[6] The deputy lieutenants of the county, who were for Parliament, wrote to Smyth asking him to send a detachment of cavalrymen to assist in strengthening the town. It is not known if he replied to either of these letters. Whether he actually attended the meeting at the Ram we do not know; possibly he sent his son, the second John Smyth of Nibley, who favoured the king's cause, in deference to his employer, Lord George Berkeley. Old John's connections lay in all directions: law, parliament, colonies, literature (George Berkeley was the patron of Robert Burton, who dedicated *The Anatomy of Melancholy* to him; Smyth quoted from it in *his Description of the Hundred of Berkeley*), and, above all from the point of view of the strategists, the households of the gentry and yeomanry – the 'middle ranke' as John Corbet called it in 1645 – of the wealthy and productive Vale of Berkeley.

Word spread of Brydges' arrangements and 'there came (to Cirencester) at least a thousand armed men to assist the townsmen, who with posts and chains fortified the town to keep out horse'. Early on Monday morning 'divers Gentlemen… and some of the townsmen' rode out to intercept Chandos on his way across the Cotswolds from Sudeley. They met him at Rendcombe Down, near the house of Sir Maurice Berkeley, and informed him that they were instructed to 'keep my Lord out of the town if he did not promise and protest that he did not come to execute the (king's) Commission of Array'. Leaving Chandos to wait on the hill, the men rode back to Cirencester to tell the garrison leaders that 'he came not with above thirty persons, and those no weapons but swords, and so he was admitted in'.[7]

Chandos conferred all day 'with the Gentlemen of the Peace for the County', and in the evening they adjourned to Abbey House, the home of Sir William Master. The town was alive with rumour; 'after dinner the Justices of the Peace and other gentlemen being in conference with my Lord, the soldiers

6 GA D2510/12: 'Letter from John George, one of the Justices of Gloucestershire, to John Smyth, in answer to the latter's enquiry as to the supply of horses, and of pay for the dragoons to ride them'.

7 This and the following is from 'A letter sent to a worthy member of the House of Commons, concerning the Lord Shandois coming to Ciceter to execute the Commission of Array. Read in the House of Commons and ordered to be forthwith printed. August 22 1642'; Beecham, *History of Cirencester*, 'Notes and Appendices', 287–8.

and arm'd men came and beset the house, and demanded of my Lord, wherefore and for what he came thither?' Chandos sent out word 'that it was only to confer with the Gentlemen'.

The implication that he had not come to confer with commoners infuriated the crowd gathered outside. Messages were sent in informing Chandos that they 'required him to deliver up his Commission of Array unto them'. Anxious to avoid violent confrontation, Masters went out and asked them what proof they required of Chandos's intentions. They replied that 'if my Lord would put it under his hand that he would never execute the Commission nor any others for him in any part of (the) County, but would oppose and hinder it to his power, and that he would maintaine the power and privilege of Parliament and the laws and liberties of the subjects with his life and fortune… (they) were content to depart'.[8] Brydges almost certainly found this notion intolerable, but there was nothing much he could do with only thirty or so men against a thousand or more in the armed crowd surrounding Abbey House.

'In extreme fear', Chandos agreed. A note was drawn up and signed by 'my Lord, Sir Robert Tracye and some others, which did in some sort pacifye' the crowd. Many, however, did not believe Chandos and his followers could be trusted, and it was only 'with very much intreaty about eleven of the clock at night [the crowd] departed to theire lodgings, intending to speak with my Lord again (in the) morning'. During the night Chandos, 'still in great fear' of what might happen the next day, was smuggled away 'on foot very privately by Sir William Masters and other gentlemen through his house, let out a back way and so departed'. Next morning the townspeople and soldiers reassembled outside the gates of Abbey House. 'Finding (Chandos) gone (they) were extremely enraged and had like to have pulled down the house, took his coach and drew it themselves into the market-place, (where they) cutt it and tore it in pieces.'[9]

John Corbet was very likely an eye-witness to this violent symbolic act, so his analysis of the social dynamics behind it is worth noting. He was in no doubt that Brydges' attempt to serve the king's commission 'was stifled in the birth, and crusht by the rude hand of the multitude'. It was his fear of the 'fury'

8 'A letter', Beecham, *History of Cirencester*, 288; Nick Poyntz, 'The Attack on Lord Chandos: Popular Politics at Cirencester in 1642', *Midland History* 35:1 (Spring 2010), accessed at mercuriuspoliticus.wordpress.com, 16–17, 29, shows that the 'conceptual vocabulary' here almost certainly derived from the Protestation covenant that originated in Parliament in May 1641, and was probably presented at Cirencester in February 1642; as he observes, this vocabulary 'further broke down barriers between the centre and localities'; an episode described in Fletcher, *The Outbreak of the English Civil War*, 320–1, suggests that this region 'had absorbed one side of the story: Pym's side', against that of 'the lord's annointed'.

9 'A letter', *ibid*; see also the leading authority on the symbolism of popular violence in the English Revolution: John Walter, *Understanding Popular Violence in the English Revolution: the Colchester Plunderers* (Cambridge 2001); Walter, *Crowds and Popular Politics in Early Modern England* (Manchester 2006).

of the 'meanest of the people' that 'constrained' Brydges to sign his agreement, and it was the 'vulgar multitude' (Corbet also used the term 'common people' as a synonym for the labouring poor) that tore his coach to pieces the next morning. 'They glory to vent their humours,' explained Corbet, 'by reason of their usuall restraint and subjection.' The puritan Corbet knew exactly what he meant when he said they required 'a more undescerned guidance of superious agents' to turn them 'to the terrour of the enemy': their employers, men like Hodgkinson Paine, Corbet's 'middle ranke'. Parliamentarians and royalist agreed that the 'common people ... were to decide the issue'. All depended on who they could be persuaded to fight for.[10] The town was now filling with trained men from all the county and more would arrive in the next few months.[11]

The uneasy peace which descended on the region after the abortive efforts of Chandos and his deputy lieutenants to muster support for the king lasted until October, when representatives of 'the country' visiting the market at Stow on the Wold set upon 'divers scholar volunteers' *en route* to join the king under the leadership of Sir John Byron, allegedly arresting or killing ten of them.[12] A few days later a crowd from Tewkesbury attacked the earl of Middlesex's estate and deer-park at Forthampton. His agent later complained that it had become impossible to collect rent from the earl's tenants. The earl's biographer calls the turbulence around Tewkesbury a *jacquerie*, which is appropriate as a description of its *countrey*-specific character, but not appropriate if it means perpetrated by peasants.[13]

10 John Corbet, A *true and impartiall History of the military government of the citie of Gloucester from the beginning of the civil war* (London 1647): BL Thomason 64: E.402(4), 8–9.

11 E.g. 'Memorialls of my deare brother John Friend', Bodleian Library, Ms. Top Oxon f. 31, repr. in S. Porter, 'The Biography of a Parliamentarian Soldier', *Trans BGAS* 108 (1990), 131–4, is a brief and moving account of a young man from Westerleigh, near Bristol, who 'took my father's Armes and went to Cirencester' in December 1642, was captured and imprisoned at Oxford, released and served as a clerk and quartermaster in the London-trained bands and several more companies in Gloucestershire before dying of smallpox at Woodchester in May 1645. By that time 'his Cloak was shot through in twenty places at least ... yet it pleased God that a childish disease should take him that Bullets could not hurt'.

12 Manning, *The English People*, 66.

13 Menna Prestwich, *Politics and Profits under the Early Stuarts: the Career of Lionel Cranfield Earl of Middlesex* (Oxford 1966), 572–6. This happened in spite of the fact that 'it was well-known that Middlesex was no well-wisher to the royalist side'. His problems almost certainly arose, firstly, because he was an efficient capitalist landlord, secondly, because as far as the people of the Tewkesbury district were concerned, he was not of their *countrey*, he was a 'foreigner'. This was a lethal combination. In more immediate terms, local resentment also had to do with the fact that this foreigner, through his local agents, 'had always taken stern measures to protect his deer and much of (his agent's) time had been taken up with bringing deer-stealers to justice'. The first raid in October 1642 brought about the 'rebellious, riotous, devilish' destruction of 600 deer. The deer-

Tewkesbury was a manufacturing and commercial centre with large numbers of poor people living in damp slums frequently flooded by the Severn. Agriculture in the district between Tewkesbury and Winchcombe meant large plantations, notably but not exclusively concerned with the production of tobacco. The manufacturing workers were subject to the usual boom-and-slump cycles of the preindustrial economy, and were doubtless adversely affected by the war. The agricultural workers (often the same people) could only ever take it for granted that they would be employed for a few weeks of the year. The Tewkesbury district is another illustration of how different conditions were from district to district, *countrey* to *countrey*.

Different conditions, different locations, meant different occasions, stimuli and different responses. Tewkesbury was just to the south of the major centres of early conflict in the West Midlands. The attacks on the earl of Middlesex's estate, while doubtless representing long-standing local resentments of his enclosures and prosecutions of poachers, were also shock-waves rippling out from the early hot-spots of conflict in the Welsh border-country to the north. Situated where the Vales of Severn and Avon converge, Tewkesbury, like Cirencester, was a way-station for migrant workers. The crowds that attacked Cranfield's property probably included itinerant workers, vagrants, deserters and retreating soldiers from both camps. In the meantime Cirencester, the gateway into Gloucestershire from the parliamentarian east, a standing offence to the king's court at Oxford, awaited its fate.

The parliamentarian leaders in Gloucestershire reinforced the garrison of country volunteers in the town, 'it being always feared that that town would be the first attempted in the county'. Matters began to approach a climax on 31 December, when the Marquis Hartford trekked his Welsh regiments across the North Wolds from Worcester to Stow and Burford, where he hoped his soldiers would find quarter. It was mid-winter. At the best of times farmers' supplies were running low at this time of the year. Because of the war, the ides of March came three months early to the regions south-west of the king's base at Oxford in 1642–3.[14]

Hartford reported to the king that his men and horses 'could not long subsist, the stores of all places (where they were masters) being neare spent and exhausted'. He urged 'that unless he might have contribution and quarter for his army (6,000 horse and foot) in Gloucestershire and Wiltshire' the cause

slayers boasted that 'they would not only destroy the remainder of you lordship's deer but rifle your lordship's house at Forthampton and pull it down to the ground and not … let a tree or bush stand in all the Chase'. Adding insult to injury, vagrants and royalist soldiers escaping from Edgehill also pillaged his estate.

14 In the parish register (GCRO P86 IN 1/2) it says 'The town was made a garrison in the year 1642 – Col. Fettiplace was made governor, who with divers gentlemen raised forces to defend it and were joined by two companies of the Earl of Stamford's regiment, but it was taken by Prince Rupert (apparently with a loss of 300 lives and 1,200 prisoners) and 3,000 arms and other considerable bootes; for it had been a magazine for the county'.

was lost. Those counties 'would never be had till the town of Cicester was taken'. At this point Cirencester's strategic location sprang into consciousness and the parties of the civil war each focused, for a few weeks, on that one place. To keep his men supplied in the coming weeks, Charles had to subdue the parliamentarian *countreys* of Gloucestershire and north Wiltshire, and to do that he had to conquer Cirencester. Prince Rupert's chaplain reported that the town was universally 'esteemed the key' to those parts.[15]

Charles gave orders that Cirencester was to be taken, and strengthened Hartford's army with five regiments of horse from the armies of Princes Rupert and Maurice. Five days later they set off up the Thames Valley. At noon on Saturday 7 January, an estimated 7,000 royalist horse and foot drew up around the borough, almost encircling it. They remained in position for two hours, 'only sending out scouts', a witness inside the town reported, 'to view our guards'. They reported 'the town (was) pretty large' and that 'some diligence had been used in fortifying it, which was indeed strong in its natural situation, being about half-way round encompassed by water, a great part with a high wall, and the remainder secured by strong works'.[16]

At 2 p.m. Hartford issued his ultimatum. He 'summoned those in the towne in the name of Marquesse Hartford, lord generall of all those forces, by a trumpet, to deliver up the towne and armes to his lordship, upon promise of his majestie's free pardon for all by-gone offences, with assurances of safety of their persons and estates'. Another trumpet sounded. Prince Rupert's herald repeated this message, adding that 'they came to vindicate and maintaine the king's rights and prerogatives'.

By any standards, it was a moment to test the strength of the citizens' loyalty to the prerogatives of Parliament. The resident population was about 3,500, two-thirds at least women, children and old people. To these had been added 2,000 volunteers, few of them trained soldiers. They were outnumbered by about three to one. Against this, Hartford had not brought any siege weapons with him. Although the royalist accounts exaggerated the strength of the town's defences – the River Churn is shallow and narrow, and the walls were those of the gardens on the edge of town, no more than 3–5 feet high – the people inside the town may have been encouraged by the observed lack of artillery. The streets were 'barricadoed up with chains, barrows, wagons of bavins or *Risebushes*'. 'Each end of the High (Dyer) Street … was secured against horse with a strong *slight-boomes*, which (Prince Rupert's) men call[ed]

15 '(Cirencester) is a town of many streets; and 2000 communicants: and (as seems) by that party esteemed the very key of Gloucestershire on that quarter': A *particular relation of the Action Before Cyrencester (or Cycester), Taken in on Candlemass Day 1642 by Part of His Majesties Army Under the Conduct of His Highness Prince Rupert, written by an eye-witness* (Oxford 1642), EEBO, 3 (henceforth A *particular relation*).
16 *Ibid*, 3.

turnpikes.'[17] The walls and hedges around the town were for the most part manned by clothworkers, yeomen, husbandmen and labourers from the villages round about, bakers and butchers, and a rich assortment of other occupations, under the command of Giles Fettiplace of Coln St Aldwyns, Robert Pleydell of Ampney Crucis, John George MP, local clothiers like Hodgkinson Paine, yeomen and trained and able-bodied men constituting a militia of at most 4,000 soldiers.

Their reply was firm. 'We do heartily acknowledge and professe ourselves to be his majestie's loyall and faithfull subjects,' they replied. They were not the *king's* enemies and were 'and shall be ever as ready with our lives and fortunes to maintaine his just rights and prerogatives as they were, or the best of his majestie's subjects'. The key qualifier was 'just'. 'The best of his majestie's subjects' was ambiguous: it could and would, under normal circumstances, be taken to mean the princes and nobles commanding the army that surrounded them. They stood against *unjust* prerogatives only 'to enjoy his majestie's peace, and the just rights and liberties of the subjects of England, according to the lawes of the land, in defence wherof and the true protestant religion only we stand to our armes'. They were 'resolved with God's assistance to defend [just rights and true religion] with our estates and our lives'. It was a modest but intransigent statement of 'independency'.

The cavaliers remained in place 'untill it beganne to grow darke', when 'they retreated to theire night quarters in the villages round about, where they did eate up all the provision of victuall, and spoiled much corne and hay'. Next morning they took up positions around the town as they had the previous afternoon. A too-cavalier royalist officer, John Villiers, brother of Lord Grandison, ventured too close to the defences and was taken prisoner. Hartford's herald stepped forward again. They were leaving now, but the town could look forward to 'a sudden return with more force, and as much fury and revenge as they could send to us with the best cannon they could bring'. Then, taking 'with them all the horses of the villages round about', they dispersed, Rupert to Oxford, Maurice to Farringdon, and Hartford to Burford. The dispersal of the three armies was essential if their men and horses were to find quarter.[18]

The garrison 'waited a fortnight for the return of the enemy', sending out for reinforcements (including a message to John Smyth Jr, which went unanswered), improving the fortifications, and taking delivery of 'four great iron pieces (i.e. cannon) from Bristol' to add to the 'two brass peeces' earlier sent from Gloucester. Intelligence reports informed them, correctly, that Prince Rupert was scouring Northamptonshire and Warwickshire for supplies and *matériel.* He 'fetched a compass from Oxford' into those counties, 'where he plundered some towns and tooke away all the armes and horses of the country,

[17] *Ibid*, 11; Corbet, *True and impartiall history*, 20, described Cirencester as 'a stragling and open towne, neither well fortified nor capable of defence'.
[18] *A Relation*, 2–3.

with which he armed and mounted all his men, except a few pikes to guard his carriage'.

Rather than passively wait upon the return of the cavalier army – and its systematic theft of all the horses within a fifty-mile radius of Oxford testifies to its determination to be, literally, a cavalry army – the garrison commanders made a fatal error. Rather than keep their forces together, they were side-tracked by intelligence reports (or rumours) that 'a strong malignant party was rising' in the Winchcombe district overlooked by George Brydges' strongly fortified castle at Sudeley, 'fourteen miles from Cicester' across the North Wolds. Sudeley, White explained, was the royalists' 'strongest hold in these parts'. That it was bound to be 'a receptacle both of the malignants' armes and treasure', was the justification offered for the decision of the garrison leaders at Cirencester to attack and take it. On Thursday 26 January 'a party of foure or five hundred greate horse and dragoons' rode out from Cirencester to meet with 'more strength from Glocester and Tewkesbury'. The following day 'two hundred choyse musqueteers, and one brass cannon' arrived from Cirencester to reinforce them, and they took Sudeley Castle.[19]

News reached Oxford within hours, and on 28 January *Mercuricus Rusticus*, the royalist news-sheet, announced that 'Sudeley Castle (had been) delivered up to (the) rebels, who occupied it and the town of Winchcombe'. To indicate what kind of men they were, the report added that the 'rebels were quartered in the church', which was 'heavily profaned'. 'They dyg up graves and disturb the ashes of the dead, hung carcases of sheep in the pulpit, covered the nave with dung of man and beast,' wrote *Mercurius*. If right-minded people had their way, this low-born and ill-educated riff-raff would be 'hanged for rebellion, their carcases exposed to the fowls of the air, and the beasts of the field, that the ravens of the valleys might have had their due portion, and never suffered them to come so near the church, as to have the privilege of Christian burial'.[20]

The attack on Sudeley was a mistake, an attempt to relieve tensions in the garrison occasioned by the long, uncertain wait for the return of the king's army. Two days later, on Monday 30 January, Rupert's army 'appeared before [Sudeley] castle', ensuring that there was no way for the men inside to get back to Cirencester in time to help in its defence. The parliamentarian account described the troops at Sudeley as 'the greatest part of our strength', and suggested that 'they tarried there (I will not say by whose neglect it was) till the town of Cirencester was utterly lost'.

On the first of February, Rupert's regiments isolated the garrison of Winchcombe by surrounding the castle, drawing up and displaying his cavalry – upwards of 2,000 mounted men – on the slopes under its walls. 'Most of his men lay all night on the hills,' but rose early 'in regard there fell that night a

19 *Ibid*, 3–4; Corbet, *True and impartiall history*, 19, has a more detailed account of the taking of Sudeley.

20 Qf. Emma Dent, *Annals of Winchcombe and Sudeley* (London 1877), 261.

great snow.' The men at Sudeley were trapped, with Rupert's seasoned cavalry at more than double their numbers situated on the snow-blanketed hills between Winchcombe and Cirencester.[21]

With the greater part of their garrison pinned down, the defenders at Cirencester stood no chance at all. Rupert met with his senior officers on Wednesday to plan their attack, and at daylight on Thursday 2 February scouts from the borough 'discovered them some two miles from the towne, where under a hedge they staied some two houres, till all theire forces drew together into one body, from their severall quarters in the villages'. Between nine and ten o'clock the army was drawn up in position around the town, and the order was passed round that 'the (pass)word was Queen Mary'.[22] There they waited for three hours, tempting the garrison to fire at them and reveal the position of their guns and cannon.

At twelve o'clock the battle began. At the stroke of noon, 'two or three regiments of foote … beganne a furious assault on the Barton, a greate farme which lay not farre from the towne westward'. It took them two hours to overcome 'some two hundred musqueteers that lay under the garden wall', after 'a very hot fight' in which the royalist 'Welchmen' were driven on by cries of 'On! On!' by the cavalry behind them, whenever 'they were seen to drop down a pace or two'.[23] At two o'clock the earl of Carnarvon's men broke through another weak spot in the northern defences of the town and the 'barricadoes' in Dyer Street were breached.

> Our greater firemen, 'twere justice to admit, [made the difference, wrote the royalist witness] for the terror and fury of the cannon muche caused the victory. At one end [of the town] the *granadoes* were terrible: especially after they had fired one house. At tother end, the ordinance were thus dispersed. One of the demi-cannons was against Poole's mount and battery: and shooting through the parapets [at the lord of the manor's mansion] forc't away the defenders.

By now musketeers had forced their way into houses in Dyer Street and were picking off defenders in the market-place.

> The other great piece [set up in the street] at randome ranged her bullets into the town, killed one cannonier in the market-place, and made a terrible rushing among the houses.[24]

The final defensive 'strong-post' was 'at the water-mills on the left hand of [John] Giffard's house, where the white and red colours stood'. Seeing the town

> taken another way, [the defenders] took down their colours and retreated to a bridge and chaine. The enemy now perceiving our horse could not pass the

21 *A relation*, 4.

22 *A particular relation*, 6.

23 *A relation*, 4–5.

24 *A particular relation*, 13–14.

> chaine, faced about and gave them a full volley: keeping their ground, till our foot came up and beate them from it. Then was Payne, (a clothier) killed, with a colours in his hand.[25]

It was the moment for Prince Rupert to make his entrance. 'Hearing some enemies to be still in Poole's house, he sent for one small piece and two petorns, to force the gate: but finding no opposition, either there or elsewhere, the Ordinance all marched into the market-place.'[26] By 'foure of the clocke the towne was wholly taken, and shooting was ended on all sides'.[27]

Before the end, fighting in the market square and in Dyer Street was hot and furious. The parliamentarian witness reported no more than twenty of the garrison were killed, but the royalist 'eyewitness' reported 'slaine of theirs, those that think fewest, judge 300, others think more. The truth is, we could see but few men left at all in the towne: plainly they hid their dead and wounded men in their houses; wherof we heard many since buried in the night.' 'Most', he thought, had 'fallen in the fields in chase.'[28] The parliamentarian account reported that 'Lord Carnarvon pursued the fugitives to the southward, killed a few, and made many prisoners.' 'Sir John Byron followed those that fled towards Cricklade, killed above a hundred, and made as many prisoners.' One of these was the Quaker, John Roberts of Siddington St Mary, who left an account of his narrow escape across the fields.[29] Two ministers were taken, 'Mr Stanfield armed back and brest, with sword and pistolls' and 'Mr Gregory … who [had] lately assured his people that he had *begged that Towne of the Lord*.' [30] Gregory, 'the minister of Cirencester', was dragged back into town, stripped of his outer clothes and 'made the butt of many insults'.[31] The leader of the rebels, 'Colonel Fettiplace' (lord of the manor of Coln St Aldwyns, later a Quaker) 'was taken at Lady Jordan's house' and 'Mr (John) George, a parliament-man, was taken elsewhere.'[32]

A note in the parish register affirms the report of 'those that thought fewest', namely that 300 of the defenders were killed. Only twelve of the 48 burials recorded in February 1643 are specified as soldiers, and they were probably members of the garrison. This may be because the men who would otherwise have kept the register were prisoners of the king for a month and the register is deficient. Alternatively, it may mean that most of the defenders who were killed in the town were not classified as soldiers, and those killed

25 *Ibid*, 11–12.
26 *Ibid*, 13.
27 *A relation*, 5.
28 *A particular relation*, 14.
29 *Some Memoirs of the Life of John Roberts written by his son Daniel Roberts* (2nd edn, Bristol 1747), 3; Rollison, *Local Origins*, 173–5.
30 *A particular relation*, 15 (emphasis original).
31 *A relation*, 5–6.
32 *A particular relation*, 11.

on the roads leading away from it were buried elsewhere. The parliamentarian account reported 'some of our men lay naked foure daies after they were killed, neare the place where the enemy... kept his utmost guard, and none durst bury them'. *Mercurius*'s curse was enacted. The story told in the burial register reveals other implications of the long months from August 1642 until October 1643. In the 1630s burials at Cirencester averaged 82 a year. In 1640 there were 92, in 1641 111, in 1642 159, and in 1643 278, of whom only 30 are specified as soldiers. The month of the siege has the highest number, but burials were double or triple the average from August 1642 to October 1643.

Burials began to rise in May 1642, when there were 17, and June, when there were 21. The worst months of mortality before the month of the actual siege in February occurred long before royalist soldiers descended like a plague of caterpillars on the farms and villages on which Cirencester depended for its supplies. The presence of royalist troops garrisoned around Oxford and along the Thames Valley caused shortages. Given their anti-absolutist propensities, and the tendency of agrarian societies to believe no deaths are 'accidental' or 'due to natural causes', some people would have seen the poor harvest and the minor epidemic that accompanied it, as God's judgement on the political troubles. This might be regarded as 'superstition'. But there was nothing supernatural about the extra mouths introduced into the town by the volunteers, nor about the rapacious depravations of the armies of the king with their raiding parties.[33] The brutal violence of the battle of Cirencester was the climax of hardship stretching across many months. The burial-graph tells the story and gives an impression of how it might have seemed to the people living through the period. They believed their 'country' had been invaded by an arrogant army of traitors and foreigners, and, subjectively speaking, they were right.

The aftermath was depressing. Injury was followed by days of crowing insult. All Thursday night and through the early hours of Friday morning, more than a thousand prisoners were rounded up, stripped of their outer garments and shoes, and herded into the church. The victors 'showed all the barbarous insolence of a prevailing enemy', plundering the town mercilessly, 'sparing not (even) to plunder their best friends'. 'For I can assure you,' reported our parliamentarian source, 'some of the most notorious malignants were the most notably plundered of all the towne.' Inside the church the prisoners were taunted. 'Where is now your God ye roundhead rogues!' 'You praied to the Lord to deliver you, and ye see how he hath delivered you, ye rebels!' The ministers, Stanfield and Gregory, were 'shamefully abused', and their taunters 'reproachfully imitat(ed) their manner of preaching'. Cash was obtained from families on promise that prisoners would be released. Cash and valuables were taken from their hiding places and handed over, claimed now merely as payment for sparing the parliamentarian dogs' lives. Attempts to have food and water

33 E.g. GRO TRS 128, in which Robert Rowden, later rector of Coberly, records that he was 'abus'd' by a royalist soldier in 1643, while travelling from Northleach to Dursley.

passed into the church for the 'wounded and weary' prisoners were denied, the food eaten by the hungry victors, the water poured on the ground.[34] While regretting any excesses that may have taken place, Rupert's chaplain thought the fact of 'prisoners [that] were brought away 1200' demonstrated his master's benevolence. They were not slaughtered. This 'show[ed] the Prince's and the Cavaliers' mercy, as the captives themselves acknowledged'.[35]

It could have been worse. There is no mention of rape, and after Carnarvon's and Byron's slaughter of fleeing members of the garrison there was no more bloodshed. Plundering occurred. 'Some particular men's houses ... were purposely set on fire after the towne was won' and 'many hundred families' had their possessions taken or deliberately destroyed. 'The Barton Farme ... and all the corne, hay, and other goods and cattle..., which amounted to three thousand pounds, was burned to the ground,' probably by accident, since it would have defeated the express reason for taking Cirencester to have burned supplies on purpose.[36]

It also helps explain heavy mortality in the following months. There would be no more grain until the May harvest; what there was would be commandeered by occupying forces. On Friday royalist cavalry rode out 'into the countrey, and tooke away all the horses, sheepe, oxen, and other cattle of the well-affected that inhabited neare Cirencester'. On Saturday they went further afield, taking away 'cloth, wooll, and yarne, besides other goods from the clothiers about Stroudwater, to the utter undoing, not only of them and theirs, but of thousands of poor people, whose very livelihood depends on that trade'.[37] They punished the whole country. Dependence of the 'poor people' on the clothiers and other employers was axiomatic in the rhetoric of both sides. The only difference between parliamentarian and royalist versions was that for one employing the poor was a sincere, self-sacrificing, honourable duty, and for the other the relationship was coercive, exploitative and hypocritical. The number of deaths caused directly and indirectly by this temporary shattering of the regional economy is unknown.

Only a systematic examination of local parish registers, many of which were not kept up over the next few years, could tell us if the story told by the Cirencester registers was repeated throughout the region. At Stroud, where the registers have been aggregated, 1642 and 1643 were years of crisis mortality as they were at Cirencester. Many hundreds probably died as an indirect consequence of the invasion, which in the coming months moved deeper into the county, where it centred on the more famous siege of Gloucester. Until the earl of Essex retook Cirencester and relieved Gloucester some months later, direct resistance by the people of the smaller villages and market towns was

34 *A relation*, 6.

35 *A particular relation*, 14.

36 *A relation*, 6–7.

37 *Ibid*, 7; it is difficult to imagine how the people of the region fed themselves over the ensuing months.

futile, indeed suicidal. Corbet reported that 'the whole country was quickly full of this disaster' and 'thousands of men armed and unarmed flocked together, and resolved to undertake the enemy under the conduct of a grave and well-minded patriot'. The patriot (possibly Nathaniel Stephens) refused, knowing 'well they made a loud cry afarre off, but if once brought up to the face of the army they would never abide the first onset'.[38]

On Friday 3 February *Mercurius Aulicus* informed Oxford of the taking of Cirencester. 'So easy a purchase did they make of so great a prize,' wrote its editor, Peter Heylyn, 'that seldome any towne hath been surprised at a cheaper rate.' The long-term consequences for the royalist cause were not at issue in this day of celebration. Was this to be a repeat of a military occupation like that of 1066, re-enslaving of the working population and restructuring society, always under the supervision of forces of occupation? Were Stroudwater, the Vale of Berkeley, Kingswood Chase, the Forest of Dean, the most populous parts of the county, and the most industrious and crucial to the regional and national economy, to be depopulated, restored as hunting forests for squires, knights and barons, as they had been when, supposedly, the king's and his magnate's ancestors came to England centuries earlier? Heylyn informed his readers that 'neare 1200 prisoners' including 'the most practicall promoters of the Rebellion in that part of the countrey' were on their way to Oxford, accompanied by George Brydges, lord Chandos of Sudeley, who was about to enjoy his Triumph. None of those who observed this march of the defeated through the villages and towns to Oxford could have failed to notice its blatant symbolism.

Seven months earlier, in August 1642, these same men had defied and humiliated the young Lord Chandos, when he tried to serve the king's commission of array. Chandos's prerogative as the king's lieutenant was dismissed, he was personally humiliated, forced to slink away in the night through the dark garden of Abbey House, leaving his coach in the market-place to be cut to pieces the next morning by the triumphant crowd. Chandos's conception of social order was embodied and imposed by an army led by two princes, four earls, six barons, dozens of knights, hundreds of esquires and at least two thousand men on horseback. In this company Chandos was no more than a colonel, but on him was bestowed the honour of a Triumph. The king of the Cotswolds was restored. Etiquette was observed in the sad parade of the defeated to Oxford. Chandos rode proudly in front, followed by the rebel gentlemen 'on horseback'. Behind them, barefooted and undergarmented Alexander Gregory, bearing the brunt of the insults. Behind him 'the inferiour sort', barefoot, without coats, roped together, utterly defeated. At this point it was impossible to know that Brydges' triumph would be short-lived.

The 'men of quality' among the defenders 'were permitted to ride on horseback, the rest of the inferiour sort following on foot, and being for the most

38 Corbet, *True and impartiall history*, 21–2.

part bound together by two and two'. It was a neat and characteristic reversal of the royalist battle array during the siege, where the foot went first to clear the way for the swashbuckling cavalry. Cavaliers did not humiliate gentlemen in front of their inferiors. They would be needed to restore order. Heylyn thought the most active perpetrator of this rebellion had been

> Gregory the late Lecturer there, a man first placed in Cicester by the Feoffees for buying up Impropriations … at the first setting up of that mischievous project, and ever since conformable to their mischievous purposes … Twas most fit [thought Heylyn] that [Gregory] should leade [the prisoners on foot], as their Captain, to the place of punishment, which had been their ringleader so long, to animate and excite them unto this rebellion.

Literate and articulate men of the cloth were much given to exaggerating the social importance of the ministry, puritan or otherwise. The royalists' instinct was to separate the gentlemen from the commonalty by leaving them their horses.

Sadly, Sudeley was still in the hands of the mob. Heylyn explained Prince Rupert's failure to take back Chandos's castle on the way to Cirencester 'as that he was not willing to batter and deface an house belonging to so honourable and brave a gentleman' as he who had brought the prisoners into Oxford 'in this triumph'. If Cirencester, Bristol, Gloucester and Tewkesbury fell, the rest would follow. Accordingly, the parliamentarian rabble at Sudeley 'did presently on the first newes that the Towne was taken, betake themselves to their heeles … as also the soldiers which had been garrisoned (by a detachment from Gloucester) in Berkeley Castle, the seat and Barony of the Lord Berkeley'. Events would show that parliamentarian tacticians learned from the mistake made by the Cirencester garrison when it divided its forces. By concentrating all their forces at Gloucester they were able to hold out until the trained bands from London could come to their assistance. Naturally, all this may have been very far from the thoughts of the 1,200 prisoners in February.

They were jeered through the streets of Oxford to the town centre and straggled into the market-place. On the afternoon of Monday 6 February 1643, 'his Majestie rid forth to take a view of the Prisoners', watching from his horse as their spokesman, on his knees, petitioned to be set free and allowed to return home. 'Dread Sovereign,' he intoned, 'the inhabitants of poor distressed Cirencester acknowledge their submission' to Charles's 'justly incensed army'. 'Prostrate … at his majesties feet' he begged the king's forgiveness and mercy for their 'inexcusably faulty' behaviour. 'Oh Sir,' he cried, 'the God of Heaven hath given you unto us our God upon the Earth.' They had all 'grievously sinned against (God) by (their) undutiful carriage against their Sovereign King, God's vice-regent'. Prostrate in the slush of the market-place, 'they prayed the king' to forgive them. 'Lying before (him) acknowledging and from (their) hearts detesting the foulness of (their) offense,' they begged for their lives. Such were their sins that only Charles's 'divine vertue' could contemplate forgiveness. They begged to be allowed to 'securely returne to, and abide at, (their) severall homes'.[39]

The prisoners begged to be sent home, that 'many hundreds of people of our towne, who have no other livelihood, may be againe set on work and relieved'. Note the collective persona of the speaking voice, the silent assumption that the body of the prisoners consisted of Cirencester's *employers*: it was important they be released and sent home so that 'many hundreds of people ... may be againe *set on work and relieved*'. The petition implied a dialogue between two parties who, for all their differences, shared a prescription within a description, namely that production was the business of *employers*. The employer class, I have suggested, stretched to accommodate 'the gentlemen of town and country', wealthy mill-owning, precociously capitalist merchants and clothiers, artisans and husbandmen who occasionally hired labour, in the form of servants, apprentices and journeymen, broadly (and vaguely) those whom, for the time being, were 'independent', 'inhabitants'.[40] In the reigns of James I and his son, this 'economy' of 'employers' came to form a more or less tenacious and confident social bloc, united by what they opposed (Catholics, courtier-magnates who put their own honour and glory ahead of that of the 'common wealth', 'undeserving poor') and inspired by the lasting effects of the generation of Philip Marner and John Coxwell and the grand vision that informed their policies and practices. The communal revival led by Marner, Coxwell, Philip Jones and their contemporaries of the employer class (the 'better sort' and the more independent 'manuary workers' and 'householders'), in turn, involved reawakening precepts that had driven communal movements at Cirencester for centuries: namely that certain abiding, practical, realities underpinned the existence and the *weal* of the commune.

Two potentially conflicting worlds were implied in the theatre and rhetoric enacted at Oxford. One, symbolized by the king's dramatic appearance in the last act of Lord Chandos's 'triumph', enacted the traditional hierarchy of degrees, lords, lesser gentry and commons. The petitioners' plea implied another, radically simplified commonwealth constituted by all the hands-on work, markets, connections and networks – in a word, the 'economy'. Both sides assumed that this 'common' world consisted, essentially, of two simple classes: *employers*, virtuous (or, in royalist versions, hypocritical, pretentious,

[39] *The Petititon of the Inhabitants of Cyrencester whose names are subscribed presented to His Maiestie at Oxford with His Maiestyes Answer, printed at Oxford February 28th, 1642*, EEBO.

[40] *Ibid*; 46 names, clearly of the 'better sort', were appended; they included Andrew Sollace (churchwarden 1637–8, 1648), Rowland Freeman (1621, 1631), Thomas Litton (1648–50), Edmund Freeman (1658–9), Amos Daunsey (1660–1), Virgil Crippes (1642), Michael Sharp (1633–4), William Groves (1639), three members of the Man family (wealthy butchers) and other prominent names of the late sixteenth and early seventeenth centuries like Sollace, Stone, Chance, Ferribee and Webbe: see Vestry Minutes, GA P86 VE 2/1, and Index, VE 3/1.

false-pious and self-interested) organizers of labour, who, in their own eyes, put their hard-earned capital at the service of the 'common people', the 'labouring poor'. The latter, the petitioners implied, were *dependants*. Employers of labour alone guaranteed the common wealth on which the whole nation depended.[41] The two worlds could and, in practice, had to coexist, but ideas and feelings hardened as the many branches of the English 'puritan movement' became stronger and the authority of king and court weakened.

In reply, 'the God upon the earth ... graciously accepted the submission' of his cowed inferiors. Sadly, 'it was not in his majestie's power to prevent' sufferings they had brought upon themselves. After a pause, the king graciously dismissed all those who had not been marked for imprisonment. 'Demeaning themselves with that duty and obedience to his majestie's just and necessary commands,' agreeing, in future, to supply whatever 'his majestie's necessities demand', they trooped off into the night with their tails between their legs.[42]

Historians have long disagreed about the role of the the 'multitude', those whom, the petitioners implied, had to be organized to labour and, if physically unable and in need. There was general agreement after the event that, as royalist Thomas Hobbes put it, 'the common people... were to decide the controversy' and that, as puritan John Corbet put it, 'common people know nothing of right or wrong by their own meditation'. That was what preachers, ministers and the 'better sort' were for. My impression is that the term 'common people' came, in the 1640s, to mean what later generations would call 'labouring poor' and later still, 'working class'. The reification of the employer class implied it, and class terminology emerged to fill the gap. One assumption was that the multitude was, on the whole, mobile. It comprised many young adults, still 'dependants', but maybe not forever: not yet 'settled down'. Wherever large numbers of young apprentices gathered, as in London, they formed the nucleus of the 'mobility' in motion: the 'mob'. Apprentices may not have formed a large enough group to serve such a function at Cirencester, although, as we have seen, the journeyman weavers were organized within the Weavers' Guild. Corbet took for granted that the 'undescerned guidance of superiour agents' was necessary to turn the allegedly volatile multitude 'to the terrour of the enemy'.[43] What determined for whom the 'vulgar multitude' (Corbet's – and before him, Shakespeare's – term) fought?

The cavalier 'eyewitness' emphasized 'three things [that] would not be forgotten' about the conduct of the rank and file defenders of Cirencester in their moments of defeat:

> One, how the dying men in the very fight cryed out 'that Robert Cooke, Mr [Nathaniel] Stevens, Mr George, and their preachers *had undone them*.... The

[41] The emergence of the 'political economy outlook' is the subject of Rollison, *A Commonwealth of the People*, part III, 'The English Explosion'.

[42] *The petition of the inhabitants*, 299.

[43] Hobbes, *Behemoth*, 181; Corbet, *Historicall Relation*, 9.

> Seconde … some of the prisoners confessed (and others have made it good) how that the gentlemen and clothiers threatened them they should have no work. Others that they should be plundered. Others were violently fetch't from their houses by dragooners, and made to get up behind them. Others were dragged from their ploughs, and others coming into the town about businesse, there were detained, and threatened to be shot.[44]

'This is the liberty of the subject,' he concluded. These were articles of faith. The mass of the subject population, in this interpretation, don't care about the great issues of the day unless they are indoctrinated or inveigled into involvement by superior officers and NCOs. If it was true that common people are inherently limited and dependent upon others for their world views and ideas, and this fact was the reason of reasons why established, traditional, absolutist hierarchy was correct and necessary, then conservatives were bound to believe lesser sorts were forced or meanly seduced into rebellion. The prisoners had an urgent awareness of what their conquerors wanted to hear: that rogue gentlemen like Mr Cooke, Mr Stephens and John George were the real culprits. The multitude went Parliament's way because its representatives in this region happened to live in the vicinity of Parliament-men and preachers (Stephens and Cooke were Members for the Shire, John George for the borough). Others were simply *forced* by their employers and the professional soldiers. Peter Heylyn thought this was necessarily so. As they passed through the streets of Oxford, the prisoners were asked 'why they tooke up armes against his majesty'. They replied that they 'neither did it on hope of pay, or out of any ill affection to the King's Majestie'. Rogue gentlemen had led the way. 'They were inforced unto it by the Deputy Lieutenants of the County, who made them goe into (Cirencester) whether they would or not.' Those who agreed to this version of events were allowed to go home.[45]

The memorial to Hodgkinson Paine, clothier, who died clutching Parliament's colours, confirms the royalist account of parliamentarian social relations but put a different spin on relations between employers and the 'poor' defenders of the town. 'Warre' had 'made rent' in (torn apart) the employer's special 'calling', 'the poore's supplie'.[46] Both sides agreed that the relationship between employers and employees was critical, the difference being whether that relationship was patriarchally or paternally familial, or greedily coercive. In the absence of direct testimony, all that can be said is that both sides saw 'the poor' as essentially passive and, in principle, uncommitted to either side.

Paine was not forgotten. His wife, Elizabeth, lived for another twenty-five years. Although we know nothing of her activities, it is likely she continued the clothing business through her long widowhood. Theirs, it seems, had been

44 *A particular relation*, 15 (emphasis original).

45 *Mercurius Aulicus*, report dated 'Munday February 6' (1642/3).

46 See above, Chapter 14, 000.

what sociologists of the family call a 'companionate marriage'.[47] This is what she wanted posterity to remember:

> One was our thought one life we fought
> One rest we both intended
> Our bodies have to sleep one grave
> Our souls to God ascended.[48]

Elizabeth Paine's memorials to herself and her husband offer flashes of insight into hidden driving forces of the 'puritan revolution', i.e. what was genuinely 'revolutionary' about its rank-and-file enactors. In my reading, the strongest of Elizabeth Paine's carefully selected words are 'thought', 'fought', 'intended' and 'ascended'. In the eyes of God their souls were equal. Their duty was to raise independent, God-loving children with a strong sense of responsibility towards the wider community. Love of God imposed on them a duty to work and to help others get the work they needed to sustain themselves and their families in pious, companionate independence. However weak their neighbours might be in their practices, their souls too were equal in the eyes of God. Theirs was the loving God of *Piers Plowman*, Julian of Norwich and Tyndale's *New Testament*; its powerful, proverbial injunction was, simply, 'love God and thy neighbour'.

Souls are not gendered. Gender is contingent, part of the vocational mix endowed by God on every individual soul. In Elizabeth Paine's mind, marriage is a collaboration of two souls and two minds into 'one thought' and, looking back on the circumstances of the early 1640s, 'one fight'. It was worth engaging in and even losing one's life for this cause, for its reward would be eternal rest and ascension to God. Elizabeth Paine's memorials pointed to the domestic and communal heart of the Puritan Revolution.

In its millenarian and messianic manifestations, this communalist soul- and vocation-centred theocracy drew on apocalyptic traditions, in which the 'saints' were perennially persecuted by wealthy and powerful forces for evil. Its most radical elements were traditional: let me conclude the revolutionary phase of Cirencester's history by identifying three of its elements. Firstly, it eschewed what Tyndale's *James* called 'respect of persons'. God loves souls, not powerful, ostentatious 'personalities'. Secondly, gender prejudices, like 'steeple-houses' and 'hat respect' for the Quakers, were 'institutions of men', contingencies of vocation, not the eternal soul. Thirdly, these generations valorized *work*. Once it became clear what one's vocation was, it only remained to practise it in every aspect of one's life. The Paines' household gods were companionate

[47] For an interpretation of the historical emergence of 'companionate marriage', see Lawrence Stone, *The Family, Sex and Marriage in England, 1500–1800* (London 1977), 325–404.

[48] Once again we have Rudder to thank for recording Elizabeth Paine's memorial: *History of Cirencester*, 264.

marriage, hard work, plain public words and service to the community. The cold, analytic John Corbet called them 'middle rank', but that was not how they saw themselves.

When Hodgkinson Paine left the house on the morning of 3 February 1643, they both knew he might never return. He in fact did return, mortally wounded, and died a few hours later. It was a sad, challenging yet also triumphant moment, for what, finally, Elizabeth Paine's memorials witness is her absolute confidence that, wherever events on earth led, their souls were destined for eternal bliss.

Another committed partisan, John Friend, joined the garrison at Cirencester in December. He was one of those who, like Gregory and Stansfield, were sent to Oxford gaol, where they remained until April.[49] As the son of a freemason from Westerleigh, near Bristol, Friend he also falls into Corbet's 'middle ranke', who, in his view, *were* 'discerning', the 'only *active* men'. The line between capacity and incapacity for rational thought and decision, in the rhetoric of both sides, more or less coincided with the line between 'independent' employers and 'dependent' employees. Committed parliamentarians framed their godliness in terms of what would later be seen as an entirely secular, economic relationship. They were the natural rulers of the 'vulgar multitude' insofar as they were its employers and (as instruments of local government) managers. A third account of the 'misguided zeale' of the defenders and 'the motives by which they have been drawne into rebellion', purportedly written by one who was converted by the experience of defeat, was that it had been a battle between 'the Cavaliers, whom we see with our eyes to be the flower of the Parliament, Nobility and Gentry' and 'those such as were not knowne to us by any Vertue, but only Crossnesse to Superiours'.[50]

The royalist cliché was that cynical, self-serving, troublemaking employers and preachers stirred the volatile, irresponsible multitude for their own hidden and hypocritical purposes. Gentlemen, momentarily caught up in the movement, led and fought with their parliamentarian communities in 1642–3, and then retreated. In his horror at where, in January 1649, it had all led, Calvinist firebrand Alexander Gregory probably spoke for most but not all the inhabitants of town and country. 'Non separatists', people broadly contented with the monarch's nominal headship of church and state, had always outnumbered 'separatists'. (Ana)Baptists, Independents, Congregationalists and Presbyterians became 'routinized' (organized themselves institutionally); seekers like

49 Porter, 'Biography of a Parliamentarian Soldier', 133; for a parliamentarian account of their treatment, see Edmund Chillenden, *The Inhumanity of the King's prison-Keeper at Oxford, Or, a true relation of the most transcendent cruelties* (London 1642/3): GCL 23.8326, 10/1.

50 *A warning piece to all his majesties subjects of England, being the lamentable complaint of them that were brought prisoners from Cyrencester, being 1160 and odde, told in the view of all for their misguided zeale. Containing the motives by which they have been drawne into Rebellion* (Oxford 1642/3): GCL 8326/47, 2, 4.

John Roberts reminded them that in the not too distant past they, too, had been 'rebels'. 'Dissenters' and 'Nonconformists' were not people who blamed social superiors for believing and acting as they did, but they too wanted to forget how far it had gone. Like Elizabeth Paine, John Roberts never resiled from his partisanship for the commonwealth. He continued to draw his contemporaries' attention to certain 'inventions and traditions of men' they too had once fought against. In Roberts's view, the 'English Revolution' had changed very little.[51]

In 1681 Sir William Dugdale doubted 'that the actions of our late times, chiefly from the year 1637 till 1660, can be easily forgotten'. 'That there is any need of reviving the memory of them to this present age,' he wrote, ''tis not to be imagined.'[52] In 1679, cavalier poet Abraham Cowley thought otherwise: erstwhile rebels very quickly 'forgot' what had happened in the darkest months of the winter of 1642–3:

> What fights did this sad winter see each day,
> Her winds and storms came not so thick as they!
> Yet naught these far lost rebels could recall,
> Not Marlborough's nor Cirencester's fall.[53]

For Roberts, 3 February 1643 was the day God saved his life from the slashing swords of Sir John Byron's cavalry.[54] In return for his unwelcome testimony, Roberts received his share of 'the rage and fury of our persecutors, which', as fellow Quaker Theophila Townshend testified in 1687, 'was against us for several years'.[55] It had become more prudent to forget than to remember.

51 For details and discussion of the events of the first civil war in Gloucestershire, cf. Rollison, *Local Origins*, 123–63; A.R. Warminster, *Civil War, Interregnum and Restoration in Gloucestershire, 1640–1672* (London 1997); Brian Hawkins, *Taming the Phoenix: Cirencester and the Quakers 1642–1686* (York 1998); and for Roberts, cf. Rollison, *Local Origins*, 164–98: for 'the inventions and traditions of men', *ibid*, 166.

52 Sir William Dugdale, *A Short View of the Late Troubles in England* (London 1681), Wing catalogue D2492, EEBO, 1.

53 Abraham Cowley, 'A Poem on the Late Civil War', in *Essays, Plays and Sundry Verses*, ed. A.R. Walker (Cambridge 1906), 476; Lauro Martines, *Society and History in English Renaissance Verse* (Oxford 1985), 107, writes that 'the example of Cowley's *Civil War* helps us to see that there are realities – in crisis above all – which poetry dare not look at too directly or it capsizes'.

54 Rollison, *Local Origins*, 173–4.

55 'Theophila Townshend's testimony concerning the life, death and sufferings of Amariah Drewett lately deceased', in *Some Testimonies of the Life, Death and Sufferings of Amariah Drewet of Cirencester in Gloucestershire* (London 1987), EEBO, 8.

Johannes Kip, 'Cirencester the Seat of Allen Bathurst Esq,' from Sir Robert Atkyns, *Ancient and Present State of Gloucestershire* (Gloucester 1712): courtesy of the Gloucestershire Archives.

Afterword

Rural sunrise

> … we soon arrived within the limits of Gloucestershire, in the Eastern parts swelled up into hills called Cotswold, which feed innumerable flocks of sheep, the wool whereof is much praised for its fineness; the middle parts consist of a fertile plain, watered by the Severn: and the Western part, where lies the Forest of Dean, is much covered with woods…
>
> Travelling over this delightsome region, the first place of any remark we came to was Cirencester *alias* Ciceter.… 'Tis now beautified with a very handsome church, having a high spired steeple (sic.) and hath once a week a market, and has been enriched with the trade of clothing, though that with other privileges and immunities they enjoyed, are now impaired and gone to decay.[1]

The theme of this Afterword is the emergence of a new epoch in the town's (and nation's) history. It had a distinctive mythology, enshrined in its twilight years by the great country writer Richard Jefferies, in a chapter of *Hodge and His Masters* entitled 'Fleeceborough – A Despot' (written c.1870). The accompanying illustration, 'Cirencester the Seat of Allen Bathurst Esq.', engraved by the much-travelled Dutch craftsman, Johannes Kip, captures an in-between phase. It was published as one of a fine series of gentry power houses in Sir Robert Atkyns' *Ancient and Present State of Gloucestershire* (1712). Kip represented Cirencester from the perspective of a hill east of the town where no such hill exists. It is the town as Gulliver might have viewed it striding along one of the old roads from the East. Bathurst's Jacobean mansion is the physical centre, but the converging roads compromise its centrality by creating a more natural focus on a place, closer to the church, where the roads (and 'passingers') converged. Here Kip placed a sign-post. The historical commune was a 'field of force', in which two great buildings compete for the viewer's focus, one a late Tudor mansion, the other 'perhaps (the largest) of any Perpendicular church anywhere'.[2]

1 James Brome, *Travels over England, Scotland and Wales giving a true and exact description of the chiefest cities, towns and corporations*, (London 1700), EEBO, Wing B4861, 8–9.

2 David Verey, *Cotswold Churches* (London 1976), 74.

The church still advertised the wealth and confidence of Cirencester's merchant, craftworker and retailing communities. It signalled their presence to travellers miles before they reached the outskirts of the town. It said, 'call in here'. At the centre of Kip's study, an observer's line of sight flicks between the two dominant buildings, the mansion and the church, and comes to rest on the 'island' of houses between the two, situated in what looks as if, before houses were first built there in the late thirteenth and early fourteenth centuries, it might have been a great open forum market-place. Crossroads are places for decisions and choices.

The church, the crossroads, the market-place and the mansion signify a slow-moving level of history. They are monuments to abiding structural continuities combined in a field of forces. The elementary particles remain the same; their relative power changes from time to time. The neatly laid-out gardens ('backsides') of the houses in the streets, and the geometric market gardens and small farms on the outskirts, signify well-ordered 'tillage', arable husbandry. Kip shows no sheep, cattle and horses grazing in the pastures and on the rough, hilly country that is the backdrop. A real Gulliver would have noted hundreds of sheep and scores of horses, dairy and beef-cattle, some belonging to locals, some available for hire, others fattening for the next market. When Kip's English contemporary, James Brome, thought of Cirencester, he saw 'innumerable flocks of sheep' and 'the trading of cloth' (which he thought 'now impaired'). In Kip's idealized representation of power, the *matériel* of even the pastoral sources of the town's immemorial dynamism is absent. There are no wains, carts, coaches, packhorses, riders or travellers by shanks' pony on the roads or in the streets, no stalls, traders, musicians or entertainers in the market-place. Commerce and traffic, movement and population are absent. It is the ideal of a culture yearning, not for change, but for an end to change.

Social historians study what is absent from Kip's engraving. Nearly two centuries later, Richard Jefferies added an unchanging society to Kip's vision of a timeless, monumental hegemony. Jefferies covered the Cirencester district as a reporter for the *North Wilts Herald* and the *Wiltshire and Gloucestershire Standard* in the third quarter of the nineteenth century. He does not say 'Fleeceborough' is Cirencester but certain details make clear it was his model.[3]

[3] Quotations in the following paragraphs from Jefferies, *Hodge and His Masters*, Vol. 1 (London 1880), Ch. XI, 256–77; Jefferies' accounts of rural life in the district merit a full-scale study; on the parallel with Cirencester, Jefferies mentions 'a famous poet who sang in the woods about the park' of the lords who, in Jefferies' myth, had dominated life in the district for centuries. 'His hermitage remains, and nothing is lost that was his.' This was Alexander Pope, who laid out the grounds of Cirencester Park, home of the Bathursts (see Map 2) since they purchased it from the Pooles in 1695. Pope built himself a small shelter at the centre of its radiating avenues, a visible symbol of

The Fleeceborough district is 'a distinct land'. Neighbouring districts are 'separate countr(ies) … almost … foreign'. Every male inhabitant is 'a citizen of Fleeceborough … it is his centre; thither he looks for everything'. 'The place is a little market town, the total of whose population in the census records sounds absurdly small; yet it is a complete world in itself; a capital city, with its kingdom and ruler.' Its constitution is organic. 'Soil and substrata are characteristic,' he writes. The 'flora is distinct'. The wood and stone from which the people build has a grain, texture and colour all its own. A solid but proud native imagination meshes with centuries of stone-cutting from local pits, and a specialized masonry, to produce an impressive vernacular achitecture. Its constitutional culture (for that, essentially, was Jefferies' subject) has emerged from centuries, possibly millennia, of organic interaction with the land. They all have 'plentiful food, and of the best quality' and, not least, 'their ale! No-one knows what English ale is till he has tasted this.'

Jefferies' myth implies continuity of settlement, which he regards as natural to humanity. 'When men have first settled,' he writes, 'they and their descendents remain, generation after generation.' They 'have been stationary for a length of time, and the moss of the proverb has grown around them'. He ranks them into five sorts: the lord or 'prince', the gentry, the farmers, the shopkeepers and tradesmen, and the farm labourers. Following his abstract of Fleeceborough and its satellite farms, hamlets and villages, contained within a radius of 'thirty miles or so' from the town, he introduces the 'despot' of his chapter-heading. The 'demesnes' of the 'prince' are surrounded by a 'vast wall', spread out around a mansion, which 'gives an air of power and authority'. These are the 'private demesnes of a prince and ruler of Hodge – the very highest and most powerful of his masters in that part of the country'.

In this aspect, Jefferies' Fleeceborough and historical Cirencester are very different places. Across the centuries explored in this book only one family exhibits the continuity of settlement Jefferies had in mind. The Georges of Baunton, possibly thirteenth-century merchants, then classic *liberi homines* and country gentlemen for at least nine generations, deserve more extended treatment than is practical here. They were definitive 'inhabitants'. Of all the gentlemen of town and country, indeed of all the inhabitants, they alone, demonstrably, generation after generation, had served commune, country and commonwealth.[4] They had not sought greedily to 'add land to land, lordship to lordship', aspired to higher status, or lived aloof from their

the enlightened self at the centre of the universe, and of the order that noblemen of conservative Augustan vision, like Allen Bathurst, could impose on it.

4 GA P86, CH 1.9–23 refers to a George family settlement in 1275 and leases for joint lives, 1300–88; CH 1.2 includes a marriage settlement dated 1403 between John George and Elizabeth, a daughter of William Tanner – for Tanner, landlord of the Ram Inn, see above, Chapter 5; CH 1/1–3 refer to family settlements 1338–1453; for further family

community. A study of the Georges would be a study of a highly exceptional, yet widely distributed and massively influential, class of families: country gentlemen of the sixteenth and seventeenth centuries, distinguished from other gentry families by the fact that their affinities were always, first and foremost, to their countries. The Tudor–Stuart Georges were very far from the stereotypical rustic boors encountered in the writing of Henry Fielding and nineteenth-century progressives like Marx. In a society that held service to the commonweal in such high esteem, they were preeminent, and highly exceptional.

Otherwise, in every generation, new names continued to appear on the walls of the nave and chapels, in the lists of jurymen, expropriated burgesses, rebels, bailiffs, taxpayers, mustered men, parish registers, dissenters and nonconformists, churchwardens and so on. Continuity of settlement for more than one or two generations was the exception rather than the rule, at all levels and among all 'sorts'. It hardly needs saying that different classes experienced and practised their social and geographical mobility in very different ways. The gross, systematic inequality that determined the town's underlying class structure was not changed by the English Revolution. When, after the restoration of monarchy in 1660, efforts were made to institutionalize flows of labour (the mobility of the 'mobility' or 'mob'), men of property and substance were not to be subject to interrogation by vestries and overseers of the poor whenever they changed their location. The images of absolute settlement in Kip's engravings and Jefferies' writings aroused pangs of recognition in people who knew that reality meant unpredictable change and movement, not monumental balance. Ideals of settlement and equilibrium were esteemed because they were so difficult to achieve and maintain.

As with Kip, the apex of Jefferies' country constitution is a 'despot' with 'private … dominions … almost coextensive with the horizon'. He acknowledges a popular element. The inhabitants are 'personally free': the 'citizens of Fleeceborough' are always granted 'free entry' to the 'despot's' park in the nutting season. The 'prince' owns most of the farms belonging to the farmers and minor gentry of the surrounding countryside. Such an arrangement is the result of the rational choices of past generations. The farmers 'have long since discovered that it is best to rent under a very large owner, whether personal as in this case, or impersonal as a college or corporation':

> A very large owner like this can be, and is, more liberal. He puts up sheds, and he drains, and he improves, and builds good cottages for the labourers. Provided, of course, that no serious malpractice comes to light, he, as represented by his

settlements of various dates from the fourteenth to seventeenth centuries, see CH 1.4–5, 1.6–8, 1.24–5.

> steward, never interferes, and the tenant is personally free. No-one watches his comings and goings; he has no sense of an eye for ever looking over the park wall. There is a total absence of the grasping spirit sometimes shown. The farmer does not feel that he will be worried to the last shilling. In case of unfavourable seasons the landlord makes no difficulty in returning a portion of the rent; he anticipates such an application. Such immense possessions can support losses which would press most heavily upon comparatively small properties.... It is well understood that no change will be effected. The tenure is as steady as if the tenant had an Act of Parliament at his back.

They do not need 'an Act of Parliament' to protect their interests. Parliamentary enclosure, which affected Cirencester's North Wold hinterlands as much as any part of England, is not mentioned.

Despite the prince's nominal 'despotism', local politics run deep and engage many classes, factions and interests. The farmers have their own informal councils and regard attendance at their 'hostelries ... on market days' as a 'religious duty'. Their meetings have an aura of formality. 'No-one finally settles himself at the table till the chairman arrives.' The chairman is 'a stout, substantial farmer, who has dined there every market day for the past thirty or forty years'. Each farmer has 'his own particular hostelry', to which entry is granted by inheritance. 'He is expected to dine in the same room... (as) his father and grandfather.' The farmers keep their councils on market days, when the shopkeepers and tradesmen are at their busiest. The townsmen have their meetings in the evenings, when they stroll down to their hostelries to consult with their neighbours. All adult males are entitled to attend, 'the rich and the moderately well-to-do, the struggling and the poor'. Every adult male has entry to 'the common hall – the informal place of meeting'. Every man has his own 'hostelry', where, naturally, 'the drinking is extremely moderate' because 'it is here that the real government of the town is planned'.

These are what Stuart churchwardens called the 'better sort': husbandmen, artisans and shopkeepers, few if any of them owning their own homes, gardens and farms. The 'prince' never attends their informal yet routine meetings, yet his presence abides in every discussion. Everyone asks 'What will "he" do? What will "he" say to it?' 'He' is an absent presence in every discussion of 'the cottage hospital; the flower show; the cattle show and agricultural exhibition; the new market buildings; the artesian well, sunk that the town might have the best of water'. 'The whole list of town affairs,' he writes, is 'at [the prince's] expense.'[5] Although 'the real government of

5 The Bathursts were great patrons of the Bristol and Gloucestershire Archaeological Society, e.g. after a meeting held at several places in the Seven Hundreds on 25 May 1925, 'from Ampney Crucis members drove to Cirencester Park, where the President, Earl Bathurst, who was unavoidably absent from the meeting, entertained them to tea': *Trans BGAS* 47 (1925), 25.

the town is planned' in the 'hostelries', which form an informal adult male suffrage, the townspeople also have a formal council to co-ordinate decisions, the local equivalent of Parliament. Its legitimacy as an ancient institution is established by images Jefferies paints of the building in which it is held. The Elders meet 'in an ancient wainscoted hall, with painted panels and coats of arms, carved oaken seats black with age, and narrow windows from which men once looked down into the streets wearing trunk hose and rapier'. The men who come here are 'the respectable men of Fleeceborough'. They discuss and decide what is needed: the prince provides whatever financial support is needed. The 'despot's' policy is 'perfect freedom, with support and substantial assistance to every movement set on foot by the respectable men of Fleeceborough, or by the tenant farmers around them'.

It is what Jefferies' contemporary, Ferdinand Tonnies, called an 'associational community', governed, not by laws and contracts, but by custom and association. Formal institutions are insignificant compared with arrangements outside the formal structures. The 'respectable men' are not required by any formal law to consult with their lesser brethren in the hostelries. They do it as a matter of course. If his tenants are having difficulties, the prince simply forgoes his rent. Rather than rely on formal institutions and laws, the citizens 'walk down to their inns' every evening voluntarily, restrain their drinking voluntarily, consult with each other voluntarily, and defer to the prince because they love him. The farmers at the hostelries wait voluntarily for the 'chairman' to arrive. There is nothing mysterious about how all this is achieved. It is empirical common sense, a matter of observing local life and keeping an eye and an ear open to what other people think and say.

How could anyone be against it? Yet 'there is a section which is all the more vehemently rebellious because of the spectacle of its staid and comfortable neighbours':

> This section is very small, but makes a considerable noise. It holds meetings and utters treasonable speeches, and denounces the 'despot' in fiery language. It protests against a free and open park; it abhors artesian wells; it detests the throwing open of nut-woods that all may go forth a-nutting.... It asks why? Why should we wait till the park gates are open? Why stay till the nut-woods are ready?... Why not take our own?

'Dissenters' are few 'but make ... considerable noises'. They ask 'why?' Jefferies touches lightly and ironically on a great paradox of English constitutional history. If the system is so perfect and organic, the shrewdly and assiduously accumulated wisdom of generations, why the constant, continuous bass-line, the equally well-documented great tradition of dissent and debate, protest, resistance, rebellion and even revolution? Jefferies' answer, like that of the royalists after their victory in February 1643, was: a few deluded (or self-interested) troublemakers.

Jefferies was probably thinking of Chartists and socialists. For the proto-Tories of the 1640s, enemies of the natural supremacy of kings and lords had been religious fanatics who used scripture to question 'traditions of men', lauded commonwealth-minded businessmen, taught common working people to read, write and listen to sermons dealing with subjects that only kings and lords had any right (or ability) to think about. Over and again, they had urged common people to apply the principle of commonweal/th to traditional authorities and institutions. Jefferies was probably right. Consistent, active dissenters are always a small minority. The interesting question is why, in some periods, their ideas spread and take hold. The history of Cirencester suggests they take hold when existing authorities manifestly fail to convince their subjects that they are motivated by love of the common weal.

*

Kip's etching and Jefferies' *vignette* set the commune of the generations of Philip Marner, Elizabeth Whiting, John Coxwell, John George, Elizabeth and Hodgkinson Payne, in sharp relief. More research and thought is needed on the long transition from industrious, mercantile, bourgeois and parliamentarian borough – always, it seemed, at the sharp end of economic, social and constitutional life – to the parochial, rural capital idealized by Kip and Jefferies. Here are some suggestions.

From 1643–5 the town played reluctant host, successively, to soldiers of both sides. A majority of the inhabitants continued to baptize their infants at the parish church and bury their dead in the churchyard. Alexander Gregory returned, but in the later 1640s 'the dissolution of Presbyterian power, and growth of Independents' opened sharp new divisions, 'whereupon ensued the nefarious murder of King Charles'.[6] Non-separatist churchwardens and vestrymen continued to meet, appoint officials and generally manage the parish. They paid agents in London (men from local families) to keep them informed of what they needed to know of national affairs.[7] They were troubled by sects, which began to routinize in the late 1640s and 1650s. The children of several 'Anabaptists' are recorded in the burial registers of 1655–6.[8] From the 1650s the testimony of persecuted Quakers

6 Sir William Dugdale, *A Short View of the Late Troubles in England* (London 1681), EEBO, Wing D2492, 4.

7 A Vestry Minute of 26 June 1647, 'ordered that Edward King shall have for his journeys to London wch he hath taken, for his charges'; and a meeting of 18 October 1651 'requested [Edward King] to follow the town's business, and if he stay any longer in London than his own business requireth, then he is to be payd by the p[ar]ish': GA P86, VE 2/1.

8 This paragraph based on Vestry Minutes and entries in GA P86, IN 1/2, Burials 1637–1799; the latter include many deaths of soldiers in December 1644 and January–February 1645, Gregory's cry of pain (January 1649) and, on 2 June 1654, 'A child of Robert Wilkins Anabaptist'; 17 August 1655, 'A child of Alexander Neale, Anabaptist';

suggests that, as Abraham Cowley observed, the right-thinking majority passionately wanted to forget where the inspired, enthusiastic populism of the early 1640s had led. 'O England what didst thee do the 30th of this month,' wrote an agonized Gregory in the burial register the day after the king was beheaded in the name of the commonwealth.

Sources of the later seventeenth century support Jefferies' view that overt dissenters from the sacraments and institutions of church and state were never more than a small minority. The Compton Census of communicants in 1676 enumerated 6,500 'conformists', 18 'papists' and 236 (3.49%) 'nonconformists' in Cirencester Deanery. Of these, the borough contributed 1,745 conformists, no papists and 155 (8.1%) nonconformists. The town was not congenial to papists. It would remain the passionately protestant town it so suddenly became in 1570, until the ecumenical movement of the late twentieth and early twenty-first centuries. Among the protestants, conformists outnumbered dissenters by nearly ten to one. The parish of Cirencester held 27 percent of the adult population of the deanery and 66 percent of the 'nonconformists'. Yet nonconformity was a feature of town *and* country. The highest nonconformity rates in Gloucestershire were in 'rural' deaneries west of the Severn Vale, in or on the edge of the Cotswolds.[9] Statistically, like trained men in the musters of 1608, nonconformists were lightly but quite evenly spread: 24 (57%) of the 42 parishes in the deanery had at least one open 'nonconformist'. There were nine each at Siddington St Peter and Bibury, six in the tiny village of Harnhill, 27 at Northleach (where, as at Cirencester, no papists resided), but only six and seven at Fairford and Lechlade respectively.

A survey of 1682 employed a much wider definition of 'nonconformity'. It named 49 'Anabaptists that go neither to church nor sacramant', 65 'Quakers that disown the sacrament', and an eccentric individual, 'John Aston, one that disowns the church and keeps Saturday Sabbath'.[10] These

1 September 1655, 'A son of Richard Burges Anabaptist'; 24 January 1656, 'A son of Henry Archer Anabaptist'; 23 August 1656, 'a son of Henry Chance Anabaptist'.

9 The Compton Census 1676, Photocopy 377 at GA, yields the following data: Gloucester deanery had the lowest nonconformity rate (1.46%); the highest rate in the county was in Stow deanery (7.55%), followed by Deerhurst (where Tewkesbury was an influence, 7.11%), Hawkesbury (6.49%), Winchcombe (4.3%), Cirencester (3.49%) and Stonehouse (3.3%); on the Compton evidence, 'nonconformity' was less prominent in 'Tyndale country' (Dursley deanery, 2.36%).

10 This is based on a paper book later sown into GA GDR 243; the survey concentrated on the Cotswolds and the book contains no data for the Stroudwater Valleys, the Vale of Berkeley or Longtree hundred; nonconformity and non-attendance were highest in the Cotswolds, particularly the deaneries of Winchcombe and Cirencester and – to a lesser extent – Fairford. The book reports 34 non-attenders at Sherborne and ten at Southrop. It employs the following categories: 'Anabaptists that go neither to church nor sacrament' (49); 'A loose sort of careless persons, who go not to the Sacrament and seldom to the church (35); 'A loose poore that neglects both the church and the sacrament' (23);

114 active dissenters were lumped with 35 'loose sort of careless persons, who go not to the Sacrament and seldom to the church', 23 'loose poore that neglects both the church and the sacrament', 22 'careless poor that come not to the sacrament and seldom to the church' and 80 more, mostly couples, who 'come to church but neglect the sacrament'; among the latter were a dozen 'young, mean beginners but frequent the church'. The survey ignores Presbyterians, who presumably were not absenting themselves from church at this time. In 1682, 275 (15%) of an adult population of 2,000 either refused or simply neglected to go to church. Of these, 114 (5.7%) were dissenters, active 'nonconformists'.

They were defined in relation to a society whose basic structures were unchanged by the civil wars. Sources for the later seventeenth, eighteenth and nineteenth centuries are excellent. Hearth tax listings of the 1660s and 1670s reveal that gentlemen were at least as ubiquitous and numerous as they had been before the civil wars. About a dozen gentlemen had apartments or houses in the borough. The listings for Crowthorne and Minety, encompassing the villages closest to the town, list 15 gentlemen.[11] Eleven gentlemen had residences in the eight complete parish listings for Brightwells Barrow.[12] Of four complete listings in Rapsgate, two had resident gentlemen;[13] ten listings for Bradley record another ten.[14] Apart from the Georges of Baunton, whom we know from other sources always had a house at Cirencester, only William Dutton Esq. definitely had a town house (with ten hearths at Northleach) as well as his main country residence, Sherborne House, the largest in the county with 56 hearths. The largest house at Cirencester, yet to be immortalized by Kip, was headed by Sir Henry's widow, Lady Poole; the old Poole power house at Sapperton (30 hearths) was now the residence of Sir Robert Atkyns, father of the Gloucestershire historian.

'Careless poor that come not to the sacrament and seldom to the church' (22); 'Come to church but neglect the sacrament' (80); 'Quakers that disown the sacrament' (65) and 'One that disowns the church and keeps Saturday Sabbath'.

11 Driffield: George (Illeg), 12; Harnhill: John Nicholl, 7; Ampney Crucis: Mr Masters, 6 & Robt Pledwell, 14; Ampney Peter: Henry Trinder, 7; Down Ampney: Hungerford Ducie Esq., 21; Coates: Mr Partridge, 14; Siddington: George Brill Rector, 7; South Cerney: Widow Jones, 6 & Richard Jones 6; Stratton: Mr Kinge, 13; Duntisbourne Rous: Sir Robert Atkyns, illeg.; Chesterton: Mrs Franklyn, 9; Duntisbourne Abbots: Mr Dowle, 7; Baunton: Illeg. George, 10.

12 Kempsford: Sir Henry Thynne (44); Hatherop: John Blomer Esq. (25); Coln St Aldwyns: Giles Fettiplace (12), Henry Powle Esq. (15); Lechlade: Mrs Bathurst (12), Mr Singe (10), Mr Lander (10); Fairford: Mr Barber (25 in 2 houses); Barnsley: William Bourchier (16); Aldsworth: Mr Wheler (6).

13 Elkstone: Thomas Horton Esq. (12); Brimpsfield: Miles Sandys Esq. (13).

14 Northleach: William Dutton Esq. (10); Whittingham: Lady Denham (6); Brockhampton and Sevenhampton: Mr Doudswell (8), Mr Rogers (10), Edward Rich Esq. (13); Notgrove: Sir Clement Clark (6); Withington: William Haynes (10), John Hew Esq. (18).

Even industrial Bisley hundred lists at least eight gentlemen and several candidates for membership of the select fraternity of 'gentlemen clothiers' (still a contradiction in terms in the eyes of older families). It is clear enough from the 1608 muster and the hearth tax listings that gentlemen regarded the Cotswolds and the Oxford Clay Vale, close to Cirencester, and within easy striking distance of London, as desirable places to live.

Table A1. 1671 Hearth Tax[15]

Ward	H/H	Tax	Ex	% Ex	1H	2H	3H	4–5	6–9	10+
Castle	74	47	27	36	17+22	15+4	3+1	5	5	
	(12.3)				54%	26	6	7	7	
Cricklade	98	52	46	47						
	16.25									
Gosditch	95	68	27	28	19+24	22+2	14+1	9	2	2
	15.75				46	26	16	10	2	2
Lawrence	67	28	39	58	6+37	15+1	3+1	4		
	11.11				64	24	6	6		
Inst. & C.	39 (6.5)	17	22	56						
Dollar	101	61	40	40	16+36	14+4	10	12	6	1
	16.75				52	18	10	12	6	1
Dyer	129	92	37	29	19+36	19+1	13	9	8	
	21.4				52%	19	12	9	8	
Totals	603	365	238	39	232	97	46	39	21	3
	(2713)				52.9%	22.1%	10.5%	8.9%	4.8%	0.7%

4 Rural	1309	764	545	41.6	755	199	122	67	29	23	1195
Hundreds					63%	15%	10%	6%	2%	2%	

Table A1 shows that hearths were as unequally distributed as possessions and capital in the assessments of 1327, 1522 and 1579. Including ineligibles, more than half the assessed (52%) lived in one-hearth accommodation. Another 32.6 percent paid on two or three. A mere 14 percent lived in a household with more than three hearths. A total of 39 percent of households in the town and 42 percent of villagers were exempt on grounds of poverty. 'Poor' was always a fluid term, but when every qualification is made, the housing data comfortably fits the pattern we encountered first in the

15 Discrepancies between total HH in col. 2 and totals for cols 6–12 due to illegibility in the source of 2 in Castle; 5 in Cricklade; 8 in Dollar; 28 in Dyer; percentages in cols 6–12 based on legibles. The analysis is exploratory, not least because it is based on only one far from perfect assessment (1671); David Levine and Keith Wrightson, *The Making of an Industrial Society: Whickham 1560–1765* (Oxford 1991), Ch. 3.1, 'The householders of Whickham in 1666', exemplifies what can be done when the most complete listings are seen in the context of other contemporary records; see also Tom Arkell, 'A Student's Guide to the Hearth Tax: Some Truths, Half Truths and Untruths', in N. Alldridge (ed.), *The Hearth Tax: Problems and Possibilities* (Hull 1983)

tax list of 1327: a tiny elite of 'magnates' with 10+ hearths, a substantial 'better sort' with 4–9, a 'lower middling' group of inhabitants paying on 2–3 hearths and the multitude with one. Immemorial class distributions were still in place.

In the town, exemptions varied quite considerably from ward to ward. The most prestigious streets were Dyer and Gosditch, but even they had 29 percent and 28 percent exemptions. More ineligibles lived in Lawrence (58% exemptions), Dollar (40%), Instrop and Ciceley (56%) and Castle Wards (36%). Overall, exemptions for the town, as the table shows, were slightly higher than the average for the county of Gloucestershire in general (36%). Two-hearth households were much less likely to be able to convince assessors they should be exempt. Twelve two-hearth households were granted exemption, and no exempt household had more than two hearths.

Deducing social structure from such statistics requires more information than the statistics provide, even if they were complete, unassailably accurate and conducted with complete honesty by the assessors and the taxed. Wealthy men with a need to do business at Cirencester may well have rented small 'apartments', which show up as two-hearth households. Poorer families might scrimp and save enough, in good times, to rent three- or four-hearth accommodation. At any one time in the history of the town from the thirteenth to seventeenth centuries, there were rich, upper and lower 'middles', and 'the multitude' or 'mobility'. In qualification of the impression these static sources leave us, it is evident that, up to a point, local society was socially as well as geographically mobile. At no time in the history of the town is it impossible to imagine penniless immigrants moving in and up the time-worn hierarchies. We have seen that mortality crises regularly created openings at all levels of the community. As we saw in the exemplary cases of Robert Strange and John Coxwell, longevity was an ambitious man's greatest ally in this epoch of slow accumulation. The move from lower to upper middling was, for many, a stage of life: from journeyman or servant to master-craftsman or tenant farmer. Wealthy clothiers with six or more households were often on the verge of losing their capital. Openings there were, but for most of them, a little 'seed' capital was needed. Philip Marner and John Coxwell knew this, and had institutionalized short-term loans to deserving, aspirant households. From the fourteenth to mid-seventeenth centuries the town was in the vanguard of that ultimately immeasurable world revolution, 'capitalism'. The managerial revolution instituted by the generation of Marner and Coxwell was routinized and developed after the civil wars.

Strong women like Elizabeth Whiting and Theophila Townsend begin to force their way into the archival record with greater frequency than in the past. The inhabitants Kip failed to describe did not become any less enterprising, industrious or willing to engage in national and local politics. Presbyterian, Baptist, Independent and Quaker congregations flourished and were institutionalized. The later seventeenth century was an age of what

Max Weber called 'routinization', in which once evangelical, even messianic religious and social movements lost evangelical fervour and became, themselves, institutions. The parish revival of the late sixteenth and early seventeenth centuries provides the exemplary case: the preachers went, but the managerial reforms of c.1570–1640 were consolidated, routinized and developed. Around the end of the seventeenth century the handwriting of local officials changed from village Secretary to Copperplate. Printed forms begin to streamline the monitoring of labour mobility in the eighteenth century. A workhouse was built. As elsewhere, the workload of parish officials in managing, seeing to the employment of, relieving and institutionalizing the labouring poor, monitoring and controlling migrant labour, multiplied.

New benefactors of commune and parish continued to be honoured in death on the walls of the church. Wealthy old men continued to dominate the Vestry, probably still in nominal consultation with the 'better sort', who continued to provide most of the parish officials. New family names on the memorials suggest the tradition of generational turnover of the wealthy elite continued well into the eighteenth century. My impression is that high standards of probity were maintained in parish affairs, but much research remains to be done on the history of the town from the civil wars to the First World War and, indeed, up to the present.

Comprehensive occupational listings make it possible to dissect and classify the economy of the town on the eve of the industrial revolution. Rudder offers typically judicious clues to what was happening in the late eighteenth century. Four of the Seven Hundreds were markedly affected by parliamentary enclosures. Parliamentary surveys of the poor in the 1770s and 1803 suggest that these hundreds had unemployment rates of 20–30 percent around 1800. Part of the reason was that in the later eighteenth century the strategic orientation of English traffic shifted north, a new meaning was given to the word 'industrial' and places like Cirencester became, for the first time in their histories, 'rural'. The process was not without pain.

The occupations in Table A2 refer to the male inhabitants polled in a parliamentary election in 1768. Although 167 of the 717 polled men are not assigned occupations and the list excludes inmates, sojourners and persons in receipt of alms, the table certainly gives an accurate impression of the services offered by the town 160 years after the earlier lists associated with the muster of 1608. Rudder writes that 'an exact account', taken in 1775, recorded '838 householders and the inhabitants 3,878, besides 110 in the workhouse, making together 3,988, something more than four and a half persons per house'.[16] The 717 men polled and enumerated in 1768

16 Rudder, *History of Cirencester*, 331: in 1741 'after the smallpox had left' there were 3,798; in 1758 'after a severe visitation of the same kind the people were numbered 3458'.

comprised more than 80 percent of householders. The list excludes inmates, sojourners and persons in receipt of alms. It is therefore an excellent guide to the functions served by the town on the eve of the Industrial Revolution, more comprehensive than, yet comparable with, the lists associated with the muster of 1608.

Table A2. Occupations in 1768[17]

Agriculture		
Yeoman	3	
Husbandman	1	
Farmer	1	
Gardener	9	Total 14
Food processing and marketing		
Cheese Factor	3	
Cheese Monger	1	
Grocer	4	
Baker	15	
Maltster	10	Total 33
Meat		
Butcher	8	Total 8
Animal hides		
Tanner	2	
Currier	4	
Saddler	4	
Glover	11	
Cordwainer	25	
Shoemaker	8	
Fellmonger	2	Total 56
Wool, cloth and clothing		
Woolcomber	53	
Woolstapler	25	(78)

17 Occupations from *The Poll of the Borough of Cirencester, taken March… 1768* (Samuel Rudder, Cirencester 1768), 8–31; asterisked items from 'Cirencester Directory', GCL J20.27; an appendix to *The Poll…*, 32–40, also contains valuable material: it lists an additional 253 'names of such persons whose votes were rejected, as being Inmates, occasional Inhabitants, certificated Persons, receiving Alms, not Parishioners, under Age &c': of these, 46 places of origin are given for 125 persons, including London (43), Gloucester (9), Bristol (6), Tetbury (5), Bath (4), Chippenham (4), Cerney (3), Tewkesbury (3), Ampney (3), Painswick (2), Northleach (2), Warwick (2), Wotton under Edge (2), Stroud (2); only 35 of the 125 came from places in the Seven Hundreds; for the political context of this election, see Jenkins, 'The Cirencester Contest', 161–2, 168.

Frame Knitter	6	(6)
Shearman	1	
Yarnmaker	1	
Carpet Weaver	1	
Weaver	14	
Dyer	2	
Scribbler	1	
Spinner	1	
Clothier	1	
Mercer	9	(31)
Tailor	15	
Collarmaker	5	
Perukemaker	6	
Breeches Maker	1	
Staymaker	2	
Hosier	2	
Milliner	1	
Haberdasher	1	
Hatter	3	(36)
Ragman	2	(2)
		Total 153
Wood		
Joiner	6	
Millwright	5	
Carpenter	13	
Cooper	4	
Wheelwright	6	
Sawyer	1	
Chairmaker	1	
Cabinet Maker	1	
Woodcutter	1	
Basketmaker	2	Total 40
Stone/building		
Slatter	10	
Mason	14	
Painter	2	Total 26
Glass		
Glazier	3	Total 3
Metals		
Brazier	4	
Ironmonger	1	
Sieve Maker	1	
Cutler	3	
Blacksmith	7	

Farrier	1 + 1	
Silversmith	1	
Edgetool Maker	17	Total 36
Transport		
Carrier	5	
Waggoner	1	
Peddler	1	Total 7
Alcohol, food and entertainment		
Distiller	1	
Winemerchant	2	
Drummer	1	
Ostler	1	
Innholder	11	
Brewer	1	
Victualler	15	Total 32
Shopkeeper		
Chandler	3	
Tallowchandler & Soapboiler	1*	
Apothecary	2 + 1	
Shopkeeper	1	
Barber	7	
Snuff-man	1	
Salesman	2	
Bookseller/Stationer	1*	Total 18
Local official		
Bailiff	1*	
Sergeant at Mace	1	
Sexton	1	
Parish Clerk	1	
Gatekeeper	1	Total 5
Services		
Printer	1	
Surgeon	4	
MD	1	
Attorney	5*	
Schoolmaster	4	
Minister	3	Total 18
Labourer		
Labourer	77	
Porter	16	
Servant	7	Total 100

Gent		
Esquire	1	Total 1 (550)
Occupation not given		167
Total (incl. not given) 717		

Additional	
Whitesmith (polisher and finisher of metal goods)	1
Gunsmith	5
Watchmaker	1
Pattern Drawer	1
Wontcatcher	1

Although the number of occupations has more than doubled, the town remained the industrious and enterprising regional market and service centre it had been two or even five centuries earlier. The occupations, while more numerous, are still entirely connected into the networks and culture of what Professor Wrigley calls 'advanced organic economy'. One change, however, is noteworthy. Wrigley observes that

> in the transition from a traditional society where income levels are low to a modern economy with high average incomes … the absolute level of demand will rise for the products of all the three main employment categories, but the rate of growth will be least in the primary sector and greatest in the tertiary sector.

Tertiary employment, he explains, relates to

> the production of services rather than material products: the professions, government service; the arts and entertainment; the provision of food, drink and lodging; and transport, for example.[18]

Allowing for 125 men who were certainly lodging in the town at the time of the poll, it would appear that the town depended on 'tertiary' employment to a significantly greater extent in 1768 than in 1608.[19] By 1768, these

18 Wrigley, 'Country and Town', 218.

19 For this calculation I include the following categories in Table A2 as 'tertiary': transport (7); alcohol, food and entertainment (32); local official (5); services (18); barbers (7); apothecaries (3); bookseller (1); the 1608 figures for transport (13) and A/F/E (14) are comparable and, with the single named local official, produce the considerably lower average of 7.9 percent overall.

'tertiary' employment categories made up 13.2% (73) of the men whose occupations were listed.

As its tertiary sector increased, the 'secondary' declined. The process of its becoming a 'rural' capital and district began with the ebbing away of its traditional connections with mass manufacturing. The making of cloth was now vestigial; the town lost its role as a manufacturing, finishing and distribution centre to Stroud, which grew very rapidly in the late seventeenth and early eighteenth centuries. Cirencester became a 'rural capital' in relation to the Industrial Revolution and the geographical–economic changes associated with it. The Seven Hundreds were no less transformed by the Industrial Revolution than new cities like Liverpool, Manchester, Leeds and Birmingham, but in an opposite way.

Rudder saw this happening and suggested some causes. Division of labour was more extensive in 1768 than is evident in the 1608 listings. The largest occupational grouping (as in 1608) is labourers (77), followed by woolcombers (53) and woolstaplers (25). 'Clothing declined,' confirmed Rudder, 'because of the lack of rivulets on which to erect fulling mills... Demands increasing beyond what the clothier could supply, he naturally quits his residence [in the town] and settles where mills might be erected.'[20] The Weavers' Guild continued to meet 'in their hall in St Thomas's Hospital' but would 'admit new members without regard to their line of business ... not any of the company transactions have the least relation to weaving'. Rudder noted that the town's cloth fairs had been long discontinued.[21] In 1768 one clothier, probably running a fulling mill on the Churn, was providing work for 14 weavers and two dyers. Nor was the wool trade bringing any wealth into the town. Rudder noted that the wool market Defoe had marked as having (since 1608) recovered to be one of the greatest in England in the early eighteenth century, had declined to nothing: 'the wool dealers travelling the country and buying that commodity at the farmhouses, soon reduced the market to a mere nullity', he observed.[22] The woolcombers and woolstaplers were now supplying the Stroudwater Valley clothiers with yarn. This final connection was about to be lost.

The occupational listing of 1768 occurred at the beginning of a sharp decline in the prosperity of the town and, to an even greater extent, the Seven Hundreds. Calculations from the parliamentary *Abstract of Returns Relative to the Expense and Maintenance of the Poor* (1803) show that from 1776 to 1803, increases in expenditure on poor relief were sharpest in two districts of Gloucestershire, the north Cotswolds and the Vale of Tewkesbury (see Table A3).[23] The four hundreds included in Table A3 were the

20 Rudder, *History of Cirencester*, 171.
21 *Ibid*, 171–2.
22 *Ibid*, 149.
23 Commons Papers (1803).

most rural of the Seven Hundreds, and three of them, Brightwells Barrow, Crowthorne and Minety, and Bradley, were intensely affected by parliamentary enclosures after 1760.[24] In Gloucestershire as a whole, 17 percent of individuals were in receipt of some kind of relief in 1803. Hundreds recently affected by parliamentary enclosure had much higher figures, ranging from Crowthorne and Minety's high of 37 percent receiving some kind of assistance, to Brightwells Barrow's 22 percent. Those receiving occasional relief were also highest in Crowthorne and Minety, which encompassed the villages closest to Cirencester, i.e. those that, in 1399, had still been included in the hundred of Cirencester itself.

Table A3. Expenditure on poor relief in four rural hundreds, 1776 and 1803[25]

Hundred	1803 as % of 1776	Total relieved as % of total population	Relieved occasionally as % of total relieved	Average expenditure per inhabitant
County mean	244	17	25	.576
Crowthorne and Minety	313	37	48	.768
Bradley	333	31	12	.905
Rapsgate	259	26	21	.811
Brightwells Barrow	341	22	29	.834

A document of 1815, relating to the Estcourt estates at Shipton Moyne (a centre of agricultural and social innovation), details one aspect of the problem. In July 1815 the estate required the labour of ten men for a total of 86 days, six women for 35 days and four boys for 24 days. The following January, however, only six men were employed for a total of 25.5 days, two women for three days and two boys for a total of eight days.[26] Seasonality of agricultural employment was probably exacerbated by other effects of wholesale enclosure, though further research would be necessary to determine what, exactly, those effects were. Enclosure was only part of the problem.

[24] Based on calculations from W.E. Tate, 'Gloucestershire Enclosure Acts and Awards', *Trans BGAS*, 64 (1943).

[25] It is difficult to calculate unemployment and underemployment rates from the *Abstracts* because it is not clear how far the figures in different columns (e.g. 'permanently out of work', 'over sixty or disabled') are overlapping. However, in order to obtain a rough and ready estimate the total population of each hundred in 1801 has been divided by four (to give an approximate figure for heads of households) and the number given in the column headed 'permanently out of work' is expressed as a proportion of it. The figure obtained by this procedure for the county as a whole is 18 percent. The results for Bradley (39%), Rapsgate (35%), Crowthorne and Minety (30%) and Brightwells Barrow (24%) are much higher.

[26] GA, Estcourt Papers.

Industrial by-employments had been an important element in the domestic economy of the labouring poor of town and country since the emergence of the cloth industry in the fourteenth and fifteenth centuries. Rudder made special note of the decline of woolstapling and woolcombing, which the 1768 listing shows to have been one of the most important employers of local labour. 'Forty or fifty years ago,' he wrote, 'the town enjoyed a considerable share in the wool-combing business', but it had since dwindled to nothing. 'The woolstapler', wrote Rudder, 'simplifies the clothier's business by supplying him with that particular sort of wool which his trade requires.'[27] The change of urban identity was not due to any loss of enterprise and vitality.[28] As clothmaking ebbed away, Cirencester's woolstaplers stepped in. They had not been 'confined to the [supply of] manufacturers of Gloucestershire, but were connected with [those of] Wiltshire, Somerset and Devon'. This source of income vanished in the later decades of the eighteenth century.

> A machine for spinning was brought into use in Yorkshire, and having found its way into these parts, almost totally superseded the former practice of spinning by the single thread [wrote Rudder]. This gave a fatal blow to the yarn business at Cirencester, and proves, we fear, an irreparable loss to the industrious inhabitants of the villages round about, to whom it had furnished constant employment and a comfortable maintenance.[29]

We need to know more about how these losses were experienced in the households of the tradesmen, farmers and 'poorer inhabitants' of the town and its surrounding villages. Did the Industrial Revolution marginalize and reduce the traditional enterprise and vigour of Cirencester's business community? Rudder made no bones about the attitude of the gentry: they were no help at all. 'Rendcombe, Compton, Stowell, the Ampneys, Driffield, Ashton, Somerford, Oaksey, Sapperton, Pinbury, Side and Miserden,' he explained, 'are all villages within the boundaries of a small circle round the town.' 'In most of these, within memory, the tradesmen found a valuable customer, the farmer a friend and adviser and the poor inhabitants hospitality' at the manor house. Now they preferred to fritter away their rentals

27 Rudder, *History of Cirencesteer*, 173–4.

28 Analysis of the 1768 listing yields one significant new industry: the edge-tool manufacture, which provided employment to 17 men and a whitesmith (a polisher and finisher of metal goods). Rudder commented that 'curriers knives' manufactured in the town 'find a market all over Europe and America'. Whether the seven blacksmiths were in any way connected to this speciality is not clear. They and the edge-tool makers were also meeting expanding demand from farmers in the surrounding villages, just now affected by various kinds of 'improvement' centred on parliamentary enclosures.

29 Rudder, *History of Cirencester*, 174.

and profits at fashionable spas and resorts like Cheltenham, Bath, Brighton and Newmarket.[30]

What was needed had not changed. The commune worked best, in all its dimensions, when town and country, farmers, tradesmen, 'the poor inhabitants', 'sojourners' and 'passingers', manor and vestry, were united. Uniting them was never an easy matter, but efforts were especially strong and successful in the fifteenth century and then, again, from 1570 to 1643. The challenge was always to persuade a community riven with gross class inequalities that those in authority had *all* their best interests at heart. As the case of Cirencester shows, some generations did better than others.

*

Throughout this book I have noted continuous interrelations between a strategic town, its region, nation and wider connections. The town's population may well seem, as Richard Jefferies put it, 'absurdly small'. We have seen that in Jefferies' sense, 'continuity of settlement' was exceptional. Yet in another, easily ignored but highly significant sense, the 'settlement' or 'commune' of Cirencester *was* continuous. The continuity of the commune was not inevitable. It was so, I have shown, because generation after generation of inhabitants actively and consciously maintained and participated in the buzzing networks of traffic and communications that were such distinctive features of late medieval and early modern England, an unusually integrated society. For these reasons, the study of medieval and early modern towns must be measured, not by their size but by their connections and networks. These related to and formed those deceptively simple contemporary contexts and identities: 'commune', 'country' and 'commonwealth'. The latter was sometimes used to mean 'nation' and, from the 1640s, 'republic'; but in its evaluative sense, I have suggested, 'commonwealth' also carried a moral and political charge that applied in every context: the notion that government was only acceptable if authorities were able to convince subjects of their dedication to the common good. Overt resistance and rebellion were not always practical when this was not so; but whenever it was, as we have seen, the phoenix arose.

The history of 'absurdly small' English towns, then, is not and cannot be simply 'local' history. It is an opportunity to study the responses of all ranks of society, living, permanently or temporarily, in often highly distinctive communities, to widely dispersed themes of social, economic, religious

30 'There the young, the gay, and unthinking of both sexes are initiated into the mysteries of gaming and intrigue; and to these may be attributed the numerous instances of incontinence, so much and so frequently exposed in our courts of justice; and the alienation of so many family estates as soon as their heirs come into possession': *ibid*, 179. One is minded of the novels of Jane Austen; Rudder's moralizing statements could easily be converted into hypotheses concerning the *mores* of the minor gentry of the Seven Hundreds in this period, and tested by archival research.

and, in both narrow and broader senses, constitutional history. To my mind the main importance of local studies is that they touch on *all* ranks. Most decisively, the heterogeneous, hierarchical commonalty emerges most fully in local records (for localities, of course, were where the work went on). This, clearly, is crucial, for the rise of the common people is what makes the modern epoch different from any that preceded it.

Bibliography

Primary Sources

Gloucestershire Archives

P86/1 Cirencester parish records: P86, IN 1/1: Cirencester Parish Registers: baptisms 1560–81, marriages 1560–81 and 1585–1637, burials 1560–80 and 1585–1637; IN 1/2: baptisms 1637–1781, marriages 1637–1776, burials 1637–1799

Vestry Minutes 1613–1886 (P86 VE 2/1)

MSS of the Reverend Joseph Kilner (P86/1 IN 6/3–4)

Index of Baptisms, Marriages, Burials 1560–1636/7

Inventory of Ornaments of the Lady Chapel in 1457 (MI 1)

Accounts of Master of (Cirencester) Workhouse, 1753–4 (P86a OV 2/1)

'Cirencester Seate Booke' (P86 CW4.1)

George Family Settlements (P86 CH 1.1–25)

View of Frankpledge for Borough of Cirencester, 1560 (GCL RV 79.7)

View of Frankpledge … 1564 (D1322/1)

Vill Court with View of Frankpledge (D1375/208)

Manor Court Roll 1550–2 (D1375)

Presentments of Butchers, Alesellers, Tanners, Glovers (D1375/496)

'Whitmore of Lower Slaughter', seventeenth-century Slaughter Hundred Court Rolls (D45)

'Benedict Grace Papers' (D8, Z1)

Coxwell Family Papers (D269)

'Strange Family' (D4871; D2957)

EN R. Strange 1970

'Heads of Evidence about the Mill Stream' (D674b, L1–2)

'Strange Family Pedigree' (D2930/3)

'Thomas Straunge for lands in Myntie. Release of tenement with lands called Scarletts in Myntie, with Thomas Straunge of Chesterton, Gent.' (D205A (1.2)

'The charter of King Philip and Queen Mary, 18 May Anno Regni 4' renewed as 'The charter of Queen Elizabeth, 8 February 1558 (dated 'AD 1576' with 'began 1558' in Elizabethan hand) (D 4590 1.2)

'Customs and constitutions of the Journeyman Weavers' ('by voluntary agreement' written on reverse in an eighteenth-century hand) (D4590 1/3)

Cirencester Weavers' Book (D4590 2/1)

Tewkesbury Borough Records ('Black Book')

Gloucester Diocesan Records
Wills
Inventories
GDR Volumes:
GDR 1552 GDR6.15
GDR 1554/110
GDR 1555/81
GDR 1556/29
GDR 1557/69
GDR 1557/81
GDR 1557/166
GDR 1557/150
GDR 1557/145
GDR 6.15, 30–1
GDR 17
GDR 20
GDR 26
GDR 20.57 1563 Visitation
GDR 381A ('Benson Survey', 1750)

Manuscripts, Transcripts and Photocopies
George Dutton's notes and transcripts on nonconformity in Gloucestershire (D2025)
E. Wraight, 'Religious Movements from the Reformation onwards, illustrated from the history of churches, chapels and other meeting places in the Vale of Berkeley' (D.2940/1)
Parochial list of dissenters' families from GDR 285B (1735) (D.1762/4)
Episcopal report of Gloucester Diocese, 1750 (D1762/7)

Avening parish register aggregates (Cambridge Group)
Stroud parish register aggregates (Cambridge Group)
Minchinhampton parish register aggregates (Cambridge Group)
Fairford parish register aggregates (Cambridge Group)
Winchcombe parish register aggregates (Cambridge Group)
Tetbury parish register aggregates (Cambridge Group)

Gloucestershire Subsidy Roll, 1 Edward III, 1327
1671 Hearth Tax (D383)
1381 Poll Tax (D1874/1)
Compton Census 1676 (Photocopy 377)

The National Archives (TNA)
PRO Stac 2/19/38, 36 Henry VIII
Gloucestershire Hearth Tax Assessment, Lady Day 1664 (E179/247/16)

Calendar of Close Rolls 4 Edward II
Calendar of Close Rolls, Richard II
Calendar of Patent Rolls, Richard II
Calendar of Patent Rolls, Edward III

Calendar of Patent Rolls, Henry IV
Calendar of Close Rolls, Henry IV
Calendar of Patent Rolls, Henry V

Abstract of Returns Relative to the Expense and Maintenance of the Poor (Commons Papers 1804)

Secondary Sources

Printed Sources, Books, Articles Relating to Cirencester

A letter sent to a worthy member of the House of Commons, concerning the Lord Shandois coming to Ciceter to execute the Commission of Array. Read in the House of Commons and ordered to be forthwith printed (London, 22 August 1642)

A particular relation of the Action Before Cyrencester (or Cycester), Taken in on Candlemass Day 1642 by Part of His Majesties Army Under the Conduct of His Highness Prince Rupert, written by an eye-witness (Oxford 1642): EEBO, 3

A relation of the taking of Ciceter in the county of Glocester, on Thursday, Febru. 2, 1642, by seven thousand of the cavaliers, under the command of prince Rupert, prince Maurice, the earls of Northampton, Carnarvon, Denbigh, and Cleveland, the lord Digby, lord Andevour, lord Wentworth, lord Taffe, lord Dillon, lieutenant-general Wilmot, sir John Byron, colonel Gerrard, colonel Kyrke, colonel Dutton, and captain Legge, and divers others. Sent to a friend in London, by one who was present at, and some days after the taking of it. Published because of many false reports that were in print concerning that businesse. Printed at London, February 20 1642/3: BL, Thomason Tracts 16: E90/7

A warning piece to all his majesties subjects of England, being the lamentable complaint of them that were brought prisoners from Cyrencester, being 1160 and odde, told in the view of all for their misguided zeale. Containing the motives by which they have been drawne into Rebellion (Oxford 1642/3): GCL 8326/47

Atkyns, Sir Robert, *The Ancient and Present State of Gloucestershire* (Gloucester 1712)

Austin, Roland, 'Philip Jones of Cirencester', *Trans BGAS* 44 (1922)

Baddeley, Welbore St Clair, A *History of Cirencester* (Cirencester 1924)

Baddeley, Welbore St Clair, A *Cotteswold Manor, being the History of Painswick* (Gloucester 1980)

Beecham, K.J., *History of Cirencester and the Roman City of Corinium* (1887, repr. Stroud, 1978)

Briggs, K., *The Folklore of the Cotswolds* (London 1975)

Brill, Edith, *Life and Tradition on the Cotswolds* (London 1973)

Chillenden, Edmund, *The Inhumanity of the King's prison-Keeper at Oxford, Or, a true relation of the most transcendent cruelties* (London 1642/3): GCL 23.8326, 10/1

Clutterbuck, R.H., 'State Papers Respecting Bishop Cheyney and the Recusants of the Diocese of Gloucester', *Trans BGAS* 5 (1881)

Corbet, John, A *true and impartiall History of the military government of the citie of Gloucester from the beginning of the civil war* (London 1647): BL Thomason 64: E.402 (4)

Domesday Book: A Complete Translation (Penguin, London 2003)

Elrington, C.R., 'Open Fields and Inclosure in the Cotswolds', *Proceedings of the Cotteswold Naturalist Field Club* 34 (1964)

Elrington, C.R., 'The Survey of Church Livings in Gloucestershire', *Trans BGAS* 83 (1964)

Evans, A.K.B., 'Cirencester's Early Church', *Trans BGAS* 107 (1989)

Evans, A.K.B., 'Cirencester Abbey: From Heyday to Dissolution', *Trans BGAS* 11 (1993)

Fallows, W.C., *The Brasses of Cirencester Parish Church* (Cirencester 1985)

Finberg, H.P.R., *Gloucestershire: an Illustrated History of the Landscape* (London 1955)

Finberg, H.P.R., *Gloucestershire Studies* (Leicester 1957)

Finberg, Jocelyn, *The Cotswolds* (London 1977)

Fisher, P.H., *Notes and Recollections of Stroud* (1871)

Fuller, E.A., 'Tenures of Land by the Customary Tenants in Cirencester', *Trans BGAS* 2 (1877–8)

Fuller, E.A., 'Cirencester: the Manor and the Town', *Trans BGAS* 10 (1884–5)

Fuller, E.A., 'Cirencester Guild Merchant', *Trans BGAS* 18 (1893–4)

Fuller, E.A., 'The Register of the Chapel of the Blessed Virgin Mary in the Parish Church of Cirencester', *Trans. BGAS* 18 (1893–4)

Gairdner, James, 'Bishop Hooper's Visitation of Gloucester', *Eng Hist Rev* 19 (1904)

Glanville, John, *Reports of Certain Cases Determined and Adjudged by the Commons in Parliament in the 21st and 22nd years of the Reign of King James the First, collected by John Glanville Esq., Sergeant at Law, then Chairman of the Committee of Privileges and Elections* (London 1775)

Glasscock, R.E., *The Lay Subsidy of 1334* (London 1975)

Hadfield, Charles and Q.M., *The Cotswolds: a New Study* (Newton Abbot 1973)

Haine, C., 'The Cloth Trade along the Painswick Stream', *GHS* 10 (1979)

Harmer, W.S., 'Cirencester Weavers' Company: a Review of its Records', *Wilts and Glos Standard* (29 December 1917)

Hart, Gwen, *A History of Cheltenham* (Oxford, 1965)

Hawkins, Brian, *Taming the Phoenix: Cirencester and the Quakers 1642–1686* (York 1998)

Heatley, H.R., 'Annals of Ampney Crucis: Amenities of Social Life in 1640', *Wilts Standard* (28 July 1912)

Hill, Canon Rowland, *Cirencester Parish Church – An Account of its History and Architecture* (Cheltenham 1985)

Hilton, R.H., 'Winchcombe Abbey and the Manor of Sherborne', in H.P.R. Finberg, *Gloucestershire Studies* (London 1955)

Hilton, R.H., *A Medieval Society: the West Midlands at the End of the Thirteenth Century* (London 1966)

Hodgson, Eric, *A History of Tetbury* (Gloucester 1978)

Hoyle, R.W. (ed.), *The Military Survey of Gloucestershire, 1522* (Stroud 1993)

Jefferies, Richard, 'History of Cirencester', *Wilts and Gloucestershire Standard* (12 March–29 October 1870)

Jefferies, Richard, *Hodge and His Masters* (London 1880)

Jefferies, Richard, 'Cirencester Weavers Company: A Review of its Records', *Wilts and Gloucestershire Standard* (29 Dec. 1917 & 12 Jan. 1918): GCL 10600/3

Jenkins, R.W., 'The Cirencester Contest', *Trans BGAS* 92 (1973)

Jones, Philip, *Certaine Sermons preached of late at Ciceter in the countie of Glocester, upon a portion of the first Chapter of the Epistle of James: wherein the two several states, of the riche and poore man are compared and examined, the differences in quality, and duety betwixt them shewed... Penned at the earnest request of divers well affected inhabitants of the place: and now published as well for the use of others, as for the further profit of that particular congregation. By Philip Jones, Preacher of the word of God in the same Towne. Allowed by authoritie. Imprinted at London by T.D. for Thomas Butter 1588* (London 1588, copy at GCL)

Kimball, E.G. (ed.), 'Gloucestershire Peace Rolls', *Trans BGAS* 62 (1940)

Kingsley, Nicholas, *The County Houses of Gloucestershire*, Vol. 1: *1500–1660* (Cheltenham 1989)

Maclean, Sir John, 'Chantry Certificates, Gloucestershire', *Trans BGAS* 8 (1883–4)

Maclean, Sir John, *Calendar of Sherborne Muniments* (1889)

Maclean, Sir John, and Heane, W.C., *The Visitation of the County of Gloucester in 1623* (London 1885)

McGrath, Patrick, 'Gloucestershire and the Counter-Reformation in the Reign of Elizabeth', *Trans BGAS* 88 (1969–70)

Mayhew, N. and Viner, D.J., 'A Civil War Coin Hoard from Weston Sub Edge, Gloucestershire', *Trans BGAS* 105 (1987)

Morris, Colin, 'A Note on the Troubles under King John', *Trans BGAS* 87 (1968)

Origo, Iris, *The Merchant of Prato: Francesco di Marco Datini* (Harmondsworth 1963)

Percival, A.C. and Sheils, W.J., 'A Survey of the Diocese of Gloucester, 1603', in *An Ecclesiastical Miscellany*, BGAS Records Section XI (1976)

Perry, R., 'The Gloucestershire Woollen Industry, 1100–1690', *Trans BGAS* 66 (1947)

The Petititon of the Inhabitants of Cyrencester, printed at Oxford February 28th, 1642, repr. in Beecham, *History of Cirencester*, 299

Playne, A.T., *A History of the Parishes of Minchinhampton and Avening* (Gloucester 1915)

Porter, S., 'The Biography of a Parliamentarian Soldier', *Trans BGAS* 108 (1990), 131–4

Powell, K.G., 'The Social Background to the Reformation in Gloucestershire', *Trans BGAS* 92 (1973)

Price, F.D., 'The Commission for Ecclesiastical Causes for the Dioceses of Bristol and Gloucester, 1574', *Trans BGAS* 59 (1937)

Price, F.D., 'Gloucester Diocese under Bishop Hooper', *Trans BGAS* 60 (1938)

Price, F.D., 'The Administration of Gloucester Diocese 1547–1579', B. Letters, Keble College, Oxford, 1939

Price, F.D., 'Bishop Bullingham and Chancellor Blackleech: A Diocese Divided', *Trans BGAS* 91 (1972)

Price, F.D. (ed.), *The Commission for Ecclesiastical Causes Within the Dioceses of Bristol and Gloucester*, BGAS Records Section (Gateshead 1973)

Ramsay, G.D., 'The Distribution of the Cloth Industry in 1561–2', *Eng Hist Rev* 57: 227 (July 1942)

Reece, Richard, 'The Abbey of St Mary, Cirencester', *Trans BGAS* 81 (1962)

Reece, Richard, and Catling, Christopher, *Cirencester: Development and Buildings*, *British Archaeological Reports* 12 (Oxford 1975)

Ross, C.D., *The Cartulary of Cirencester Abbey*, Vol. 1 (London 1964)

Rudder, Samuel, *A New History of Gloucestershire* (Cirencester 1779)

Rudder, Samuel, *The History of the Town of Cirencester*, 2nd edn (Cirencester 1800)

Rudge, Thomas, *The History of the County of Gloucester* (2 vols, Gloucester 1803)

Simpson, J.J., 'The Wool Trade and the Woolmen of Gloucestershire', *Trans BGAS* 53 (1931)

Smyth, John, *The Names and Surnames of all the Able and Sufficient Men in Body fit for his Majesty's Service in the Wars, in the Month of August, 1608, in the Sixth Year of the Reign of James the First*, ed. Sir John Maclean (Gloucester 1902)

Stenton, D.M. (ed.), *Rolls of Justice in Eyre (Gloucestershire, Warwickshire and Staffordshire 1221, 1222)* (Selden Society, London 1940)

Tawney, A.J. and R.H., 'An Occupational Census of the Seventeenth Century', *Econ Hist Rev* 5:1 (1934–5)

'Transactions in the Fairford District', *Trans BGAS* 22 (1899)

VCH Gloucestershire, Vol. 2: *Ecclesiastical History etc.*, ed. William Page (London 1907)

VCH Gloucestershire, Vol. 9: *The Northleach Area of the Cotswolds*, ed. Carol Davidson, A.J.C. Jurica and Elizabeth Williamson (London 2001)

VCH Gloucestershire, Vol. 11: *The Stroud Valleys*, ed. N.M. Herbert (London 1976)

Verey, David, *Cotswold Churches* (London 1971)

Verey, David, *Gloucestershire*, Vol. 1: *The Cotswolds* (London 1971)

Viner, David, 'A Civil War Coin Hoard from Ashbrook, Ampney St Mary', *Trans BGAS* 110 (1992)

Warminster, A.R., *Civil War, Interregnum and Restoration in Gloucestershire, 1640–1672* (London 1997)

Williams, W.R., *Parliamentary History of the County of Gloucester,... 1213–1898* (privately printed, 1898)

Willis, Browne, *Notitia Parliamentaria: or, an history of the counties, cities and boroughs, containing an account of the first returns and incorporations... that send Members to Parliament* (London 1750)

Wilson, Beckles (ed.), *Life and Letters of James Wolfe* (New York 1909)

Wyatt, John, 'Men and Armour for Gloucestershire in 1608', *GHS* 4 (1970)

Wyatt, John, 'Occupations and Physique in 1608', *GHS* 6 (1972)

Wyatt, John, 'Trades and Occupations in Gloucester, Tewkesbury and Cirencester in 1608', *GHS* 7 (1973)

Wyatt, John, 'How Reliable is Men and Armour?', *GHS* 9 (1978)

Wyatt, John, 'Industry in Gloucestershire in 1608', *GHS* 10 (1979)

Zweigman, L.J., 'The Role of the Gentleman in County Government and Society: the Gloucestershire Gentry, 1625–1649', Ph.D. thesis, McGill University (1987)

Other Printed Sources and Secondary Works

Appleby, Andrew, *Famine in Tudor and Stuart England* (Liverpool 1978)

Bossy, John, 'The Character of Elizabethan Catholicism', in T.H. Aston (ed.) *Crisis in Europe 1560–1660* (London 1965)

Bossy, John, *Christianity in the West 1400–1700* (Oxford 1985)

Brenner, Robert, *Merchants and Revolution: Commercial Change, Political Conflict and London's Overseas Traders, 1550–1653* (Cambridge 1993)

Britnell, R.H., *Growth and Decline in Colchester, 1300–1525* (Cambridge 1986)

Calder, Isabel McBeath, *Activities of the Puritan Faction of the Church of England 1625–33* (London 1957)

Campbell, Bruce M.S., 'Nature as Historical Protagonist: Environment and Society in Preindustrial England', *Econ Hist Rev* 63:2 (May 2010)

Clark, P. and Hosking, J., *Population Estimates of English Small Towns 1550–1851* (Leicester 1993)
Collinson, Patrick, 'Episcopy and Reform in England in the Later Sixteenth Century', Ch. 6 of Collinson, *Godly People: Essays on English Protestantism and Puritanism* (London 1983)
Collinson, Patrick, 'The Elizabethan Church and the New Religion', in
Christopher Haigh (ed.), *The Reign of Elizabeth I* (Basingstoke 1987)
Collinson, Patrick, *The Birthpangs of Protestant England* (London 1988)
Cressy, David, *England on Edge: Crisis and Revolution 1640–1642* (Oxford 2006)
Cross, Claire, *The Royal Supremacy in the Elizabethan Church* (London 1969)
Dent, Emma, *Annals of Winchcombe and Sudeley* (London 1877)
Dewar, Mary, *Sir Thomas Smith: A Tudor Intellectual in Office* (London 1984)
Duffy, Eamon, *The Stripping of the Altars: Traditional Religion in England, 1400–1580* (New Haven and London 1992)
Duffy, Eamon, *The Voices of Morebath: Reformation and Rebellion in an English Village* (New Haven and London 2001)
Duffy, Eamon, 'Religious Belief', in Rosemary Horrox and W. Mark Ormrod (eds), *A Social History of England* (Cambridge 2006)
Dyer, Christopher, *Lords and Peasants in a Changing Society: the Bishopric of Worcester, 680–1540* (Cambridge 1980)
Dyer, Christopher, *Standards of Living in the Later Middle Ages: Social Change in England, c.1200–1520* (Cambridge 1989)
Dyer, Christopher, *Making a Living in the Middle Ages: the People of Britain 850–1520* (London 2003)
Fisher, F.J., 'Some Experiments in Company Organization in the Early Seventeenth Century', *Econ Hist Rev* 4:2 (April 1933)
Fletcher, Anthony, *The Outbreak of the English Civil War* (New York and London 1981)
French, Henry, *The Middle Sort of People in Provincial England* (Oxford 2007)
Fryde, E.B., *Peasants and Landlords in Later Medieval England* (Stroud 1996)
Given Wilson, Chris (trans.), *Chronicles of the Revolution, 1397–1400* (Manchester 1993)
Grassby, Richard, *The Business Community of Seventeenth-Century England* (Cambridge 1995)
Haigh, Christopher, 'Anticlericalism and the English Reformation', in Haigh (ed.), *The English Reformation Revised* (Cambridge 1987)
Haigh, Christopher (ed.), *The English Reformation Revised* (Cambridge 1987)
Haigh, Christopher, *English Reformations: Religion, Politics, and Society under the Tudors* (Oxford 1993)
Haigh, Christopher, *The Plain Man's Pathways to Heaven: Kinds of Christianity in Post-Reformation England, 1570–1640* (Oxford 2007)
Hill, Christopher, *Society and Puritanism in Pre-Revolutionary England* (London 1964)
Hill, Christopher, *Puritanism and Revolution* (London 1968)
Hill, Christopher, *The World Turned Upside-Down: Radical Ideas during the English Revolution* (London 1972)
Hill, Christopher, 'From Grindal to Laud', in Hill, *Religion and Politics in 17th Century England* (Brighton 1986)
Hill, Christopher, *Antichrist in Seventeenth-Century England* (London 1990)
Hilton, R.H., *Class Conflict and the Crisis of Feudalism* (London 1990)

Hilton, R.H., *Towns in Feudal Society* (Cambridge 1992)
Hindle, Steve, 'Persuasion and Protest in the Caddington Common Enclosure Dispute, 1635–1639', *Past and Present* 158 (Feb. 1998)
Hindle, Steve, *The State and Social Change in Early Modern England, 1550–1640* (Basingstoke 2000)
Hindle, Steve, 'Dearth, Fasting and Alms: the Campaign for General Hospitality in Late Elizabethan England', *Past and Present* 172 (Aug. 2001)
Hirst, David, *The Representative of the People: Voters and Voting in England under the Stuarts* (Cambridge 1975)
Holstun, James, *Ehud's Dagger: Class Struggle and the English Revolution* (London and New York 2000)
Hoyle, R.W., 'Taxation and the Mid-Tudor crisis', *Econ Hist Rev*, New Series, 51:4 (Nov. 1998)
Hughes, Ann, *Politics, Society and Civil War in Warwickshire, 1620–1660* (Cambridge 1987)
Kirby, Ethyn W., 'The Lay Feoffees: a Study in Militant Puritanism', *Journal of Modern History* XIV (March 1942)
Knowles, David, *The Religious Orders in England* (Cambridge 1950)
Knowles, David, *The Religious Orders in England*, Vol. 2 (Cambridge 1955)
Knowles, David, *The Monastic Order in England … 940–1216* (Cambridge 1963)
Lang, R.G. (ed.) *Two Tudor Subsidy Rolls for the City of London* (London 1993)
Levine, David, *At the Dawn of Modernity: Biology, Culture and Material Life in Europe after the Year 1000* (London 2001)
Levine, David, and Wrightson, Keith, *The Making of an Industrial Society: Whickham 1560–1765* (Oxford 1991)
Litzenberger, Caroline, *The English Reformation and the Laity: Gloucestershire 1540–1580* (Cambridge 1997)
Maitland, F.W., 'The Corporation Sole', *Law Quarterly Review* 16 (1900)
Mann, J. deL., *The Cloth Industry in the West of England, 1640–1880* (Oxford 1971)
Manning, R.B., *Religion and Society in Elizabethan Sussex: a Study of the Enforcement of the Religious Settlement, 1558–1603* (Leicester 1969)
Manning, Brian, *The English People and the English Revolution* (Harmondsworth 1978)
Miller, Edward, and Hatcher, John, *Medieval England: Towns, Commerce and Crafts, 1086–1348* (London 1995)
Mollat, M. and Wolff, P., *The Popular Revolutions of the Late Middle Ages* (London 1973)
Muldrew, Craig, *The Economy of Obligation: The Culture of Credit and Social Relations in Early Modern England* (Basingstoke 1998)
Patterson, Orlando, *Freedom*, Vol. 1: *Freedom on the Making of Western Culture* (New York 1991)
Perkins, William, *A Treatise on the Vocation or Calling of men*, in M.J. Kitch, *Capitalism and the Reformation* (London 1969)
Pitt-Rivers, Julian, *People of the Sierras* (Chicago 1954)
Plumb, J.H., *The Growth of Political Stability in England, 1675–1725* (Harmondsworth 1967)
Postles, David, *Naming the People of England, c.1100–1350* (Cambridge 2006)
Postles, David, 'Religion and Uncertainty in Four Midlands Urban Centres', *Midland History* 34:1 (Spring 2009)

Postles, David, 'The Politics of Diffuse Authority in an Early Modern Small Town', *Canadian Journal of History/Annales Canadienne* (Spring 2010)

Postles, David, 'Relations between the Laity and the Parochial Clergy during the Henrician Reformation: the Case of the North and West Midlands', *Nottingham Medieval Studies* 54 (2010)

Postles, David, 'The Decline of Late Medieval Monasticism in its Sociological and Anthropological Context', unpubl. MS (courtesy of the author)

Poyntz, Nick, 'The Attack on Lord Chandos: Popular Politics at Cirencester in 1642', *Midland History* 35:1 (Spring 2010)

Prestwich, Menna, *Politics and Profits under the Early Stuarts: the Career of Lionel Cranfield Earl of Middlesex* (Oxford 1966)

Ramsay, G.D., *The English Woollen Cloth Industry 1500–1750* (London 1982)

Rollison, David, *The Local Origins of Modern Society: Gloucestershire 1500–1800* (London and New York 1992)

Rollison, David, 'Exploding England: the Dialectics of Mobility and Settlement in Early Modern England', *Social History* 24:1 (January 1999)

Rollison, David, 'Only the Poor Will be Saved: a Theology for the Artisans of Elizabethan England', in Ellen Warne and Charles Zika (eds), *God, the Devil and a Millennium of Christian Culture* (Melbourne 2005)

Rollison, David, *A Commonwealth of the People: Popular Politics and England's Long Social Revolution, 1066–1649* (Cambridge 2010)

Ruigh, Robert E., *The Parliament of 1624: Politics and Foreign Policy* (Harvard 1971)

Runciman, W.G., *Social Science and Political Theory* (Cambridge 1969)

Sacks, D.H., *The Widening Gate: Bristol and the Atlantic Economy 1450–1700* (Berkeley 1991)

Sackville-West, Vita, *Berkeley Castle* (n.d.)

Saul, Nigel, *Knights and Esquires: The Gloucestershire Gentry in the Fourteenth Century* (Oxford 1981)

Seyer, Samuel, *Memoirs Historical and Topographical of Bristol and its Neighbourhood* (Bristol 1821)

Sharp, Buchanon, *In Contempt of all Authority: Rural Artisans and Riot in the West of England, 1586–1660* (Berkeley 1980)

Sharpe, Pamela, *Population and Society in an East Devon Parish: Reproducing Colyton, 1540–1840* (Exeter 2002)

Shaw-Taylor, Leigh, and Wrigley, E.A., 'The Occupational Structure of England, c.1750–1871: A preliminary Report', Cambridge Group for the History of Population and Social Structure (Department of Geography, University of Cambridge, 2006, 2008)

Slack, Paul, *The Impact of Plague in Tudor and Stuart England* (London 1985)

Smith, Alan G.R., *The Emergence of a Nation State: The Commonwealth of England 1529–1660* (New York 1984)

Smith, Richard, 'Plagues and Peoples: the Long Demographic Cycle, 1250–1670', in Paul Slack and Ryk Ward (eds) *The Peopling of Britain: The Shaping of a Human Landscape* (Oxford 2002)

Smith, Sir Thomas, *A Discourse of the Commonweal of this Realm of England, attributed to Sir Thomas Smith* [1549], ed. Mary Dewar (Charlottesville 1969)

Smith, Sir Thomas, *De Republica Anglorum* [1560s], ed. Mary Dewar (Cambridge 1982)

Stephens, W.B., 'The Cloth Exports of the Provincial Ports', *Econ Hist Rev*, Second Series, 22:2 (1969)

Stone, Lawrence, *The Family, Sex and Marriage in England, 1500–1800* (London 1977)

Stratford, Joseph, *Great and Good Men of Gloucestershire* (Gloucester 1867)

Tawney, R.H., 'The Rise of the Gentry 1558–1640', *Econ Hist Rev* XI (1941)

Thirsk, Joan, *The Rural Economy of England: Collected Essays* (London 1984)

Tittler, Robert, 'The End of the Middle Ages in the English Country Town', *Sixteenth Century Journal* 23:4 (Winter 1987)

Walter, John, 'The Social Economy of Dearth in Early modern England', in J. Walter and R. Schofield (eds), *Famine, Disease and the Social Order in Early Modern Society* (Cambridge 1989)

Walter, John, *Understanding Popular Violence in the English Revolution: the Colchester Plunderers* (Cambridge 2001)

Walter, John, *Crowds and Popular Politics in Early Modern England* (Manchester 2006)

Walter, John, 'The English People and the English Revolution Revisited', *History Workshop Journal* 61 (2006)

Waugh, S.L., 'The Profits of Violence: the Minor Gentry in the Rebellion of 1321–2 in Gloucestershire and Herefordshire', *Speculum* 52 (1977)

Withington, Phil, 'Views from the Bridge: Revolution and Restoration in Seventeenth-Century York', *Past and Present* (2001)

Withington, Phil, *The Politics of Commonwealth: Citizens and Freemen in Early Modern England* (Cambridge 2005)

Wood, Andy, *The Politics of Social Conflict: the Peak Country 1520–1770* (Cambridge 1999)

Wood, Andy, *Riot, Rebellion and Popular Politics in Early Modern England* (Basingstoke 2002)

Wood, Andy, *The 1549 Rebellions and the Making of Early Modern England* (Cambridge 2007)

Wrightson, Keith, *English Society, 1580–1680* (London 1982)

Wrightson, Keith, 'Estates, Degrees and Sorts: Changing Perceptions of Society in Tudor and Stuart England', in P. Corfield (ed.), *Language, History and Class* (Oxford 1991), 30–52

Wrightson, Keith, 'Sorts of People in Tudor and Stuart England' in Jonathan Barry and Christopher Brooks (eds), *The Middling Sort of People: Culture, Society and Politics in England, 1550–1800* (Basingstoke 1994)

Wrightson, Keith, 'The Politics of the Parish in Early Modern England', in P. Griffiths, A. Fox and S. Hindle (eds), *The Experience of Authority in Early Modern England* (London 1996), 10–46

Wrightson, Keith, *Earthly Necessities: Economic Lives in Early Modern Britain* (New Haven 2000)

Wrightson, Keith, and Levine, David, *Poverty and Piety in an English Village: Terling, 1525–1700* (New York 1979)

Wrigley, E.A., 'Country and Town: the Primary, Secondary and Tertiary Peopling of England in the Early Modern Period', in Paul Slack and Ryk Ward (ed.), *The Peopling of Britain: the Shaping of a Human Landscape*, (Oxford 2002)

Wrigley, E.A., 'The Transition to an Advanced Organic Economy: Half a Millennium of English Agriculture', *Econ Hist Rev*, 59:3 (August 2006)

Wylie, J., *History of England Under Henry the Fourth* (London 1884)

Index

Acelin the Priest (11th century), 19
America, North, colonies, ix, 121, 139 n19, 148, 184, 219
Anabaptists, 109–10, 182, 201, 253
Apprenticeship, 167, 209, 241
Aristotle on constitutions, 13–14, 189–90
Arminian, 221–4
Array, Commission of (1642), 225–29
Artisans, *see* Ranks, Social
Atkyns, Sir Robert, (1647–1711), 212–3, 217, 246–7
Awakening, Great, 148

Bagendon, 1
Bailiff, *see* Manor
Bastardy, 77, 173–4
Bathurst family, 246
Becket, Thomas, cult of, 65–6, 78, 80–1, 91
Berkeley, family, 30, 51, 55–6, 59, 74, 140 n20, 150, 159, 193, 215, 218, 226–7
'Better sort', 10–11 and n.13, 177, 205, 209, 251
  See Class
Biological regime, 7
  See Mortality, Crises of
Borough of Cirencester, 9, 20–21
  Corporate Traditions, 21, 45–6
  Parliamentary, 211
Bossy, John, 68, 84, 98
Bristol, 3, 30, 36, 40, 98, 133, 233
Brydges family, lords Chandos of Sudeley, 159–61, 168, 192, 218, 225–30, 238–40
Businessmen, business community, 11, 72–3, 118, 137, 191–207, 219, 265

Calvin, Jean, 'Calvinism', 13, 108–9, 195, 203–4
Capitalism, 35, 84, 91, 167, 187–8, 198–200, 204, 257
  Communal, 11, 196–200, 204
Catholics,
  'Papist', 100, 109–113, 118, 133, 177, 254
  'Survivalist', 84–6, 95–102, 111–13
  'Vernacular', 64–88
Chantries, 53, 64–88
Cheltenham, 3, 100
Church, St John the Baptist, Cirencester parish, 8, 70–1
  Altars, 74–8
  Bells, 80, 206
  Books, 75
  Disrepair, 109
  Finances, 9, 11, 64–88, 190–205
  Jesus, brotherhood of, 76
  Lights & torches, 75–81
  Memorials, 73–4, 258
  Porch, 81
  Rebuilding of, 64–88,
  Rood, 77–8, 83
  Seating, 100, 206
  Singing, 76–77, 82
  St Mary Chapel, 64–5, 86
  Treasurers, 83, 190–206
  Trinity Chapel, 66–7, 70, 73–5, 193
    See parish, institutions of
Class, classes, 3, 5, 39, 53, 65, 93, 121–2, 135–6, 160–1, 177, 183, 185–6, 204, 212, 229, 238–40, 244, 256–7, 266
  Conflict, struggle, 3, 73,118, 137, 192, 225, 244
  Language, 134
  See Ranks, Social; Employers, valorization of
Cloth, woollen,
  Manufacture, 37, 47, 71–2, 79–83, 120–2, 126–7, 164–67, 175, 248, 263
  Trade, 37, 47, 73–8, 120, 125, 131, 248
Collinson, Patrick, 68, 78
'Common people', 3, 229, 241, 267

Commonalty,
Classes of, 23, 33–43, 211, 214, 266
'Third Estate', 17–19, 23, 52–3, 62–3, 119
Commerce, *see* Traffic
Commission for Ecclesiastical Causes, 110–18
Commonwealth ideology, 3, 11–15, 39, 67, 71, 93, 137, 139, 145–6, 165, 169–70, 192–3, 203, 209, 213–14, 266
Commune, communal, 'communalism', 1–3, 5–6, 8–9, 23–24, 86, 88, 103, 191, 196, 218 247–8, 252
'New communalism', 11, 189–224, 240
Communications, 1–5
See Traffic
Constitution, constitutional, 4, 10–12, 26, 46, 57, 249, 267
Corbet, John, 228–9, 241
Cosyn, John, (d.1403), 53–65
'Country', 13, 208
As collective identity, 79, 208, 249
Seven Hundreds of Cirencester as, 2–3
Cowley, Abraham, 245
Coxwell, John, 11, 127, 145, 168, 192–205

Dependency, notions of, 91
See Independency
Dutton family, 158–61
Dissent, Dissenters, 87, 103–18, 245, 252–4
'Nonconformists', 254–5
Domesday Book, 17–18
Duffy, Eamon, 68–9, 76
Dugdale, William, 245
Dutton family, 213, 218

Elders, 22–3, 145
Employers, valorization of, 192, 198, 206–7, 209–10, 237, 240–3
Enclosure
Parliamentary, 251, 258, 264
Piecemeal, 28–9, 56
Erastians, 221–4

Family, 179, 181, 185–6, 202–3
Feoffees for Impropriations, 11, 219–20, 239
Fettiplace, Giles, 230 n14, 235
Florence, Italy, 42, 47
Fortescue, Sir John, 187
French, Henry R., 133, 149, 217–18
Friend, John, 244

Gambling, 104
George family, 94, 98–101, 108, 111, 117, 127, 134–6, 190, 218–19, 223–4, 232, 235, 249–50
Gloucester, City of, 1, 36, 115, 133, 160, 233–4
Gloucester, diocese of, 3, 103–9, 118–19, 146–7
Gregory, Alexander, 219–20, 235, 236, 238–9, 244, 254
Guild Merchant, 9, 65, 71, 86, 117, 128, 134–7
Guns, gun-culture, 7, 153–4, 232–35
Gurney, Ivor, 171

Haig, Christopher, 68, 110
Highways, 1, 74–5, 83, 100
Maintenance, *see* Parish, Surveyors of the Highways
Hill, Christopher, 106, 114, 175
Hill, Rowland, 67
Hilton, R.H., 29
Hindle, Steve, 12, 189 n1
Hooper, John, bishop of Gloucester, 86, 97, 103–8, 123
Hoskins, W.G., 173
Household, 41, 93, 139, 163–70, 176, 178–85, 217, 255–7
See Elders; Family; Independency; Parliamentary Franchise
Hoyle, R.W., 89

Ideas, popular, 137–8
Immigrants, immigration, *see* Mobility, geographical
Independency, notions of, 11, 25, 91, 93, 139, 162–70, 181–3, 224, 232
See Employers; Household
Inhabitants, Inhabitancy, 1, 11, 18–19, 23–4, 43, 49, 86, 134, 162, 169, 190, 215–17, 249–50, 258–60
Inns, taverns, alehouses, 47, 50–1, 59, 100, 104, 145, 152, 223–4, 226, 249

Jesus, images and representations of, 66, 69, 76, 83, 85, 142–4
Jones, Philip, 129, 138–48, 175–6
Journeymen, 166–7, 183
Jefferies, Richard, 106 n9, 180, 247–53

Kip, Johannes, 246, 253
Knowles, David, 17

Labourers, 155–6, 177, 180, 263

Langland, William, 69, 85, 243
Language, vernacular, 51–2, 66
Levellers, 162
Levine, David, 55
Literacy, 166, 183, 204, 222–3
    Reading, 141
Lollards, 51, 66,
London, traffic with, 3, 36, 79, 110, 124, 166–7, 209, 217

Macintosh, Marjorie, 12
Magistracy, 227
Manor of Cirencester, institutions of,
    Bailiff, 31, 46, 96, 103, 133–4, 216
    Constable, 133–4, 174
    Estate, 96
    Labour services, 19, 23, 58, 82–3
    Lordship, 6–7
        Bathhurst, Allen, 246
        Danvers, Sir John, 95, 118
        Kingston, Anthony, 95
        Poole, Henry, 196, 235
        St Mary's Abbey, 17–32, 44–49
        Thomas Seymour, 95–6
        See Atkyns, Sir Robert
    Sergeant, 31, 106, 110
    Wardsmen, 133
    Other, 133
Manufacturing industry, 160
    See Cloth
Market, local, 22–3, 35
Marner, Philip, 11, 140, 145, 192–7
Marx, Karl, 7, 39, 187
Master family, 196, 215, 227–9
Memory, social, 5, 45–6, 55–6, 64
Mercantilism, 87
Millenarianism, prophecying, 118, 137, 141, 145, 195, 243
Mobility, Geographical,
    Immigrants, immigration, 5, 11, 22–23, 38, 40–1, 121, 171–88, 230
    Motivation for, 174
    'Passingers', 133, 171, 206, 247
    Quotidian, 171–2, 181
    Sojourners, 22, 35, 133, 259 n.17
    Strangers, 173, 185
    See Journeymen
Mobility, Social, 37, 71, 91, 97, 145, 167, 203, 257
Monarchs, Monarchy, 142
    Ideal forms, 14, 25, 30–1, 38, 65–67, 219, 232, 239–42, 249–51
    Charles I, 160–1, 211–12, 223, 239–41, 253
    Edward II, 26, 30, 57, 65
    Edward III, 34, 211
    Edward VI, 103
    Elizabeth I, 102, 106, 212
    Henry I, 20
    Henry II, 20, 44
    Henry III, 21
    Henry IV, 51–2, 54–7
    Henry V, 62
    Henry VIII, 18, 94–6, 187
    James I, 211–12
    John, 22, 44
    Mary, 97
    Richard I, 20, 44
    Richard II, 50, 57, 65–6
More, Sir Thomas, 83, 187
Mortality, crises of, 7, 38, 40–1, 94, 119, 124–32, 173, 235–8
Mortmain, 29
Munden, John, Tailor, 178–85
Music, Musicians, 123, 186–7

Names, personal, 29, 62–3
Nicholas the Proctor, 28–9, 44
Nottingham family, 61, 71, 76, 84

Paine, Elizabeth and Hodgkinson, 206–7, 209, 235, 242–24
Painswick, 4, 154, 164, 168, 213
Parish, 9, 66, 71, 86–7, 104, 189–207
    Beadle, 174–5
    Chest, 206
    Churchwardens, 80–83, 103–6, 112, 124, 174, 190, 197, 205–6
    Minister, Priest, 1, 11, 24, 45, 64–88, 104–8, 112–14
    Surveyors of the Highways, 83
    Vestry, 10, 77, 112, 169, 176, 192–207
Parliament, Commons House of, 11, 106
    Constituencies, 160
    Elections, 57, 161, 213–17
    Electorates, expansion of, 208–24
    Franchises, 11, 117, 133, 208
    Prerogatives of, 211, 226, 232
Patriarchs, patriarchy, 23, 176, 190–207
Perkins, William, 13,
Pesthouse, Stow on the Wold, 172
Plumb, J.H., 209
Poole family, 110, 115–17, 158–61, 168, 196, 215, 218, 235
Poor, definitions and ambiguities, 8–9, 15, 32, 44, 109, 110, 139–42, 185, 256–7
Poor, relief of, 66, 72, 75–6, 80, 84, 93, 169, 196–7, 201, 241, 263–4

Employment of, 206–7
Workhouse, 258
Poor, 'undeserving', 138, 170, 174
Population,
Local, 38, 120–132, 212, 231, 258–9
National, 26, 119–20
Postles, David, ix–x, 18
Preachers, preaching, 10, 13–15, 196, 200, 204–5, 241
Predestinarianism, 140
Price, F. Douglas, 111
Proctor, institution of, 28, 64, 137
Protestants, Protestantism, 68, 103–18, 141, 254
Congregational, 9, 222, 253
Evangelical, 103, 133–48, 222
Limitations of wills as evidence for, 97
Sects, denominations, 9, 244–5, 253–4
Puritans, Puritanism, 193

Rank, middle, 161
Ranks, Social, 142, 149–70, 221–2, 238–9, 244
Artisans. 10, 41, 91–2, 109, 118, 137–40, 152, 169, 217
'Barony', 31, 51–2, 149, 152, 168, 225
Esquires, 149, 152, 159–61, 213
Gentlemen, 30–32, 97, 99, 042, 149, 152, 158–61, 168, 213, 255–6, 265–6
Husbandmen, 152, 162–3
Knights, 31, 149, 152, 159–61, 213, 225
Merchants, 37, 41–2, 50, 72, 74, 97, 167
'*Proletarii*', 41, 90, 93, 149, 153
Servants, 152, 167–8
Sir Thomas Smith on, 149–50
Yeomen, 74, 101, 108, 149, 152, 190, 227
Rebellion, resistance, riot and, 12–13, 22, 30–1, 48–9, 57, 69, 160, 239, 252, 266
Recession, economic, 94, 128, 191
Reformation, 9, 17, 67–8, 103–118, 130, 210
Dissolution of Abbey, 69, 84, 95
Dissolution of Chantries, 84
Renaissance, 47
Resurrection, 195, 203
Revolution, 65, 148, 191, 243
Industrial, 265
Rich, excoriation of, 142–47
Roberts, John, 235, 245
Rudder, Samuel, i, 65, 74, 258
Rupert, prince, 231–7
Rycardes, Robert, 81–4

Sapperton, 4
Saxton, Christopher, 4, 180
Schools, 24
Selwyn, Giles, 108–9, 117, 137
Shopkeepers, 5, 112, 118, 135, 137, 157, 261
Smith, Sir Thomas, 3, 13–15, 149–50, 212
Smyth of Nibley, John, 3, 150, 182
Soldiers, trained, 150–1
Southampton, 3, 42
Strange, Robert, 9, 84, 95–102, 134–5, 190
Stroud, 4, 7, 79, 154, 167, 237
Stroudwater Valleys, 79–81, 126, 130, 152, 160, 163, 168, 179
Sudeley, castle, 233–4, 239
Surnames, 29–30

Tawney, A.J. and R.H., 150, 122, 162–5
Tawney, William, 171–2
Taxation, 7
Classes, 33–43, 89–94, 185–6, 254–7
Tewkesbury, 3–4, 90–1, 229–30, 233
Thirsk, Joan, 123
Townsend, Theophila, 245
Tradition, 114
Traffic, 1, 26, 33, 36, 40, 123, 248, 266
Tyndale, William, 69, 83, 243
Tyranny, theory of, 14–15

Unemployment, 125–6, 191, 264–5

Vestry, *see* parish
Violence, 26–8, 30–1, 49, 50 2, 54–7, 69, 85, 99–100, 129–30, 207, 222–3, 228–9, 232–43
Vocationalism, 13, 193–6, 204

War, civil, 50, 207, 225–45
Wealth, distribution of, 7, 33–43, 89–94, 177
Weavers' Guild, 61, 71, 80–1, 131, 165–6, 175–6, 241, 263
Wilson, Thomas, 10, 153, 168
Winchcombe, 3, 226–7, 233
Women, 19, 69, 75, 83–4, 78–81, 84, 100–3, 106 n.9, 110, 112–16, 164, 171, 242–3, 245, 257
Wool,
Shearing, 158

Sorting and Combing, 259, 263–5
Spinning, mechanical, 265
Trade, 34–6, 42, 47, 75, 90–1, 157–9, 248, 263
Wrightson, Keith, 12, 119, 173
Wrigley, E.A., 120
'Advanced organic economy', 93, 154–7, 262
Tertiary employment, 262–3, 263
Wyatt, John, 150 n.4